KNOWING LITERACY: CONSTRUCTIVE LITERACY ASSESSMENT

PETER H. JOHNSTON

State University of New York at Albany

LIBRARY

STENHOUSE PUBLISHERS

York, Maine

Stenhouse Publishers, 431 York Street, York, Maine 03909

www.stenhouse.com

Credits are on page 352.

Library of Congress Cataloging-in-Publication Data
Johnston, Peter H.
Knowing literacy : constructive literacy assessment / Peter Johnston.
p.   cm.
Includes bibliographical references (p.   ) and index.
ISBN 1-57110-008-3 (alk. paper)
1. Language arts—Ability testing. 2. Literacy—Evaluation.
3. Educational tests and measurements—Social aspects.   I. Title.
LB1576.J596   1996
372.6′0287—dc21   96-52720
CIP

Cover and interior design by Geri Davis, The Davis Group
Typeset by Technologies 'N Typography
Manufactured in the United States of America on acid-free paper
01 00 99   9 8 7 6 5 4 3

To Tina, Nicholas, Emily, and Samantha
and to the memory of John G. Nicholls

CONTENTS

Acknowledgments   viii

Introduction   1

PART ONE

BASIC ISSUES

1 Starting the Conversation   5

2 Being a Constructive Evaluator   11

3 It Takes Two: Evaluation as Social Interaction   17

4 Sanc Self-Assessment   26

5 Shaping the Reflective Lens   34

6 What Makes Literate Activity Easy or Difficult?   42

7 Controlling the Ease of Literate Activities   50

8 Choosing and Erring   57

PART TWO

NOTICING DETAILS

9 Meaningful Literacy   69

10 Constructive Literacy   76

11 Concepts of Being Literate   86

12   Concepts About Print   98

13   The Sound, the Look, and the Feel of Words   113

14   Being Strategic   122

15   Children's Concepts of Competence and Success   130

16   Under Construction: The Patterns of Development   138

PART THREE

DOCUMENTING AND KEEPING TRACK

17   Opening Conversations   159

18   Conversations in Print   168

19   Interviews and Conferences   178

20   Learning from Listening   186

21   Recording Oral Reading   192
Co-authored with Marie M. Clay

22   Interpreting Oral Reading Records   212
Co-authored with Marie M. Clay

23   Telling Thinking: Evaluation Through Thinking Out Loud   232

24   Questioning, Cloze, Retelling, and Translating   239

25   Observation Records and Checklists   250

PART FOUR

TALKING ABOUT CHILDREN'S LITERACY DEVELOPMENT

26   Beginning Portfolios   263

27   Talking About Portfolios   277

28   Writing Case Studies   288

29   Opening Pandora's Grade Box   297

30   Synchronizing Our Conversations: Moderation in Assessment   311

31   Keeping Track Without Losing Our Way   320

Contents

VI

APPENDICES

A   Alphabet Knowledge Record Sheet   325

B   "Why Do Boys Say Girls Are Afraid of
     Creepy-Crawlers?" by Emily Johnston   327

C   Some Interview Questions   329

D   Sheet for Running Record Analysis   331

E   Practice Running Records   332

References   341

Index   353

Contents

VII

ACKNOWLEDGMENTS

Many people have helped me with this book. I am particularly indebted to Philippa Stratton for her patience and thoughtful comments. But I would not have been able to work with Stenhouse at all if not for the generosity of Longman Publishers' vice president, Roth Wilkofsky.

Mary Unser, our department secretary, helps me maintain sufficient sanity in my work life, and Dick Allington, Lil Brannon, Jim Collins, Jim Fleming, Ginny Goatley, Sherry Guice, Cy Knoblauch, Anne McGill-Franzen, Frank Vellutino, Sean Walmsley, and Rose-Marie Weber, my colleagues at SUNY-Albany, have always been supportive, providing stimulating conversation and intriguing ideas. I also owe thanks to a wonderful group of graduate students who raise questions and confront me with cases and examples, keeping me rethinking what I know. I am particularly indebted to Barbara Gioia for her many insights, thoughtful feedback, and interesting conversations about teaching and learning.

Marie Clay has contributed in a number of ways, through direct and indirect conversations and through her support of my efforts. Barbara Watson gave detailed feedback on the running records chapters; any errors or confusion that remain are of course my responsibility.

Teachers in local school districts have helped me beyond measure with examples, counterexamples, enthusiasm, commitment, and questions. Teacher groups in the Guilderland, Hudson, Schenectady, and Troy school districts have been particularly helpful.

Of course much of the time I spent on this book came out of family time, and many of the examples came from family members. I could not have written the book without them. But their most important contribution has been, and will always be, their sustaining love.

*I*NTRODUCTION

*T*his book is about the evaluation of literate activity. The emphasis is on transforming literacy assessment from the classroom out. Its companion volume will be more concerned with the issues involved in public debates about assessment practices. Together, these two books will comprise a complete revision of my book *Constructive Evaluation of Literate Activity*, published by Longman in 1992.

I begin with an introduction to the premises upon which the book rests: the social and educational bases of literacy assessment. One of my premises is that assessment and literacy are both fundamentally social and situational. Another is that self-evaluation is the most important form of evaluation. A third premise is that assessing literacy demands that we teachers have an intimate knowledge of literacy and its development so that we can make sense of the literate things students do and the circumstances under which they do them. Consequently, Part Two of the book describes the nature and development of literacy in some detail. There I describe literacy as a way of knowing the world, our neighbors, and ourselves. At the end of each chapter I propose some assessment questions that might be asked relating to the aspect of literacy addressed in the chapter.

Within this framework, in Part Three I provide practical techniques for recording and representing literacy learning. In Chapters 21 and 22 Marie Clay and I explain step-by-step how to make running records of oral reading. These chapters are supported by an audiotape of children reading. Although this section emphasizes the "how to," I hope to make it clear throughout that the issues of "how," "why," and "so what" are closely related to one another and dependent on local circumstances. To do this, I describe the effects different techniques have on students' learning and the conditions that will make these techniques most useful.

In Part Four, I examine the language and conversations used in evaluation. As teachers, we develop rating scales, standards, rubrics, and the like in an attempt to communicate with each other about children's learning. These conversations are full of complications that must be untangled if we are to improve our assessment practices. Changing the conversations requires that we come to understand our own part in perpetuating the older, less successful ways of talking about literacy development and to imagine some alternative ways of talking.

In this book I use the terms *evaluation* and *assessment* rather than *measurement* and *testing*. The latter terms have unfortunate connotations from their origins and their current use. *Testing*, for example, is too restrictive a concept. Most of what I describe in this book does not involve tests in the modern sense at all. The word *test* is derived from a Latin word *testa* meaning "a piece of burned clay or skull." The word *test* arose from the practice of testing metals by incineration in a clay vessel that resembled a skull. (Current tests are not so far from this origin.) The word *measurement*, too, is restrictive in that it implies a concern for comparability and standardization, and a belief that the measuring process is somehow amoral, nonreactive, and linear. I hope I make it clear that it can be none of these.

The word *assessment*, however, has a more pertinent origin. It derives from the Latin word *assidere*, meaning to sit alongside (Hewitt 1995). This is a useful metaphor for assessment, particularly in the classroom. The word *evaluation* also carries useful connotations. It has a common root with the word *value* and thus recognizes overtly the value-laden nature of the activity. The Latin root is *e* meaning "from," and *valere* meaning "strength" or "worth." Throughout this book I emphasize the importance of valuing strengths. Also, although a distinction is commonly made between the notion of assessment and that of evaluation—that assessment is the gathering of data and evaluation is the interpretation of that data—I use the terms interchangeably. Since the entire process is interpretive and consequential, and hence value-laden, I argue that trying to differentiate the terms is misleading.

In writing this book I have tried to keep in mind that assessment must serve to optimize education, and education must be in the service of a just democracy. The most critical aspect of a democracy is the responsible political engagement of its citizens—the ongoing conversations that lead to new possibilities, new realities. In the spirit of democratic engagement I have written this book in a conversational manner. I hope that you take up the conversation with me. I have left wide margins so that you can heckle, question, and record connections. I hope also that you carry on these conversations with friends, colleagues, and students.

*I*n Part One, I contend that assessment, or evaluation (I use the words interchangeably), is not so much a technical problem as it is a people problem. It concerns the ways we represent ourselves and each other as literate individuals. I argue that evaluation is always interpretive—that we *make* sense of literate activity—and that it is always social. Evaluators give as much information as they get. I also explain the importance of self-evaluation. I argue that if evaluation is to be improved, we must start with teachers

*B*ASIC ISSUES

and students, and we must create conditions in which they will be likely to evaluate their own literate activity critically and constructively. I describe two kinds of knowledge that can help our evaluations of children: knowledge of what makes reading and writing easy or difficult, and knowledge of how to make sense of children's (and our own) errors

*S*TARTING THE CONVERSATION

*W*hen we assess literacy development we choose the words, numbers, or symbols that we think best represent literacy learning for the purpose at hand. We might describe a child's writing as an "A," as "at the 60th percentile," as "evidence of a learning disability," as "emergent," or as "the result of extensive revision that led to a believable character and a more careful selection of verbs than in earlier pieces." Each representation will be part of different conversations and relationships, and each has different consequences for those involved. Assessment conversations are about how we construe each other as literate people and consequently how we treat one another as human beings.

Try this. Make two copies of a first grader's piece of writing. At the top of one copy, write "first-grade student" and at the top of the other, "sixth-grade student." Assemble a group of people—parents, teachers, administrators, school psychologists—and give half of them one piece and the other half the other, with instructions to make a list of their observations about the writing. Then notice what happens. One group will be smiling and pointing, while the other group will be shaking their heads and speaking in dark tones. The lists they produce will be starkly different. One will include enthusiastic expressions of interest and observations of what the student can do. The other will feature statements about what the student *cannot* do and will likely include such terms as "learning disabled." Ask the two groups what should be the instructional response to the author of the piece and you will again get very different answers. The same piece of writing elicits different assessments and different conversations. As children become involved in those conversations, their learning—their development—changes.

My goal in writing this book is to help generate productive assessment conversations around children's literate learning—in classrooms, in schools, and in the wider community. Productive assessment involves using some practical procedures for data gathering and the like, but it also involves thinking about the nature of literate development, the language we use to represent children's learning, and the goals we serve with our assessments. As teachers, our responsibilities to our students and to our society are the same: increase each child's ability to participate in and contribute to a just, caring democracy. Our classrooms must provide children with literate experiences consistent with this responsibility. Since our assessment practices are an integral part of these experiences, they too bear this responsibility. For example, we should welcome practices that help children become more reflective and engaged and more in control of their learning, or that develop independence of judgment and collaborative engagement. We should be skeptical of assessment practices that lead children to be uncritical of what they read and unreflective about their experience, or that convince children that their own experience (or that of others) is irrelevant or that they are incompetent or helpless. Assessment practices that lead to large motivational differences between children, or to a more divisive or restrictive curriculum, will not be satisfactory.

This, then, is our compass as we negotiate the task of literacy assessment. We require our notion of literacy and our approaches to assessment to be sympathetic to these larger values.

Rehumanizing Assessment

American children are the most tested in the world (Resnick 1982), and the poor and the less competent are the most tested of all. We keep trying to improve literacy learning by developing new tests with better technical characteristics. Unfortunately, all of this testing has had, if anything, the opposite effect. Our error has been in approaching the matter as if it were merely a technical problem—as if it were possible, even desirable, to exclude human judgment and values from the assessment process, and as if it were reasonable to treat children as psychological objects. Assessment, we shall see, is a profoundly human, social phenomenon, thoroughly value-laden; it cannot be otherwise. All human science is like that, despite pretenses to the contrary (Knoblauch and Brannon 1988), and we will not improve education by pretending otherwise. Tests are constructed and interpreted by people, and are used on people. Social interactions are an integral part of assessment, and tests are always part of social interactions. It matters whether we describe a young writer as "emergent" or "low-ability," as "dyslexic" or "a prolific writer who often reverses letters." It matters whether a teacher's efforts are represented by descriptive comments, by an average test score, or by a portfolio the teacher has composed. It also matters whether that representation is public or not, and who decides.

Rethinking assessment in social terms requires breaking with the tradition in which the very humanness of teachers is viewed as a problem to be avoided through the use of tests. In this book I hope to capitalize on, and shape, the power of the human instrument rather than lament its imperfections. I do not wish to suggest that teachers are all finely honed assessment instruments, that their ability to care and to feel is always turned to best advantage, or that there is not a technical aspect to assessment. But the fact is that most educationally significant assessment takes place in classrooms, moment to moment, among teachers and students. Teachers make instructional decisions on the run at an alarming rate, with little time to reflect, and mostly without recourse to formalized sets of data such as test scores. The most important contribution to improving assessment, then, is to help teachers make these rapid decisions in the most productive and thoughtful ways—ways that will expand their students' literate competence while helping them to maintain caring, responsive relationships with (and among) their students, their colleagues, and the wider community.

Although individual teachers engage in assessment, we do not do it alone. Our assessment practices arise from the practices and conversations of the communities in which we live and work. Different conversations do not mesh easily: ask any teacher who has sent a narrative report card home to parents who expect normative grades. Assessment conversations that sustain inquiry and learning are very different from those that sustain blame, reward, and punishment. Different words are used, different relationships and motives are invoked, and a different view of humanity is at stake. The word "accountability" is part of many current assessment conversations. It implies a relationship that is very different from "responsibility," particularly with respect to trust. March (1972) points out that "a demand for accountability is a sign of pathology in the social system" (p. 428). Consequently, although I present all assessment as social, I also advocate particular kinds of assessment conversations and interactions. I advocate viewing assessment as a matter of inquiry done by and within communities as they explore the nature and circumstances of learning in their community.

Language and Literacy

Recently I was chatting with a fourth grader near my home. After a while he said, "You ain't from 'round here, are you?" I conceded that my linguistic roots lay in New Zealand rather than in the United States, to which he replied, "Yeah. You've got a accent."

"So do you," I pointed out.

"No I don't!" he protested.

We are immersed in language from birth. Just as we do not normally feel the air that surrounds us, we are normally unaware of the language we use to render the world sensible. It is transparent. This language that we did not choose gives us the power to name the world and to know ourselves. At the same time, though, it imprisons us in its own borders. We become trapped within the words and stories of our culture, with all of its stereotypes and prejudices.

The transparency of language is easily missed, particularly by those in the dominant culture. What is considered literate language in the dominant culture of the United States is very direct. Style manuals and editors are quite clear on this: "Get to the point." Yet in other cultures such directness would be considered extremely rude. Writing in Indonesia, for example, is marked by circularity and deference. There, indirectness and passive constructions are characteristic of *good* writing. Indonesian students often have a difficult time with writing when they come to universities in the United States. Changing their writing requires not simply learning new rhetorical techniques, but a whole different way of thinking about knowledge and their relationships with others—in other words, changing their culture, or at least becoming bicultural (Fox 1994). Literacy is not simply an isolated set of skills, but rather a very complex way of interacting with the world, with others, and with oneself (Ferdman 1990; Heath 1991). Being literate is as much something one *is* and *does* as skills one *has*.

Although literacy certainly has cognitive (indeed, biological) dimensions, it is fundamentally social, which means it is also situational. Robin, a fifth-grade student being tutored in our practicum lab, impressed all of us with her caring, unassuming presence and her commitment to her reading and writing. We were stunned when her mother told us that at school she was considered a nonreader with serious behavior problems. Robin's literate actions were very different in the two different contexts. In order to evaluate literacy development, then, we will need to describe the circumstances under which people engage in literate activity as much as the nature of their engagement.

Common Metaphors

In many ways, evaluating is just like reading and writing: it involves noticing both details and themes and patterns. Good writers are able to describe believable characters because they notice the details of people's behavior and have a wealth of observations to draw on. Good readers construct detailed meanings from a similar wealth of observations. Good writers write with audiences in mind, and readers read with authors in mind. They also read and write with a concern for the consequences of the meanings they construct. These qualities are all equally true of good evaluators.

One day my two-year-old daughter, Samantha, came to me and said, "I e a hou?" to which I replied, "You want to eat a house?" She hesitated, then said, "Yes!" and giggled uncontrollably. The big joke lies in her realization of the power of language. With language, she realized, you can construct a world that could never exist (Chukovsky 1963). This ability to create multiple realities is central to language, but it is also at the heart of reflective teaching and evaluation. It is this ability that allows teachers to do mental experiments to consider the possible consequences of particular changes in their instruction. In his book *The Reflective*

Practitioner, Donald Schon (1983) points out the importance of the teacher's "capacity to hold several ways of looking at things at once without disrupting the flow of inquiry" (p. 130). This ability to construct multiple realities is also what Mihalyi Csikszentmihalyi (1981) defines as wisdom which, he says, "does not lie in becoming mesmerized by that glimpse of reality our culture proclaims to be ultimate, but in the discovery that we can create various realities" (pp. 18–19). Benjamin Barber (1984) contends that this imagining of alternate realities is also a key feature of the citizens in a democracy: the ability to imagine others' lives and to collectively envision a future.

Teaching and Assessing

Most books on teaching and assessing literacy provide some sort of listing of necessary skills. I have done some of that in this book. For example, I argue that the ability to listen is a teacher's most important assessment skill. Actively listening to what a child has to say about her own reading and writing enables us to understand the logic of her literate behavior. Understanding the logic of errors is what enables us to focus instruction. I also believe that active listening is at the heart of literacy. It is what allows us to build a social imagination: the ability to imagine characters, to predict audience reaction, and to protect ourselves from unscrupulous writers by imagining the motives underlying their rhetorical choices. Yet listening is as much a disposition as a skill. When you genuinely believe a person has something interesting to say, you do not have to be taught to listen. Although I will try to teach you to listen, I will try harder to convince you that children have interesting things to say and that the more you listen, the more you find they have to say.

The more independent literate activity that goes on in the classroom, the easier it is to observe it, and the more consistent evaluation will be. The more students are reading and writing and talking about their reading and writing, the more examples are available to be observed, and the less critical it is for the teacher to notice every single one. In addition, the more commonplace it is for students to talk about and analyze their literate activity, the more capable they become of participating in their own evaluation. In a classroom where students are supposed to work quietly on their workbooks, briefly read to the teacher in a reading group from the same book, and do only single-sentence-response writing, a teacher will be hard pressed to talk coherently about students' literacy development. The more students can generate and choose among books, strategies, topics, and audiences, the more useful information they will provide about their reading and writing processes.

The notion of *independence* is critical. Teachers obtain the most useful information in one-to-one conferences with students, and from stepping back and watching how students make choices and manage their literate activity when they are self-directed. These activities require students to be able to manage themselves independently. If they cannot, they will be constantly interrupting teacher-student conferences to get help. Their teacher will also be unable to step back and observe classroom activity. By "independence," however, I am not referring only to students doing things alone. Much independence involves an *interdependence* with others. Indeed, since literacy involves the conversations around text as much as the text itself, conversations among students are important both instructionally and as a source of information.

This book is entitled *Knowing Literacy* for several reasons. First, I hope to show you that literacy involves knowing and representing the world, ourselves, and each other. Second, assessing children's literate development requires knowing how literacy works and how it is acquired so that you can notice the details of your students' learning. Without this knowledge a teacher cannot respond to the subtleties of children's literate activity or adapt instruction to their individual needs. Teachers cannot gain this knowledge without listening carefully to individual children, and this in turn is possible only in a classroom where children take responsibility for managing their own behavior. In addition, the personal nature of the interactions necessary to gather such knowledge is more likely to be part of a caring relationship.

In other words, assessment, literacy, and teaching cannot be reduced to sets of technical skills. Although there are certainly skills to be learned, they are learned and practiced in social situations that strongly influence how children know literacy and themselves as literate individuals.

$\mathcal{B}$EING A CONSTRUCTIVE EVALUATOR

$\mathcal{M}$y goals for both literacy and assessment are ambitious. I want students to be keenly observant of how people do things and why, and to actively seek patterns and relationships. For example, rather than my teaching a child the patterns of letters and sounds and the many exceptions to the patterns, I want children to actively seek patterns for themselves. I want them constantly to notice and theorize about all aspects of language. This is also what I hope for teachers: that they notice the details of children's development and theorize about why particular children do what they do. I also want both teachers and students to notice what they themselves do in their reading, writing, teaching, and learning, and to notice and theorize about the consequences of those practices.

Noticing Patterns

One requirement of assessment expertise is that one know a lot about the domain to be assessed, which in this case includes literature, reading, writing, children's development, and procedures for keeping track of their development. But there is more to expertise than simply having extensive knowledge; one must use it in a coherent, integrated way (Glaser 1988). When they are solving problems, experts are not distracted by the surface features of the problem, but instead recognize the underlying principles needed to solve or redefine it.

For example, consider the chess expert. A grand master recognizes about 50,000 board configurations, a good club player about 1,000, and a novice only a few (Chase and Simon 1973). A master can look at the pattern of pieces on a board for a few seconds and be able to replace the pieces in their original positions if the board were upset (a very functional skill for those of them who have young children). However, if the pieces are placed on the board in a way that would never occur in a game, the grand master can no longer replace the pieces. Only familiar patterns are recognized and remembered.

Teachers act in similar ways when they observe children engaging in literacy behavior. They remember and respond to patterns they recognize, but they will not remember and respond to those they do not recognize. The aim is to move beyond what is merely familiar: to see patterns and not treat them as though they are all the same, but to see them instead as an individual's way of organizing domains of experience and then to consider ways of responding appropriate to that pattern. One pattern should not be viewed as identical to another, but rather as a good metaphor to explore for this child in this situation. The more patterns and possible responses you have available, the more flexible you will be at problem-solving, and the more able to envision possibilities and predict their consequences.

The analogy between a chess player and a teacher is stronger when the grand master plays exhibition matches against twenty or thirty club players simultaneously, going from board to board around the room. Even grand masters lose some of these games. However, the teacher's job is even more complex, since chess players only have to attend to the board and the inert playing pieces. Teachers deal with people, whose actions and thoughts are influenced by the contexts of their lives. Teachers must also deal with changing relationships among the students in a context that produces motives far more complex than the simple win or lose of a chess game.

Bird-watching is another analogy. A skilled bird-watcher recognizes a yellow-shafted flicker on the basis of a small flash of yellow on the bird in flight and the pattern of the flight, the size and color of the head when the bird is not in flight, and so forth. But bird-watching requires not only rapid pattern recognition on the basis of partial information, but a knowledge of where and when to look for the particular bird. If you want to see a snowy owl it is not enough to know what it looks like; you also need to know where to look for it. You might hang around California for a long time looking for snowy owls without success, but you would be wrong to conclude that they do not exist. Similarly, teachers can fail to see a student's development if they do not know what that development would look like, but they will also fail to see it if they know what it looks like but are unable to set a classroom context in which it is likely to appear. Independent literate activity will not be seen if there is no opportunity in the classroom to engage in it, or if there is time but an unsatisfactory supply of appropriate books.

The point is that both an expert and a novice might look at a child's activity, but the expert sees more patterns and relationships in it—makes more meaning out of it. The novice might look at the sample of a child's writing shown in Figure 2.1, for example, and see only scribbles, whereas the expert might see a letter written in spelling that is partially invented and partially derived from visual memory, with an appropriate opening, a message (a rainbow) in the middle, and a signature at the end. The expert might also observe that the child has used print

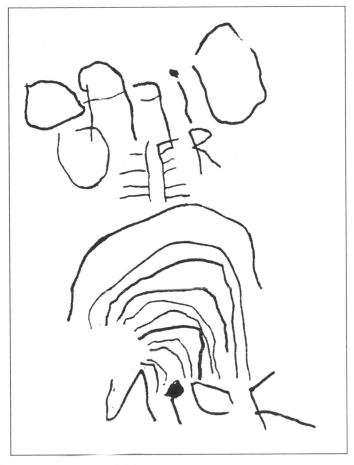

FIGURE 2.1   *A Thousand Words?*

for those parts of the letter for which only print can be used, and graphics to convey a message that is simply too laborious to produce in words. In this case, a picture may in fact be worth a thousand words.

Experts are distinguished by their knowledge: its extent and structure and the way they go about making knowledge. Two experts on a controversial issue such as nuclear power plants might each know a great deal, but their knowledge may be organized differently. If they both visit the same new power plant, what they each see, remember, and report may lead their audience to assume that they visited entirely different places. Teachers with many years of experience in the classroom have a lot of knowledge. But sometimes it is not organized into theories of how children learn to become independent readers and writers, but into theories of how to control and organize children to learn a series of skills. This is a different kind of knowledge involving different kinds of patterns. To return to the chess example, the master can only put all the chess pieces back in their right places if they could have been in those positions in a game. If the pieces are put in nongame positions, the master's pattern recognition falls apart. Similarly, a teacher viewing a classroom from the perspective of "time on task" and "efficiency" will very likely not listen to the patterns of dialogue in students' classroom talk; he or she will only be concerned that there is too much talk.

The Language of Assessment

Differences in what people see are reflected in, and determined by, their language. Indeed, it is in conversations with others that we learn what to see. The Inuit have an extensive language for describing snow, whereas mainstream Americans, even avid skiers, do not notice, much less describe, such differences. Such contrasts can also be found among teachers. Teachers have different predispositions of perception (Johnston, Afflerbach, and Weiss 1993). For example, a teacher who knows children's literature well tends to see children through that knowledge. For example, a teacher who had a substantial knowledge of children's literature described the literacy development of one of her students in these terms:

> So he would stick to those kinds of books or these kinds really—you know, *Three Bears, The Business Letter*, those kinds of books. Then gradually he branched out a little bit to the . . . *Fortunately* is one of Mercer Mayer's books, and the *Clifford* books, and that type of thing. [Later] he was again sticking with the things that he felt secure with, like *Frog and Toad Together* . . . And now, I guess he'd have to be considered one of the Patricia Riley Giff experts. Because those books are not real easy for him. But he just likes the character so much. I think he's in love with Ms. Rooney—with her classroom—that he's willing to spend that extra time getting to know more about those children in that room, in that book, and he really tries very hard to be very self-sufficient reading those books of hers . . . He's tried the mystery ones that she's come out with . . . [This is only one quarter of the description of that one child.]

Another teacher, whose knowledge of literature was more limited, described a child she knew well in the following way:

> From the beginning of his coming into my room he could not read. He's eleven years old, in third grade, and very little sight vocabulary. Now he's able to read, not fluently, but he can read. And he's real proud of himself. He's made progress. He'll still be placed in special ed in a couple of weeks, but I do see progress. [This was the entire, prompted, description.]

Knowledge of literacy activity is one kind of knowledge that determines what teachers notice and how they describe it. For this reason alone it is important for teachers themselves to read and write regularly and broadly. But this kind of knowledge is also critical if teachers are to provide optimal instruction for students, who approach literacy in a variety of different ways. Without this knowledge, teachers are apt to assert absolute control in the classroom in an attempt to make all literacy activities be done the same way.

The way a learner's development is described influences the way others understand and treat him or her. There really is a difference between describing a cup as half empty or half full. If we describe a learner as a failure, he or she will tend to perform that role for us; but if we describe that same person as a successful, literate learner, that is how he or she will generally act. Describing learners through their strengths means that we must put them in situations in which they will behave in a competent, literate manner. A classroom in which children are all required to read the same book is guaranteed to make some children look and feel incompetent and to make constructive assessment of their literacy very difficult.

Other conditions also make a difference. For example, although one teacher had a substantial knowledge of children's literature, her classroom was dominated by the district's insistence that students complete the basal reading program with all its workbooks and tests. As a result, this teacher described a child's literacy development without reference to literature at all. When prompted, however, she was able to describe what a more able student was reading. The reason was that, in her classroom, children were able to do free reading only after they had finished their workbooks. Thus, only the more capable readers got to read and talk about books. The others never finished their workbooks.

What teachers see and remember of students' development is what influences their interactions with the students, and the relationship is reciprocal. Teachers who refer many children to special education are distinguished from those who refer few children by their relatively brief descriptions of children's literacy development (Broikou 1992). Their knowledge or circumstances prevent them from noticing details of their students' literacy development.

Looking and Listening

You might think that noticing patterns is simply a matter of constant exposure, but a moment's reflection will demonstrate otherwise. Most people have many birds around them, but they do not even notice that there are birds, let alone the length of their tails, the details of their wing bars, or the pattern of their flight. Noticing requires looking and listening. Listening involves not just cocking an ear, but opening it to the many possible things that can be heard, tuning it to the speaker and responding in such a way that the speaker tells a detailed, accurate, and focused story. For a classroom teacher it means making polyphony out of cacophony. At the heart of listening is empathy.

Both looking and listening involve taking time and being non-egocentric. The more people are absorbed with their own needs, the less they take the time to listen or to observe. Consequently, the more stressful and ego-involving we make teaching, the less teachers are able to look and listen. A teacher who is required by mandate to use materials that specifically preclude children's choosing literature to read will not evaluate those children through their selection and reading of literature (Johnston, Afflerbach, and Weiss 1993). Children in such a class will, as we shall see, learn only a very narrow and controlling concept of literacy. This is not to say that simply making teaching less stressful and less ego-involving will make teachers into good listeners and observers, but it would increase the likelihood. Neither do I want to suggest that teachers somehow "naturally" will develop a constructive practice if they are allowed to use children's literature. Most of us have learning histories that would militate against it. Looking and listening are dependent both on personal learning history and on the situation.

There is one final, and critical, aspect of constructive assessment practice. The old saw "There is none so blind as those who will not see" rings true. People who are welded to their own theories of learning often conveniently and systematically ignore evidence that does not fit their theory. A constructive evaluator is aware that each person constructs his or her own knowledge. Nobody has a corner on truth. Our responsibility to ourselves and to our students involves listening to each one and critically examining our own knowledge and theorizing as well as that of others. This requires that we maintain for ourselves a situation of undefensive "intelligent unrest" (Graves 1983) in which we constantly reflect on our own evaluations. In other words, pattern recognition is fine, but seeing some patterns often means that we are not seeing others. What if the patterns that we automatically see are inaccurate, stereotypical, or incomplete?

Part of assessment expertise, then, involves our being able to collect data that will help us to confront our own knowledge, and actually restructure it. This critical reflectiveness is the most important dimension of a constructive evaluator's expertise, since it is the one that helps increase expertise and produces self-correction. Critical reflectiveness is grounded in open conversations with others who think differently from ourselves. Echoes of these conversations can help free us from our own tunnel vision and can sometimes produce observations that neither party alone could have made. Constructive evaluation is thus best viewed as a property of learning communities, particularly democratic communities—not authoritarian or adversarial ones. Such communities are characterized by a productive use of difference and a deep investment in inquiry.

*I*T TAKES TWO: EVALUATION AS SOCIAL INTERACTION

*M*ary, a white professional in her early thirties, is a dedicated, caring literacy volunteer who is meeting her client for the first time. Raymond, her client, is an unemployed man of color who can neither write nor read with facility. They sit down opposite each other at the table and introduce themselves. To begin their first learning session, Mary uses a test to find out Raymond's reading level. The test materials are set up between them on the table so that Mary can see the questions and answers, and Raymond can see only the text he has to read in order to answer Mary's questions. Raymond reads what he can and answers the questions as best he can until he has demonstrated (and experienced) a level of consistent failure. Following the test directions, Mary then decides what "grade level" he is at and "diagnoses" his "problem." Her analysis of the test results suggests that his "phonic analysis is weak."

What understandings have been constructed in this situation? Mary understands Raymond to be "a nice man who is nearly illiterate—well, reading at a low-first-grade level—and whose problem is deficient phonics, particularly in medial vowels." This understanding is laden with affect. Mary has volunteered her time and effort in order to help another human being, and she can see that Raymond really needs her help. Her understanding is colored with pity, but at the same time with feelings of power: she knows more than this person, and may be able to give him the gift of literacy, which will in turn give him access to work and perhaps to the pleasures of literature. Mary records the numbers from the test in the record book so that her supervisor, or some other person who was not present at the time, can construct an understanding of Raymond and his "needs."

Raymond is also busy making sense of the situation. Although he and Mary began with a difference in social status, with each step in the process the power difference between them becomes greater. Raymond begins to understand that in this situation he is powerless, and even more incapable and ignorant than he thought (as incapable as a first grader). He imbues this experience with anxiety, a certain amount of frustration at being unable to demonstrate some things that he thought he could do, a certain degree of feeling oppressed, and later perhaps some anger. He begins to understand that whatever he learns in their instructional sessions, his relationship with Mary is likely to be remain embarrassing and demeaning. His role will be to receive knowledge from this person, to whom he must remain indebted since he has nothing to offer in return. He also learns that reading is even harder, less comprehensible, and less interesting than he thought, and there appears to him to be even less reason to engage in it and learn about it than he thought before.

There are consequences to Mary and Raymond's understandings. On the basis of her diagnosis, Mary begins an intensive phonics instruction program, which requires Raymond to alter his dialect when he participates in the instruction. Essentially, he is forced to deny his cultural heritage in order to participate in the instruction. As a result of the understanding he has constructed, Raymond quits the program. Mary, in self-defense, decides that Raymond is unreliable and not particularly motivated to become literate. But at the same time, she has a nagging doubt about her own ability as a teacher.

In short, in the course of the evaluative interaction, the participants constructed knowledge about themselves, each other, their relationship, and the nature of the activity in which they were engaged. Their subsequent actions were guided by these understandings.

Whenever we evaluate someone, we are engaged in a social interaction. The interaction can take a variety of forms, but it is always a social activity in which each participant constructs an understanding of what is going on. The example I have used may seem a little extreme, but similar ones occur all the time in schools. Children generally do not have available to them such a response as physically leaving (though they can mentally leave), but they will respond to their understanding. At first glance, it may seem that group tests are immune to these problems. A little reflection will prove otherwise. Most of us at some point have experienced tests along with the feelings that accompany them. These feelings often have to do with our own self-worth, fears that our performance will be made public or won't "measure up."

When a standardized test is given to students to evaluate their performance (and that of their teachers), the experience will help students decide what school is about, what reading (if it is a reading test) is about, and what kind of knowledge is valued; and it will contribute to their understanding of themselves as learners and knowers. The experience will contribute to teachers' understanding of who they are, what kind of knowledge is valued, and their relationship with those responsible for the administration of the test. They might learn that administrators, and possibly the public, believe that teachers are not capable of monitoring their own performance or not responsible enough to do so. The largely female teaching community might construct knowledge about its relationship to the largely male community of administrators, and about the "place" of women. The administrators might construct knowledge about the quality of particular teachers, about their power over the teachers, and about their prestige in the community or the security of their jobs given the test scores.

Most assessment is not as overt as a test, and most easily passes unnoticed. A kindergartner brings to her teacher a story she has written. The look of the story is "AATLLLcpNoOWWIX," but the sound of it is "Yesterday we went to the beach and I went swimming with my sister, and we went in a boat and caught a fish." The teacher, hoping to preserve the oral version of the story, writes it correctly underneath the child's writing. This may not be intended as an evaluative act, but *under certain circumstances,* which we will explore in later chapters, it can be interpreted as one by a child—ample evidence that she did not do it right, with the outcome being a lack of desire to try it again. A good analogy to this situation is when an eighteen-month-old toddler speaks to a grown-up with her best attempt at language. To repeat it back to her in correct English would not encourage the continued conversation that is central to the child's development. But responding in proper form to what she has said will provide her with both a conventional model of the language along with a motive to attend to it, and a set of beliefs about the uses and value of language.

Dimensions of Assessment Interactions

Given that the evaluation interaction is a social interaction, how can we engage in it in such a way as to maximize the benefits for all concerned? To begin with, I must clarify the directions in which I consider maximum benefits to be found. I look for interactions that produce in the person being evaluated greater reflectiveness or self-evaluation and greater confidence and commitment to proceed; and in both parties an increased understanding of the learner and what is learned.

Trust

The foundation of clear communication in assessment (or anywhere else) is a trusting relationship along with shared knowledge. If the student does not trust the teacher, even nonjudgmental, reflective comments such as "Uh-huh" or "So you feel that . . ." are likely to be interpreted as equivalent to "Wrong!" or "Oh boy!" (with roll of eyes). Unfortunately, current evaluation practices in most schools work directly against the development of trusting relationships; rather, their adversarial nature fosters mistrust and suspicion of dishonesty. When this happens, students are apt to avoid the obvious interpretation of the situation and search for an alternative, more devious one. If the teacher asks a simple question, such as "How did you feel about the mouse?" but the student hears "What do I think are the correct feelings you should have about the mouse?" the entire communication (and hence the assessment) will be misleading.

If we lose trust, all is lost. Yet a sense of mistrust is pervasive in educational assessment. Teachers are held accountable because they cannot be trusted to be responsible. Teachers deliberately avoid reading previous assessments of their students so that they will not be prejudiced by other teachers' (untrustworthy) commentaries. Students are deeply worried about their report cards because they do not trust the teacher's comments or their parents' responses. John Nicholls and Susan Hazzard (1993) report a conversation about parent conferences by Susan's second graders:

> "They talk about us," Dan declares.
>
> "They talk about the bad things," says Tim.
>
> As the children murmur anxiously, Sue says that she would tell them if there were bad things, that conferences are for her to brag about them and show how well they are doing.
>
> "That's different," says Peter. "Some teachers just say what you need to do."
>
> Dan follows up, wondering how third grade teachers will be.
>
> "They're all different," says Dan. (p. 39)

Assessment practices must be based on trust, respect, and assumed good intentions rather than on assumed incompetence and irresponsibility. However, while trust implies openness, it does not imply gullibility. The aim is to develop a trust based on the assumption that each of us—teachers, parents, and others—cares and will consider judgments and evidence with a sensitive and critical eye. Engaging all the participants in the inquiry is one way to increase the level of trust. We also seek trust in how we gather data.

POWER AND CONTROL

Closely related to the issue of trust is the consideration of power and control. The assessment relationship can be embodied in the physical stances adopted by the participants. Physical posture and orientation say a lot. More power is assumed by standing or sitting in a higher position, and power is emphasized by standing with hands on hips or with arms folded. Evaluators should avoid these postures. Sitting next to someone is generally more comfortable and less confrontational than sitting opposite someone. Thus, it helps for participants to sit next to each other rather than across from each other in most evaluation interactions in order to minimize the differences in power status. Unfortunately, most individualized reading tests, such as the *Woodcock Reading Mastery Test* (Woodcock 1973), require the assessor to sit opposite the student, higher up, and to hold the answers that the student is to match. A rare exception to this is the *Concepts About Print* test, designed by Marie Clay, in which evaluator and student sit alongside each other, share the same book, and share the same activity. Running records, described in more detail later in this book, also promote more equal roles. The evaluative relationship should be considered one of advocacy, in which the assessor sits next to the student, at the same height, makes lots of eye contact, and waits to be offered the student's writing (Graves 1983). By contrast, an adversarial relationship is projected when the assessor sits opposite the student in a higher chair, takes the student's writing without waiting for it to be offered, makes little eye contact, and has all the answers.

Adopting an advocacy relationship does not deny that there is a power difference between teacher and student in the classroom. There is. The point is that this difference need only apply to certain domains and in certain situations. In matters pertaining to physical and emotional safety in the classroom, the teacher clearly has a dominant position, though even this responsibility is better shared. Steps can be taken to minimize the power imbalance through establishing clear rules that have been agreed on by the classroom community and through maximizing community responsibility. Power differences can also be minimized by treating students' views as seriously as you expect them to take yours. This is just as true at the school-community level as it is within the classroom.

Teachers often ask questions in order to gather information. Indeed, the format of testing, and the instruction based on it, demands extensive questioning. However, questions have at least two facets to them. One is to request information; the other is to demand a response. Most questions asked in the classroom are ones to which the teacher already knows the answer. These are asked primarily as a means of control, and they affect the development of the instructional relationship. For example, once in middle school my son was assigned as homework a set of articles to read, accompanied by a set of multiple-choice questions of similar length to answer. He began reading the questions and finding the answers without reading the articles. I suggested that he read the articles, which were really very interesting. He said he would do one or the other, but not both. He added that the questions were there for control purposes—to check that they read the material—and that he would humor us (his parents) only so far. I mentioned my son's analysis to his teacher, who agreed that my son was right, but that students would not read the material unless he forced them to by requiring them to answer the questions. Few of the students who answered the questions, though, actually read the articles, none engaged in the issues raised in them, and I would guess that the teacher's relationship with his students was not enhanced in the process.

When children consider a question genuine they are more likely to focus on the request for information. Otherwise they interpret it as an assertion of control. If there is a likelihood that students will misinterpret the question this way, we can help them focus on the request for information by helping them understand our genuine interest in, or need for, the information. Asking questions about controversial topics is a great place to start (Nicholls and Hazzard 1993; Nicholls and Nelson 1992). Maximizing trust also goes a long way. Remember, too, that asking questions is not the only way to get information. Giving information can frequently be a better way. For example, to respond to a student's writing with your sincere reaction to it ("The part in the middle about the horse made me feel very sad, but I felt a bit confused about the part where you were going home") can have a more productive effect than asking direct questions ("Why did you write the part about going home in that way?") or making assertions ("This is badly written"). The personal response at once gives a reason for clarification and shows respect for the writer and the piece of writing without necessarily invoking a power differential.

TIME AND TIMING

When two people talk to each other, each has to decide when the other has finished. There are cultural differences in the amount of time people will wait for further comment, and there are substantial individual differences within a given culture. Each of us also waits a different amount of time before responding, depending on our interpretation of the other person and the social situation we are in. Often cultural differences between student and teacher can result in a teacher's not waiting long enough for a response, which may result in minority children's having less opportunity to speak (Cazden 1990). Even more often, teachers wait longer for responses from students who are seen as more able than from those who are seen as less able (Allington 1983). Indeed, their wait time is a reflection of their expectation of the child's ability to respond adequately. This increases the likelihood that less capable students will say little, be defensive, feel inadequate, and be dependent. So it is important to take your time with students—to wait that extra few seconds for a response to a statement or question. This can be hard, especially with students who are not doing well. We often conclude that such students will not be able to respond; and, with the best intentions, we jump in quickly to save them from embarrassment, thereby rendering them powerless. Of course, good timing requires a very fine balance. No one likes to be left with the floor when they really do not have anything to say. This makes it imperative that we reduce the likelihood of such situations arising, and that the teacher-student relationship allow the student to get out of such situations, for example by saying, "I don't understand." In other words, "I don't understand" must be a valued, not a humiliating, response.

Often in schools we hustle kids along and try to keep them on our schedule. At the same time the schedule keeps getting more and more packed. In our family we often have trouble with our youngest, Sam, who is often on a different schedule, sometimes in a different galaxy. Once when Sam was in kindergarten, amidst the bustle of morning preparations, her schedule and the school bus's did not coincide. I had to drive her to school, which disrupted my own overscheduled schedule. After a lecture on the importance of pace, efficiency, and focus, we arrived at school, had our hug and kiss, and she got out of the car. To my frustration, she wandered a few paces toward the school building and became engrossed in watching another child get out of a car, interact with his parents, and look for his things in the car. Unperturbed by the fact that the school schedule was already under way, she ambled a few more feet, still watching the other family, eventually turned, and, obviously still thinking about what she had been watching, skipped into the school building. I raced off to work, shaking my head, trying to get back on my schedule.

Four days later it occurred to me to ask Sam what she had found so interesting. She said, "You probably noticed [??] that the boy was not allowed to kiss his father good-bye. He had to go like this [makes thumbs up sign]. And the mother was like the Simpsons' mom. She worries a lot." Sam went on to describe other details of this family's life, which I have now forgotten. Her observations are those of a serious writer. Indeed, her ability to notice details, particularly in social situations, showed up in her writing. For example, that year, when writing a letter to a friend, she used both sides of the paper. Realizing that the receiver might not know to turn over the paper, she wrote, "turn over."

As schools intensify the pressure on teachers through increasing demands for accountability, "add-ons," and "higher standards," teachers become less able to take children's observations seriously. If we don't take the time, it is hard to listen and so to make careful inquiries. It is easy to forget that the word *school* is derived from the Latin *scola*, meaning "leisure" or "quiet reflection," particularly as schools are urged to become more like businesses, the roots of which are in the idea of "busyness" (Jacoby 1994).

Focus

The focus of our responses to students' reading and writing influences their understanding of the nature of literacy and their understanding of themselves as literate people. For this reason, responses to reading and writing should first be concerned with what the student has to say. Such a focus not only establishes a productive relationship, but also improves the quality of the student's reading and writing by establishing literacy as a communicative activity and the student as a person who has something to say. Do not mistake this for the common practice of asking students "factual" questions about what they just read out loud to you, to which you in turn respond "Good" or "Correct" or "No." Such a practice gives the message that the teacher has access to the single meaning of the text. This eliminates the basis for dialogue about a book or story and, while it might imply a communicative function, it also suggests that the student has nothing of his or her own to say. Similarly, if we regularly praise the neatness of particular children's handwriting, we can say to the class that handwriting neatness is unimportant until we are blue in the face, but the students will know otherwise. Children are very good at reading nonverbal and incidental cues.

Focus is also an issue in assessment at the program level. Certain tests focus on particular areas of literacy while avoiding others. This alters the balance of classroom instruction and the ways the community views what happens in schools. For example, when a district evaluates its early reading program with a test that focuses primarily on children's knowledge of letters, sounds, and spelling, that affects the conversations people in the district will have about the teaching of literacy.

A focus on the process of reading and writing can change the assessment relationship, too. Such a focus reduces the possibility of students making counterproductive comparative judgments of who is better than whom. It keeps their attention on where they are going and how they are getting there. Outcomes are obviously important, but when the focus in assessment is on how the outcomes were arrived at, the relationships involved and the student's subsequent engagement are positively influenced. For example, examining the process makes it easier for teachers to see and respond to responses that are partially correct. This not only affirms to the student what is already known, but provides energy for him or her to pursue that which is yet to be known. Equally important is the effect of a positive focus on the relationships involved. Cynthia Rylant (1992), in her book *Missing May*, nicely captures the consequences of focusing on the positive in her description of May:

> May was the best person I ever knew . . . She was a big barrel of
> nothing but love, . . . She understood people and she let them be
> whatever way they needed to be. She had faith in every single person
> she ever met, and this never failed her, for nobody ever disappointed
> May. Seems people knew she saw the very best of them and they'd
> turn that side to her to give her a better look. (pp. 15–16)

STAKES

The stakes involved in assessment can make an enormous difference to the process and outcome, and to the relationship as a whole. For example, when districts or states make teachers' salaries contingent on test scores, the relationships among teachers, students, and administrators change. Teachers become more likely to assist students in taking tests and to take over the selection of materials for writing portfolios (M. Smith 1991; M. Smith et al. 1991). Furthermore, the higher the stakes, the more likely teachers are to become controlling and authoritarian (Renshaw and Gardener 1987).

Another way to raise the stakes in assessment is to make performance more public. Some of my teachers used to announce our grades to the class or hand our papers back in order of performance. My memories of these experiences are not positive. The effect of such practices is to increase students' ego-involvement in the outcome, which changes the nature of their engagement in learning. Students who are concerned about their performance will adopt ego-defense strategies (more on this later). Similarly, teachers whose average class test scores are made public are likely to adopt similar strategies and are also not likely to appreciate diversity in their classrooms. Such circumstances also lead to a change in the tone of the conversations, from inquiry to blame-placing. In highly controlled, high-stakes situations, teachers use more restricted, less personal language to describe children's literate development (Johnston, Afflerbach, and Weiss 1993).

OBJECTIVITY AND DISTANCE

Assessment practices can be seen as "objective" or not. "Objective" testing may depersonalize the assessment and hence the relationship between the participants—a situation that can have more or less productive consequences. For example, people behave more positively in personal, enduring relationships than they do in impersonal ones. On the other hand, negative assessments that are seen to be grounded in clear, external, "objective" criteria are less likely to be "taken personally." Questions of objectivity come back to the issues of trust and control.

So What?

The meaning that is made in any assessment is based not only on what we say and do, but on how we say it and the context and relationship in which it is said. Our assessment interactions with students tell them who we think they are, what we think learners should do, and what we think it means to be literate (how literate people behave). Assessments are not simply outcomes, they are part of the process and product of social activity. The literacy interactions in which we are immersed contain the genes from which our literate thinking evolves. As Uri Bronfenbrenner (1979) points out, the relationship between a teacher and a student has an effect on the student's development. The nature of the effect is determined by the extent to which the participants in the relationship evince a positive regard for each other and the degree to which the balance of power can be shifted in favor of the student. Implicit in the relationship is a valuing of the child and her responses. This valuing makes it possible for children to ask questions. Indeed, the frequency with which children are prepared to say "I don't understand," or to admit as much through their questions, is probably a reasonable indicator of the health of the teaching-learning relationship for some children. The reciprocity of the relationship is critical to the assurance of a credible evaluation. When we assess, our goal should be to understand the subjective reality of the task and the situation for the learner. This is much easier to do if the learner is willing, where possible, to correct any misconceptions we might have. As Bronfenbrenner observes:

> In the absence of persons able to recognize unwarranted interpretations based on misperceptions of fact, the unwitting investigator can, in all good faith, arrive at false conclusions. Once such persons are involved in the scientific enterprise, the risk of errors is appreciably reduced. (pp. 31–32).

The essence of the relationship is active listening.

CHAPTER 4

SANE
SELF-ASSESSMENT

I guess I could be called a "late bloomer": my academic career was not healthy for quite a long time. Figure 4.1 is the last of my high school report cards. Some years after I received that report card, at the insistence of my younger brother, I reluctantly attended a high school reunion. One of my math teachers, a Scotswoman, a little tipsy, approached a small group of us, most of whom had been in her class. She asked us each in turn what we were now doing. At the time I was teaching undergraduate statistics—not very well, but that was what I was doing. Her amused response was "Pull my other leg; it's got bells on it."

I cannot blame her or the other teachers for their evaluations, written or oral. They were trained in particular ways and were caught in a system that was not conducive to alternative views of evaluation. And I was not the kind of student that inspires teachers to look for positive attributes. There was a time in my schooling (around eighth grade) when the most important evaluation for me, and the rest of the group I inhabited, was the number of notches in my belt, which indicated the number of times I had been caned by the principal or vice-principal. By the end of high school, my criteria for judgment had changed. I had moved on to more inventive pranks. My evaluation of my schooling career was actually quite positive based on the principal's call to my parents the night before the graduation ceremony asking for their assurance that I would not pull any pranks at the ceremony. How could I count that as a failure?

Alas, others were looking at different indicators of the successfulness of my schooling (or rather different indicators of my success in schooling). They took my grades to be important indicators of my academic prospects. Things did not improve immediately after high school, either. Ultimately, the University of Wisconsin at Madison rejected my application to their doctoral program in educational

HUTT VALLEY HIGH SCHOOL

REPORT FOR TERM ½-Year ENDING 13 Dec. 1968 NAME: Peter H. Johnston

Half-days Absent: 6. FORM: 6A

	Number in Form	Place in Form	Term Marks	Exam. Marks	Remarks	
English	15	14	41	48	Has difficulty getting his good ideas down on paper.	H H.
French						
German						
Latin						
Greek						
History						
Geography						
Mathematics	19	18	37	20	Has made little effort to improve this subject.	VP
Additional Mathematics						
Physics	32	31	26	22	Not a good effort.	N Lh.
Biology	10	8	84/11	43	Appears to have made little effort. Results are poor	AM.
Chemistry	13	9	55	31	Often somewhat puzzled, but has made some genuine attempt	B76
Bookkeeping						
Economics						
Com. Law						
Physical Ed.						

Conduct: ....

General Comments: ....

Form Master/Mistress: H.M. Henderson   J. McLea Principal

FIGURE 4.1 *My Report Card*

psychology because of my undergraduate grades. Indeed, I shared their view of my prospects. I had applied to do doctoral work only because when I had returned to university from teaching to do graduate work, my advisors, Richard Barham and Terry Crooks, believed that I was capable of doing doctoral work and had so advised me. I applied to doctoral programs out of a sense of responsibility to them with no expectation of being successful.

The point of this story is that others evaluate us and we evaluate ourselves, and the two evaluations are related to each other, sometimes in subtle ways (Crooks 1988). Sometimes, for survival, we reject the criteria others apply to us, but we usually reject more than just the criteria. The most important evaluation in the long run, for any learner, teacher or student, is self-evaluation. When we evaluate our students' literacy, we have to keep in mind how our evaluations can affect children's evaluations of themselves. The voices of the classroom reverberate in our sense of self—of who we are as literate people (Gilyard 1991).

In a way, teachers' evaluations provide children with a mirror through which they can examine their learning. When we look in a mirror, many things influence what we see. The kind of mirror we use affects what we see. Sometimes we look into a distorting mirror, like the ones at fairgrounds that make us look fat, thin, or dumbbell-shaped. Sometimes the mirror is small and only lets us see parts of ourselves at a time. Sometimes it is hung on the wall leaning forward, making our feet look small and our head big. Our reflection is rarely seen through a perfect full-length mirror, and even when it is, we rarely see ourselves clearly. Sometimes, self-consciously, we focus on the pimple on our nose or the mole on our neck, not even seeing the rest of the image. How we see ourselves also depends on the context: whether we are going on a first date with a person we think is perfect or out to build a fence in the backyard; whether the principal is observing us or whether a teacher trainee is observing us.

How we see ourselves is influenced by the way others interact with us. If a man has only one arm and that is the first thing everybody notices and acts on, then this feature is likely to dominate the man's own view of himself. It is one thing to be a blind person who reads and quite another to be a reader who happens to be blind. If the major feedback we get on our writing focuses on the neatness of our penmanship, then neatness is likely to be distorted into the largest part of the image we see—rather like the teenager going on a date whose pinhead-sized pimple has expanded in his mind to the size of quarter. If the teenager is not confident to begin with, this distortion in perception may cause him to cancel the date. As teachers, we can help children develop healthy self-evaluation systems or unhealthy ones.

There are two kinds (or perhaps emphases) of self-assessment that can be considered. One has to do with the ways we take stock of our progress, skills, knowledge, and accomplishments—what we know and can do. An example of this kind of self-assessment would be the following: "This year so far I have completed only nonfiction pieces. I can write newspaper-style articles, but I have yet to finish one piece of poetry. I have some good beginnings from my journal and I have some good words for poems; I just can't figure out how to finish them. I've written some good dialogue for characters, but I haven't got any plot yet for them. I need to know how to make a good plot." The second kind of self-assessment involves naming or categorizing oneself in more generic, judgmental terms. We might call this "self-judgment." An example of this kind of assessment would be "I am really smart at math but really stupid in reading." The first kind of self-assessment is helpful; the second is not. Although a child who feels he is "really smart at reading and writing" might have "positive self-esteem," this evaluation gives neither direction nor motive for growth.

Valuing Self-Evaluation

There are several reasons for valuing self-evaluation. First, independence in literacy should be part of teachers' long-term goal for students. We will not be around to give our students feedback forever. Second, in the long run self-evaluation is more immediate than having to hang around waiting for others' evaluations. Third, when you discover a problem for yourself, there is a greater likelihood that you will respond to it constructively than when someone else points it out. Fourth, when children are encouraged to be reflective about their learning they become able to talk about it. When they are used to being asked what they do well as readers and writers and what they have difficulty with, they become able to talk intelligently about such things. These conversations are productive for all members of the learning community.

How can we help students (and ourselves) to become good self-evaluators? To begin with, don't get in the way. We often prevent children from evaluating themselves by correcting them as soon as they make an error. If, when a child becomes stuck on a word or reads it incorrectly, we immediately leap in and give the correct word, we will deprive the child of the opportunity for self-correction, and she will gradually become passive in her reading (Allington 1983; McNaughton 1981). If we continually make it clear that we think students are incapable of self-correction and that we have the correct way and theirs is simply a poor imitation, they will always look to us for evaluation. They will evaluate themselves as being incapable of that function. A common feature of children who have difficulty in reading and writing is a failure to monitor and to correct their own errors. As soon as they attempt a word, their head turns to their tutor to see if they did it right. They do not feel capable of evaluating their own responses. The first source of the problem in this case is that the task is too difficult. After that, how the teacher interacts with the students should be examined.

We can encourage self-evaluation by recognizing it when it occurs. When a student becomes aware of a problem, we can say, "I like the way you noticed that yourself. That kind of self-awareness is a sign of a good writer." Self-evaluation can be also encouraged by reflective responses that turn questions back to learners. Jack Easley and Russell Zwoyer (1975) describe "questions that teach." For example, when a student looks to a teacher for evaluation, the teacher might ask, "What do *you* think?" Of course if the student then hazards an opinion and the teacher responds, "Wrong," or words to that effect, the student is likely to avoid such invitations next time and to feel insecure in self-evaluation. A response from the teacher such as "How could we check that?" might provide more assistance, since it opens up possibilities for self-checking. In addition, the student's response to such a question is likely to give the teacher information about the strategies he or she has available. In other words, such questions do triple duty. They prompt self-evaluation, tell us what strategies the student has available, and at the same time turn the student's attention toward the literate process.

Self-evaluation can also be encouraged by making portfolios a central part of the classroom. A portfolio includes items from the semester (or year or quarter) produced and selected by the student to represent his or her development. Each item can have attached to it a statement of why it is important, or what it represents in terms of the student's development. This not only gives the teacher information about what the student values, but requires the student to be reflective, and in doing so encourages greater commitment on the part of the student. (Portfolios are discussed in greater detail in Chapters 26 and 27.)

Regaining Consciousness

As adults, things we have done many times before are automatic for us. We don't think much about the letters on the page as we read, and we don't think about most of our teaching while we are in the process of doing it. But unless we become conscious of what we do, examining and changing it is hard, so part of self-evaluation involves finding ways to make automatic activity conscious or nonautomatic. Usually videotaping or audiotaping myself as I teach allows me to juxtapose what I think I am doing with what I am actually doing, and that exercise is enough to prompt me to make changes. Often I don't even need to listen to or watch the tape. Just being aware that the machine is running causes part of me to step outside myself and observe myself while I am teaching.

Evaluating our own practice can also be facilitated by having a colleague visit the classroom and watch us teach. When I am so observed, part of me watches myself teach through my colleague's eyes. It is not necessary for him or her to say anything about my teaching for me to see grounds for improvement. Knowing the colleague and his or her approach to teaching and watching myself through that person's lens gives me a different image of my own practice. In a way, it gives me stereoscopic vision. Having a colleague observe our teaching gives us a particular kind of audience—one that is detached somewhat from our own assumptions, yet one of comparable status to ourselves. This audience is also reciprocal. If we have gone out on a limb and allowed them to watch us, they must be open to the same: "You show me yours and I'll show you mine" or, rather, "You show me mine and I'll show you yours."

In a similar way, getting children to read their own work out loud to themselves can help them notice things they hadn't noticed before, particularly if they can imagine an audience. Sometimes, when imagination fails, a friend can listen to us read what we have written but say nothing. We can help children remember to take these steps by including a list of ideas in their folders or on the classroom wall. But, like our students, we teachers often forget to "read" our own teaching out loud to ourselves (perhaps through a videotape) before being observed by an outside audience. We often forget the outside audience idea, too, of course, except when an observation by an administrator is required, and outside observations under those conditions are less than optimal for promoting change, especially since an administrator is almost always less qualified to observe, let alone pass judgment on, your teaching practice than is a competent teaching colleague or yourself.

Further reflection can occur if I talk to my colleagues about a video of my practice. In that case I view the video of my practice in a slightly different way, and the need to talk about my practice increases its coherence for me. I am most likely to be secure about discussing my practice if I can choose the part of the video to show and talk about. Indeed, the very process of deciding which section to show and how to talk about it is a learning experience, in part because we must approach our own work from the perspective of a new audience.

We might take this notion of audience and look at self-evaluation through the metaphor of writing. Good writers write with an internalized notion of their audience, which they gather from either eliciting numerous responses from an audience or knowing well particular people whose responses they can imagine. Teaching is also a composing activity in which one revises and edits one's efforts. We build our compositions from the collected experiences we have had in the past.

The most common way in which "reflection in action" comes about is when something we do results in something we did not expect. Normally, we predict what will happen, without being conscious of doing so, and when events happen as we unconsciously predicted, we carry on without thinking about it. Surprise, however, pleasant or unpleasant, often makes us aware of something previously left unexamined. If we create situations in our schools in which teachers cannot afford to be surprised, they will not look for surprise; and the fewer surprises, the less awareness. The same is true for children. If classrooms do not allow the opportunity for them to savor and study surprise, opportunities for reflective self-evaluation will be lost.

Keeping a journal about one's own teaching almost guarantees reflection. Whenever we write down something that is on our mind, it allows us to take a step back from it and view it from another angle. Thus, if you are having trouble with a student in your class, write down what the problem is—what you see and how you feel about it—so that you can share the problem with a colleague. You may find that simply writing the problem down helps you think your way through it. In addition, the student with whom you are having a problem is very possibly classified, or going to be classified, as "learning disabled." Such students are notoriously unreflective and impulsive. Involving them in writing is a powerful way to influence their reflectiveness.

The Context

Different contexts make self-evaluation more or less likely to occur, and alter the focus of the evaluation in important ways. For example, when children have folders in which they collect their writing, they are encouraged to examine their own development simply by the presence and use of the collection. They will be confronted with more and less successful efforts that are not simply good or bad, but each of which has good features and bad features. Teachers can obtain great insight into children's evaluative criteria by asking them to describe why they rejected certain pieces of writing. These pieces have already been removed from the student's ego-involvement, so he or she will find it much easier to talk about self-evaluation. Indeed, talking about such pieces can help students to clarify their selection criteria for themselves and think about ways to carry their work past those criteria. We can encourage children to reflect on their own work and how and why it changes. We can make their own criteria more explicit and available for reflection by trading our students' writing folders with those of the students of another (trusted) teacher and then discussing what we each see in the writing.

In contrast, competitive contexts reduce the likelihood of reflection, and when reflection occurs in these contexts it is rendered useless because it focuses on aspects of learning that tend to be irrelevant to the child's development. In competitive contexts, learners do not consider their own previous performance, and they concern themselves less with the process than with the outcome (Ames and Ames 1984). But it is reflection on the process that will help them improve their performance. This is true for teachers as well as students. The ego-threatening situation produced by competitive contexts has little to recommend it, yet the assessment systems used in schools, basal readers and standardized tests, invariably produce competitive contexts by reducing literacy to simplistic linear scales (see Chapter 15 for a more detailed discussion of the consequences of these contexts). Tests and basals are not the only way to produce competitive contexts. Valuing the "best" interpretation, the most, the hardest, or longest books, or the longest writing in a classroom filled with children's literature can have the same consequences. A productive classroom setting presents literacy as sufficiently complex that students can each document their improvement yet not compare their work in simplistic ways.

In order for children to become self-evaluating, they must feel themselves to be able knowers and evaluators. As teachers, what we say can either make us appear to have all the answers and to be the all-powerful final arbiters, or suggest that our students can be knowledgeable and able judges of their own learning. For students to be self-critical and to develop reflective commitment to their reading or writing, they need to have confidence and self-respect, and they need to value their own knowledge. These conditions are likely to occur only when children feel that they have something to contribute. In other words, they must feel that their experience is important and worth talking about. This feeling comes about when other people listen to them, and when it is clear that different perspectives are accepted. In such an environment, the teacher can help the student develop "intelligent unrest" (Graves 1983), a stance from which learning is most likely to take place. But a student must first feel intelligent.

We teachers have only limited control over many of the factors described in this chapter, and over those not mentioned here. Among other things, some children are simply more compulsive than others. Children also differ from each other because of birth order, cultural background, and many other factors outside of a teacher's control. We can't simply explain all these as differences in learning styles and work around them. A measure of reflectiveness is important for all of us. In many ways, reflectiveness—self-evaluation—is essential to being an independent learner. Failure to monitor your own progress means that you must be dependent on someone else for your learning. Any process, including learning processes, needs a feedback system to give it direction. If the feedback system is taken away, the process is without guidance and is dependent on someone or something else to provide that guidance. It is thus critical that children monitor their own activity and reflect on what it means.

Balance

Becoming conscious of our practice can help both teachers and students become more effective in self-evaluation. But it is possible to become so reflective as to lose track of the activity. If I become overly conscious of my typing while I am typing, my fingers tend to trip over one another. Too much conscious awareness may be incompatible with fluent complex activity—with reading or writing, for example, or intense discussion such as might occur in a classroom. Thus in some situations, in some contexts, involvement and conscious reflection may be in opposition. A sense of balance is required in order to optimize the benefits of both activity and reflection.

CHAPTER 5

SHAPING THE REFLECTIVE LENS

*E*lwyn Richardson (1962), in his book *In the Early World*, tells the following story:

> I watched Stuart, a small boy in the infant room [kindergarten], show and tell with the twist and shaping of his small fingers all about the size and habits of a small insect that he had seen on a nature ramble:
>
> "The flicky things were a dark colour, not black. They had little, little wings and long, long legs; they were so little nobody could see them—only me."
>
> Each wing, each leg was itself a thing that he had to explain with his bodily movements, and his painting of this delightful "species" was also full of the same child excitement that his teacher quickly recognised. She wrote down the story and praised him for it. However, another person was there at the time, a person who was concerned that such a loose inaccurate description had been allowed to go unchecked.
>
> "Was it an insect, Stuart?" he began. "How many parts did it have to its body? Did it hop? Why do you say it was a 'flicky thing?' Did it fly?" Of course there could be no answers. Stuart became more and more subdued, and when he was told to look more carefully in future when he was doing nature study, I saw that he was about to cry . . . How often children can rise above such assaults on their imagination is not hard to guess. (pp. 126–127)

The assault is doubtless on Stuart's imagination, but the effect is more pernicious. Ongoing conversations such as these shape the reflective lens through which we view ourselves and our literacy efforts. Let's consider some of the dimensions of the lenses and their construction.

The Criteria of Self-Evaluation

Self-evaluation is based on complex images, models, values, and melodies. Most of these we are unaware of because they arise naturally from immersion in the conversations and contexts of our lives. When I listen to the music I grew up with, I find the harmonies very satisfying. I notice when someone's harmony is off. I have melodies in my head that I constantly, and unconsciously, refer to, which I use to monitor my own singing, and to judge music I listen to. I recall my son trying to sight-read as he practiced a piece on the piano. He played the same phrase several times, trying to get it right, but knowing that it sounded wrong. In despair, he said, "It doesn't make sense." Indeed, he knew what made sense in the musical world, and that the sequence he was playing did not. When a child's reading does not make sense, we expect that he or she will similarly notice and try to do something about it. If it doesn't sound right—if it violates the reader's language rhythm or notion of appropriate syntax—the reader will notice the discrepancy and act on it. If a book I am reading is too difficult, I notice that it doesn't feel right and do something about it—perhaps shift to something more manageable.

Children develop the criteria for evaluating their reading out of the conversations in which they are immersed. Marie Clay (1993b) suggests that teachers ask reflective questions as children read orally, such as "Does that make sense to you?" or "Can we say it that way?" or "You said ———. What letters would you expect to be there?" or "Does that look right?" Such questions help the child focus on sense, structure, print detail, and letter-sound relationships respectively. If a child does not monitor his reading independently to be sure it is making sense, asking him to reflect on the sense will be helpful. However, asking "Does that make sense to you?" only when it does not make sense to you is exactly the same as saying "That does not make sense!" Consequently, it is important to ask such questions both when it does and when it does not make sense to you. The student must also understand what is meant by "making sense." The conversations in which we contruct our reflective lenses can not only make the participants more or less reflective, they also focus our reflection.

Conversations about literacy, then, can also cripple children as learners by limiting the extent of the self-evaluation they do and by making them repeatedly evaluate themselves as having failed, or worse, as being failures. This happens when children set evaluative criteria that they cannot attain. The easiest way to draw students' attention to what they can't do is to view them through a set of external standards, particularly normative ones. Students who are furthest from accomplishing the standards are the ones who will have the most negative image reflected back to them. Children are different from one another, though, and problematic criteria can arise in a variety of ways. For example, a child who learns about the separate sounds that make up spoken words and about print detail before muscle development allows easy control of a pen can easily set evaluation criteria that will make writing singularly frustrating. A child who is unaware of such details may find it easier to set more manageable performance criteria.

Portfolios are a wonderful way of examining the criteria that students have developed. As they reflect on their work in their portfolios and make decisions about what to put into the portfolio and what not to, students reveal the criteria they value and provide an opportunity for conversations about these values. As we shall see, their criteria can be quite diverse and have quite complex sources.

All of this is also true of teachers. If they feel that there is only one way to teach, that there is a single correct way to evaluate progress, they will be likely to feel that they are not doing it correctly but that someone else is, or at least that one of their colleagues is better at it. This breeds insecurity, which tends to deprive them of the conditions necessary to talk comfortably about their own practice and to be self-critical. Insecurity produces defensiveness and, in turn, backbiting, which is destructive in every way. It must be clearly understood that *all of us* can improve our teaching practice and that there are many ways to do a good job. This is exactly what we would want our students to understand about their literacy. Teaching is like writing a novel: there is more than one good thing to write about and more than one good way to write about it.

Just as with reading and writing, some of the criteria for evaluating teaching come from our observation of others as they teach. The models need not be "better" in any sense, just different. It is the juxtaposition of one's own practice against someone else's that produces the tension needed to rethink, especially when we can talk about the differences and similarities and the theories underlying them.

Emphasis on the Positive

If our assessments are to result in increased learning and productive self-evaluation, they must emphasize assets—what a student does well. I cannot stress this enough, so I will explain the reasons why it is so. First, emphasizing a student's assets builds a positive basis for the relationship between teacher and student and between student and literacy. Second, it confirms the student's existing knowledge. Third, it allows the student to attend to any difficulties from a position of strength. The idea is to see in detail what the student has done and hear the motives and feelings that come with it. From this, we help the student attribute to him- or herself the best that is there. This does not mean avoiding difficulties, but rather framing them with what is done well. Nel Noddings (1984) put this clearly when she said:

> What the teacher reflects to [the student] continually is the best
> possible picture consonant with reality. She does not reflect fantasy nor
> conjure up "expectations" as strategies. She meets him as he is and
> finds something admirable and, as a result, he may find the strength to
> become even more admirable. (p. 179)

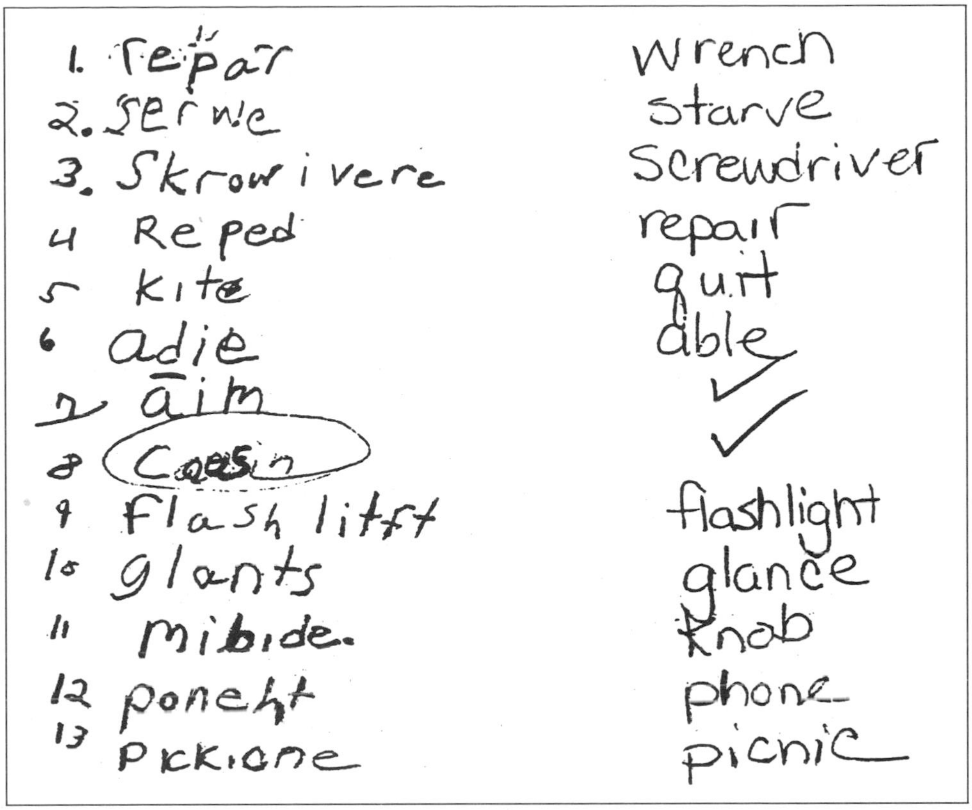

1. repar	wrench
2. serwe	starve
3. Skrowivere	Screwdriver
4 Reped	repair
5 kite	quit
6 adie	able
7 aim	✓
8 (Coesin)	✓
9 flash litft	flashlight
10 glants	glance
11 mibide.	knob
12 poneht	phone
13 Pckione	picnic

FIGURE 5.1 *Matt's Spelling Test*

Let me give you an example. Matt, a sixth-grade student who is classified as learning disabled, did his weekly spelling test of words selected from his own writing. When he got his test back from the teacher it looked like Figure 5.1. His interpretation is that he got two right out of thirteen and, since this is one in a series of such performances, he is dispirited. Since he tried hard and failed anyway, Matt's interpretation is that he lacks the ability to spell. Increased effort would thus be futile. This kind of feedback is thoroughly unmotivating! (More on these motivational issues in Chapter 15.)

But let's look at what Matt actually did as he took this test. Start with item 2: *serwe/starve.* He has written the *s,* included a vowel and an *r,* used a *w* for the *v,* and has finished with the final *e*—that is, he has represented three of the four sounds in the word plus the final *e,* which does not represent a sound.

He moves on to *skrowivere/screwdriver.* There are eight or nine sounds in this word, depending on pronunciation, and Matt has represented seven of them. The *c/k* error is plausible. The *ow/ew* substitution is also understandable. Although the *dr* is missing, the *ver* is correct. Finally, his awareness that words often have an unpronounced *e* at the end shows up again. Good knowledge, just overapplied.

Next, *reped/repair.* If Matt heard *repaired* instead of *repair,* he has represented all of the sounds. Later in the test he goes back and "corrects" the wrong word so that his second spelling is *repar* (item 1), which has all the sounds represented and only one letter missing from the conventional spelling.

Kite/quit. Here again Matt has all but one of the sounds represented, and he is determined to use his knowledge of that elusive final *e.*

Adie/able. One reversed letter would make this so close. I wonder why he put the *i* instead of the *l.*

Aim and *cousin* are conventionally spelled. Furthermore, Matt corrected *cousin* himself.

Flashlitft/flashlight. Matt spells *flashlit,* then thinks, "No. The ending has that weird stuff." Then he remembers about the lesson they had on *gh* and how it sometimes has the *f* sound, so he adds the *f,* looks at his word and is sure that the word *flashlight* ends with a *t,* so he adds one. All the sounds are represented, even ones that require two letters; there is just one confusion here.

Glants/glance. Sounds like *pants.* All of the sounds are there, only the wrong word family was used as a model.

Poneht/phone. Matt remembers that, for some inexplicable reason, *phone* starts with a *p* instead of the sensible *f,* then spells the rest of the word *(one)* conventionally (with his final silent *e* knowledge coming in handy at last). But the word doesn't look right. He knows there is an *h* in it somewhere, so he adds that. But he also knows that the *h* is not by itself. Usually an *h* comes with a *t,* so he adds that as the final touch. Lots of knowledge and lots of self-correction here.

Pickicne/picnic. Matt knows that *c* usually has a *k* after it and spells the first half of the word with that in mind. He finishes with *ic,* realizes he forgot the *n,* adds that, and, since it still doesn't look right, adds that important *e* again as a finishing touch.

Some of my interpretation here is my assumption, because Matt's concerned teacher showed this test to me some days after it had been done. If I had spoken with Matt at the time he took the test I am sure he could have filled in the details more accurately. Asking him to do so, and pointing out all the good things he did along the way would be a most productive assessment. It would be productive because it would be positive and specific. It is not enough just to be positive.

It is easiest to help students focus on assets if there are a lot of them to notice. In Matt's case a more manageable set of words would change the testing situation some. Choosing words from his written work makes sense, but choosing them bearing in mind what he knows would be even better. Perhaps fewer of them would be a good idea too. In the same way, an assessment of a child's reading will be more productive if he or she begins by reading something successfully and proceeds to more challenging, but manageable material. I don't mean that the child should have a brief period of success followed by extensive failure. The majority of a session specifically concerned with evaluation should be spent engaged in activities the child can manage moderately well, though sometimes with a stretch. Marie Clay (1993b), in describing tutoring sessions that accelerate the reading development of children experiencing difficulty, advocates spending several sessions "roaming the known." By this she means engaging the student in activities that require minimal teacher intervention, in which the student explores and becomes more comfortable with what he or she already knows and can do.

Specificity

In some classrooms, when children publish books they leave space in the back for responses. This offers the chance for ongoing feedback that might expand a child's understanding of audience. But consider some of the comments made by teachers in the back of one of these books:

> "Real nice story."
> "Great book!"
> "What a wonderful story about Tiff. Nice job!"
> "I really loved this and all of your books! Keep writing!"
> "You did a super job!"

Although attending to the positive is important, it is equally important that the response be focused. General praise, such as "Good work" and "Correct," communicates mainly that you, the teacher, know what counts, and this often leads children to read and write for praise rather than for what the reading and writing can do to and for *them*. Specific feedback makes it possible for the child to apply the criteria subsequently in your absence. Furthermore, nonspecific praise makes possible a breakdown in trust. A friend of mine in her thirties observed that as a teenager she used to get dressed up to go out on Saturday night and her mother would say, "You look really nice, dear." After a while, she became suspicious of her mother's constant reaction and decided to run a test. She put on an ugly outfit. When she got the same response as always from her mother, she decided there was nothing her mother could say to her in the future on the subject of dress that would have any significance for her. She discredited the source of information as untrustworthy.

The Process

Sometimes, the positive aspect of a piece of writing is a single word that works really well, or a sentence or metaphor. Sometimes there is little in the produced piece of writing that is positive, but the process the student used was admirable. For example, when Matt was doing his spelling, sometimes he sounded out the words, sometimes he checked to see if it looked right, and sometimes he made an effort to correct an error when he found one. Each of these practices is admirable and worth drawing his attention to—more important than the word he got right the first time.

Evaluating the process helps us see what strategies we can help students learn or use more effectively. In doing so, we draw students' attention to the "how" of the matter. We might say, "I notice that you spelled the sounds in 'screwdriver.' How did you know to put an *e* on the end?" or "I noticed that you decided to change the way you wrote 'cousin.' How did you know?" or "How did you know to put the *f* in the last part of 'flashlight'?" When assessing students' reading, we can say, "How did you figure out . . .?" or "When you read this part, you noticed that it did not make sense, so you went back and fixed it so that it made sense. Good thinking."

The Trajectory

Children (and adults) are inclined to attend only to their current state of knowledge and competence—a small window in their learning. When students put together a portfolio of their work, or for some other reason return to work they did a while ago, they have the chance to notice changes in their competence. Their attention can be focused on their development in other ways, too. Jane Hansen (1987) asks children, "What have you learned most recently in writing?" Don Graves (1994) refers to students having "a sense of history" about their learning. In other words, children begin to see their learning as changing and growing. As they gain a sense of history, they also gain a sense of possibility, a sense that their learning has a trajectory. This means they break free of the small window through which most of us catch glimpses of our learning. When Hansen also asks, "What are you working on learning next?" she reinforces this sense of possibility. Asking "What will you do to learn about that?" takes the matter a step further by asking students to take control of their learning. Self-evaluations that develop this sense of possibility and control are productive both because they are motivating and because they draw attention not only to the literate process, but also to the learning process.

Keeping these ideas in mind can help us produce classroom conversations that enable children to develop useful reflective lenses. By way of example, my children's soccer careers have featured many coaches. Some scream from the sidelines (as do parents). They offer lots of advice (reducing the children's own self-evaluation and problem-solving), use bad timing (shouting when the kids' attention is needed on what they are doing), and often focus on the negative. The outcome of such practices is not positive. They largely produce habitual second-guessing and feelings of incompetence. One coach, however, took a different tack. At the beginning of the game she reviewed what went well in the last game and mentioned one or two aspects of the team's play that needed work. Throughout the game she said little, allowing the girls to concentrate on their game. However, she would regularly substitute players, and as the player came off the field she would ask, "What did you just do?" She noticed the player doing something, usually something right, and helped the player notice it for herself and celebrate it before sending her back into the game and bringing someone else off. For the team reviews at half and full time, she took the same tack: asking "What is going well?" followed by "What will you do differently in the second half [or next time]?" This is good assessment practice. Stay out of the way, help students see what they are doing well, and help them focus and take control of their own learning.

The Trajectory

41

$\mathcal{W}$HAT MAKES LITERATE ACTIVITY EASY OR DIFFICULT?

$\mathcal{J}$erome Bruner (1985) has observed that "it is possible to construct not only experimental studies but 'real life' situations that make people (or pigeons, for that matter) look stupid or clever, generative or passive, combinatorial or rote" (p. 5). If we are to document children's literate activity, particularly if we are to emphasize their assets, we must be able to arrange situations in which they will behave in their most literate ways. For example, it would probably not be a good idea to ask a first grader to read from a college physics book so we could find out how she goes about reading. If we want to see the nature of her competence, we must arrange a situation that allows her to display that competence and describe both the circumstances and the competence. In this chapter and the next, I explore what makes literate activity more or less difficult, so that you can recognize and prevent problems associated with inappropriate difficulty, and understand the limitations of some of the ways teachers have tried to do this in the past.

Readability

For decades people have tried to answer the question "How can I tell how difficult this text is so that I can find material easy enough for my student?" Readability formulas were invented in the 1920s in an attempt to solve this problem (see Klare 1984 for a historical review of readability formulas). The idea was that if we can administer a test to find out how difficult a text a student can read, and if we can measure how difficult the texts really are, we can perfectly match student with text. A 3.3 grade level text should fit a 3.3 grade level student, and a 3.1 level text should be easy reading for such a student. Although this idea is intuitively appealing, it really has little to offer.

The recipe for making a readability formula is as follows. First, select a set of texts that seem to be of varying levels of difficulty. If you want the formula to work well, choose texts that range from extremely easy to extremely difficult. Second, have a large number of people read these texts (the wider the range in age the better your results will appear) and measure their ability to read them, usually by asking comprehension questions or having the readers perform cloze (fill in the missing word) activities. Third, describe the texts with as many different quantitative indicators as possible. You will need measures of word difficulty, sentence complexity, and any other factors that seem important. For example, you might include the number of words per sentence, letters per word or sentence, syllables per word or sentence, polysyllabic words, and low frequency words (those not on high frequency word lists), as well as the percentage of words with over a certain number of letters, abstract words, and pronominal modifiers. Now feed all this information into a computer and have it determine which set of these numerical indicators best predicted people's scores on the comprehension questions or cloze test. This will give you a formula like the Flesch Reading Ease formula (see Klare 1984):

grade level = .39 (average words per sentence) + 11.8 (average syllables per word) − 15.59

Some states still use formulas such as this to decide whether or not basal reading companies have set their reading materials at the appropriate level of difficulty. The U.S. military services also use them to decide whether their suppliers are writing manuals easy enough for their personnel to read. We can also find on the cover of many children's paperback books a grade level indicator based on these formulas so that, for example, an eighth grader will know what he or she should and should not be able to read.

The general notion behind readability formulas makes so much intuitive sense to so many people that it seems almost foolish to question it. It is so logical and scientific. Indeed, these formulas, applied to books in general, can produce a rank ordering of difficulty that will apply to the average performance of a large number of people who are reading texts in order to answer questions about them. But there are large differences between individuals, so that for any individual the ordering might be quite different. This is particularly so in kindergarten and first grade. It is one thing to talk about an average level of difficulty for a large number of students and quite another to apply that ordering to a particular student. It requires qualifying the ranking with "all else being equal," which is simply never the case. This and other problems will become apparent presently, as I describe the many factors that cannot be included in formulas (see also Klare 1984 and Davison and Kantor 1982).

The Responsibility of Choice

The appealing idea behind readability formulas is that if we could just have an accurate measure of a child's competence and a good measure of a book's difficulty, we could match readers and books perfectly. But even if it were possible to have a test provide a clear measure of a child's reading "level" and to measure the readability "levels" of books accurately (and it is not), it would be inefficient, time-consuming, and dependency-producing. Students must learn to judge for themselves in the end, and the kind of framework that formulas create restricts their opportunity to learn how. Loss of choice also results in a reduction in motivation. To have chosen a book to read does not feel the same as having been told to read that book. The formula framework also does not take individual students' interests into account—another blow to motivation. Besides, how often would we have to test reading competence (which we hope changes continually)? Currently, many children are misassigned to materials that are either far too difficult or far too easy for them; those most likely to be misassigned are the less competent students, who are generally given material that is too difficult (Gambrell, Wilson, and Gantt 1981)—often deliberately! I have heard school principals assert that every student in their school reads grade level material. They are not allowed to "read off level." Some of the currently popular basal readers are also based on this thinking. Apart from being inhumane, this is a terrible misunderstanding of both the properties of the formulas and of how to encourage reading competence.

A more productive way to match readers with texts is to have students choose a book and have them develop a sense of whether or not it is of an appropriate difficulty. Teachers can keep track of the extent to which students are accomplishing this. We might listen to their oral reading, simply ask them whether or not they think the book is too difficult, or engage them in a conversation about the book. We might call this method of letting students choose their own texts the "library model." The idea seems almost too simple to be taken seriously. The diagram shown in Figure 6.1 compares the two approaches to matching reader with text.

How did we get ourselves and our students into such a fix? The belief that children are incapable of making reasonable choices and knowing what's good for themselves has been around for a very long time. It fits well with the belief that teachers have the knowledge to deliver to the children, who (unless they are learning disabled) are sitting around waiting to absorb it. Suppose the local librarian decided to determine all the library patrons' reading levels before allowing them to take out books (which of course would have readability indexes to match). This plan would not be received well by the general public, I think. Yet we try desperately to do this in schools though, by and large, children are quite good at selecting books of an appropriate level of difficulty on their own if given the chance, the options, and some guidance (Spiro and Johnston 1989). If a book is too easy, a child is likely to get bored and put it down; and if a book is too hard, he or she is likely to get frustrated and put it down. The trick is for teachers to keep track of what *is* being read, and to make sure that when one book is put down another is picked up. There are, of course, conditions under which children will

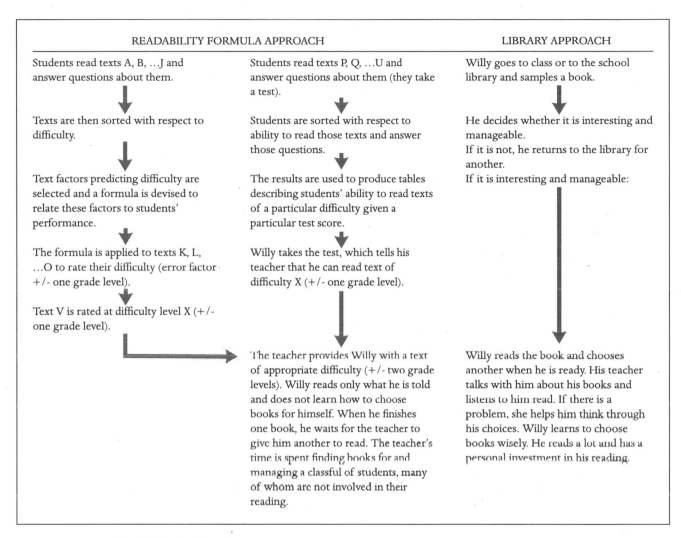

READABILITY FORMULA APPROACH		LIBRARY APPROACH
Students read texts A, B, …J and answer questions about them.	Students read texts P, Q, …U and answer questions about them (they take a test).	Willy goes to class or to the school library and samples a book.
Texts are then sorted with respect to difficulty.	Students are sorted with respect to ability to read those texts and answer those questions.	He decides whether it is interesting and manageable. If it is not, he returns to the library for another. If it is interesting and manageable:
Text factors predicting difficulty are selected and a formula is devised to relate these factors to students' performance.	The results are used to produce tables describing students' ability to read texts of a particular difficulty given a particular test score.	
The formula is applied to texts K, L, …O to rate their difficulty (error factor +/- one grade level).	Willy takes the test, which tells his teacher that he can read text of difficulty X (+/- one grade level).	
Text V is rated at difficulty level X (+/- one grade level).		
	The teacher provides Willy with a text of appropriate difficulty (+/- two grade levels). Willy reads only what he is told and does not learn how to choose books for himself. When he finishes one book, he waits for the teacher to give him another to read. The teacher's time is spent finding books for and managing a classful of students, many of whom are not involved in their reading.	Willy reads the book and chooses another when he is ready. His teacher talks with him about his books and listens to him read. If there is a problem, she helps him think through his choices. Willy learns to choose books wisely. He reads a lot and has a personal investment in his reading.

FIGURE 6.1 *Book Selection Procedures*

make unsatisfactory choices, and I discuss these in Chapter 8. If children are not able to choose well, that is a problem to be taken seriously in our instruction, rather than avoided by always choosing for them.

What Makes Literate Activity Easy

Knowledge of what makes reading and writing more or less difficult is invaluable for teachers. In one case, Terry was asked, "How do you decide what books to read?" His response was that it has to be "easy, but not too easy" and that it should have "not too many words on the pages—and a few pictures to make it interesting." When asked about type of book, he said "Oh, less than 100 pages maybe, but with chapters so it would look hard . . . It has to look like the books the other kids are reading, but I'll really know it's easy enough for me." In another, Steven was not enjoying writing at school. His writing was done in booklets the teacher provided. He mentioned his dislike of writing to his teacher, and she asked him why. He said that it was just too much to write, that "there are too many pages." His teacher, realizing Steven's confusion, pointed out that he did not have to fill all of the pages in the booklet; he only had to write what he wanted. Later, when the children were asked what they had learned in writing that day, they said all sorts of things, but Steven said, "I learned that writing is fun." The apparently small change in his conception of the goal of the activity was Copernican in its consequences. For a while it was popular in educational circles to talk about "time on task." In some circles it still is. But, as many have noted, children are always on task; the important question is, what is the task? In Steven's case, the change in his understanding led not so much to a change in his time on task, but to a change in the nature of the activity he was engaged in, and the feelings he had while being engaged in it.

Knowing how a literate activity can be made more manageable for a novice is useful for both instruction and evaluation. For example, if a student is struggling with a book, it helps the teacher to know that reading the book to him or her first might result in the student's being able to read it independently. It is also useful if we can show that a student is able to manage increasingly difficult reading, because then we can make an argument that he or she has learned something. For example, if it were possible to come up with measures of text difficulty, there is the promise of being able to show progress by showing that a student is able to read more difficult books than before.

There are numerous ways to make a text easier or more difficult for children to read. As just mentioned, simply reading the book to the child first will make it easier to read. The more readings, and the more recent the readings, the greater the memory the child will have for the text, and the easier the text will be. Also, familiarity with the topic helps. If a child knows a lot about farms or dirt bikes, then books about farms or dirt bikes are likely to be easier to read than books on topics about which he or she knows little. A well-illustrated book is generally easier than one without illustrations. Of course, there are always caveats. For example, the "authors" of some reading series deliberately try to make the pictures give no clue to the meaning of the text in order to force children to attend more to the print. In addition, if children are made to think that reading does not necessarily involve seeking meaning, illustrations may be irrelevant to them.

These and many other factors that determine the readability of a text are listed in Table 6.1. Knowing what makes a text easy means that it is virtually always possible to obtain a reading sample, even when a student is relatively new to literacy. For example, when a text is read to the student first it will make it easier, especially if it is short, predictable, melodic, and interesting. Similarly, even relative novices can read back a sentence that they have just dictated, especially if the criterion for success is preserving the meaning of what was dictated rather then exactly replicating the words.

TABLE 6.1

Some Factors that Affect the Ease of Reading Activities

Text Characteristic	Factors Affecting Ease of Reading
Student's history	Familiarity of the specific text from previous readings Familiarity of the concepts in the text Recency of the experience with the concepts or the text itself Successful experience with the text or related text Extent of own relevant personal experience

Language in text	Familiarity with book language
	Familiarity with the structure (e.g., the commonalities in narrative form across familiar stories)
	Complexity and diversity of the syntax
	Naturalness of the language
	Repetition of sequences of language
	Melody and rhythm of the language
	Pattern of the language:
	  • rhyme
	  • cyclical patterns (e.g., repeated episodes)
	  • size of unit in cycle
	  • cultural patterns (counting, days of the week, months, etc), idioms

Structure	Narrative vs. nonnarrative Plot complexity Inference load (especially causal and motivational)
Vocabulary used	Simplicity Decodability Repetition Density of new vocabulary Vividness or memorableness *(continued)*

If I read about Taoism having never encountered the term before, I will have a difficult time understanding what I am reading. Similarly, if I have not experienced the joy of reading a tax form many times, I will have considerable trouble with that. The more times I read a given tax form, the easier it is to read it the next time. The more experience I have reading tax forms in general, the easier they will tend to become. A four-year-old can read all 1500-odd words of Bill Peet's *Cowardly Clyde* if it has been read to him enough times so that the memory of it is almost perfect. Similarly, a child can read material that is substantially beyond her usual performance level if it has been rehearsed. Children are very sensitive to the natural rhythms and melodies of the language, and as the melodies become internalized, they can be used to help children determine, for example, how many

TABLE 6.1

continued

FORMAT	Lines per page Complete message on each page vs. each page only part of narrative Diversity and complexity of page layout Sheer quantity of print/number of pages
ILLUSTRATIONS	Aesthetic stimulation Contextual support Intellectual stimulation
IMMEDIATE FUNCTIONALITY	Practical objectives (construction, entertainment, etc.) or select menu items Relationship to desirable activities
READER REACTION	Desire to return to the text/context Intellectual stimulation Aesthetic stimulation
AUDIENCE REACTION	Interest Support
PERSONAL CONTROL	Of reading rate Choice of material Choice of response
CONTEXT AND GOAL	Comparative vs. cooperative focus of class Public performance vs. private experience Definition of success or failure (e.g., word level accuracy vs. meaningfulness) Consequences contingent on failure or success
TEACHER INTERVENTION	Prompting strategy use, monitoring, etc. Supplying missing information Highlighting success

Sources: Holdaway 1979; Peterson 1988; New Zealand Department of Education 1980.

syllables should be in a given word or phrase. "Patty cake, patty cake, baker's man" is readily distinguished from "Twinkle twinkle little star" aside from the words, and the knowledge that allows this distinction can be used to support a child's reading of many kinds of books. Rhyme, too, can make words much easier to read. The predictability that comes from these rhythms and patterns makes oral language, with its the familiar patterns, initially more readable than "book language," with its less familiar patterns.

Determining difficulty of writing assignments is also complicated. A group of students assigned to write about "my vacation" will not find it equally easy to do.

One perhaps remained indoors watching television, while another went to Disneyland. The memorableness of the experience will make a difference both to the child's recall and to the ease with which an audience can be engaged. At the same time, when there is a lot to say a writer may find it hard to focus and select relevant detail. In addition, a child raised in an authoritarian household will find it more difficult to write a persuasive letter than will a child raised in a household that tolerates or values negotiation, even though both have similar knowledge of the topic.

The point is that the ease with which a particular person reads or writes on any given occasion is influenced by a range of factors. A sensitivity to these factors is critical if we are to help readers and writers be successful and document their development. Although there are predictable patterns of task difficulty "on average," there is also a great deal of individual variation.

CHAPTER 7

CONTROLLING THE EASE OF LITERATE ACTIVITIES

When teaching children to read, we do what we can to ensure that they read material of just the right difficulty. Children learn most when they are operating in what Lev Vygotsky (1962) called the "zone of proximal development." By this he meant those activities that a learner can do with some support: the area between what he or she can do independently and what he or she cannot do even with support. Support can come in the form of collaboration with a teacher or a peer, and the providers of support need not be more competent than the learner; their collaboration need only bring the activity within reach of the learner. For example, when two children write together on a computer, one often takes on the role of transcriber, while the other takes more responsibility for composition. The support each provides allows the other to muster all of his or her resources on one role, rather than having to split them between two.

Not only do children learn most when operating within the zone of proximal development, but as they do so, they display the most instructionally useful information about their learning. Setting up contexts in which children may often find themselves operating within this zone is thus a critical part of a teacher's job. This is one reason why teachers' knowledge of their students and of literature is critical. The more the teacher knows about both, the easier it will be for that teacher to find a book that is both manageable and interesting for a particular student. The more a teacher knows about what makes books more or less difficult, the easier it is to make more difficult books accessible. This is particularly important for students whose interests are beyond their competence.

A teacher must know, then, how to adjust the difficulty of literate activity. But, as we shall see, it is easy to make mistakes. Fortunately, if our relationship with our students is good, and the situation is not ego-involving, students will help correct our errors of judgment. This will not happen in a testing situation, though, and testing brings up another reason for controlling the difficulty of literate activity. In order to ascertain whether children have become better at reading, we commonly make a test, administer it twice, and look at changes in student performance. A skeptic might say that any improvement in performance from the first time with the text to the second was explained by the fact that, on taking the test the second time, the students were simply familiar with the test. To avoid this problem, psychometricians try to construct parallel or alternate forms of a test—tests that have the same form, but are different in content while being equivalent in difficulty. I will return to this in the companion book to this volume, but for now let me say that creating parallel forms is not so difficult for *groups* of children. We can say that *on average* two activities are comparable in difficulty, and there is a very large branch of measurement theory busily engaged in trying to produce such tasks and the mathematics to justify them. However, as established in the last chapter, it is impossible to say in advance that two activities will be equally difficult for two different children, or even for the same child, one reason being that a student can change from day to day. So with that in mind, let's examine the consequences of manipulating some of the different aspects of literacy, and the problems that can arise.

Context, Motives, and Goals

A teacher can make a given story, or any literate activity, easy or difficult simply by changing the context or the goals of the activity. Consider the following two cloze activities that accompany a certain text. Which is more difficult?

    a.   We went to the shop to buy some _____.
    b.   We went to the shop to buy some b_____.

The answer depends on what is required. If we simply require a response that fits the information given in the text, then *a* is easier because it is more open-ended, with fewer constraints to be satisfied. There are many possible answers for *a*, and fewer for *b*. If, however, the child thinks the task is to find *the one right* word, the one the teacher has in mind, then *b* is easier than *a* because there is more information available to find the right answer.

The child's understanding of the nature of the activity also influences the difficulty of writing. For example, I have seen few children as reluctant to write as Jimmy. Jimmy was in third grade, and my assignment was to improve his reading. After reading *Teach Us Amelia Bedelia* (Parish 1977), we began a session on writing. I told him that we were going to do some writing, and I asked him if there was anything that he could think of to write about. He began to talk about his summer vacation in New Brunswick. Until that point in our association, Jimmy had said very little without prompting, but he sallied forth into a lengthy description of his vacation. It clearly meant a lot to him. So I expressed great interest in the topic and set about finding and writing down a topic by thinking out loud about some ideas. I told him that the rules for writing were that we had to concentrate on writing the story and that we could spell words any way we wanted. Spelling didn't matter. He said "O.K." Then, while I wrote, he wrinkled his face into thoughtful, composing expressions while not touching his paper. After a while the pretense wore off and he just stared blankly at the wall. I looked up from my work and asked, "What's the problem?"

He said, "I can't write."

"You just told me a fascinating story, Jimmy. Remember what you told me about?"

"My vacation."

"O.K.," I said. "Write that down as best you can: 'My Vacation.'"

I resumed my writing, but again Jimmy just sat there, staring. After a few minutes, I said, "Are you having trouble?"

He replied, "We had to write a story about this before, but my mom had to help me with all the words like 'New Brunswick' and stuff."

I asked him if he did any writing in class; he said he did. I asked him what he did when he came to a word he didn't know. He said, "We can look it up in a dictionary or the teacher will tell us." I explained that we do things differently here and that spelling really doesn't matter when we are composing a story. "You can write the words any way you like. We can clean it up later. This is just a draft."

He then began to write, but erased his first word three times before I explained that writers are allowed to be messy. I showed him my paper, which had cross-outs and corrections, but Jimmy was clearly uncomfortable about risking invented spelling. So I suggested he just leave blanks for the words he didn't know. While I wrote, he wrote the following:

My _____ of the _____.
i _____ in a _____

I took a break from my writing to help Jimmy. He read what he had written to me: "My vacation of the year. I left in a . . ." But he could not remember what he intended for the last blank. Then he realized that he had meant to write "on a Sunday" and began to erase *in*. I suggested he just modify the word to *on*. We then began to figure out how to write *left*.

"What letter might start the word?"

"L."

"Can you hear any other sounds in the word?"

"F."

"O.K. . . ."

"E."

"'Left'—how could you end it?"

"T."

And so we got *lFet*. We moved on to "Sunday."

"How would you start it?"

S, he writes, then pauses; *U* , he writes, then pauses; *N*, he writes, then pauses; then he writes *day*: he spelled the word accurately and conventionally.

We moved on to "vacation." He wrote *Vak* and then was stuck. I said, "Va-caa," stretching the sounds, and he said, "I already have the *a*" (of course he did: when you say the letter *k*, an *a* sound is built into the letter name). So I said, "-*tion*. What would start that?"

"C. No. S." He then wrote *c*.

"And what does it end with?"

"*Shun*. N. I-N-G." Jimmy recognized the common ending *ing*. His analysis of the sounds of words took him so far, then his visual memory of words took over. (More on this in Chapters 21 and 22.) So we ended up with *Vakcing*. We moved on to "year." With no prompting he wrote *yere*. He then proceeded to extend the story by writing *i dov for 7 or 8 orers* (I drove for 7 or 8 hours).

Jimmy made quite clear at the outset his definition of the activity and his criteria for success, or rather for failure. To misspell a word constituted failure at writing, and his goal was the avoidance of failure rather than the achievement of success. Avoiding failure meant not misspelling any words. Jimmy's definition of the task, which arose from the context in which he normally wrote, made it extremely difficult for him to write.

Another child with a similar problem was Mickey, who began writing *I have a dog*, all words he thought he could spell. He wrote *I have a go* and realized he had gone wrong. Instead of crossing out *go* and writing *dog*, he said, "Wait. G-o-d—that's a word. *I have a god*. [He finished writing it.] There!" Having selected a low-risk sentence to write, Mickey was content to sacrifice even the intended meaning so as not to mess up his page. Making writing easier for these students involves changing their definition of what it means to write.

The Consequences of Control

The factors I have described contexts, motives, and goals influence not only the ease or difficulty of the literate activity, but also the manner in which it is done—the strategies used along the way. For example, a child reading a text for amusement has a different goal from reading to find specific information, which in turn is a different goal from reading to answer questions about the text, or reading it aloud to an audience. Writing a list because the textbook requires it is different from writing one to make sure that you take all the things you need to camp. Having to write something formal within a time limit is likely to cause you to choose words that you are sure of, and that are easily spelled, unless you have a secretary or a spelling program on your word processor. When the goal of the reading or writing, or the context, is different, the strategies the reader or writer uses are likely to be different.

Because of the interrelatedness of goals, contexts, and strategies, trying to control the difficulty of literate activities can result in problems for the unwary. Educators have tried to make texts easier by using various combinations of these factors for a long time. Sometimes they have relied too much on particular techniques, causing children's reading development to become distorted in one way or another by restricting their way of viewing reading and the strategies they use to read. For example, a child who has been learning to read by using texts that have been controlled for phonic regularity is likely to read example *a* below with some ease, yet have difficulty with example *b* because his or her decoding strategies will simply not be adequate for handling the words (Bartlett 1979; Clay 1991; Juel 1988). Similarly, a child whose reading experience is limited to material like example *b* will likely have difficulty reading example *a* because the prediction strategy that he or she is used to simply will not work. Neither will self-correcting from meaning, since text *a* is not highly meaningful.

a. The man and his cat can get in the pit.
    The tan fan is in the can.
    The man and his cat can not get at the fan.

b. Rachel ran up the stairs,
    Rachel knocked over chairs,
    Rachel tore out her hairs
    When the ghosts came out on Halloween.

As we control difficulty using one means, such as the highly decodable words in example *a*, we can deprive the reader of interest (and hence motive), meaningfulness, and relevance of prior knowledge, and increase the concern over accuracy of word pronunciation, thus achieving an overall increase in the difficulty of this activity, and possibly similar activities in the future. The material read can also act as a model of authorship for readers; thus students' writing can wind up resembling the kind of text they are reading (Eckhoff 1983; McGill-Franzen and Allington 1991). (I will return to this idea in Chapter 11.)

The context of the activity is very important. Even such texts as "The man on the land can get tan fog from the log" can have their place. If they are read as nonsense, which children enjoy immensely, they are fine and may well encourage children to play with language themselves. Indeed, it may heighten their comprehension ability by allowing them to explore possibilities and by helping them to define more clearly the boundaries between sense and nonsense. But if such texts are presented as serious reading material, children are likely to get the impression that that is what reading really is and that it has little to do with making sense. They may try desperately to make sense out of the nonsense and produce oral reading errors that reflect such attempts. In short, systematic control of children's reading material through any simple means is rather like the Japanese art of bonsai. It systematically distorts the growth of a child's reading. The result is rather less desirable in a child's reading than in a houseplant.

Another way to alter the difficulty of the task is for the teacher to provide some support. Teacher intervention as part of evaluation has been advocated by many researchers of late in the name of what is called "dynamic assessment" or "interactive assessment" (Feuerstein 1979; Vygotsky 1962). A common term for such assistance is "scaffolding." The idea is that an activity that would normally be out of reach of a given student can be accomplished if the teacher helps by providing certain kinds of support or instruction until the student can take these functions over independently. For example, when a student is reading and cannot figure out a word, the teacher could either provide the word or offer a prompt, such as "What would make sense there?" or "What does it start with?" or "How could you figure that out?" Each of these kinds of support is appropriate in certain conditions and can supply the teacher with information about what strategies the student has but does not automatically use, which the student does not have at all, and so forth.

But giving support also has potential drawbacks. Under certain conditions, it can easily result in dependency, just as can happen with the overuse of any of the other difficulty controls. Students who use only predictable language material can easily end up overpredicting, being overdependent on the predictability of the language and not using or developing the knowledge they have of the details of print. Similarly, students who learn to read only on phonetically regularized text can easily become overdependent on the decoding aspect, failing to look for and use the larger patterns in the language. Students who are continually told the word without having to work it out for themselves can readily end up dependent on the teacher, and at the same time suffer an erosion of their confidence. Loss of confidence makes any task psychologically more difficult. This problem occurs most commonly when children use a basal reading program in which the teacher controls most of the reading. When children spend a fair amount of time reading material they select for themselves, the teacher is unable to help them all, and the children are more motivated to figure things out for themselves both because there will be less disruption of the story (they will not have to wait their turn for the teacher's help) and because it is *their* story: they selected it, they are involved in it.

Recently, a different kind of difficulty management has become popular. Some of the newer basal readers, for example, are based on the premise that all children in the same grade should read things that are at that grade level. The teacher's job is to bring the text into the range of all students in the class by using various techniques—rereading, "buddy reading," shared reading, and so forth. I imagine the reason behind this approach was to avoid ability grouping, certainly an admirable goal. But the consequences of this approach to difficulty management are possibly even more problematic than the others. Aside from the fact that the approach ignores individual interests, it guarantees that the most competent readers in the class will become bored, and the least competent will constantly be faced with material that is too difficult for them. Some of these less competent readers will find "buddy reading" uncomfortable and tedious, and they will sit back and let the more competent student do the reading, thus ensuring the continuation of their lack of competence.

An important side effect of helping a child engage in manageable literate activity is that she comes to know what it feels like to learn within her own zone of proximal development, and to distinguish that from the feeling of literate activity that is too difficult. This means that teachers should set up situations in which students often, with support, become involved in literate activities at a level just beyond what they can normally manage by themselves. And teachers can apply this principle to themselves as well as their students. If you attempt something far beyond your current capacities, you will likely become frustrated. Frustration leads to changes in emotional and cognitive activity, and this leads to reduced effectiveness and ability to solve problems, and hence a destructive cycle (Argyris and Schon 1974). At the other extreme, if individuals continue to attain goals that require no new learning, their behavior becomes increasingly repetitive, routine, and primitive. Because they are not expanding their possibilities, their freedom of choice is also reduced, with predictable consequences for motivation (Argyris 1970). In the long run, we want children to take responsibility for managing the difficulty of their literate activity, and understanding the consequences of the choices they make.

There is, however, one thing to bear in mind. The more we overtly focus on the relative ease or difficulty of particular literate activities, the more we draw children's attention to that characteristic and away from engagement in the activities themselves. An overemphasis on ease or difficulty can invite comparisons with others, overconcern for ability, and ego- rather than task-involvement. In general, it is much better to focus children's attention on engagement.

CHOOSING AND ERRING

*C*hoice is important in the classroom. It is important to us and to our students both for its role in motivation and for the information choices yield about ourselves and our students. We do not always make good choices, nor do our students, but errors can be even more informative than good choices. The more we understand our choices, the reasons for them and their consequences, the more we can understand ourselves and our students as readers and writers, teachers and learners.

Choosing

It feels quite different to do something when you are forced to than it does when you have chosen to do it yourself. When children choose what books to read, whether to finish a book, and what interpretation to have of a book, they will read in a different way than if they cannot make these choices. They will also read more often. The same is true of writing. When I began writing one book, I signed a contract with a publisher to complete it in approximately two years. I said at the outset that I did not want a deadline, but they had paid me an advance on the royalties so that I might buy myself a word processor. As the deadline approached I found I was forcing myself to write. I walked with a stoop from the burden I felt, and I ultimately could not write at all. After discussing the problem with my wife, I decided to take a loan from the bank, pay back the advance, and write the book on my schedule instead of the publisher's. As soon as I had made this decision, I was able to write again. It is the feeling of free choice that matters. Thus it is also possible for a teacher to tell a student what to do, offering no choice, and for the student to do it joyfully because he has chosen to trust the teacher's judgment.

When readers and writers make choices, they reveal important information about what it means for them to be literate—for example, how they deal with constraints, what knowledge they have about audiences, what conventions they are familiar with, and what strategies they are apt to use. When you highlight the reasons for students' choices, and help them consider these reasons, they become more aware of the possibilities open to them and more able to choose wisely in the future. They become more in control of themselves as literate people. Thus a large part of our job as teachers is to help students increase their options, predict the consequences of their choices, and attend to the choices they make.

When people write and read, they make choices within their set of beliefs and a framework of socially sanctioned language conventions. They make choices among letters, words, sentences, books, authors, strategies, topics, audiences, goals, genres; about what to include and what to leave out of their writing; about what to finish and what not to finish. A student who reads the sentence "We all rushed into the pool" as "We all raced into the pool" is demonstrating not so much an inability to decode the word "rushed" as an intention to make meaning predominate over her desire to match all of the conventions of printed language. The same is true in writing. A writer intends to accomplish something and makes use of language and the conventions of the discourse community in a way to best attain his or her goals. A big part of the teacher's job is to help students accomplish their intentions by helping them make sensible choices, and by providing options among which they can choose.

People do not always make the best choices. In general, students are quite capable of choosing their own books; they are likely to choose ones that are interesting to them and of an appropriate difficulty. They even know to choose an easier book to read aloud than they would to read to themselves (Danner, Hiebert, and Winograd 1983). However, children who have been in the bottom reading group for the bulk of their school career are unlikely to be reading independently outside of school. They read only what they are told to read in school. Thus, not having had the experience of choosing their own books, they will not be good at it (Spiro and Johnston 1989). Furthermore, being in the bottom group, they very likely have been given material that is too difficult. As a consequence, they may never have experienced the feeling of reading something manageable and satisfying. With only their reading-group experience to guide them in their decisions, they are likely to make unwise choices.

Other factors can also influence their choices, for better or for worse. In some literature-based classrooms, a nasty rumor gets spread that there are such things as "baby books." This is most likely to occur in competitive classrooms and in classrooms in which there is a clear (and inappropriate) transition—for example, from illustrated books to chapter books. Children who do not find reading satisfying for one reason or another, or who feel insecure, sometimes find success or security in placing themselves above other children who appear less competent. Children who are not reading well in those classrooms will either choose books that are too difficult for them or will (more frequently) choose not to read at all.

Both choices are unhealthy ones. Any setting that produces a simplistic linear ranking of ability and of texts will produce this sort of problem.

Sometimes students will consistently choose "low risk" books—books they know they can read well. They do not challenge themselves to struggle with more difficult ideas and more complex language. Most children will be inclined to do this at times—adults too. It is not a problem unless a child chooses never to venture into more challenging books. In these cases, teachers can encourage children to choose "challenging books" or "brave books," and to have more than one book going at once. But as Nancie Atwell (1987) demonstrates, when students trust the teacher's judgment (a trust that has to be earned) they are very likely to read books the teacher suggests for them even though they could easily choose something else to read. Framing a challenge well can also help. For example, Don Graves (1991) suggests saying something like "I wonder whether you are ready for this . . ." (pp. 152–154).

The learner's decision-making process reveals his or her priorities. For example, when a child chooses a word he or she can spell, rather than misspell the word he or she really wanted to use, look it up in a dictionary, or ask someone, it says a great deal about the child's conception of the task in which he or she is engaged. This type of choice is one thing in a form letter and quite another thing in a draft of a piece of expressive writing. Understanding the thinking behind children's choices is thus instructionally indispensable. Listening to children think through their choices can be especially informative. For example, Jane Hansen (1987) listened to a student trying to decide which book to share with the class, Donald Hall's *The Man Who Lived Alone* or Patricia MacLachlan's *Arthur, for the Very First Time*. Mark said, "If I share *The Man Who Lived Alone*, I could read it all, but *Arthur* has some funny parts and they might like it better" (p. 160). In this statement, Mark tells us what he thinks his options are and on what grounds he is making his choice. He tells us that he understands the concerns of his audience, the constraints of time, and the trade-offs between presenting an entire work and excerpts. A child saying that he has chosen not to continue with a piece of writing because it did not have enough action, or a child who chooses to keep a character description and discard the rest of a piece of writing because "I can really feel myself being Betsy, and I just think that she would never do what I had her doing" tells us about what they think counts for readers and authors. Hansen quotes another student explaining the basis for her choices:

> I like both [writing with someone else and by myself]. If I'm writing
> about my kittens or my family I'd rather write by myself, unless a
> friend was along with me on a trip. If I'm writing a mystery or
> something, it's fun to have a friend. (p. 223)

This comment shows an awareness of the consequences of particular choices of topic and writing situation.

People make choices in their writing in order to accomplish a particular goal.

Asking a student at the beginning of a writing conference "What are you trying to do with this piece?" or "Where are you with this piece?" will get the intention out on the table. Once we understand a student's intention, we can help him or her accomplish it. But that is not all. Simply asking students such questions asserts that you expect that they are trying to do something with their piece, and that your role as teacher is to help them realize their intentions.

When choices do not accomplish intentions, or have unintended consequences, then the choice might be considered an error. If we intended to write using conventional spelling and form, but failed to do so, then we erred. If we did not intend to write using conventional spelling and form, but the social situation—a job application, for example—calls for it, and we fail to accomplish the purpose of our writing—getting the job—because we ignored the context of the writing when choosing the form our writing would take, we erred again.

The intentions we ascribe to readers and writers have a lot to do with how we perceive their command of the conventions. In other words, it matters whether we think they can represent language conventionally and choose not to, or if we think that they cannot and are therefore incompetent. A first grader taking the liberties with language that e. e. cummings did in his poetry is unlikely to receive comparable acclaim. The first grader is likely to be seen as erring, but it is a bold critic who suggests that cummings has done so. Indeed, when we read published books we look for voice in the way the writer uses and violates conventions and in the choices he or she has made.

Erring

If "to err is human," then why are people so afraid of making mistakes or, having made one, so keen to call it something else? Error is often the consequence of exploration. Error-free learning is very rigid learning. The advantage of mistakes is that you stand to learn something new when you have made one and noticed it. The best definition I have found is "A mistake is an event, the full benefit of which has not yet been turned to your advantage" (Senge 1990, p. 154). In fact, a good way to improve your teaching is to document at least three interesting errors you make each week. This takes the edge off making errors, and at the same time makes them instructional. Students too, might be interested in this approach.

For teachers, the most useful aspect of errors is that people do not make them randomly. There is always a reason for them. If you can figure out the reason, then you know where to use your instructional expertise without further confusing the student. Children's choices regarding literacy are based on the hypotheses they have developed through past and present literate experience, and on their various motivations and goals. Furthermore, what turns errors to advantage is identifying in them the partially correct. This is what we must help our students see.

In order to learn from your students' errors, you have to assume that others do not experience the world the same way you do, and then set out to see what it is like in their particular universe. Adults often make the mistake of assuming that children think like small, but mistaken, adults. But in many ways, children inhabit a different world put together with a different set of assumptions. Although we often mistakenly assume that children have the same logic as we do, it is even easier to assume that other adults have the same logic. But even small cultural differences can produce big differences in the way people think about themselves and others, the world, and literacy. The logic and intelligence of students' errors may be impeccable, but inconceivable from the teacher's perspective. Consider this story dictated by a three-year-old:

> My old cat was dead because he was probably sick. He was sick because I was not born yet. When I wasn't born yet, he wanted three children, so he died.
>
> We had three cats. One was my parents' cat and now, one we have right now. I liked number one better than number two.
>
> My mom's parents cat died and Opa ran over it. Opa was sad because that cat did not scratch.

This story suggests the limitation of our own system of thought, and the impossibility of being able to imagine how a child thinks. Yet children make such seemingly odd connections all the time, and teachers are constantly faced with exactly that imaginative challenge of figuring out their logic.

Standing where the learner stands in order to see his or her world is not easy, and it is something teachers must want to do. This is no more than we ask of students when we ask them to write (understand their audience), read (understand the author's use of language), and edit their writing from the perspective of a person who uses conventional language.

The critical parts of understanding errors and choices, then, are:

- The knowledge that people understand the world, and literacy, differently.
- The mind set to look for intentions and patterns of choices or errors.
- The imagination to envision how a pattern of choices or errors could be related to those particular intentions.
- The recognition that *error* does not mean *failure*.
- The understanding that learning without error is learning without exploration and is likely to be very narrow and inflexible learning.

Teachers often reach a point at which they understand intention and the positive nature of error, but lack the imagination to construct the possible ways in which the error could have occurred. This imagination develops as many different students explain the stories behind their particular errors and as teachers learn how literacy relates to the diversity of people's lives.

Helen Fox (1994), struggling to understand the logic of a graduate student's writing, drew on her experiences living in other cultures to understand a persistent error in his writing. Her student, Tony, repeatedly overgeneralized. For example, he generalized from the statements of individuals such as Spike Lee and Malcolm X to the opinions of the entire American people. In the United States, an individualistic country, this was a serious error of logic. But Tony was brought up in a collectivist culture, where public figures speak for everyone "in solidarity." The rules of evidence in the two cultures are quite different, and their effects spill over into Tony's writing.

We learn from our students' errors by reading them to understand their meaning, in just the same way as we might carefully read a book, attempting to make meaning of the particular uses of the language the author has made: the way in which the author has pressed the language into the service of her intentions. In doing so she uses the uniqueness of her own language along with the conventions of the culture. When a teacher knows how a student knows the conventions, she can be helpful in straightening out misconceptions (best done one-on-one) and introducing new knowledge about conventions and techniques (often best done in a group).

A key to understanding errors is often inferring intent, which is a lot harder to do from simply reading a piece of writing than it is from talking with the writer shortly after the writing was produced. The writer's *intention* is what organizes the writing. Thus, error analysis involves being able to take the perspective of the student so as to be able to imagine what produced that particular pattern. That is why a writing conference is often begun by asking the author to talk about the piece and what he or she is trying to accomplish with it. Intention also organizes reading, and teachers must similarly infer a reader's intentions in order to make sense of patterns of reading errors.

Suppose a child writes a letter: "U kld my frg. I hat U and U ar suped." She gives it to her friend. Her friend throws it on the ground and won't play with her the next day unless the letter is destroyed. Did the writer err? She may have not spelled the words conventionally, but the letter probably served her purposes well without her having to take the time to spell her words conventionally. At the same time, the child's choice to put her message in writing rather than simply saying it suggests her awareness of the powerful and permanent nature of print. If a child writes "A cat is on a bus. A hat is on a man," has he erred? If he writes this after talking at length about an exciting event in his life about which he was keen to communicate, then he has probably erred. His error is either in misperceiving the function of writing or in being led to believe (by his teacher) that convention takes precedence over meaning. In other words, he may have accurately perceived the nature of literacy in his classroom, and the error may not really be his.

In analyzing errors, there is lots of room for error. If we analyze incorrectly, we may end up reinforcing the source of the error. For example, consider a student who tries to "sound out" each word when he is reading orally, but is not particularly successful at it. We can interpret his performance as representing a particular kind of decoding problem—for example, that he "has trouble with consonant blends and medial vowels"—and set about trying to rectify this problem, with the probable result that he will focus even more on phonic analysis over the construction of meaning. Alternatively, we might interpret his performance as an indication of an erroneous perception of the nature of reading. If we do, the problem to be solved is how to help this student see that his intention in reading should be to make sense rather than to sound out each word correctly. Or, if we look further, we might find that the error lies in his selection of books that are too difficult, which results in his missing too many words and consequently lessening the possibility of his making sense from his reading.

Intentions arise in part from one's history. Often, adults who are having difficulty in reading and writing say that they want help with spelling and decoding problems, which are what they were taught they were not good at in school. While their stated intention is to learn to spell, concentrating on this alone means they will have a hard and unsatisfying road to becoming literate. Nonetheless, the sensible teacher will concede instructional time to the individual's perceived problem, rather than deny the value of that perception.

It is also very important for teachers to notice which errors a student knows how to detect and correct. Students need practice detecting and correcting errors, so that the correct form or choice becomes more automatic. Errors that the student can detect but not correct are the perfect place for instruction. But although this recognition is important, it is equally important for teachers to know whether the student has strategies for detecting and correcting errors. For example, reading their paper aloud to themselves helps some writers, reading it from the bottom to the top helps others, reading it to another student with the understanding that their partner say nothing helps others. We look for the kinds of errors a student can detect unaided, or within an identified sentence, and whether he has a feeling for the types of errors he commonly makes. When a student is aware of the kind of choices and errors he is likely to make, he can go about locating and subsequently preventing them. For example, when he is aware that he is inclined to leave -ed off the end of words, and that he tends to run sentences together, he can make an editorial pass through his work looking specifically for those errors. He might even keep a brief, and changing, list of these personal hurdles. Such a list, including changes, is most useful for evaluation purposes. Getting students involved in studying their own reading and writing puts them more in control of themselves as language users, rather than leaving them victims of a language they do not control.

Some of the errors evident in young children's writing, such as the confusion of word boundaries in *our next store nabor*, may also be found in the writing of graduate students (for example, I recently encountered the term *fact simily*). Each student has a particular pattern of errors, but teachers need to determine how common a particular pattern is before beginning instruction, since they need to decide whether individual or group instruction is warranted. Glynda Hull (1986) differentiates between "those things that the majority of students don't do in their writing," which are appropriate for group instruction, and "those things that they do incorrectly (which require both learning and unlearning)," which are better dealt with individually (p. 222).

One kind of error is produced by the mind's going faster than the pen or the eye. Other errors arise when a student tries on a language which he does not yet master. This can produce errors of all sorts, such as *all of the sudan* and *imput*. But of course the error might be simply a typo. In order to decide on the logic of the error, we need to, first, talk with the author and, second, expand the sample we have. For example, Glynda Hull (1986, p. 209) provides an example of repeated use of a particular sentence pattern in a student's work:

1. My response to this story I feel work that SFC Robert Cooley had such a big influence in my work he always kept me busy "every" minute.
2. My response from this story I felt that she was pressured by her own peirs who never understood Ruth's Viewpoint.
3. My first impression toward Victor Bean I felt he was all right, but as work proceeded I got to know him and his emotions toward younger people.
4. My future employment, I want to advance myselv in the clerical or business field, because I feel their will be openings and advancement, high paying salary.

Hull provides six additional examples of this writer's use of a "topic/comment" strategy, in which he joins a topic to a comment on that topic spatially but not syntactically.

Other kinds of error arise when a student either generates or is taught problematic rules. Mike Rose (1980) has provided some lucid examples of this in his analysis of writers' block. He describes Ruth who, in high school, learned the rule that an essay must always grab the reader's attention immediately. This, along with her rule that you always begin writing at the beginning, and her rule that ungrammatical sentences are forbidden, effectively shut down Ruth's composing process. Making choices that meet all of these constraints at once is extraordinarily difficult. Martha, on the other hand, has learned to plan essays. She will not write a draft until she has spent a couple of days preparing an outline that looks, Rose says, "like a diagram of protein synthesis or DNA structure." Unable to convert this complex outline to a short essay, she would reach her deadline, scrap the whole thing, and throw together whatever she could to hand in. Her failure to translate her outline into an essay was made a certainty by another rule which asserted that humanities papers must scintillate with insight, images, and ironies.

The notion of an error arises from the contrast between an intended text and an actual text. In writing, teachers have to imagine what the intended text would look like—what the student was trying to accomplish—in order to infer the misconceptions that underlie different patterns of errors. The more extensive the teacher's experience with a particular student's writing and the better the teacher knows the student, the more likely it is that the analysis will be accurate. We need to ask ourselves, "What does she know and what did she do that produced the error?" We must assume a logic and set out to find what it is. Error is not to be feared, but ennobled. As Donald Schon (1963) puts it:

> The formation of new concepts treating the new as the old can perhaps best be understood as a form of error. Coming to form a new concept involves in several ways making a mistake. A new hypothesis, however fruitful, is typically at least partially wrong. The account of a discovery is typically partly false . . . the formation of new concepts typically leads to error. Every good new scientific theory is surrounded with error, as appears abundantly in retrospect. It is typical of insights that they are overstated. What is more, error often leads to the formation of new concepts. (p. 26)

We must not assume that error is the privilege of children. Analyses of teachers', administrators', and parents' errors are best done in the same way. Often simply describing the error in as much detail as possible sets the conditions for developing a deeper understanding of it.

I asserted in Part One that the patterns and details a teacher notices are the central aspect of assessment. In Part Two I give a brief description of the nature and development of literacy and highlight some important features to notice. Texts about literacy are often organized by starting with "basic" details about print and the relationship of speech to print before working "up" to the "higher levels" of "comprehension." I hope to convince you that such a hierarchy is a bad idea in the first place, and that if anything is "basic" it is the meaning-making aspect of literacy. Thus, my presentation begins with the social and psychological aspects of making meaning and the larger issues of what it means to be literate and to make sense of and in print. I then bring up details such as the conventions of print and the relationships between speech and print as they fit with the social and psychological aspects of making meaning.

*N*OTICING DETAILS

The last two chapters in this part address the strategic aspects of literacy and the nature of its development. Although tests and curricula would have us believe otherwise, there is no nice, even sequence to literacy development, though there are some predictable sequences.

Each chapter in Part Two ends with a limited set of assessment questions that the chapter suggests. These questions are intended to help focus inquiry into literate learning in the classroom.

*M*EANINGFUL LITERACY

One of my favorite children's books is *Faithful Elephants* by Yukio Tsuchiya. Towards the end of World War II, the zookeepers in Tokyo are ordered to destroy their animals in case Allied bombing allows the animals to escape into the city. The zookeepers reluctantly poison the animals, but the elephants, with whom the zookeepers have a mutual affection, avoid the poisoned food. The elephants slowly starve to death. In the process they beg and do all their tricks to entice their friends the zookeepers to feed them, which the keepers have been forbidden to do. When the elephants are finally dead, as bombers roar overhead, "Still clinging to the elephants, the zookeepers raised their fists to the sky and implored, 'Stop the war! Stop the war! Stop all wars!'" The book never fails to move me to tears. The elephants' and the zookeepers' suffering provokes a profound antiwar sentiment in me. But not everyone reacts to the book the way I do. I sent a copy to a dear friend who, it turned out, hated the book. As a veterinarian, he viewed the slow, painful death of the elephants as unnecessary and cruel. For him, the zookeepers' failure to provide a quick and merciful death for these creatures was unthinkable.

Meaning and Experience

For me to say that I understand a book means that I have connected it with other experiences I have had, with all of their emotional nuances, and constructed a new experience. Because your experiences and mine are different, your understanding of a piece of writing will be different from mine. Indeed, when I read a book for the second time the meaning *I* make is different, first because I have already read the book and, second, because between the two readings I have had further experiences. There are, of course, similarities in the meanings I make. But there will be differences.

Readers whose cultural backgrounds differ can make radically different meanings from the same text. Pigs are viewed in some cultures as dirty, stupid animals, whereas in others they have religious significance and are seen as clean and intelligent. A book such as *The Piggybook* by Anthony Brown will not mean the same to people from these different cultures. In addition, men and women can make considerably different meanings from the same book because of their identifications with different characters and their history of different experiences within the same culture. Emotions also influence the kinds of connections a reader makes. A person who is depressed is likely to identify with a depressed character in a book and thus make different connections (Bower 1978). In short, a single book does not have a single meaning. The closer we are to the writer in terms of cultural and personal experience, the more we are likely to make a 'common sense,' and the less detail a writer must supply in order to evoke shared images in readers. But two readers with different experiences are likely to create different meanings for any given text. The subtlety of these differences is nicely captured by Hector Mailot in *The Foundling:*

> It is only those who have lived in the country with peasants who can understand the distress of those three words: "Sell the cow."
>
> The cow has a different meaning for different people, but for peasants it is everything. No matter how big the family, and they have a cow in their byre, they know they can't go hungry. We had our butter, and milk to moisten the potatoes, and until the time I am talking about I had hardly ever eaten meat. Our cow not only gave us nourishment, she was our friend. Some people seem to think that a cow is a stupid beast, but that is not true for a cow is full of intelligence. When we talked to ours and patted her she understood us, and with her big soft round eyes she knew well enough how to tell us what she wanted and what she did not. She loved us and we loved her, and that was all there was about it. (p. 4)

When I first began to study how we make sense when we read people wrote about how we "make connections with prior knowledge" as if knowledge were a stack of cold propositions, some of which might be missing. But experience is much more lively than that. The term "breech birth" has a very clear meaning for my mother, who had three of her five children born bottom first into the world, doubled over, expanding their girth to test the limits of their mother's endurance. Although the doctor who advised her to breathe deeply might also have shared the dictionary definition of the term, his experience of breech birth was not the same as my mother's. And the two will not make the same meanings when they read a book about childbirth. A book's meaning cannot be reduced to a stack of propositions, either.

Words do not make meaning themselves; they provide a vehicle for making meaning. Language is full of gaps and ambiguities that we must resolve through connections with our experience. Different readers will make more or less different meanings. Consequently, when we assess their understanding we will want to know *how* they understood what they read rather than *whether* they understood it. I mean this both strategically (how they went about it) and experientially (what kind of meaning they made).

"Well, O.K.," you might say. "For fiction, yes; but for nonfiction? Different meanings?" Yes, for nonfiction too. Making sense of language requires making connections with experience and to the extent that experience differs, so does the meaning that is made. This is a property of language, not merely a property of one or another genre or use of language, and "nonfiction" is simply a way to frame language when your purpose is to appear factual. Books categorized as nonfiction are simply those whose purpose seems to be to inform about a particular subject. It is not that they are necessarily true. In five years they will still be filed as nonfiction even though the author's assertions of fact might have been proved otherwise. Similarly, when we read "fiction" we are often struck by how true the story seems to be. Indeed, since authors draw on their experiences to weave their illusions, perhaps it is.

When we note differences in interpretation, we often assert that one meaning is less adequate than another without considering how different experiences would lead to the different meanings and how we might be enriched by having access to multiple meanings. It is particularly easy for those in a dominant culture to view their language use and experience as the standard from which others deviate. Standardized multiple-choice tests insist on this, and their "scientific" aura perpetuates the myth. I do not mean to argue that there are no facts. There are certainly things about which most people in a given culture agree and count as facts. But the significance, the meaning, of those facts is a matter for negotiation in the context of people's experiences. For example, two plus two equals four (at least in base ten). We can count on it. Discussion about the matter is probably neither interesting nor valuable. The fact has no particular significance. But as soon as those numbers are cast into the real world—for example, whether the lives of two children and two police officers are equivalent to those of four convicted murderers—the fact becomes much more likely to generate disagreement (and interest).

A Range of Connections

Making meaning means making connections with experience. But just as experiences vary, so too can the kind of connections we make when we read. I remember reading to my youngest daughter when she was two or three and she commented, "This is the one who did the caterpillar one," meaning that the book was by Eric Carle. In this case, she was mistaken; it was written by Margaret Wise

Brown. But what is important is that she knows that connecting books by authorship and style is something literate people do. When children read, they can make connections with:

- Their own personal experience. ("That happened to me when my brother was born, too.")
- Their experience as writers. ("I wonder how many drafts she made of this?")
- Others' experiences and interests. ("Emily will love this. She loves mysteries, and she has been researching Native Americans.")
- Other books. ("*Sleeping Ugly* reminds me of *The Paperbag Princess.*")
- Other plots, themes, characters, and genres. ("*Sleeping Ugly* is another parody like that poem we learned.")
- Other authors. ("This guy writes like Roald Dahl.")
- Illustrations or illustrators. ("These illustrations remind me of Quentin Blake's illustrations.")

When we assess children's understanding, then, we should notice these connections. We might even formalize how they are noticed, so that students, in groups or individually, can map themes or other connections among books or authors that they have read. Such maps can provide useful, lasting assessments that are by-products of interesting learning activities.

Not all readers actively pursue connections with their experience. Some children do not understand that reading is primarily a matter of making sense. Others draw distinctions that prevent them from making sense—for example, making a clear distinction between personal experience and "academic" work and systematically excluding their personal experience from their school reading. This unfortunate conception is particularly common among children in low reading groups or lower-track programs, those from lower socioeconomic communities, and those classified as having disabilities (Anyon 1981; Page 1991; Nicholls, McKenzie, and Shufro 1995). Although counterproductive, the problem is hardly surprising when schools lean heavily on such distinctions. In a similar way, children who do not view books as the result of personal efforts by particular people are unlikely to make connections with authors. Since connections are the source of understanding, beliefs that restrict them are a source of reading difficulties. If a child never makes connections with other authors, we might consider helping her make such connections.

Of course the connections readers make on any given occasion are influenced by their immediate situation and by the personal and collective histories of the community. For example, Kathy Short and her colleagues found that an Eric Carle book read as one of a group of Eric Carle books would elicit different connections than it did when it was read as one of a group of books about animals. Helping students make different connections, then, partly involves providing them with a different set of circumstances or a different set of conversations.

Among any group of readers there will be a range of different understandings of a particular book. The more diverse the experiences of the group, the greater the diversity of understanding, and thus the richer the meaningful possibilities for the group when they discuss it. When my friend and I read *Faithful Elephants*, we made different meanings—the same book, but different connections and different meanings: not so much more or less, or truer or less true, meaning, but different meanings. The conversations that follow from such differences are a critical part of the reading experience. I shall return to these conversations in the next chapter.

Recognizing and Seeking Patterns

A major difference between experts and novices is that experts recognize automatically, without effort, patterns that novices have to laboriously figure out. A grand master chess player can recognize the patterns of pieces on a chess board so fast that after a brief five-second look he or she can replace all of the pieces of a knocked-over chess game. Expert readers are just like that with words, themes, styles, genres, and arguments. When patterns are recognized automatically, they actually take an alternate route through the brain, one that does not require conscious attention (Luria 1970). Once that happens, we recognize the patterns even if we don't want to. Ever tried *not* reading the print that is in front of you?

Recognition can become so detailed and automatic that we don't even need to see the whole pattern for it to be recognized. Context helps, but as readers become more competent their recognition of individual words reaches a point where it is so fast and automatic that the benefits of context are limited (Nicholson, Lillas, and Rzoska 1988; Shany and Biemiller 1995). Readers still predict words and seek contextual agreement, but recognition proceeds so very quickly and accurately that context and phonetic analysis are used primarily for verification. Thus, a simple indicator of one part of reading expertise is the number of words recognized instantly. It is only an indicator, though, and as an indicator, it is helped by the fact that word recognition expertise is developed by reading a lot. In other words, good word recognition implies a considerable amount of other knowledge too. In a similar way we recognize entire story structures and other familiar elements of our culture. Writers of television series such as *The Simpsons* and *Animaniacs*, and books such as *The Stinky Cheese Man* (Scieszka 1992) and *Ten in a Bed* (Ahlberg 1983), count on their audience's knowledge of these familiar story structures in order to make the violation of them funny.

There is no substitute for reading as a means of getting more adept at recognizing these patterns. This is even true of the patterns of letters that occur in words, as Connie Juel (1988) has demonstrated. For example, let's say Karen's basal reader program contains many words with the letter patterns *fl* and *oun*, but Daryl's program has more words with the patterns *thr* and *rd*. These two students will recognize more readily those letter patterns they have seen more frequently.

In reading, pattern recognition ranges from letters, through letter patterns, words, word patterns, plots, characters, styles, genres, stories, and lines of argument, to feelings (we learn to recognize and name feelings, and we learn their significance too). Five-year-old children can recognize different authors' styles of writing (Green 1981): if they have had sufficient experience with, say, Bill Peet's writing and Dr. Seuss's writing, children that young can recognize a new book as being by one or the other author. Clearly if they have not had extensive experience with one author they will be unable to distinguish between them in the same way. But if they are regularly involved in conversations about differences in authors' styles and they are read two new books by different authors, they are still likely to notice the difference.

But simply encountering patterns is not always enough. People can be surrounded by flowers every summer and never learn to recognize a single one. Most people cannot read flowers. However, if they spend time planting or arranging flowers, pretty soon they come to recognize more of them and more of the details of each. Of course it helps if they spend time talking with people who are interested in, and who know a lot about, flowers, particularly while flower gardening or visiting gardens. Just so with reading and writing. Reading and writing *together* and having conversations about reading and writing also help learners pick up significant features of the patterns to be read and written. But once they know the important features of a new pattern, just increased exposure to it makes a difference. Once a child knows to attend to letter order, simply reading more words will increase her recognition of the patterns of letters that commonly occur and the locations at which they occur.

Patterns are ways of organizing experience, and some patterns are more helpful than others. If a child notices that a particular letter is usually associated with a particular sound, that is one thing; but if a child notices that letters often have consistent relationships with speech sounds, that is another thing. The latter understanding is likely to lead the child to seek more examples. As a teacher, I want students to actively seek patterns in their literate environments. Having a classroom full of such seekers certainly helps.

Although automatic pattern recognition is useful, it has several costs. First, people often assume that what is obvious (and automatic) to them is obvious to others. Once, at a national teacher conference, a troupe of deaf children performed for the audience. At the end of the performance, the audience applauded in their usual (automatic) manner, with their hands at waist level, out of sight of the performers, not realizing that the performers had to see the applause. Similarly, as teachers, the connections we make with a story can be so automatic, so "obvious," that we cannot conceive the possibility that a child might make different connections. Equally common is the child writing about a personal experience who assumes that the reader was there too and so excludes crucial information.

Second, sometimes people automatically leap to inappropriate conclusions (connections). When we hear that a young nurse broke down in tears after having an affair with a famous doctor, we picture immediately (automatically) the sex of each (though we might be wrong). Automatic connections can reflect—and maintain—cultural stereotypes.

The third danger of automatic recognition is that people are often satisfied with having recognized the larger pattern and do not take the trouble to notice smaller details and changes. When I first shaved off my beard, my wife didn't notice, and the only person at work who noticed asked if I had grown a mustache (which had been there all along). The same thing happens in reading. We sometimes substitute one word for another that makes sense but is not quite what the author intended; and when we read an article in which we recognize the general ideas, we are apt to skim it and fail to notice interesting nuances that the author might have included.

These natural blindnesses that result from efficient recognition—that is, familiarity—must be counteracted, particularly if we are to have a just society. And children in the dominant culture are in some ways most vulnerable to having their experiences remain transparent—unexamined and unexpanded.

Assessment Questions

When we as teachers assess our literacy instruction, we will want to know the answers to questions such as the following:

- What kinds of connections do students make when they read?
- Under what circumstances do students actively seek to make connections?
- What kinds of patterns does each student recognize automatically?
- In what ways does the student's past experience influence the meaning he or she makes while reading?
- Under what circumstances is the student's automatic recognition not balanced by a consideration of details?

CHAPTER 10

Constructive Literacy

*L*inda Rief, an eighth-grade teacher in New Hampshire, engages her students in reading, writing, and literate conversations that produce deep understandings both of what they read and of the processes of reading and writing. Listen to Nahanni, one of her students, describe a mural-collage she did in collaboration with her classmates Jay and Sarah in response to their reading of the book *Night* by Elie Wiesel:

> We brainstormed what the book was making us feel . . . it was difficult because we don't have much practice brainstorming pictures. After we succeeded in getting our feelings portrayed in shapes and pictures, we put together some of our ideas: a triangle, upside down to show rising growth that finally got out of control, a growing sense of disorder and helplessness. We worked to get the image artistically interesting and show contrast, not just in the art form, but in the book. The black and white. The full pages to the ashes . . . We decided to burn pages of *Night* and fasten them to a triangular board. In the bottom of the triangle the pages were orderly and gradually got more burnt and unorganized. We traced our hands and made them reaching up from organization to chaos. We revised our original idea of the clenched fist. People weren't fighting back. We skipped the people and the barbed wire that we had originally planned because we decided it would be distracting and split the picture, stop the movement.
>
> In the book I saw Wiesel going from not believing anything would happen, even after he was warned by an old man, to almost becoming that old man . . . I think the painting means something different to each one of us . . . but all the ideas worked together and are related. The important thing is that people can look at our painting and feel

something . . . for their own meaning . . . Art, literature and music all
mean something different to everyone. (Rief 1992, p. 143)

What can we say about Nahanni's understanding of the book she read? Is it
useful to say that she had "80 percent comprehension" of it? This would surely
trivialize her experience. Saying that Nahanni "got the main idea" would be no
better. It would be counter to her understanding of reading. She believes that
multiple understandings are a given and that they are to be valued as resources for
deeper understanding. Did Nahanni read the book with the intention of making
sense? Absolutely. Is it likely that Nahanni will read another book without striving
to make sense? Probably not. Will it be necessary for us to check each book she
reads to see whether she "got it"? Probably not. Indeed, to do so would not merely
be a waste of time, it would destroy the conditions necessary for producing the
experiences she has had.

I am content that Nahanni's experience with *Night* was productive, not because
she understood the book the way I did, but because of the nature of her experience with the book and her understanding of what it means to know. Nahanni
respects her own experience, and the experiences of the other readers, knowing
that they will be different. She does not seek or accept a single meaning from the
book but rather seeks to understand the experience of the characters and the
experiences of other readers. She is able to listen carefully to other readers in the
expectation of expanding, but not displacing, her own experience. Her attentive-
ness to the characters and to her fellow readers is an important aspect of her
literate development.

Nahanni and most of her classmates are literate in a very particular sense.
They show all the signs of *constructive knowing,* which Mary Belenky and her colleagues (1986) characterize as "the opening of the mind and the heart to embrace
the world" (p. 141). Theirs is a connected and expansive knowing. They know the
value of literate conversations for understanding themselves, each other, and the
world. And the conversations they involve themselves in are not just any conversations. These students value conversations in which people share ideas, particularly
incomplete ones—conversations that involve a collaborative construction of knowledge, that expand both their individual and their collective experience. This kind
of literacy expands their consciousness and increases their sense of connectedness
with and respect for others—a literacy that turns "different perspectives into intellectual and social challenge, even adventure" (Nicholls and Hazzard 1993, p. 52).
Making meaning for them involves meaningful relationships. Their experience with
literacy will influence their interactions with others and their expectations for the
nature of their working lives beyond school. This is the literacy of democracy.
These students would be unsatisfied with hierarchical competitive monologues,
with cut-and-dried facts; they have been spoiled for authoritarian living. They will
only be satisfied by living in a democracy.

Contrast this with another group of high school students described by Allison Jones (1991). Unlike the students described by Rief, these young women insisted on being given lists of facts or sections of books to copy and memorize. If their teacher tried to get them to share their knowledge, to engage in discussions, or to work collaboratively, they felt that the teacher was not doing her job. One of them explained "We never talk if she wants us to say things . . . talk about something, you know? Everyone shuts up" (p. 80). Indeed, these students insist that the teacher deliver and enforce sterile, uncontroversial facts, preferably broken up into bite-sized pieces (see also descriptions by McNeil 1987). That, they believe, is the teacher's job. Their job as students is to receive those facts. These students think of receiving information, not of making meaning. They assiduously keep their personal experience separate from their literate learning in school, and they resist any attempt to get them to take responsibility for their own learning. They denigrate their own experience, and often that of their fellow students. They believe that knowledge is uncontroversial and is produced by authorities somewhere. They themselves have no authority, no knowledge.

These students are literate in a quite different way from those in Linda Rief's class. They have different theories about language, about knowledge, about themselves, and about acceptable ways of living. They are reasonably well prepared to live in an authoritarian community. Indeed, they insist on doing so in school in the face of some of their teachers' efforts towards making the classroom community more democratic.

Social Imagination

The quality of Nahanni's literate experience, her "comprehension" if you like, is not limited to her connections with the words or the book. She and her fellow students also learned about each other (and themselves) in important ways. Sarah, one of her collaborators, reports:

> I learned about the sensitive sides of Jay and Nahanni. We had very
> serious discussions about how to do a certain part—the design, paint,
> color—would this help? Hurt? How does this make you feel? Working
> together on such a serious project really let me get to know both of
> them in a different way. (Rief 1992, p. 160)

This experience of others is not separate from the experience of reading the book and must not be ignored when we assess these students' learning. Indeed, this ability to "read" others, what I call a *social imagination,* is, I believe, a very basic literate skill.

Writers of fiction often assert that it is their characters that drive, and often take over, their writing. We might expect Nahanni's knowledge of others to influence her writing, too. In order to write a novel or short story, a writer must imagine herself as each character, thinking, feeling, and acting. For example, in the span of her hundred-page book *A Couple of Kooks and Other Stories About Love*, Cynthia Rylant opens to us the lives of a couple of sixteen-year-olds who share a pregnancy, a divorced grandfather of a bride, a senior citizen who experiences a passionate marriage and the death of her spouse in a brief period, a retarded person who learns about loving and giving, and many others. She can imagine these people, and through careful selection of details she can compel us also to briefly, but completely, take up residence in their minds. Not only do we find the immediate experience powerful, but our lives are subsequently enriched. Rylant opens the possibility of understanding our own and others' experiences from that many more vantage points.

Writing or speaking to persuade or to amuse also requires knowing your audience. Attempting to persuade a tired child through rational, logical argument, for example, can accomplish the opposite of one's intentions. Even the apparently mechanical task of editing your own writing involves reading it from the perspective of someone else. The purpose of editing is to ensure that we have used conventions such as spelling, grammar, and punctuation to obtain the desired effect in the reader. Notice how easy it is to miss things when you read your own writing and how you pick them up when you read your writing to someone else. People who speak a "nonstandard" (nonprivileged) dialect find it particularly hard to edit their own writing into "standard" English. To do so they must read their work as if they were speakers of the privileged dialect.

Social imagination is fundamental to the development of critical literacy. Reading critically involves imagining why a writer would use certain words, stylistic devices, or formats—creating a narrative about the writing of the piece. For example, I might ask why a writer has decided to use the term "wealth generator" rather than "opulent parasite" to describe a corporate executive.

The development of social imagination is one of the reasons diversity is so valuable in the classroom. Valuing, exploring, and appreciating multiple perspectives develops the ability to imagine the worlds of others: what it is like to walk in someone else's shoes. When we can stand only in one place or see from only one perspective, we get a flat image. We see only a part of what we are looking at. We have two eyes in order to experience depth of vision through having two discrepant images. Considering more than one point of view gives us similar richness. In addition, such an attitude toward literacy is compatible with the kind of personal characteristics and relationships required in a democracy. It fosters the development of the individual without fostering individualism. It fosters understanding through connection, and critical analysis without an adversarial stance. It makes possible our seeking new meanings and new solutions rather than simply choosing among existing options. We would seek a different literacy for an authoritarian society. For that we would seek a technical, impersonal, passive literacy.

Meaningful Relationships

The meaning Linda Rief's students make when they read and write intimately involves their relationships with others and their understanding of those relationships. Her students read with these relationships and people in mind. According to Mary Belenky and her colleagues (1986), we can think of this as *connected knowing,* which involves active listening and social imagination grounded in empathy. In a college senior's words:

> You shouldn't read a book just as something printed and distant from you, but as a real experience of someone who went through some sort of situation. I tend to try and read the mind of the author behind it, and ask, "Why did he write that? What was happening to him when he wrote that?" (p. 113)

Another college senior observed that to sort out conflicting interpretations she would

> read them both very closely and try to recreate that person's reasoning, see if I could follow the path. I try to think as the author does. It's hard, but I try not to bias the train of thought with my own impressions. I try to just pretend that I'm the author. I try to really just put myself in that person's place and feel why is it that they believe this way. (p. 121)

For connected knowers, book discussions are collaborative explorations of meanings and possibilities. They withhold judgment in order to understand more fully. They listen to each other because they know that the range of contributions enriches their understanding of the book. However, they also listen to each other to learn more about each other. This expanded understanding of others contributes to both reading—by expanding the possible meanings they can make and perspectives they can take in the future—and writing—by helping them better anticipate audience responses and create more detailed representations of characters in their writing.

Connected knowing is quite different from *separate* knowing. The distinction hinges on the relationships between the knower and the known, and among the people involved. Separate knowers develop ways of distancing themselves from the object of study, emphasizing indifference towards a subject rather than involvement with it. Classic examples of this are the "scientific method" and its equivalent in literary analysis. Separate knowers emphasize rules and external criteria for evaluation and often write more to manipulate readers than to express themselves meaningfully and personally. They are inclined to view readers as "potentially hostile judges" and to adopt a technical approach to understanding books or world affairs. Indeed, because of their beliefs, they themselves are inclined to be judgmental and can in turn become hostile judges of others' work. Belenky and colleagues give the example of Faith, who dealt with "the Iranian crisis, like *Wuthering Heights,* as a technical problem, . . . [as a] 'math problem with humans'" (1986, p. 110).

The separate knower, say Belenky and her colleagues, asks, "'What standards are being used to evaluate my analysis of this poem? What techniques can I use to analyze it?' . . . The orientation is toward impersonal rules." The connected knower, by contrast, asks "'What is this poet trying to say to me?' The orientation is toward relationship" (p. 101). In critical reading, the separate knower might ask, "What rhetorical techniques have been used here?" The connected knower might ask, "Why would the author choose those words and that format?"

Connected literacy is not merely a property of individuals, however. As Belenky and her colleagues point out, "Connected knowing works best when members of the group meet over a long period of time and get to know each other well" (p. 119). The problem in part is one of establishing the necessary trust to share fragile, fledgling ideas that might not yet fly.

Ginny Goatley (1996) provides a case study that illustrates these issues well. Stark, a fifth-grade student who is new to a book club discussion group,

> did not appear to value the opinions expressed by other members of the group, focusing instead on what he thought to be the right answer and often simply yelling over others to express his view when they were talking or when his answer was challenged. [In one case] Yelling over the others, Stark was firm in arguing for what he perceived to be the correct answer. The other students argued that they could think of different interpretations, implying, as they had during the first meeting Stark attended, that they were allowed to do that in this group. (p. 202)

Sustaining Relationships

For Nahanni and her classmates, being literate is a thoroughly social matter. Indeed, one way to consider Nahanni's literacy development would be through the conversations in which she engages. For example, with others in her class, she keeps a dialogue journal in which she carries out some of her conversations about literacy. Consider her response to *The Runner* (1985) by Cynthia Voigt:

> Sometimes this book really frustrates me. It's not that it isn't interesting, but sometimes I just don't *get* it. Bullet seems to have dealt with things in a strange way, burying himself. Burying himself from everyone else . . . Bullet and Katrin have learned to sort of remove themselves and not get too involved in things they care about, so they never get hurt . . . I think I'd rather live through some of the bad times than never see any good times. Sort of like in *The Little Prince,* the taming of the fox. I'd rather love, lose, get hurt and go away with memories than never love and never know the difference between happy and sad. What words! Happy? Sad? When I was little I thought

happy meant a smile and going to the circus. Sad was a frown and
sitting home on a rainy day. (Rief 1992, p. 140)

Nahanni examines her own experience, her own values, but also considers the experiences of others through the characters she meets in her books. This is the basis for the development of self-knowledge and autonomy. Notice, too, how she examines the words she is using and their adequacy for capturing her experience. She takes her own experience and her own use of language seriously, just as she takes the language and experience of others seriously.

Nahanni is not alone in these matters, as we see when her colleague Jay responds to her reading log:

> I never thought of Bullet burying himself, I guess I thought of him
> isolating himself, in the boxes he always talks about. Isolated, being
> able to see out, but no one can see in. Do you think people, like Bullet
> and Katrin *really* know what happy and sad are? In their boxes? I guess
> you and me would rather have loved and lost than never to have loved
> at all. There is a point though where the lost overcomes the loved and
> you (collectively, not just you, Nahanni) end up feeling like cuckies. At
> least for me—Have you read *Sons from Afar?* By Cynthia Voigt. That,
> and I guess *Homecoming,* too, show how similar Sammy is to Bullet.
> Them and their boxes. Scot is like that too. I guess he has good
> reason. His parents both left him in the lurch. But he doesn't let
> himself get too involved, because he always got hurt. (p. 140)

Nahanni's notion of reading is formed within this sort of literate exchange, an exchange that respects her experiences, one that is connected. She comments:

> In order to be a good reader I think you must read a lot and think
> about what you are reading—how it relates to you, what the writer
> wants you to think, versus what you really get out of it. I think the
> responses I got to my reactions to books were written or asked in such
> a way that I feel my ideas are important and that makes me think
> more. (p. 140)

The ability to engage in such exchanges is an important literate skill. It sustains a literate community. When Nahanni moves to a new community, her ability to initiate and sustain such conversations with others will determine her continued development as a literate person.

As we have seen, the individual mind arises and is nurtured within the conversations of society. The more diverse, connected, and nurturing those conversations, the greater the possibilities for the individual mind. Consequently, it is in the individual's interests to expand the thinking of others. In a democracy people view each other, in part, as resources for expanding their own experience and for solving individual and collective problems in more mutually satisfying ways. The more capable one's neighbor and the more different his or her experience, the better. In this context, the ability to help others expand their literate skill and experience is itself an important literate skill. Thus, in a democracy we must value not only the ways in which an individual's literacy develops, but the relationships that enable the expansion of collective literacy. Relationships that involve individuals asserting power over others will not be helpful and might not count as literate achievement.

Consider the literate relationships among a group of elementary school children as they converse with a classmate about his writing:

> "'Wind-silent dogs' is beautiful. It makes me try and say something good, such as . . . er . . . river-wet cows . . . But that's not so good is it?" . . .

> "I like your beginning Ron. It's just the best writing you ever did, but I think you went astray after a good beginning."

> "It's like David's story of yesterday about his motor bike bits. The way he said it, I mean" . . .

> "Sort of flows" . . .

> "'Rock fall' is a lot better than a lot of rocks."

> "I like the way you brought your thinking into it, Ronny . . . You've made the story part more real because of that." (Richardson 1964, p. 206)

These young children are able to provide a thoughtful critique of a classmate's writing, and to do it in a manner that foregrounds what he has done well, a feat many adults find difficult. Because of this and the trust of the classroom community, the critique is not seen as a threat, but as useful assistance. As one child commented after receiving such critical-supportive advice, "It was good of him to get me going again . . . and I don't help him much" (p. 204). These are citizens in a democratic classroom.

Not only have these children learned to notice specific features of writing, but they are part of a community that values each member's work and learning. They notice what has been done well, but do not shy from constructive critique, which is made possible by the underlying trusting relationship. They have learned a particular kind of conversation about writing that allows their observations to be received, indeed sought after. These children have also learned to value productive critique and, equally important, they have learned to construct conversations that will sustain their learning. The conversations they have are predicated on a relationship of empathy and respect for the person and his or her work. To these children, writing is both individual and social.

Like Linda Rief's students, these children are practiced collaborators. Collaborative literacy is common enough in the adult world, though most people find it difficult. Anyone who has tried to write a committee report will attest that it is no picnic. Of course the individualistic, competitive approach to schooling that most of us experienced did not allocate much time or value to such an orientation. As one third grader I knew observed, "Once we wrote in pairs in school. We wrote one story together. I didn't like it because it was hard . . . We had to, like, get in each other's heads to share ideas. It really took a long time."

Critical Literacy

One kind of critical literacy involves simply noticing a discrepancy between realities. For example, a second grader in Ellen Adams's (1995) class commented, "This book was stupid. A train changes into a tree? Give me a break" (p. 113). He considers what an author appears to be presenting and, in fitting it with his experience, finds it unacceptable. A basic approach to critical reading involves juxtaposing two possible realities, stories, or images, and judging which is more acceptable. Writers, even those not intent on doing so, can seduce a reader into an entertaining, but unexamined world. When children begin to notice disjunctures, they are beginning to develop critical literacy. For example, another child in Ellen Adams's class observed, "Did you ever notice that lots of books have wolves in them?" (p. 116), and another declared, "When books have spaceships and stuff like that on them, that means they're for boys. I hate books like that" (p. 115). This is where critical conversations begin.

Critical conversation is not merely a feature of "higher" literacy; it is basic. I have one son and two daughters and, like the rest of us, they are constantly battered by the media with cultural stereotypes of men and women. I am always on the lookout for books that will help my daughters tell themselves useful stories about their lives, and that will give my son productive narratives about women. I also seek stories about the lives of those who are different from my children. Such books are in short supply, in part because as authors we write about what we know and can imagine, and we live in a society marked by gender and racial inequities (among others), most of which seem natural to most people and are unconsciously reproduced through our language. Although I try to find books that do not perpetuate roles and stereotypes, in the long run my selection (censorship) of the books my children read will never be enough. My only hope is to help them see how their lives are being framed and shaped by what they read and view and to help them to open the possibilities and make their choices more conscious. In this sense, critical literacy is basic. Failure to develop this kind of literacy leaves children at the mercy of writers and speakers who, wittingly or unwittingly, will control the sense children make of the world and of their lives. When a cigarette company states its brand name on a billboard over an image of an attractive, athletic couple engaged in a sexually provocative activity, it invites readers to conclude that smoking these cigarettes will lead to the kind of reality portrayed. Not very subtle, but quite effective. For a generation awash in media invitations, critical literacy is not optional. Children must learn to read these invitations through the eyes of those composing them, understanding why an author would choose those particular words, and an illustrator those particular images. Fortunately, even quite young children are able to understand when someone is trying to sell them something and why a company might peddle their breakfast cereal the way they do. In spite of their supposed egocentricity, children are able to stand on both sides of the writing. They are capable of invoking a social imagination and wielding it as an evaluative tool.

Rejecting the invitation to buy a product, however, is the easy part (even though it might not seem so when you are in the cereal aisle with your child). More demanding is to use one's imagination to unravel the gender roles and stereotypes that we live with daily. Authors write from their experience to produce plausible characters and circumstances, but their experience, as with our own, is within a gendered and racially unbalanced society. The more engaging and comfortable the writing, the more difficult it is to notice the replication of the stereotypes and inequities. Unless we are careful, our own writing is also likely to replicate those parts of our lives and culture that on reflection we would rather not replicate. But it is hard to read against the grain of our own writing—to read it critically. The experience is ours and the language is ours. To do so requires reading it from the perspective of someone whose experience, language, and assumptions are quite different from ours. This is the particular value of diversity in the classroom.

Assessment Questions

When we as teachers assess our literacy instruction we will want to know the answers to questions such as the following. In what ways, and under what circumstances, do students:

- view reading and writing as meaning-making activities?
- respect and value their own experiences as significant sources of understanding?
- respect and value others' experiences as significant sources of understanding?
- understand a situation from more than one perspective and write with more than one voice (as narrator and as characters)?
- give and make use of constructive feedback?
- sustain engagement in literate activity over an extended period of time?
- initiate and sustain conversations that will extend their literate competence?

CHAPTER 11

CONCEPTS OF BEING LITERATE

What does it mean to be literate? One evening Samantha, at the time a two-year-old, sat at the table and produced the literary work shown in Figure 11.1. She worked with considerable earnestness, muttering "R, S, T, oy, M," and so on. These marks and mutterings were interspersed with erasures and disgruntled comments, such as "I can't do it." When asked what she was doing, she replied, "I doing my homework." Apart from the pitch of the voice, it might have been a tape recording of her older brother doing his homework. Children infer what it means to read, to write, and to be literate from the pattern of literacy interactions surrounding them and from responses to their attempts to try it themselves. Her understanding of literacy has different shades of meaning from the understandings in which others are immersed. Maori writer Witi Ihimaera notes that, as a child, for him "books were things other people had, not us. They were Pakeha [European] things set in a landscape other kids were already accustomed to, the same landscape that was such a nightmare for us" (cited in Smith and Elley 1994, p. 119).

Children's notions of what it means to be literate include ideas about the amount of time literate people spend reading and writing, when and where they read and write and for what purposes, whether worthy bonded people (as opposed to "other people") engage in such activities, and what kind of activities they are. Becky, an eight-year-old, tells me that "a good writer is someone who knows how to choose good topics and how to write the best words to express your ideas." She states her need for conferences and distinguishes between ones when she is "stuck for ideas" for editing or revising, and ones in which she just wants to share what she has written up to that point. She often gives the listener some idea of the background to the story and where she is headed with it. By contrast, Stephen, a ten-year-old, tells me that "a good writer writes fast and neat, and doesn't make mistakes . . . You have to know punctuation and, like, where you put the address

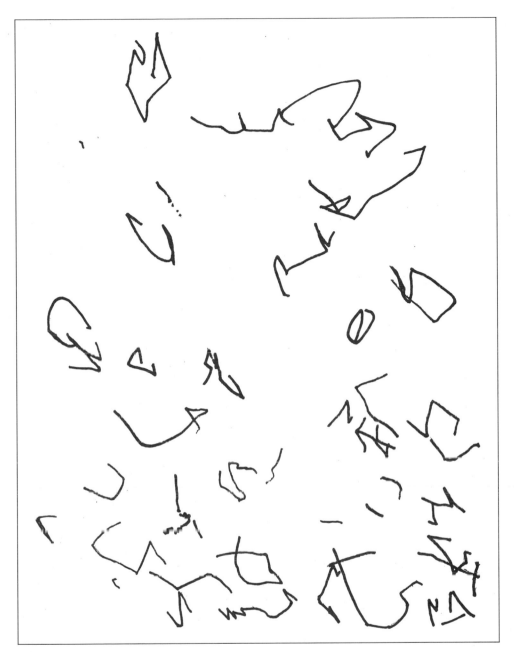

FIGURE 11.1 *Samantha's "Homework"*

on a letter." If you ask the least competent first-grade readers to tell you the characteristics of a good reader, they often mention social graces, such as being quiet or raising one's hand (Lyons, Pinnell, and DeFord 1993).

Different experiences and circumstances produce different understandings. In some classrooms, children develop separate notions of what it means to be a reader and a writer. As one of Ellen Adams's students commented, "Writing is too slow and boring and it's too easy to make mistakes. Reading is more fun and

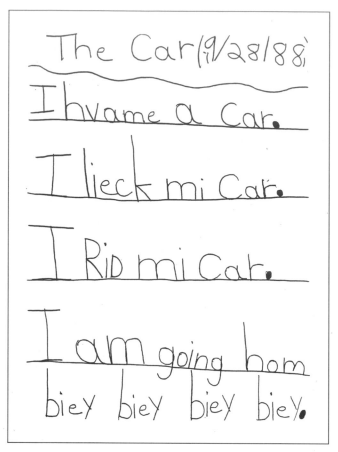

The Car (9/28/88)

I hvame a Car.

I lieck mi Car.

I Rid mi Car.

I am going hom

biey biey biey biey.

FIGURE 11.2 *"The Car" by Nicole*

people can't always tell if you miss a word like they can when you write" (personal communication). Understandings of what it means to be literate grow from the conversations of the classroom (and the home), and they determine the ways children engage in literate activity, and even whether they engage in them at all.

Different children in the same classroom can develop different conceptions of themselves as literate individuals. Elizabeth Bondy (1985), in studying first graders' conceptions of themselves as readers, found substantial differences between children placed in high and low reading groups. Children in the high group viewed reading as primarily a social activity, a private pleasure, and a way to learn things. Children in the low group viewed reading primarily as saying the words correctly, as schoolwork, and as a source of status (two of the upper group children in this ability-focused setting also viewed reading as a source of status).

Similar patterns can be found in writing. Sometimes children get the idea that writing is "getting the words right" (in the sense of spelling them conventionally as opposed to choosing them well). Under these circumstances, they are likely to produce writing such as the piece by Nicole shown in Figure 11.2. In reading this piece, I am given no hint of the vibrant young person who wrote it. This writing has no voice at all. It is devoid of all traces of authority. Given the blank piece of paper, Nicole first drew neat lines, and then wrote ever so neatly her "story":

> THE CAR
> I have a car.
> I like my car.
> I ride my car.
> I am going home.
> Bye bye bye bye.

Given Nicole's concept of what it means to write, these were the best (safest) words she could come up with. There is no voice in her writing, once the page is full the writing is complete, and the punctuation is about as terminal as you can get. These details tell us about what Nicole thinks it means to be a writer, and what sort of writer she thinks she is.

A young writer can readily get the idea that writing is something that is "done" when the page is full. Another inventive young writer, halfway through writing a single sentence, realized that it would not fill the page, so he wrote the word "IN" large enough to fill most of the page, and then stuck the last three words down at the bottom of the page. A similar conception often persists into graduate school, represented by the "How many pages does it have to be?" question about assignments.

But these concepts need not be final. When the response to Nicole's writing changes, so does her concept of authority, and her writing along with it. Figure 11.3 is a piece she wrote about a month after she began working with someone who responded only to the content of her writing, not the form. This story reads:

> MY NEW FRIEND
> I have a new friend. His name is Patrick. I like him very much. He and
> I write letters back and forth. He is funny sometimes.
> The end.

Nicole's writing has begun to reflect her changed concept of what it means to be a writer. As she wrote this piece the decisions she made along the way reflect a commitment to content, to what she has to say, more than convention. The lines are not as carefully drawn, the little punctuation that she uses is much less terminal, she crosses things out (the first indication of her changing something to make it better represent what she intended to say), and when I read this piece I start to hear some of the resonance of her voice. The bottom of the page still defines the end of the story, however, and she even formally closes her piece with the words "The end" (a page period?). However, there is clearly a change from her earlier effort.

A month after "My New Friend," Nicole wrote the story in Figure 11.4. It reads:

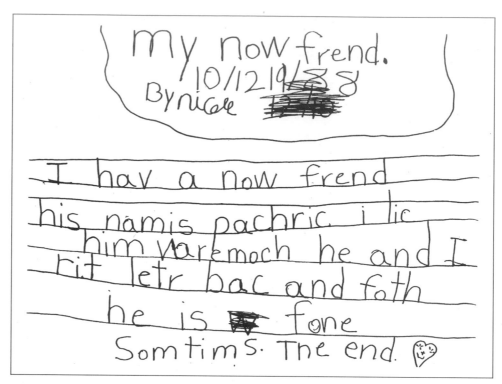

FIGURE 11.3   *"My New Friend" by Nicole*

THE TRIP TO THE PALACE

I am going on a trip to the Palace. My friend is going too. Her name
is Kari. She is my best friend in the world. We are going to sit on the
balcony. Our moms are going to sit below us. And we will be funny
too. We are going to have food.

Several developments are apparent in this piece of Nicole's writing. The lines are
gone, and the print is a little less neat and is a bit smaller. She no longer needs to
use large print to fill the page because filling the page is not the point and because
she is confident that she has something to say. As we read Nicole's piece we see
that she has revised it in a couple of places without fear of the mess ("No, that's
not how I wanted to say it" . . . "Wait. There's more"). The piece is longer (though
it took her about as long to write as the first piece shown in Figure 11.2). It has
substantial detail and a clear voice. I get a strong sense of the author, that she has
something to say, and that she thinks so, too.

Although these changes appear on the surface, they reflect much deeper
changes, not only in Nicole's conception of what it means to write, but in her
understanding of who she is. Now she is a knower and a writer. Literacy instruction that avoids these issues can produce college students who write like the earlier
Nicole. Children do not simply "grow out" of this. Mary Belenky and her colleagues (1986) give the example of Faith, a "successful" college student who said of
her writing, "You learn how to sound like you know what you're talking about,

The trip to the palis.
I am going on a trip to the palis.
my fren is going to.
hre nam ie kare
she ie my best faen in the wrld.
We are going to sit on the becine.

MoM
are momsare going to sit below os.
and we will be to the end
and we will be fone to. The end
We are going to have fod.

FIGURE 11.4 *"The Trip to the Palace" by Nicole*

even if you don't" (p. 108). Faith has learned that she can make herself heard, but has learned at the same time that she has nothing to say.

Conceptions of Knowing

Children's theories of what it means to be literate involve an understanding of what it means to know. As deeply philosophical as it might seem, children have theories about such matters. When I went to school we read texts rather than books. By this I mean we read words that contained facts. Where the facts came from and who said they were facts were not our concern. Our job was to get the facts, and the teacher's job was to tell us whether we got them. We brushed aside conflicts with our own experience by either keeping the facts separate from our experience or assuming that our experience did not count as knowledge—or both. We read poetry and plays that were written by someone, but the someones who wrote them were not human. They were gods. Their work contained a deep meaning, the teacher knew what it was, and our job was to extract it in a complex feat of detective work and have it verified by the teacher. Many of us emerged from college with this same understanding of reading. Writing was similar: the focus was on form, not on meaning, commitment, or relevance to one's life.

In spite of the fact that many adults continue to think this way, some quite young children are more enlightened. Consider the comments of Allan, a second grader in Pat McLure's class, on the matter of critical reading:

> Before I ever wrote a book I used to think there was a big machine, and they typed the title and then the machine went until the book was done. Now I look at a book and know that a guy wrote it. And it's been his project for a long time. After the guy writes it, he probably thinks about questions people will ask him and revises it like I do and xeroxes it to read about six editors. Then he fixes it up like they say. (Newkirk 1986, p. 113)

Allan realizes that writing is making knowledge. It is done, he believes, by ordinary people like himself, who put their pants on one leg at a time and who work strategically and persistently at their writing, taking into account other people's perspectives as they go.

The consequences of how one conceives of literacy are very important. If a reader cannot think as Allan does, and cannot ask questions about what was included by an author and why, he is what Tom Newkirk calls "deferentially literate." There are times when it is appropriate to read or write deferentially, but it must be by choice, just as in any social situation there are times to ask frank questions and times not to. But if a person does not know how to ask the necessary questions or feels unworthy of asking them, then he or she is likely to be trampled upon by authors and scriptwriters who wish to impose their own agendas. A deferential literacy does not serve the individual well; neither does it serve the community. Democracy requires a stronger literacy (Dewey 1966) as, incidentally, do business organizations (Senge 1990).

Mary Belenky and her colleagues have described five different conceptions of knowledge that provide a useful way of thinking about the ways people make sense of the world and of themselves (which is what Paulo Friere and others argue is the point of literacy): silence, received knowing, subjective knowing, procedural knowing, and constructed knowing. The differences among these conceptions involve beliefs about language, mind, knowledge, and self.

SILENCE

In the position of silence, one experiences oneself as without mind or voice, responding to the whims of authorities. People in this position have a difficult time thinking beyond the present, imagining what might be or what might have been, imagining alternative motives, generalizing, or contextualizing. These people experience themselves as knowing nothing and having nothing of consequence to say, their own experiences being irrelevant. They expect authorities to show them what to do, and they do not expect to understand why they must do it. They have no confidence in their ability to make meaning, and they do not see words as particularly relevant to knowing. Many children classified as learning disabled experience schooling and literacy this way (Nicholls, McKenzie, and Shufro 1995).

RECEIVED KNOWING

Some people see themselves as able to receive knowledge from authorities, and possibly even able to pass it on to others, but not to make knowledge themselves. Their own experiences and feelings do not count. Indeed, their deference to external authority is such that they turn to others even to gather knowledge about themselves. They believe books, teachers, and other authorities have all the answers. If they find that these authorities differ from one another, a prospect that makes them very uncomfortable, they invoke a hierarchy of authority to know which is right. Received knowers have limited tolerance for ambiguity. Knowledge is right or wrong, good or evil, us versus them. There are no gray areas. Teachers who present more than one perspective without saying which one is correct are viewed by received knowers as irresponsible and bad teachers. Right answers exist, and a teacher's job is to deliver them. The student's job is to work hard to acquire these facts from the authority figure and master them. Every book has a single meaning to be absorbed, and received knowers feel it is reasonable that they should be tested on whether or not they got that meaning.

In this view, controversial knowledge has little place in school. As readers and listeners, received knowers prefer authoritative lectures. Indeed, when teachers try to involve them in discussions they often resist, forcing teachers to deliver the facts as they are supposed to.

Although this position is called received knowing, which suggests an emphasis on listening, once these people receive knowledge (truth), they are inclined to pass it by assuming an authority from the source of the knowledge. Conversations among received knowers are inclined to be hierarchical and, when differences arise, confrontational. Although language is important to them, its importance has to do with its being the pipeline through which knowledge is delivered in neat, factual bundles of objective truth.

SUBJECTIVE KNOWING

In contrast to the passive, outward-facing received knower, subjective knowers' listening is turned inward. Their attention is focused on their own feelings and behavior. They see knowledge as personal and intuitive. The knowledge of others is relevant only if it matches their own personal knowledge—if it "feels right." In other words, subjective knowers shift the center of authority to themselves, valuing their own experience and moving away from the domination of external convention and control. For the subjective knower, truth is no longer absolute, but rather a matter of individual experience and history. Different people have legitimately different realities. Belenky and her colleagues quote a subjectivist in her sixties who comments:

> If I read something, and if it agrees with my senses, then I believe it, I know it. If it doesn't, I'll say, "Well you might be right, but I can't corroborate that." For me, proof is usually a sensory one . . . One

doesn't have to be told in words. That's the point. That's the thing
that's very hard for word people to believe—that there are other ways
of telling. (Belenky et al. 1986, p. 75)

This distrust of print and preference for direct experience and personal involvement is characteristic of subjective knowers. There is no need for subjective knowers to negotiate meaning. Their understanding is as good as that of others. There is thus no need to choose and no need to negotiate.

PROCEDURAL KNOWING

Procedural knowers are deeply concerned with systems or strategies for obtaining and communicating knowledge. They consciously and systematically analyze. They see form and reason as more important than content. Thus, procedural knowers might value their writing because it has tight logic and fits the conventional form but couldn't care less about the topic and may even deeply disagree with the conclusion.

CONSTRUCTED KNOWING

The position of constructed knowing is one in which the learner views all knowledge as constructed by individuals with their own experiences and perspectives. Constructive knowers value both personal and procedural ways of making sense and value themselves and others as sources of knowledge. Within this view of the world, knowledge is always bound to a particular frame of reference, so constructive knowers are very concerned with understanding the nature of the frame of reference. To do so they often step outside the situation and view the matter from a different perspective. They are not satisfied with simply answering questions and solving problems; they want to pose the questions and the problems, and when others pose questions they want to know why the question is important and how answers are arrived at. This way of thinking has been suggested as a stage of thinking beyond the stage of formal operations (often viewed as the highest level of thought) (Belenky et al. 1986, p. 139).

Rejecting hierarchical, competitive monologues, constructive knowers prefer the kind of talk in which people share ideas—even, or perhaps especially, incomplete ones—so that the group becomes involved in collaborative, mutual construction of knowledge, extending each individual's knowledge and opening new possibilities for the group. To the constructive knower, ambiguity is not a threat but an opportunity. These people view others as allies for their own thinking, and when they make judgments they take into account context and the consequences for others.

Although these conceptions of knowledge have been studied mostly in adults, they are also evident in children. They are not stages in the sense of a developmental progression, although they do differ in complexity. Their differences have more to do with the social context in which a person lives than with his or her age. For example, although many adults never develop a constructivist perspective, young children can show evidence of constructivist thinking.

These conceptions of what it means to know have considerable importance for both how one goes about reading and writing and for the literate relationships in which reading and writing are embedded. For example, learning based on uncontroversial knowledge is commonly experienced as purely instrumental, as preparation for later life and work (or test performance) rather than as an integral part of life. Such knowledge is easily used to judge students as more or less "able." Students classified as having learning disabilities experience school knowledge (the focus of most of their reading and writing) as discrete, impersonal, factual, and uncontroversial (Nicholls, McKenzie, and Shufro 1995). Since these students also do not value their own experience as having anything to do with learning or knowing, there is little motive for them to read or write anything at all. Such students, when asked how their teacher can best help them, generally suggest that the teacher show them what to do, when, and how. This is a very dependent literacy that serves neither the student nor the community well.

Rethinking Literate Constructs

When we teach, our beliefs about knowledge, language, and literacy influence our interactions with our students. If we have a deep-seated belief in received knowing, we will ask children questions to assess whether or not the meaning was received. If we adopt a subjectivist approach to knowledge, we will not make productive use of differences in children's understandings. There are, in fact, many little theories that we are unaware of and that influence our literate exchanges with children, the exchanges within which they develop their conceptions of themselves as literate individuals. The traces of these theories can be hard to see because they are too close and too obvious.

For example, over the last few years my colleagues and I have asked teachers whether they have time to read, when they read, and what they read. Teachers commonly report that they have little time to read, but that when they get the chance they read Danielle Steele (or another author in the same genre). When they say the author's name, they mumble it and look embarrassed. Although these books get passed around among friends, no one actually talks about them. Teachers, like most of the rest of the population, believe that although these are books they can't put down, they are not really, well, you know, *literature.* They feel the same way about children's books. Some books are "children's literature" and must be read instead of the books that children voluntarily devour. This concept—that there are certain books that are identifiable as "real literature" that really literate people would read, and other books that really literate people would never bother to read—sacrifices a great deal. It allows people who do not now read but who once, years ago, read "the classics" to consider themselves literate, and people who read constantly but who have not read "the classics" to consider themselves not literate and to cut themselves off from conversations that would be most helpful for expanding their literacy. These concepts are easily passed on to children.

Many first and second graders think of illustrated books as "baby books," distinct from "chapter books," the real thing. This is partly a result of an overemphasis on the word as the most important symbolic medium (words are better than pictures, and more and bigger words are better). Teachers tend to talk about "moving on to chapter books" and begin reading unillustrated books to children as soon as they can. We see it as more mature, just as cursive writing is seen as the mature form of print. But also embedded in the chapter book/baby book distinction is a comparative judgment of ability such that to be reading a book with pictures is seen as an indication not merely of a lack of skill, but of something deeper (see Chapter 15). Under these circumstances, many children will either choose not to read or will choose material that they cannot read.

To break away from such narrow conceptions of literacy, children (and adults) must understand that illustrations in books are not there just, or necessarily at all, to make the story easier. Literacy, as Denny Wolf and Martha Perry put it, "involves much more than accurate inscription . . . [It involves] understanding how writing, like other forms of record making, involves sustaining a process, making thoughtful choices among symbolic languages, and being mindful" (Wolf and Perry 1988, p. 49). When children come to understand the function of symbols in these terms, they can discuss illustrations as an integral part of composition, and discuss the relationship among different symbolic representations. In the "real world," these symbolic representations are thoroughly intertwined, as they should be in the classroom.

Wolf and Perry suggest that we consider literacy in terms of the ability to sustain a recording process from inception through editing, the ability to "tune" records to particular demands, and the ability to see oneself as a mindful author capable of making a thoughtful, useful record. They give an example of a book written by Lisa Marie, a second grader, who does:

> To begin, Lisa Marie writes a short description of a salient event: "The boy has a hat he was playing with it." She is not satisfied with this rendition and uses the facing page to illustrate it, adding the dialogic "O boy" under the picture. Returning to her book later, Lisa Marie adds many more events and then comes back to the first page, adding a title ("The boy") and prologue ("This is the boy who his a yelllo hat here goes the stoy").
>
> Still later, when she reads her text over as a part of editing, she recognizes it can't be read straight through and make sense. She adds the heavy horizontal lines which set off title, prologue, and text. (p. 49)

Lisa Marie believes herself to be literate and is thoroughly and purposefully engaged in literate activity, keeping a social eye out for any difficulties her audience might encounter.

Assessment Questions

When we as teachers assess our literacy instruction we will want to know how our students understand themselves as literate people. In what ways and under what circumstances do students:

- view themselves as constructive knowers rather than, say, received knowers?
- understand what literacy can do for them?
- sustain a writing process from inception through editing, tuning it to the demands of a particular audience?
- choose to read and write?

CHAPTER 12

CONCEPTS ABOUT PRINT

A child's first attempts at writing may not look much like writing. They may only be distinguishable as such by the expressed intention. These pieces will nonetheless be the child's estimation of what adults, peers, or older siblings do, and hence what he or she must do in order to be human.

Children quickly notice that writing is different from drawing. Figure 12.1 shows two pieces done within five minutes of one each other, one of which (12.1a) is a drawing and the other (12.1b) a letter to a friend. Not visible is the fact that the drawing is in several colors and the letter is only in black.

At some point children come to understand that marks made on paper can represent speech. At this point they are likely to show their marks to an adult and ask, "What does this say?" Later, the writing may develop into something resembling that shown in Figure 12.2, as the child becomes aware of more of the details of the specific shapes of the symbols and the common locations of print with respect to illustrations.

In this chapter I describe children's development of knowledge about the distinctive features of print, and how we can notice and keep track of it.

Less-Than-Obvious Conventions

Children construct and test all sorts of hypotheses about language structure and use as they become increasingly sophisticated in their knowledge of literacy. If children are given the opportunity to write, their hypotheses about language are reflected in their writing. Marie Clay (1975) has noted, for example, that children often hypothesize that there are repeating patterns in the print, and so they busily go about repeating strings of the same letter or the same word they already know. They are thus able to produce a piece of writing of satisfying length. Over time,

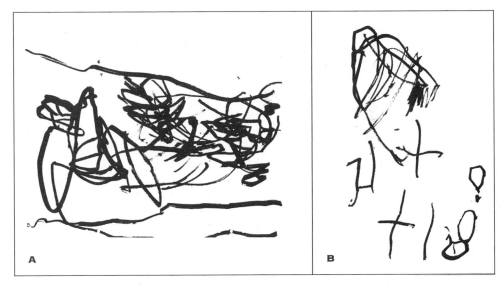

FIGURE 12.1 *Two Pieces by the Same Child. A: A Picture. B: A Letter*

FIGURE 12.2 *Recognition of Symbol Shapes and Location of Print with Illustrations*

children become aware of exactly what kinds of patterns do recur in print. In the process of exploring these patterns, children often explore the properties of letter combinations. For example, they may change a single letter on a word or write some or all of the word in uppercase, or write some parts in reverse. Starting from a handful of known letters, a child can create all sorts of patterns that look more or less like conventional words, especially if spaces are used.

But learning about letters, patterns of letters, and spaces is only a small part of the development that is taking place. As adults who have already acquired literacy, we take many features of print for granted. Let me point out some of these "obvious" features to remind you why they might not be obvious to children:

- For no apparent reason to the child (or most of the rest of us, for that matter), English requires that a writer begin at the top left-hand corner (except when the picture comes first), proceed from left to right, return to the left just underneath the first line before proceeding again to the right-hand side of the page. This pattern is repeated down to the bottom of the page (or as far as the lines go), and always proceeds from the left page to the right page (unless there is no print on the left page), beginning with the spine of the book on the left-hand side and ending with it on the right.
- Letters are made up of repeating patterns of lines and circles (except when they are in cursive or one of the "artistic" fonts). It is generally agreed that there are fifty-four distinct letter shapes (the upper- and lowercase letters and the two forms of *g* and *a*), plus eleven punctuation marks.
- Usually, it is the black shapes that are important rather than the white spaces in between.
- Spatial orientation is important for understanding letters and words. Unlike most other things, turning a letter upside down can change it to another letter or no letter at all.
- Letters can be put together to form words (though some letters by themselves can be words).
- Some letters go together and others don't. Letter patterns in writing do not include long strings of the same letter.
- The message is constructed more from the print than the pictures.
- In general, words are spelled the same way each time, and the words in print relate to the same words in speech every time they are read.
- Written language frequently has a different structure from spoken language.
- Certain letters are used to represent certain sounds (though the relationship rarely is one-to-one, and sometimes a word has to be pronounced differently in order for there to be any relationship at all).

- The relative length (temporal) of the spoken word is vaguely related to the length (spatial) of the written word.
- Print can be turned into speech and vice versa.
- One spoken word equals one written word.
- Reading something through once does not guarantee perfect memory of it.

I hope you can see after reading this list why some children may struggle a little as they learn how to read and write.

Knowing about these potential confusions is important. In school, teachers refer to the various concepts about print and language using words. If a child does not understand the meaning of a particular word, she may find the discussion confusing. For example, if a student cannot consciously analyze words into their component sounds, the distinction between *sound* and *word* will be difficult to grasp, making discussion involving those terms quite confusing. The following are just some of the concepts about spoken and written language that children must learn in order to be literate: word (both written and spoken), sound, story, letter, front and back (with respect to books), next (with respect to left-to-right spatial progression rather than time), after, before, capital letter, upper- and lowercase, sentence, author, read, write, draft, edit, revise, share, confer, publish, file, date.

Checking Up on Concepts

Children are not born with knowledge of such concepts as "letter," "word," "sentence," "story," and the like. The child's growing understanding of these concepts is very important to monitor, because confusion will affect the way the child makes sense of instruction. Marie Clay (1993a) devised a test called the Concepts About Print test (CAP) to check children's understanding of some of these critical concepts. In administering the CAP test, evaluator and student read a book together. They sit next to each other and are involved in the same activity, rather than sitting opposite each other with the evaluator silently checking the performance of the child. The CAP test checks many concepts about print: whether the child can recognize the front of the book; the right way up for the book; the beginning of the book; that print rather than pictures carries the message; directional rules, such as that one reads left to right and top to bottom; how spoken words match with written words; first and last (with respect to story and letters in words); letter order; punctuation; letter; word; and capital (uppercase) letters.

The book used in the CAP test has some strange-looking features. On one page, a picture is upside down; on another, the words are in the wrong order or reversed (*was* for *saw*); and some lines are in the wrong order. The idea is that if the child notices the inappropriate aspects of the book, he or she demonstrates a knowledge of the concept. The major limitation of this test is that it is based on error detection: it requires that the child tell the authority figure that the book is a bit weird. A child's ability to do this depends substantially on her relationship and experience with the evaluator and other adults in a similar role. Nonetheless, the CAP test is a valuable part of a detailed *Diagnostic Survey,* which can be used to select children who are having the most difficulty learning to read, so that they can catch up through intensive one-to-one instruction (the Reading Recovery™ Program).

The reason that this particular book is used in the CAP test is that the CAP is a standardized test and requires such a constraint so that norms can be generated and comparisons made. I believe that a teacher can use a child's writing and a regular book to evaluate most of these concepts, thus avoiding a formal assessment situation and a strange book. Such a procedure, being unstandardized, will not yield norm-referenced scores, which may be important for situations that require distribution of limited resources. Many of these concepts about print can be evaluated in the course of normal classroom interaction, or through an individualized interaction, using a simple checklist such as that in Figure 12.3 or a more elaborate one such as that in Figure 12.4. Although these will not produce norm-referenced

Name: _____ Date: _____

Right way up
Front of book
First page
Story/picture
Left-right through book
Left-right across page and return
Word-word match
Sentence
Word
First/last word
Letter
First/last letter
Reading makes sense
Letter/sound cross-check
Title
Author
Comments

FIGURE 12.3 *A Simple Checklist of Print Awareness*

Name: _____

CONCEPT	DATE	COMMENTS

Interest/Language

　Chooses to read _____ _____

　Chooses to write _____ _____

　Has favorite books _____ _____

　Reads a range of genres _____ _____

　Writes in a range of genres _____ _____

　Uses "book language" _____ _____

　Recalls phrases verbatim _____ _____

Concepts About Print

　Knows where to start _____ _____

　Left-right through the book _____ _____

　Left-right across page and return _____ _____

　Title (can point to) _____ _____

　Author (can point to) _____ _____

　Page

　　Top/bottom _____ _____

　　First/last/next _____ _____

　Word _____ _____

　Letter

　　First/last/next _____ _____

　　Upper/lower case _____ _____

　Sound (in spoken word) _____ _____

　　First/last/next _____ _____

　Punctuation

　　Period, comma, question mark, _____ _____

　　quotation mark, exclamation _____ _____

　　mark, sentence _____ _____

Speech/Print Match

　Words = print, not picture _____ _____

　Story/picture match _____ _____

　Spoken/print word match _____ _____

　Initial sound/letter match _____ _____

　1-1 sound/letter match in writing _____ _____

　Notices and uses multiple letter units _____ _____

Repertoire of Text Patterns

　Identifies letters of alphabet _____ _____

　Identifies 5–6 words consistently _____ _____

　Notices similarities between words _____ _____

　Notices text forms/genres _____ _____

Strategic Thinking

　Reads to make sense _____ _____

　Uses language structure as a cue _____ _____

　Uses print information _____ _____

　Integrates information sources

　　In initial attempts _____ _____

　　In self-corrections _____ _____

　Persistent in solving problems _____ _____

　Selects appropriate books _____ _____

Self and Others

　Writes and responds with authority _____ _____

　Developing a social imagination _____ _____

FIGURE 12.4　*Checklist of Book and Print Awareness*

scores, they will yield useful data that can be used to generate a criterion-referenced score, if that is desired.

Children's theories about language and print show up in their reading and writing. For example, children who are aware that the message is constructed more from the print than the pictures will point to the print rather than a picture when asked where one would start reading, or when "pretend reading" with a book (telling a story to the book and pointing at pages). When a child understands that print can be turned into speech, he or she might write "BTPEEL" and say, "This says 'home,'" or ask, "What does this say?" When a child understands the idea that certain sounds can be represented by letters, she begins using invented spelling, which usually reflects a relationship between the initial sound in the word and the letter written. But progressing this far requires knowing some letters. A child who looks at a word and says, "Oh, that starts with 'Peter,'" is confusing words and letters. A child who can take two index cards and mask all but one letter or all but one word in a sentence on request can distinguish between words and letters. However, this child might be able to recognize only a few letters.

We can learn about a child's letter knowledge by observing writing or by asking. Appendix A is a form for recording children's identification of the letters of the alphabet. A letter may be identified by name, by a related sound, or by a word beginning with it. Any of these will do if we just want to know what letters a child can distinguish.

Perhaps I can demonstrate a teacher's assessment of a child's knowledge of print with a more complete example. In the following paragraphs I describe an interaction between Dane and me. The numbers in parentheses are keyed to the list that follows the description; the numbered statements describe what I have learned about Dane (and what I can check on my list).

I began by suggesting that Dane and I read together, an opportunity he jumped at (1). I asked him to pick out a favorite book, and I had on hand some simple predictable books (2). I asked Dane if he would like to read the book he selected to me, which he also happily agreed to, though he said, "I can't really read it properly" (3). He turned the book the right way up (4), opened it at the beginning page (5), and told me the story of *The Boy Who Was Followed Home* (Mahy 1975). He matched what he said to the pictures (6), and his reading included the sentences "Robert was surprised and pleased" and "He was delighted to think he was the kind of boy that hippopotomi follow home," which was not his normal language, but "book" language (7). His telling of the story was extensive and detailed (8). At one point his story got out of step with the pictures in the book, so he corrected himself from the pictures (9). When he finished I asked him how he knew where to start reading, and he told me that the pictures had to be up the right way, and "you always start at this end" (10).

Next I asked Dane if he was familiar with any of the books I had. I chose to read to him *The Fat Cat* (Kent 1971), which was one he did not know. I asked him if he knew where to find the author and the title, which he did (11). I read them to him and opened the book to the first page. I asked him where I should start reading and he pointed to the top left of the print on the left page (12), so I read it. I asked him where to go next and he turned the page, since the second page had no print on it (13). I already knew by watching Dane write that he knew to go left to right and back to the beginning of the next line (14). I had watched him write strings of letters unrelated to sounds and with no spaces between, but written from left to right and again on a second line (15), and he had then told me a long story about what he had written (16). I continued to read *The Fat Cat,* pausing sufficiently to invite him to predict the ends of predictable sentences, which, by the end of the book, he was able to do (17). He wanted the book read again (18), so we read it to the class in the same way.

A week later I sat down with Dane again and gave him two index cards. On a book that had a single line of print on the page, I asked him to use the cards as curtains to show me one word, then to show me two words (the procedure used in the Concepts About Print test). On both occasions he showed me letters (19). I could have asked him also to show me one and two letters, but I already knew that he confused words and letters.

From these simple interactions I learned the following about Dane's awareness of print:

1. He enjoys stories and books and seeks book experiences.
2. Since he did have a favorite book, and could talk about others, I was able to learn more about his enjoyment of books, and a bit about his favorite books. I could explore this further with him later.
3. He understands that there is more to reading than just telling a story, but he is undaunted by his partial version of mature reading. I might have asked him, later, to expand this distinction. For example, I might have said, "Dane, when we started, you said that you can't really read properly. What would you do if you were reading properly?" If he had chosen to participate but not to read, I would hesitate regularly to invite him to complete lines or pages of the book. I would listen for his use of language to see whether he uses "book language" (i.e., words and sentences unlike his normal spoken language, but like the language in the book).
4. Dane knows how to orient the book. This will help a lot when he tries to learn about words. If he only orients the book correctly sometimes, it will be harder for him to discover the regularities in print.
5. He knows where to start reading.
6. He has good memory for text and knows about the relationship between text and illustration. He also knows that you read left to right through the book.
7. He has begun to develop a sense of "book language" as distinct

from his normal spoken language and a sense of when to use these two distinct registers. This will help him predict as he reads. He is also expanding his vocabulary through his book experiences.

8. Again, his memory for text is excellent.

9. He has begun to match multiple sources of information and look for mismatches. He is able to self-correct on the basis of a mismatch.

10. His book orientation is based on illustrations rather than text, but he does know to go left to right through the book.

11. He knows about authors and titles and that they are found on the front cover.

12. He knows that print begins at the top left of the page (in this case). Had he just showed me the left page and not the top left, I would have asked him where on this page he thought I should start reading.

13. He knows that print, not the illustration, is what is read.

14. He knows the left-to-right and top-to-bottom arrangement of print. Had I not known this from watching him write earlier, I could have asked him to point with his finger to show me where I should go after I started in the top left corner, and where after that, but this was not necessary.

15. He probably does not know the difference between letters and words, and he does not know that letters can be used to represent sounds.

16. He has a healthy concept of himself as an author.

17. He quickly learns a new pattern of syntax and can predict based on rhyme. This also means that he is attending to the vowel sounds in the language, and can use that knowledge, along with meaning and syntax, to predict which words will come up.

18. This is more evidence of his seeking book experience.

19. Dane's actions with the index cards confirmed my earlier observation from his writing that he confuses words and letters.

Teachers can use parts of this type of interaction to clear up specific questions about a child's awareness of print, or to gain information on a new student (after giving him time to settle in). If necessary, questions can be followed with "How did you know?" or "How could you tell?" Asking new students the question about location of author and title can reveal whether or not authorship was considered important in their previous instructional environment.

This kind of exchange may be used as standard operating procedure, a way for teachers to regularly check on the development of their students' concepts about print and literacy. Figure 12.5 shows what our knowledge of Dane's learning might look like recorded on a checklist.

Name: _____

CONCEPT	DATE	COMMENTS
Interest/Language		
Chooses to read	9/5	_____
Chooses to write	_____	_____
Has favorite books	9/5	The Boy Who Was Followed Home.
Reads a range of genres	_____	_____
Writes in a range of genres	_____	_____
Uses "book language"	9/5	_____
Recalls phrases verbatim	9/5	"Robert was surprised and pleased."
Concepts About Print		
Knows where to start	9/5	Used pictures to orient then L-R.
Left-right through the book	9/5	_____
Left-right across page and return	9/5	Writing
Title (can point to)	9/5	_____
Author (can point to)	9/5	_____
Page		
Top/bottom	9/5	_____
First/last/next	_____	_____
Word	_____	_____
Letter		
First/last/next	_____	_____
Upper/lower case	_____	_____
Sound (in spoken word)	_____	_____
First/last/next	_____	_____
Punctuation		
Period, comma, question mark,	_____	_____
quotation mark, exclamation	_____	_____
mark, sentence	_____	_____
Speech/Print Match		
Words = print, not picture	9/5	_____
Story/picture match	9/5	The Boy Who Was Followed Home.
Spoken/print word match	_____	_____
Initial sound/letter match	_____	_____
1-1 sound/letter match in writing	_____	_____
Notices and uses multiple letter units	_____	_____
Repertoire of Text Patterns		
Identifies letters of alphabet	_____	_____
Identifies 5–6 words consistently	_____	_____
Notices similarities between words	_____	_____
Notices text forms/genres	_____	_____
Strategic Thinking		
Reads to make sense	_____	_____
Uses language structure as a cue	_____	_____
Uses print information	_____	_____
Integrates information sources		
In initial attempts	_____	_____
In self-corrections	_____	_____
Persistent in solving problems	_____	_____
Selects appropriate books	_____	_____
Self and Others		
Writes and responds with authority	_____	_____
Developing a social imagination	_____	_____

FIGURE 12.5 *Checklist of Dane's Print Awareness*

There are many more concepts about print that I have not mentioned. Understanding of such terms as *vowel*, *consonant*, and *long vowel* might be needed in some classrooms (although terms like "long vowel" are potentially confusing, since the child's normal concept of long and short does not help: the /a/ in *cat* can be just as long [temporally] as the /a/ in *hate*). With substitute teachers, remedial classes, and the like, children often must get used to a variety of different instructional languages. Unfortunately, it is often the most vulnerable and confused children who must get used to more than one such language.

It may be helpful to tape-record yourself teaching occasionally and listen for the use of these terms that we teachers often take for granted. Although I have referred here only to the terminology, there are also conceptual and relationship issues involved in the ways we use language in the classroom. Talking with colleagues about teaching, listening to and observing children, and watching each other teach can help us become more aware of these issues and potential problems that may arise.

Eddies and Confusions

Some concepts about print are particularly difficult for many children, and for good reasons. For example, until children begin to encounter print, they have learned that an object is the same object no matter what its position: a cup is a cup whether it is on its side, right side up, or upside down. With print, it is as if the cup is only a cup when it is standing up with the handle on the right-hand side. A *b* is only a *b* when the round bit faces in one direction; any other direction and it is a *d* or a *p* or a *q*. For a child who cannot yet consistently distinguish one side of his body from the other, this is a difficult thing to grasp. The spatial orientation has to be in relation to something else that is constant. For example, a thing can face away from your right hand or towards it, but if you can't consistently differentiate one hand from the other, something else must remain stable, like a red margin on the writing paper (which, paradoxically, primary writing paper often lacks). This asymmetry is a complex concept because of the development of the child's awareness both of his or her own body, and of himself or herself in relation to the rest of the world, not because of neurological complications. Neither is the concept a matter of knowing left from right, but rather developing a consistent asymmetrical frame of reference. It is a *conceptual* confusion, not a *perceptual* confusion (for more on this see Clay 1991).

Many children take a while to fully grasp these concepts, and thus reverse letters, words, and even whole pages and books. For example, in kindergarten Emily made a book (kids love using staplers), which she then proceeded to write in (Figure 12.6). She began with the cover, which she wrote exactly as it should be—in invented spelling. But she wrote on the cover with the spine at the top rather than on the left. She then had to decide whether to turn the book to the left

PAGE	CONVENTIONAL SPELLING	ACTUAL TEXT
Cover	Em (Emily) dedicated to Dad (and) Mom Things I Hate	Em dAdaKAdED To DAD MOM FEW I hD
Page 1	I hate	I hD
Page 2	Writing. Nick. Nick hates writing.	RAETEN NiCK NiCK hAS rAETiEN
Page 3	(New topic) Things th-	FEN D-
Page 4	at grow.	AT Gro

One of the more amusing aspects of this piece is that, during free choice time, when she could do anything she wanted, she sat at the writing table to make this book. Furthermore, in bed that evening she picked it up and wrote another page, continuing in the same direction "I like Christmas."

FIGURE 12.6   *Emily's Backward Book. A: The Cover. B: Pages 1 and 2. C: Pages 3 and 4.*

FIGURE 12.7   *Using Periods*

or to the right in order for the pages to open properly. She made the wrong decision and turned the book so that the spine was to the right. Thus she began to write her story at the end of the book rather than at the beginning. She started at the outside edge of the (right-hand) page and went across the page, then to the next page (the left-hand page), and so forth. Having made a single incorrect decision, she managed to do everything else exactly as it should be—if the book were held up to a mirror.

A child usually picks up the concept of a convention before the details of how it is used. For example, Figure 12.7 is the work of a student who uses periods after each word. The period is, after all, a marker that separates units of text. Similarly, students are at first likely to use apostrophes in lots of places, like before every final *s* or in words that look like those that have apostrophes, such as *wan't,* which looks like *can't.* This visual similarity is idiosyncratic. Some children see likeness where we might see none. However, though they may not use the convention correctly, they are often able to describe the reason for it. Some conventions are learned very early by some children, and some are learned much later. There is no set order of acquisition. A two-year-old will often use different words and sentence structure when telling a story from a book than when telling the story without the book. The same child may not learn the difference between the concepts of *sound* and *word* until he is six. Another child might understand the differences between *sound* and *word* at two, and only later begin to "talk like a book."

Children slowly gain control over print concepts, and even as they learn they will often appear to forget them. For example, it is common for children to exercise control over conventions when they do not have to compose, merely represent. One seven-year-old tended to reverse letters in his writing, but only when he was composing. He explained this in terms of his just being too busy with writing. He could easily correct his mistakes after he was finished. Another child could read a sentence that appeared in one line, but could not read it when it was arranged in two lines.

The child's developing understanding, in both spoken and written language, of the concepts of *word, sound,* and *letter* are reflected in a variety of different ways. When a child has learned a nursery rhyme, you can bring out the written version and read it to him, pointing with your finger, and then ask the child to point to the words while you read it, or if he would read it pointing to the words (Morris 1980). You might also ask the child to find particular words on a line. Watching children do this will tell you, for example, whether they use initial sound-symbol relationships or go back and recite until they come to the word. Later, in reading, simply asking the child to "read it with your finger" will tell a great deal. Children often remain confused by syllabic divisions (which they will distinguish before they distinguish separate sounds) and by compound words, such as *today,* for quite a long time. Such confusion lasts through high school for many students (in the case of such phrases as *for instance* and *a lot,* each of which is often spelled as one word).

Persistent confusion over some of these concepts can produce devastating effects. Don Holdaway (1979) reports a case in which a child in remedial reading instruction broke down in tears because he could not make sense of "all the white rivers" (the patterns of white spaces between the words). Another example is the child who comes to believe that reading has to do with memorizing (Johnston 1985). Small conceptual confusions used as the basis for hypotheses can produce a web of incorrect hypotheses that can entangle and eventually strangle young students. Unfortunately, each new incorrect hypothesis is likely to work part of the time and hence be rewarded intermittently (the most powerful reinforcement schedule). But such confusion tends to persist only under particular circumstances. For example, when children are not allowed to experiment with and explore print, when they only read and do not write, and when they do not talk with each other about their reading and writing, they cannot consider other hypotheses about how print works so that they can build new hypotheses and get feedback about them. Such situations tend to occur in highly teacher-directed, competitive, and anxiety-producing classrooms in which there is either no time for such exploration or the risks of exploration are too great.

Assessment Questions

Many of the assessment questions relating to concepts about print have been posed in the body of this chapter. In addition, teachers should ask themselves the following questions:

- Is the student actively theorizing about the organization of written language?
- What confusions does the student have about the organization of written language?
- Is there anything in our talk about written language that might cause confusion?

CHAPTER 13

THE SOUND, THE LOOK, AND THE FEEL OF WORDS

At the same time as children are developing concepts about print, they are becoming aware of aspects of spoken language of which they had previously been unaware. A large proportion of children coming to school do not know the difference between a sound and a spoken word, or even what a word is (Clay 1991). "Spaghetti-and-meatballs" is the sort of basic speech unit that makes sense to them. Children acquire language with little or no conscious awareness of the complex analyses they must perform in the process. Although learning language required them to analyze the flow of adult speech into its component sounds, few preschoolers can consciously perform such an analysis. There is no reason for them to do so except to acquire literacy in an alphabetic language such as English. Indeed, in cultures whose language is not alphabetic, even adults cannot perform such an analysis (Read et al. 1986). Learning to read and write in English requires children to develop quite complex understandings about the relationship between speech and print.

Speech and Print

In English there is a complex relationship between speech sounds and the letters used to represent them. Learning about this relationship requires a child to understand that a relationship exists and to begin theorizing about its nature. Analyzing speech into its separate sounds (phonemes) requires learning to attend to and distinguish the sensations made in the mouth when speaking. Children begin to become aware, for example, that *MMM* is the beginning sound of the word "Mary" (which also has an *eee* sound in it). This knowledge makes it possible for children to begin writing, inventing the spellings as they go. It is certainly possible to learn to read without learning how to analyze the sounds of words (a single profoundly deaf person who can read demonstrates this). It is also true that in mature readers phonetic analysis is secondary to automatic word recognition which is much faster. Nonetheless, the evidence suggests that it is a great deal easier to learn to read and write once one has access to phonetic analysis (Blachman et al. 1994; Vellutino et al. 1996).

We can tell whether children are getting to know phonemes by telling them, "Get your mouth ready to say . . ." or by seeing whether they can articulate words slowly. I choose words that have sounds that can be extended, such as *am, man, run,* and *so* rather than words with shorter sounds, such as *cat* (try saying the *c* and *t* of *cat* slowly). Asking children to say words slowly not only allows us to find out whether or not they can do it, it also helps those who cannot, since the act of attempting slow articulation helps them to attend to the sensations in their mouths, which helps them attend to how the word is put together and hence makes them more likely to be able to do it the next time they are asked. Marie Clay describes an instructional technique that involves making boxes for the number of sounds in a word, saying the word slowly, and having the child move a penny or counter into each box as she hears each separate phoneme in the word. This is an excellent assessment device. It requires the child to hear (or feel in her mouth) the sounds and represent them without having to know the relationships between letters and sounds. A simpler way to do this is to ask the child to hold her fingers off the table and put one down for each sound she hears in a word (although using the boxes makes it easier to demonstrate to the child how particular letters are associated with particular sounds). Children's invented spelling is also revealing, although that involves not only being aware of phonemes, but also representing them with specific letters. If a child is not yet sensitive to the sounds in words, attempting to intensively teach the relationship between letters and sounds is likely to be very frustrating. But if a child is sensitive to the sounds, then teaching her to represent them, in order to record important messages, is likely to be much more manageable.

As children become aware that there is a relationship between sounds and letters, they begin to build knowledge of these relationships, and this knowledge is represented in their writing. At first, words will often be represented by initial (or final) letters only. For example, *cat* will be written "K" (or "T"). Before long, though, initial and final sounds are represented and the sounds in the middle of the word are increasingly represented, beginning with tense vowels (vowels that require greater muscle tension in the mouth, such as *came, ice, feet, hope, cue*) rather than lax vowels (those that require less tension and are thus less easily distinguished, such as *if, set, got, hat, cut*). Quickly they include blends, such as *bl,* and digraphs, such as *sh.* These developments can be seen by watching young children write. They twist their mouths into all sorts of shapes as they think about the feel of the various sounds in their mouth. At this point it is mostly these feelings that direct their representation. Indeed, if you get them to hold their tongue between their teeth, preventing them from feeling the words, their invented spelling will fall apart. It is not really that they hear the difference between two words, but that they feel the difference in the production of the words. That is why getting them to listen to you saying words slowly is less helpful than getting them to say them slowly (though watching you say the words can help them see how they are pronounced). Partly because they are articulating the words more slowly, they become aware of the different sounds within spoken words. This is when children find it fall-on-the-floor funny to switch around the sounds in words to make nonsense words. This oral play with language is not only enormously instructional, but since it has to be done our loud, it gives a useful indication when students can do it. Some great books that can get children involved in this sort of word play include *The Hungry Thing* (Slepian and Seidler 1967b) and *The Cat Who Wore a Pot on Her Head* (Slepian and Seidler 1967a). Songs like "Apples and Bananas" in *The Book of Kids' Songs: A Holler-Along Handbook* (Cassidy and Cassidy 1986) are also useful.

There is a general pattern of development for particular sounds to become represented in print. In general, children have much less trouble in English with representing consonant sounds in print. Consonants are, in general, more predictable: the number of sounds they can represent is limited. However, the number of sounds that can represent particular letters is much more complex. For example, the letter *t* in different contexts can be associated with several different sounds—as in the words *to, ratio, there, with, trap,* and *fillet*. The letter *e* can have any of a ridiculously large number of sounds: consider the words *read, dead, idea, live, weigh, weird, knew, they, eye, fern, oven, leotard, leopard*. This is why accepting children's invented spelling is so important: it allows them more easily to learn how sounds can be represented in print. It lets children use what they know (spoken language) to learn about what they do not know (written language).

Again, the pattern of development of word representations relates to the distinctiveness of the production of sounds in the mouth. The letters *m* and *n*, for example, are represented easily when they appear at the beginning and end of words, but not when they are part of a consonant blend, such as *mp, nd, nt, nk,* or *ng,* because the mouth is in the same position for the nasal (*m* or *n*) as it is for the final consonant in the blend. After some of the consonants are distinguished in a child's writing, tense vowels start to appear. The lax vowel sounds, like those in *get, bat, sit, but,* and *hot,* tend to be represented later because it is harder to feel the differences in how the mouth makes those sounds. Try it for yourself. Of course, there are exceptions. Some tense vowels, in some words in some dialects, are difficult to distinguish in the mouth (for example, the *a* in *aim* and the *I* in *I'm*), which is why they are often interchanged in children's writing for some time after the tense vowels *o (boat)* and *e (feet)* are consistently represented. This reveals the absurdity of basing initial reading instruction on all lax (or "short") vowel sounds, as in the "Dan can fan the man" type of book. These words are visually simpler, but are generally the hardest to distinguish phonetically.

As children become able to separate the sounds of the words and represent them, their efforts often include aspects of the letter name. The fact that the names of the letters *a, e, i, o,* and *u* are associated with the tense vowel sounds makes it easier for children to learn the relationships between tense vowels and their representation. Both mouth feel and letter name are distinctive. Other features of the letter name enter into development too. For example, *c* can represent the whole word *see,* and Katy can be written "KT." On the other hand, *h* ("ay-ch") is often used to represent the sound normally associated with the digraph /ch/; hence, *chip* may be written "HP." This can make it hard to read the word *tree* in invented spelling, which the child may pronounce "chree" and write as "HRE" or simply "HE."

The writing will be a representation of the child's articulation, even slow articulation. Since children's pronunciation is not as clear as that of literate adults, they tend to represent words in characteristic ways. For example, *drive* might be written "jv" or "jiv," and *three* written as "fre." Actually, many children do not acquire the sound /th/ as in *this* (voiced) or *thing* (unvoiced) until age eight or nine. Thus we get a written "dis" or "vis" and "fing" (or some variation). Lisps, dialects, and other variations also show up in written representations. Think about the places in the mouth where the dialect versions of words are spoken, and that will help you to read students' invented spellings and to understand where help is needed and where it is not. Actually, reading development tends to improve a child's standard pronunciation of words.

Visual Analysis

Parallel to developments in the child's ability to distinguish and represent sounds is the child's memory for the visual form of words. A child might learn to spell her name based entirely on the visual form. For example, "EMILY" might be written correctly—and quickly—before Emily understands much about sounds or even letters. Alternatively, she might consider "Emily" to be incorrect because it is not recognizable with lowercase letters. She might also write her name as "ELY," "EMY," "EMLIY," or "ELMY." Some or all of the right letters are there, but the letters and the order are not as they might occur in invented spelling. Some of these look like phonetic representations, since many of the appropriate sound representations are there. However, the influence of visual memory rather than phonetic analysis can be seen in several ways. In the first place, the *y* is not the most obvious form for representing the /e/ sound. Indeed, "MLE" would be a more predictable invented spelling. Second, the speed with which the word is written can suggest the influence of visual memory. Invented spellings are often slow and accompanied by much facial movement as the child concentrates on the feeling of the sounds in the mouth. Amidst a series of words labored over in such a fashion, when a word is suddenly written quickly and without facial distortion, it is very likely written from visual memory.

Visual memory is a very positive development and comes in large part from the child's reading. Its timing and rate of development depend somewhat on the nature of the child's reading instruction and the extent of reading that the child does, along with whatever predisposition the child has for attention to visual detail. In general, the more reading, the more rapidly these "sight words" tend to develop. Some children come to rely on this sight-word strategy in their writing rather than invent the spelling of words. Occasionally this can be problematic. When children invent the spelling of a word, they practice the representation process, analyze the words, and become more expert and flexible in thinking about the relationships between sound and print, and print and sound. When they use only a sight-word representation method, their development is slower, and it may be more difficult to read the writing later because it is written unconventionally and has little relationship between print and sound.

Lots of confusion can arise over why children write words in particular ways. However, if you watch them writing, and perhaps interview them about their efforts, much of this confusion will be dispelled. For example, as children slow down their pronunciation of words and start to listen to what they say, their attention is focused on the representation process, and they may lose perspective on the whole word. This explains why they sometimes add extra letters to a written word—for example, "beluw" for *blue*. The *e* represents what was pronounced as the child tried to slow down and isolate the sound of the letter *b*. Because *b* cannot be pronounced in isolation without attaching a vowel sound to it, the child used *be* to represent the single letter *b*. Similarly, the *w* at the end of the word is a result of the child's analysis of all of the mouth positions in the slowed-down spoken word.

To decide why students put particular letters in particular places you often have to be there to watch. Emerging writers often place letters out of sequence because they combine different strategies for writing the word. For example, knowing that his name is Nick, a child might write "NCI." Watching him write it, his teacher can see that the *I* is an afterthought. The *N* and *C* are representations of the initial and final sounds, but having written "NC," Nick's visual memory tells him that something is missing. Knowing that there should be an *I* in there somewhere, he adds one.

Traces of visual analysis will increasingly appear with invented spellings. For example, a child who writes "Won day" spells "day" from visual memory (phonetic, invented spelling would have suggested "da" or "dae") and "Won" from speech analysis. The two strategies may even appear within the same word—for example, writing *human* as "HYOUMIN," where visual representation of the word *you* was used for the *u*, and phonetic analysis was used for *-man;* or *cold* as "coled," which shows a realization of the common *-ed* ending to words, a visual analysis. Children will also begin to become aware of other regularities in the representation system, such as markers (like the silent *e* in *same*). The word *like* might be written "LIEK" for several different reasons. It could be a slightly inaccurate visual analysis, or it could be an overanalyzed sound analysis, or it could show a beginning awareness of the use of the *e* marker to make the tense vowel sound. We could only know which explanation is the correct one by watching the child produce the word and by asking something like "How did you know to spell *like* like that?" or "How did you know to put the *e* in *like?*" The recognition of common letter patterns is an important indicator of development, and the process through which unconventional spellings are arrived at has important implications for teaching. There is certainly no point in a teacher's trying to help a child sort out what the teacher believes is a sound analysis problem when the child's unconventional ordering of letters was produced as the result of a visual memory strategy.

Reading and Writing, Sight and Sound

Both visual analysis and sound analysis are valuable, especially if they are used as a check against each other. Most adults run into trouble with spelling at some point and resort to such strategies as writing down a set of possible ways to spell a word and then using visual analysis to choose the correct option. In the long run we want children to write and read words conventionally without sound analysis because this saves a lot of time and intellectual energy. Visual analysis will increasingly produce conventionally spelled words. In an odd switch, in visual analysis, lax vowels (like the *o* in *pot*) are conventionally represented before tense vowels. The reason for this lies in the more complex and numerous ways of representing tense vowels. For example, the sound of tense *a*, as in *hate*, can be found in the written words *hate, bait, say, fillet*. Representations of the lax vowels, however, are more limited.

As children develop this ability to represent sounds, they also develop an ability to recognize words in reading. Readers also use auditory and visual analysis, the auditory analysis being the "sounding out" of words and the visual analysis being sight-word recognition and the recognition of patterns of letters. Visual analysis in reading is a sign of the development of the mature pattern recognition that drives adults' reading. Words that children first recognize are usually what are called the "high frequency words" (because they really do occur with higher frequency than other words). The rate of development of sight-word recognition is probably related to the amount of reading the child does. Along with specific words, recognition of common suffixes develops, particularly *s, es, ing, ed,* and *er.* As in writing, both auditory and visual analyses are helpful to emerging readers, especially when they are used for cross-checking.

Deaf children often develop their awareness of print differently from hearing children, relying more on visual analysis. Cut off as they are from the qualities of sound readily available to hearing children, deaf children often develop a more detailed visual analysis of print. Thus a hearing child's spelling of *serious* might be "creas," whereas a deaf child's might be "seiruso," which has more of the actual letters, but less of the order of the sounds. Since the order of the letters in a written word is determined somewhat by the order of the sounds in the word (a time sequence mapped onto a spatial sequence), the deaf child is likely to notice more letters but less of their order. Deaf children's access (through amplification techniques) to the sounds of the language they are learning to read makes it considerably easier for them to acquire literacy.

Data on the sight recognition of high frequency words can easily be gathered from children's oral reading. Lists of high frequency words can also be helpful if you need to know which words a child can identify without contextual support. Marie Clay's technique of asking children to write down all the words they know (allowing ten minutes and prompts if necessary) can also be revealing about the words children know well (that is, ones they know better than those they can merely recognize). Children may confuse, or reverse, some of these high frequency words. However, these confusions and reversals reflect a move towards mature word recognition strategy without a concomitant attention to meaning and self-monitoring from print. While reading, it is very rare indeed for children to reverse words that cannot be written backward. In other words, expect reversals of *was/saw,* and *no/on,* but do not expect reversals of *the/eht* or *going/gniog.* Furthermore, reversals of words such as *was* and *saw* are less likely to occur when there is sufficient preceding context to clarify them. If reversals do occur in these contexts, the reader is probably not attending adequately to meaning. Notice how the reasons for various patterns suggest relevant instructional strategies. Notice also that very often the strategy that makes the most sense is simply more reading (particularly of relatively easy material) and writing.

Marie Clay (1993a) has suggested the use of two different assessment tools to study different aspects of children's representation strategies. To evaluate their visual analysis, she uses a written vocabulary test in which the child is given ten minutes to write down all the words he or she knows how to spell. Only conventionally spelled words are scored correct. To evaluate the children's sound analysis, she suggests a dictation test. The scoring of the test (if scoring is required) reflects whether the child has reasonably represented each sound in the word, not whether it is conventionally spelled. To construct your own dictation test, just compose a brief sentence or two containing a selection of words that are unlikely to be "sight words" and that contain varying numbers of phonemes. The words should include a diversity of sounds, including tense and lax vowels and consonant blends. For example, the following sentences could be used:

> My friend and I like to go and see the big sailboat. It has a blue flag.

A child who wrote "mi frend and i lyc tu go and ce ta big sal bot it has u blu flag" would have a perfect score on this test, since all 47 phonemes are represented, albeit unconventionally. The same test or a similar one could be given again several months later to provide a measure of growth in the student's ability to represent speech in print. Equivalent forms of such a test can easily be constructed, but are not generally necessary, as the same test will do just fine, as long as there is a reasonable time between the two uses. Ideally, the student's pronunciation should be taken into account when interpreting the test responses. For example, a child who pronounces *school* as "skoo" cannot arrive at the *l* in *school* by auditory analysis and must arrive at it through visual analysis. However, such accommodations make relatively small differences to scores and are not particularly relevant when you are interested only in comparing an individual's performance over time and not comparing individuals with one another.

Both visual and sound information is regularly available from students' writing. However, such information can be affected by such things as the use of environmental print and support from other students. Also, some young writers will copy their own invented spelling incorrectly, thus taking it another step away from conventional spelling. Thus, dictation tests can be useful for informing decisions that must be based on the individual's competence at translating speech to print. Dictation is, after all, a natural part of literate activity. People do dictate to other people, and this activity has the interesting property of separating representation from composing. Indeed, even when a child dictates a story to you, you will learn about their knowledge of what is required in representation. A child who knows to dictate slowly enough for you to write has more sophisticated knowledge than a child who does not.

But analyzing the sound and the feel of words does not begin and end with spelling and word recognition. Indeed, the first aspect of spoken language to which children attend as babies is the pattern of intonation. This feature of speech, which they easily master as infants, is the basis of punctuation (which many will later struggle to master in school). Yet children's awareness of intonation is rarely evaluated.

Also, interest in the sound and feel of language continues as children get older. Consider, for example, the following writing by Margaret Mahy (1985) in her book *The Man Whose Mother Was a Pirate:*

> The little man could only stare. He hadn't dreamed of the BIGNESS
> of the sea. He hadn't dreamed of the blueness of it. He hadn't
> thought it would roll like kettledrums, and swish itself on to the

beach. He opened his mouth, and the drift and the dream of it, the weave and the wave of it, the fume and the foam of it never left him again. At his feet the sea stroked the sand with soft little paws. Farther out, the great, graceful breakers moved like kings into court, trailing the peacock-patterned sea behind them.

Although discussions of the use of sound in words and the way some words sound like the thing they describe are usually put off until high school, in the study of alliteration and onomatopoeia, young children can recognize, talk about, appreciate, and use such concepts. When they do, it deserves notice.

Assessment Questions

Many of the more detailed assessment questions relating to this chapter have been mentioned along the way. The following are broader questions about the ways in which, and the circumstances under which, students notice and experiment with the sounds and visual features of language:

- Is the student analyzing the sounds of speech?
- In what ways is the student applying a sense of the sounds and melodies of language to writing and reading?
- Is the student seeking patterns in the ways letters are organized and in the ways they represent sounds and meaning?
- Is the student flexible in applying knowledge of letter-sound relationships?
- In what ways is the student integrating knowledge of the sound, the look, and the feel of words in reading and writing?
- In what ways is the student using knowledge of the sound, the look, and the feel of words to self-correct in reading and writing?
- In what ways is the student changing in his or her knowledge about and control of words?
- What words does the student completely control (that is, which can he or she read and write automatically)?

CHAPTER 14

BEING STRATEGIC

A child reading a book comes across a word he doesn't recognize. Reading suddenly shifts from recognition to reasoning. Some strategy needs to be used to render the word recognizable. Perhaps he will relate it to a different word he does know, or use some of his knowledge of the relationships between letters and sounds. Perhaps he will read on and come back later to figure it out, or ask a neighbor.

Another child finds that she can no longer make sense of what she is reading. Though she recognizes the words, perhaps she cannot sufficiently connect them with her experience to render the text sensible. She too needs to use some strategy to make the piece recognizable. She might reread a portion of the text, or she might decide to skim ahead to see where this writer is trying to take the reader, or she might decide to leave the book until she has done some background reading, or she might decide to ask someone to explain it, or she might ditch the whole thing entirely.

The more strategies a reader has, the more options are available for solving problems. The more flexibly the strategies are used, the more likely the reader is to solve problems. The more insightfully strategies are selected, the more quickly problems are solved. That is why it is useful for teachers to record the ways students solve problems as they read and write.

Suppose that a child is trying to think of a word while writing. She might:

- Find the word on classroom wall.
- Find it in a book she knows.
- Ask a neighbor.
- Ask the teacher.
- Approximate the word.
- Choose another word that she knows how to spell.

- Use a thesaurus (book or computer).
- Leave a space and go on.

Or suppose she doesn't recognize a word while reading. She might:

- Predict a word that would fit there and check to see if the letters could make that word.
- Read to the end of the sentence and come back later to check the word.
- Use letter-sound relationships to figure out what the word might be, then try it in the sentence.
- Ask a friend or the teacher.
- Try to think of a word she knows that resembles the one in the book and see if the familiar word provides a clue.

If she tries one of these strategies and it doesn't work, she might:

- Repeat the same strategy over again.
- Quit.
- Try a different strategy.
- Ask for help.

A student who uses only one strategy today will show growth by using more strategies next week or next month, or by using them more flexibly, or more persistently.

Constraints on Strategy Use

The strategies readers and writers use are limited by:

- The strategies they have available.
- The knowledge they have relevant to the topic.
- The goals they are trying to accomplish (which may change at any point along the way).
- Situational constraints, such as deadlines, audience, whether a dictionary is handy, etc.
- The person's perceptions of the cause of the problem.

Having the wrong goal is a serious problem, since this will cause a person to ignore the useful strategies of others, and may result in the development and use of inappropriate strategies. For example, teachers can tell from a running record whether or not the child's goal is to make sense. Uncorrected nonsense is a bad omen. The situation can affect both the goals and the strategies used to achieve those goals. For example, a competitive context can change the goal of writing, but even if the original goal is left intact, the available strategies may change (for example, peer assistance may no longer be available). If my goal is to remember what was said by a speaker, I am likely to take notes. If I do not have paper and pencil with me, I might use a rehearsal strategy instead. I can use the same strategies if I wish to remember what an author said in a book, but in this situation I also have the option of highlighting or underlining. If my intention in either case is to subsequently use scintillating quotes, my notes will be different from what they would be if my intention is to be able to talk sensibly about the gist of the message.

Observing a student's reading or writing generally provides teachers with good information on strategy use; however, if we don't know why the child used the strategy, we can misconstrue its appropriateness. Asking children *how* they managed to figure out a word, or how they knew to spell it that way, will often yield good information on spelling strategies (for more on this, see Wilde 1991). When descriptions of strategies are shared, either in conversations or by posting them on the classroom wall, others can add new strategies to those they already know. Thus, evaluation feeds back into learning. Simply asking students how they did something will provide a great deal of information for both teacher and students, but featuring this kind of question encourages children to become conscious of their strategies and to value them, which helps them become strategic, which is much better than just having strategies.

Availability of Strategies

Obviously, not having relevant strategies available can be a serious problem. Unless we watch our students work, we can be unaware of what strategies they do and do not have. Some strategies are not immediately obvious. For example, when composing a mystery, it helps to know that it is easier to work backward, starting with the solution and the motive, than forward. Other strategies seem so obvious that we may not think to check for them. This will sound bizarre, but it was only when my master's degree thesis was being typed for me (I could not type at that time) that I learned about cutting and pasting. Mina Crooks was typing part of my thesis and expressed surprise that none of what she had was cut and pasted. Someone might have noticed when I was in elementary school that I lacked this strategy. It would have saved me some pain and possibly changed my undergraduate grades. But no one noticed. I don't think anyone saw me writing. Now, of course, cutting and pasting for me involves a computer and software rather than scissors and tape. The problem I have now is that I often cut and paste when I should just cut, which leads us to a second problem of strategies.

Knowing When and Where to Use Strategies

Strategies all have their prices. Going to a dictionary is time-consuming (so is going to an adult, usually). There are also trade-offs in independence and ownership. How children make these trade-offs tells a lot about their notion of what it is they are engaged in.

For example, "skip it and go on" is one way to manage a difficult word when reading, but not necessarily the most efficient or most effective way. It takes little time but risks loss of meaning. It may not be appropriate when reading an instruction manual for putting together some complex piece of machinery. One adult with whom I worked would avoid using a "sound it out" strategy (even though it was available to him) in favor of "skip it and go on" and then reread. The problem was that, in order to maintain meaning, he would end up rereading increasingly larger chunks of text. This took longer than if he had used a "sound it out" strategy, which he avoided because he found it difficult and slow. In avoiding it, he ensured that his reading would be even more difficult and slow.

Sometimes strategies are simply overused. For example, self-correction is an excellent strategy. However, if a reader corrects every single mispronunciation, the strategy is inefficient. Planning, too, can be a very helpful strategy. The best writers often spend time planning, and planning certainly helps when doing research. But planning is not always helpful. It is not always what you want to do when you read or write. As Ann Berthoff (1978) points out, "If you commit yourself to one scheme, one definite plan, then anything unexpected can only cause trouble. 'Staying on the track' becomes a virtue in itself, despite the fact that that track might be leading into a swamp of the self-evident" (p. 65). The same is true for teaching. Having labored over plans, we are often loathe to part with them, even when our students' responses suggest that we should. (Here it may be worth distinguishing between *planning* and *preparation* as strategies. Planning is used to reduce possibilities, whereas preparation is done in order to manage diverse possibilities.)

Determining the Nature of the Problem to Be Solved

If, while reading, you come to a sentence that appears to state "The edible part of the banana is usually blue," you are likely to balk. What we decide is the source of the problem and what we do when we discover such a problem are very important. I could, for example, attribute the seeming lack of sense in the sentence to any of the following:

- Inaccuracies in the author's knowledge.
- Inaccuracies in my knowledge.
- Inadequate copyediting.
- My stupidity.
- My lack of effort in my reading.
- My failure to use appropriate strategies.
- The author's attempt at humor.

Having decided on the source of the problem, I would then decide what to do about it. For example, I might decide that the problem was not important and continue reading the piece. I might decide that I had missed something, some piece of context perhaps, and go back and reread a section of the text. I might decide that since the author now has little credibility because of this gross error, I would just skim the rest of the book and not take it seriously. I might decide that this was simply another example of my stupidity and I should expect such conflicts to occur because almost everybody is more likely to be right than I am. Accurate analysis of the problem facilitates productive choice of action.

These same interpretations influence the methods teachers use to solve problems. Sometimes a student does not appear to be developing as a reader or writer as quickly as we might like. We set out to figure out what the problem is, and at some point we start making decisions about what is causing the problem. These are critical decisions, as they speak directly to the kind of instructional strategy that we would then use. Dedicated teachers, having done their best and had all the other children in their class develop just fine, are likely to decide that the student who is lagging behind must have some sort of learning disability. The other popular culprit is some aspect of the child's background, be it familial or cultural. The higher the accountability pressure, the more likely it is that the teacher will see the student as the source of the problem, and the less likely that the teacher will locate the problem in his or her instruction, or that an administrator will locate the problem in the organization of the school. The goal changes from problem-solving to help the student, to self-defense. Parents, for their part, are just as likely to see the school as the problem as they are to see their child as the problem; they are less inclined to see the home setting as a problem.

There are many ways in which students can be seen as the source of the learning problem. They may be called "not very bright," learning disabled, unready, lazy, dyslexic, unmotivated, and a host of other terms. Some of these presumed causes, such as dyslexia, carry a connotation of permanence and of being not under the student's control. Thus they may evoke feelings of pity. Others, such as laziness, are conditions that may be considered permanent but are believed to be more under the student's control. Thus they evoke feelings of anger or annoyance. Each of these attributions is handled with different instructional strategies.

Clearly, the assumptions we make about causes of problems have serious consequences. For the children's sake it is very important that teachers keep an open mind, and that schools are organized so that teachers can afford to seek the causes of learning problems in their own practice.

Conditions of Strategy Use

The context in which a strategy is used is also important. Self-corrections in reading, for example, will not usually occur if the text is too difficult. Context is also important in students' use of writing strategies. For example, we might decide that it is important for our students to develop the ability to revise their writing, that it is an important step forward. We might even include revising on a checklist or on a report card list of items to grade. However, a child's decision to revise depends on a number of conditions. A child is only likely to revise if the effort involved in revision is balanced by the rewards of the outcome; the social context encourages personal response to drafts; and the writer has a personal commitment to the piece she is writing. Students' willingness to revise should also be considered in the context of how much writing they do. If a student has produced relatively little writing, she is unlikely to decide to cut anything out of it. In fact, if she does, she may end up with writers' block from trying to get all of the limited output exactly right from the start. In order to want to add information, a writer must have more to say and feel that others will think it worth hearing. Time is also a significant factor in revision: if the time allowed for writing is limited, revision is likely to be rare. Thus, if a child does not revise, it is not simply indicative of the child's development; it also relates to the student's goals and the classroom context.

This is why as teachers we must think through our own views of the goals of particular literate activities. Because of our own schooling, we often think of revising as fixing up something we have written. But *revising* actually means "seeing again," not "fixing the bad bits." In other words, fixing up is not the same as revising, and different strategies are likely to be used for these different goals.

Not All Strategies Are Productive

A distinction can be made between what I call coping strategies and literate strategies. Literate strategies are those that help you solve the reading or writing problem you have encountered. Coping strategies help you manage the situation you are in, but do not necessarily help you solve the problem. As an example of a coping strategy, consider the case of an adult student of mine. When he was quite young, he found that he was not doing as well as his peers in reading. His analysis of the problem was that he was retarded and thus had little hope of being successful. The strategy he chose was to avoid print. This relieved his frustration initially, but over the long run it ensured that he would not learn to read. He turned to this coping strategy repeatedly, and it soon became automatic. Not only would he physically try not to be caught in a situation in which he might be expected to read print, but when print was about he averted his attention. Once this strategy became automatic, it was easy for him to use it: he didn't even need to think about it. It was also quite difficult to stop.

Eliminating automatic, unhelpful strategies often requires that we bring them to the level of consciousness and then consciously override them. For example, as an adolescent I taught myself to play the guitar from books with the little black dots on the lines showing where to put my fingers. In the process, I learned some strange fingerings for certain chords. After playing in a band for a couple of years, I quit, sold my guitar, and did not play for over fourteen years. When I once again picked up the guitar I began to learn a different fingering for one chord in particular, but I had a hard time getting rid of the one I had learned so long ago. Several things helped me eventually to abandon that old strategy. First, I would consciously, and clumsily, overrule the old pattern and force myself to place my fingers in the new pattern. However, if I played with an audience of any sort (such as my children), I found that I slipped right back to the old way. But when I decided to take lessons, I was taught many different ways to play the same chord. The flexibility I gained eliminated the problem of my automatic and incorrect fingering. These principles can be applied to literacy learning as well. In particular, a wide and flexible repertoire of strategies can serve children well.

A Cautionary Tale

Most of the research over the past few years has stressed the strategic nature of literacy and the importance of children's learning multiple strategies. This view has its advantages, but I would like to end this chapter with a cautionary tale. Although most people do not know this, those who know me well know that I am disabled. I am swimming disabled. If you are a swimmer, you probably think this is kind of silly, but I come from a country in which one is never more than a few miles from water. I managed perfectly well to conceal my shameful disability by staying away from water, "forgetting" my swimming trunks, and the like. But when I came to the United States and met my future wife, who comes from a long line of swimmers (eleven children in the family—all swimmers), things became more difficult. Early in our relationship, when I most wanted to make a good impression, I was invited to join Tina and her family for a picnic at the shores of a lake. The entire family immediately swam across the lake to play. Fortunately, an inner tube allowed me to paddle across nonchalantly as I appeared to sunbathe. Unfortunately, once I got across the lake, Tina's youngest sister appropriated the tube.

Fortified by the fact that I had learned to teach swimming at teachers' college and indeed had taught a good number of children to swim despite my own inability, I decided to swim back. About halfway across the lake I realized I was going to drown. My first thought was to attract attention by waving and shouting for help, but my already established reputation as a joker precluded that strategy. Such a ploy would simply make my fellow picnickers fall to the ground with laughter. I decided to try swimming on my back, which worked fine, except that I am right-handed. The youngest in the family swam up alongside me and asked, "Why are you swimming in circles?" After painstaking adjustment of this tendency I eventually made it to shore, completely exhausted, but alive. At that point I had to 'fess up.

"No problem," they said. "We'll teach you to swim." So after lunch, they got me in the water to teach me to float. They formed a circle around me, treading water and giving me instructions   and watched me sink. My Sicilian father-in-law-to-be suggested, "Feed him more pasta." But this didn't help. I was, and still am, a sinker. They misconstrued the problem to be solved. I *know* how to swim. I can swim the length of a pool very well and very fast—but no further. It is fear that stops me from swimming. I am afraid to let go of my first breath for fear that I shall drown. To me the goal of swimming is simply to stay alive in the water. More strategies are not what I need. You might say I have a kind of swimmers' block, like writers' block.

My problems at the family picnic are comparable to the difficulties some people face with reading and writing. Strategies may be useful, but not out of the context of the individual's feelings and goals. The last thing we need are classrooms full of students who are able to check off all the strategies on a checklist but who never pick up a book or a pen.

Assessment Questions

The following are questions relating to the issues discussed in this chapter:

- Under what circumstances is the student most fully engaged and thinking strategically?
- Are the student's strategies organized around making sense and further engagement?
- In what ways is the student taking control of his or her own learning?
- When the student encounters a problem, does he or she give up easily or try to solve it persistently?
- Is the student flexible in his or her use of strategies?
- Does the student take stock of the effectiveness of strategies?
- In what ways does the student cross-check sources of information?

CHAPTER 15

CHILDREN'S CONCEPTS OF COMPETENCE AND SUCCESS

Rhoda Spiro and I (Spiro and Johnston 1989) once asked some first-, second-, and third-grade students the following question: "Suppose you had a pen pal in another school who was the same age as you, and you wanted to find out about him or her as a reader. What questions would you ask?" Predictably, their responses depended on their circumstances. Some children wanted to ask "What group are you in?" or "What book are you on?" These children's comments reveal a concern for reading as an ability (a capacity) that people have varying amounts of—a stratified notion in keeping with the basal reading programs that generally dominated their classrooms. Other children wanted to ask their pen pals "What type of book do you like?" or "Who is your favorite author?" or "Do you read a lot?" These comments reveal a concern for the other's interests and experiences rather than a concern for comparative judgments of ability. They arise from a different conception of what it means to be a literate person.

For very young children, merely completing a task is sufficient grounds for judging themselves competent. They build a block tower and they celebrate. You may point out to them that someone else built a tower faster or bigger, but they don't care. They are not interested in invitations to build the "best" construction. Below the age of about two years, it is almost impossible to convince children that they are unable. If they attempt a task that turns out to be too difficult, they simply change the task to make it manageable.

Around the age of two children begin to understand themselves as separate and autonomous, and they build identities that include notions of their own competence. They become interested in the importance of doing things for themselves. When they see someone else do something, they want to do it and can become frustrated when they cannot. Within the next year or two they begin to notice when someone accomplishes something faster than they do. In other words, over this period, they become able to adopt external criteria for success or failure. By the age of three, some children are interested in interpersonal comparisons, but they remain confident that their own work is in fact the best. By the time they are four, however, many children make specific comparisons. They notice when someone is doing something better than they, and they spend more time watching their more competent playmates than their less competent ones. This awareness may lead to arguments about the relative quality of their work, put-downs of others, boastfulness, and fights with playmates over building materials or other supplies.

As children grow older they can compare their performances with others' using increasingly complex criteria. This increasing potential for self-evaluation can provide either a turbocharge for learning or sugar in their intellectual gas tank, depending on the sense they make of their evaluation. Students may learn that differences between their own writing and that of others can be a helpful lever for skill development and revision, or grounds for exciting conversation. Such students view ability as learned competence and attend to comparisons that suggest specific ways to improve. Others, however, may view performance differences as indicators of differences in capacity—differences in smartness. These students will attend to such factors as relative difficulty, relative time taken to complete a task, and so forth.

For example, Ethan, a sixth grader, was reading a book that was a gift from his previous teacher. It was, he pointed out, a "fat book." "The good readers got the fat books and the poor readers got the skinnier books." When asked whether he attends to illustrations when he reads, he says that they are O.K., but that he does not have to have them, implying that they are only there as a crutch for less able peers. Reflecting on his earlier reading experiences, he comments that in second grade his class had reading groups and he was in the "second to worst group" which read "one big book with about a hundred pages." By contrast, "the worst kids read skinny books with only about thirty pages."

Ability as Capacity

Although very young children are incapable of comparative judgments of ability, as they get older they are increasingly able to make these normative judgments. A normative conception of ability can be made by about 30 percent of five- to six-year-olds, 75 percent of seven- to eight-year-olds, and virtually all nine- and ten-year-olds (Nicholls 1978). Although some kindergartners can make such assessments of ability, the normative framework is largely learned in school. Classrooms that emphasize normative comparisons foster this development faster than classrooms that do not (Stipek and Daniels 1987).

Once children can make comparative judgments it becomes possible for them to entertain a notion of ability as capacity, and to judge themselves unable because it took them longer than it took others to read the same book, say, or because they had to work harder, or because the book they read was not as big, and so forth. First graders who have developed the normative conception are less likely than their peers to rank themselves as highly competent—even though, on average, they are more competent (Miller 1987).

Making judgments of capacity requires controlling (in reality or in the imagination) the level of difficulty and the amount of effort involved in an activity. The more easily such dimensions can be seen as comparable, the more likely it is that judgments will be made. Indeed, the more classroom conversations are about relative difficulty, and the more classroom activities seem like a test, the more likely it is that children will be concerned about their ability.

When children make judgments within this framework, they are judging not only what they have done, but also their potential for future accomplishment and, often, their personal worth. The consequences of such assessments are worth pondering. For example, if Bill and Pete accomplish the same thing, but Bill had to work harder to do it, people infer that Pete has more ability than Bill. If Bill does not want to be judged as less able, his most likely strategy will be to work even less than Pete so that people cannot tell whether his lower performance is due to his being less able or his having invested no effort. This way, Bill can always argue that he is just not trying, and avoid the possibility that others, or he himself, will view him as unable. Of course he could invest *more* effort in hopes of performing better than Pete, but there is always the chance that he will not do better, and then he would look even worse. Once students develop a conception of ability as capacity, they are more likely to reduce their effort when they suspect they will not do as well as their peers (Miller 1985).

Just because children are capable of evaluating themselves in terms of the performance of others does not mean that they will do so. Whether children use others' performance as sources of learning, admiration, or negative self-evaluation depends on the circumstances. If the classroom focuses on discrete, uncontroversial "facts" and skills, it is easier for students to make comparative judgments of ability than if the classroom emphasizes more controversial knowledge. Controversial knowledge is also more engaging, and when people are entirely engaged in the task at hand, they do not make judgments about how able they are. Actually, they can't even keep track of time. I once observed a five-year-old in a noisy classroom, completely absorbed in making a book. After about half an hour I asked if she would show me what she was working on. I commented that such detailed work must have taken her a long time. "No," she said, "no time at all." When we are deeply engaged in an activity there is simply no space left to worry about such details as time and relative competence.

If the question children seek the answer to is "How smart am I?" they will be more likely to compare themselves with others and less likely to focus on the relevance of what they are learning, or on their developing skill. But if the question they seek the answer to is "How can I make this better (or make more sense of this)?" the performance of others will have quite different significance: it will matter to the extent that it contributes to the attainment of their goals.

What's the Point, and How Do You Succeed?

Although some children are interested in praise before the age of two, children are born with a motivation system that is strongly oriented toward mastery. At least up to age five, children generally show pleasure in their own accomplishments without being praised. In other words, their evaluations of their performance arise from their completion of the activity rather than from another person. Young children also prefer to decide for themselves which activities they will complete. They persist longer at activities they have chosen for themselves. They are more interested in achieving their own goals than in achieving goals posed by, for example, their mothers. And if another person starts to take over an activity, children are apt to lose interest in it. When another person, such as an adult, defines a high proportion of a child's goals, the child is likely to look up to that other person as soon as the task is completed to see whether he or she was successful (Stipek, Recchia, and McClintic 1992). Adults are really no different in these matters.

Children are different from one another in their orientation to learning. Some students are task oriented. They are most interested in learning to improve their personal performance. If you ask these children, "What makes you feel really pleased when you are doing schoolwork?" or, for older students, "What makes you feel really successful in school?" they will mention making sense of something, learning something new, or improving their performance as a measure of success. Other children have a strong ego-orientation and tend to focus on relative performance. If you ask them the same questions they will tell you that merely learning something new or improving their performance is not enough. To feel successful they must beat others. If schooling is to have anything to do with the creation of a democratic society, these goals and their consequences are something we must take seriously as we structure our assessment practices.

Being better than others or making sense and being engaged, then, are goals that children work toward. *How* students work toward their goals is influenced by their theories of how the world works. Task-oriented students (those more interested in sense-making) are more inclined to use "deep processing strategies" when reading and to prefer tasks that lead to learning (Nolen 1988). When they think about the purpose of school, and thus of literacy learning, they think it is to understand the world and to help them to be socially useful. Ego-oriented students are more inclined to value being superior and avoiding work. This goal is best served, they feel, by being more able than their peers and by striving to beat them. They believe that the purpose of school (including literacy learning) is to enhance wealth and status (Nicholls et al. 1989; Thorkildsen 1988). Preoccupied with their ability, these students often have unrealistically high or very low aspirations, particularly if they have doubts about their ability. Worse, the more a situation is like a test, or emphasizes their relative standing, the smaller their chances of being absorbed in and gaining enjoyment from the activity and the greater their chances of becoming uninvolved and developing unreasonable goals (Nicholls 1989).

Constructive Self-Assessment

The notion of ability that children develop regarding their literacy, then, will have a substantial impact on their motivation for and engagement in reading and writing. In classrooms that emphasize ego-involvement, students who consider themselves less able will quit when they encounter difficulties. Similar students in classrooms that emphasize engagement and more complex literacy contexts do not quit (Dahl and Freppon 1995). As teachers, we can make a difference in the ways children construe literacy, themselves, and each other through the organization and the conversations of the classroom.

Ellen Adams, a teacher-researcher, studied the conversations of her second-grade students, most of whom were perfectly capable of adopting a normative notion of ability. In their previous classroom they had been grouped by ability in a basal reading program. At the beginning of the year she recorded conversations such as this:

TEACHER: Why don't you three read together today?

NANCIE: I don't usually read with Kristy and Jenesa, Mrs. Adams. I read with Cass and Samantha, O.K.?

TEACHER: Well, Nancie. We need to read with different people . . . Go ahead. Kristy, why don't you start off and read a couple of pages.
(Teacher leaves.)

NANCIE: They're real short pages. You can read them, Kristy. I'll be your word helper if you don't know the words.

JENESA: I'll be your word helper too.

NANCIE: Gee, how can you be a word helper? You don't know too many words either, Jenesa. You read like Kristy . . . I'll read the long pages and you can read the short pages, O.K.? I'll let you read all the short pages because they don't have a lot of words, O.K.?

KRISTY: Yeah, O.K.
(Nancie reads two pages that contained a lot of text.)

NANCIE: Do you want me to read more pages?

JENESA *(looks at Kristy and shrugs):* O.K.

KRISTY: Yeah, you can read.
(1995, pp. 131–132)

Nancie's opening statement implies "My reading ability (capacity) is far superior to these other kids'." Her impatience with what she sees as their relative incompetence and her desire to assert her own competence result in her taking over the reading entirely from the other two girls, who passively concede her point. This concern for competence after emerging from an ability-grouped, basal-reader classroom was predictable enough. But Ellen Adams changes the conversations to focus children's attention on engagement, collaborative learning, and strategic competence. Later in the year the following kind of conversation was recorded.

WINSLOW: I'll start reading, Kristy. "A tiny caterpillar was coming out of a tiny, round egg. She was the last caterpillar to hold from the doz—dozens of eggs—I mean, to hatch from the dozens of eggs glud—glud—to the leaf.

KRISTY: Glud to the leaf?

WINSLOW: That don't make no sense, Kristy.

KRISTY: We need a word helper. I'll go get Arnold.
(Kristy gets Arnold.)

ARNOLD: What's the problem, guys?

WINSLOW: This book don't make sense.

ARNOLD: Why?

KRISTY: Look—Here . . .

ARNOLD: Let me start from the top . . .

WINSLOW: I read that already . . .

ARNOLD: I know, but you're supposed to start from the top when you get all screwed up.

WINSLOW: O.K. Well, let me read it, and when I get messed up then you can . . .

ARNOLD: Sure. Start reading, Winslow.
(Winslow reads the section again until Arnold steps in and says, "That word is glued, Winslow.")

WINSLOW: So the eggs wouldn't fall off, right, Arnold?

ARNOLD: Can I read with you guys?

WINSLOW: Only if we take turns, Arnold . . . and don't keep telling me the words.

ARNOLD: I won't.

KRISTY: Let's read it all together . . . like whisper reading.

ARNOLD: We'll like lay down on our stomachs together and I'll be in the middle.

KRISTY: O.K.

(The children squeeze around the book together and read it aloud.)
(pp. 132–143)

Besides developing a different understanding of what it means to read, these children have come to view their own and each other's competence quite differently.

Who's in Charge?

One day in summer my son's final report card for the year came home. It contained various grades, sometimes with a comment such as "a pleasure to have in class." I asked him to explain to me what it meant. He said, "It means I'm doing O.K." I asked him what he could do to improve in his subjects. His response was, "If I knew that, I'd be the teacher." In school he has learned that other people tell him what to learn, how to learn it, and whether or not he has done a good job. At no point in the school day does he have control of his learning, except through more or less diligent application of a work ethic. Under these conditions learning is under the teacher's control, and it must be managed through the application of rewards and punishments (mostly through grades).

Most parents have had the experience of asking their child what he or she learned at school that day and receiving the response "Nothing" day after day. But it is possible (indeed, critical) for children to take control of their learning and of the assessment that directs it. For example, children could be saying things such as:

> I write a lot more now and I use more interesting words, like in this one [piece of writing] I said "got" and "went" and "said," but in this one I wrote "winced" and "scurried." I have better topics now too 'cause I keep a journal to write ideas. Sometimes I don't even need the journal; I just see something and it reminds me. I still want to do better endings and I want to do better dialogue, but my characters sound real.

or

> Last year I didn't read much. I never read at home. This year I've been reading at home and I started reading *Goosebumps* and I read a lot of them but now I read different stuff. Like I still read some R. L. Stine, but I like some poetry like Jack Prelutsky and the kite book and other stuff like *The Chocolate Touch*. Mostly I want to get quicker at reading . . . I've published two fiction books and I am going to write a nonfiction one on fungus like the stuff that was growing on Steve's lunch. I got three books about it and I got some white and black fungus growing on some bread and cheese. And I did two poems. I didn't really do hardly any writing last year. Also I can spell better. Today I spelled *special* and *caution* right.

When children are able to notice changes in their own competence, they will be much less likely to find themselves drawn into less productive notions of competence. Because they will understand that individuals' goals, skills, and experiences are different from one another, students will not be competing to achieve the same goal at the same time. Because their goals and achievements are personal, and therefore not directly comparable, they will not be distracted from their engagement by unproductive comparisons with others.

Assessment Questions

When we assess children's notions of competence, we will want to know:

- What are the conversations in the classroom involving literate competence in literacy?
- What is the student's understanding of his or her literate competence?
- What does the student believe to be the point of literate learning?
- Who has control of the student's literate learning and its assessment?
- Can the student describe (perhaps give evidence of) specific ways in which his or her literate competence has changed?
- Can the student describe specific ways in which she would like her literate competence to change?

$\mathcal{U}$NDER CONSTRUCTION: THE PATTERNS OF DEVELOPMENT

$\mathcal{W}$hen we make checklists, tests, or report cards, we decide what are "developmentally appropriate" signs of literacy for children at different ages. We also decide what is "basic" and what is "higher level," and what evidence will suggest the need for "remediation." When we do this we often assume that we are simply documenting some natural process of development, because most children in our experience develop in what seem to be predictable ways. But thinking of literate learning as natural or developmental stops us from thinking about why it occurs in the order it does. It just *does*. Occasionally things surprise us because they violate the seemingly natural sequence, so for intellectual comfort we push them out of our memories. When my daughter Emily was eight years old, she read Katherine Paterson's *The Great Gilly Hopkins* and was able to talk about it in interesting and sophisticated ways. Around the same time, she made a "happy Easter" card on which the *p*'s were reversed. In short, literate development is less linear than we would like to think. It appears linear because the context in which it occurs, schooling, varies so little and because any variation that does exist is averaged away (Belenky et al. 1986).

Most literate learning is a process of socializing attention to particular features and uses of language in particular social situations. It appears natural because we are immersed in it and so do not see it. But the order in which literate knowledge is acquired and whether something is higher order or basic is more of our own making than not. Often schools (and states or provinces) build their curricular expectations and assessments around, for example, Bloom's taxonomy, which describes what counts as basic and what counts as higher order. This, coupled with the belief that basic must precede higher order, ensures that some children never encounter the most interesting parts of literacy. The resulting stratification of literacy development is unfortunate, particularly because it appears natural, and so inspires a critical examination of the learner rather than of the curriculum.

When we assess children's literacy development we do so within a set of beliefs about literacy and about development, and in doing so we create conditions that produce what we expect to see. Let me illustrate with two different views of literacy development.

Theories of Literacy Development

A common framework of literacy development involves the concept of "reading readiness." In the 1920s, applying Darwin's work to the concept of intelligence, Arnold Gesell (1925) and his colleagues popularized what might be called the botanical notion of human development. The basic premises of this notion are that there are sequences of physical, physiological, and cognitive stages through which individuals pass in the process of development, and that these stages are largely genetically fixed and not to be hurried. The overall process is one of neurological "ripening." Children are not ready to "blossom" into reading until their nervous system has reached an appropriate stage of development, and trying to hurry them along will only result in harm.

In 1931 Mabel Morphett and Carleton Washburne discovered that within the reading program they offered in Winnetka, Illinois, children who began instruction in reading after attaining a "mental age" of six years, six months were more likely to show progress on their reading materials and vocabulary lists than were children who began instruction before attaining that mental age. This they interpreted to mean that reading should not be taught until children have reached that mental age—the point of neurological maturity—blossom time. To prevent the damage of early instruction, teachers in Winnetka had charts on their walls to show when each child would reach the golden mental age of six and a half and thus be eligible to begin reading instruction. The mental age was calculated on the basis of IQ tests: mental age (MA) from the test performance was divided by chronological age (CA), and the outcome was multiplied by 100 (for more on this see Durkin 1978 and Teale and Sulzby 1986).

This belief system system is reflected in present-day reading readiness tests, which still enjoy enormous popularity. Current examples of such tests emphasize the most countable aspects of literacy, include items that have nothing to do with literacy (such as finding the odd-one-out in a set of complex, meaningless figures), and purport to measure the extent to which the person tested is ready to receive knowledge of literacy. From this perspective the defining and initial part of the literate skill is decoding—mastery of the alphabetic principle of the language. This makes for a rather narrow definition of literacy, which would be impossible to use in societies with nonalphabetic languages. Literacy is defined as a cognitive skill that one either has or does not have, rather than a social activity in which one can participate. Once literacy is defined in this manner, "prereading" and "reading" stages can be defined, based on whether or not one can decode. Furthermore, once the decision is made to teach the alphabetic principle first (possibly the most abstract part of literacy), there really is a chance that some children will not be ready to learn it. This unreadiness might be detected on a test and instruction denied as a result (at least in the classroom), thus ensuring that some children will not encounter literacy, and will consequently fail to develop it, just as predicted.

Recent research on children's literate development has arisen from a different set of beliefs, including the concept of *emergent literacy,* a term coined by Marie Clay (1966). From this perspective, children are believed to acquire literacy essentially the same way they learn to talk. To become literate, children require social conditions that nurture literacy, including good role models, available and manageable literature, and an environment in which literacy is clearly valued and children receive support and response. There is no specific age or stage of development at which a child is ready to become literate, except perhaps passage through the birth canal. In this view, literacy is seen as complex and multidimensional, not the product of sudden insight or neurological maturation.

This more complex view of literacy acquisition denies the value of deciding whether or not an individual is or is not literate or ready to become literate. Indeed, from this perspective, as with learning to talk, children can be thought of as always ready to learn more if placed in an environment that will support their participation. Generally (though not always), very young children learn in their homes aspects of literacy, such as that print can be used to make meaning, that stories have particular forms, that books have a right side up, that you go through a book left to right, and so forth. Within this framework children can read familiar books before they have developed a great deal of knowledge about print, provided they have had manageable books read and reread to them. The average two-year-old in the United States can read (make sense of) a McDonald's or Burger King sign at 400 paces from a moving car (600 paces when hungry).

In other words, if the school reading program is flexible enough, any child is ready for it. From this perspective we should talk about programs being ready for children rather than the other way around. Rather than having tests that children must take to determine reading readiness, we might consider evaluating literacy programs as to their readiness to accommodate particular children. If we have a very rigid notion of a reading program, we can be certain that some children will not profit from it and thus will not have been ready for it. However, if our program can accommodate considerable diversity in literate development, and emphasizes engagement, then it is likely to be ready for the children. I present, then, only partly with tongue in cheek, my program readiness test (or rather checklist) in Figure 16.1. This is to be a self-administered test in the spirit of self-evaluation.

		YES	NO
1.	Children are read to and written with often.	___	___
2.	There is abundant, well displayed, familiar children's literature, a good portion of which has rhythmic or predictable language.	___	___
3.	Children are invited, not forced, to participate in shared reading of books, often enlarged ones.	___	___
4.	The books in the class represent a range of cultures, and both genders are represented in a range of roles.	___	___
5.	Storytelling, singing, and role-plays are encouraged along with reading and writing.	___	___
6.	Language is used playfully in the classroom and attention is drawn to it.	___	___
7.	Writing and art materials are readily available.	___	___
8.	Invented spelling is encouraged when writing.	___	___
9.	Invented reading (reading from illustrations and memory, and possibly some use of print) is encouraged when reading.	___	___
10.	The classroom organization is noncompetitive, and literacy is not presented as a linear scale of sequentially more difficult skills or books to be mastered.	___	___
11.	The classroom focus is on involvement, not on relative competence.	___	___
12.	Children are grouped in a range of different ways.	___	___
13.	Exploration and experimentation with language and print are encouraged.		
14.	Errors are seen as opportunities to learn.	___	___
15.	The teacher encourages diversity in response to books, kinds of writing, and interests.	___	___
16.	Children talk a lot with each other and the teacher.	___	___
17.	The teacher listens to the children—each of them—and is often seen with his or her head at the child's level.		
18.	Some teacher time is spent with individual students and some with larger groups.	___	___
19.	Within a month of the start of school, the teacher is able to describe the literate development of individual children in the class in some detail.	___	___
20.	Children are encouraged to treat themselves and each other as authors, readers, and illustrators.	___	___
21.	Children are encouraged to help one another and to seek help as they need it, but to be independent when possible.	___	___
22.	Children are encouraged to be persistent and think strategically when solving problems.	___	___
23.	Feedback to children about their activities is focused on how something was done, and is framed positively.	___	___
24.	The classroom provides a caring, safe environment.	___	___
25.	Children do not spend large portions of time sitting at desks unless by their own choice.	___	___

FIGURE 16.1   *Readiness Test for Beginning Readers' Classrooms*

My point is that our view of literacy and how it develops informs our classroom interactions and our evaluations of children.

The Path of Development

Clearly, literacy development is not a simple journey along a straight and narrow path. One reason for this is the complexity of literacy. Development occurs along many dimensions at once, and on different dimensions in different circumstances. For this reason alone we should *expect* irregular, nonlinear patterns of literacy development. We should be skeptical of indicators such as reading tests and reading rate for their unidimensionality, if not for their dependence on average performances and widely spaced samples that hide fluctuations. Individual students do not grow in this steady manner. (Reading rate, however, probably does develop in a linear fashion, at least when considering number of words read. It might therefore be useful to keep track of words read, and since these words appear in books, the child's additional exposure to diverse vocabulary and concepts would mean that reading rate would only be a small part of the actual development taking place.)

Sometimes children will seem to have mastered some print conventions, for example, and then appear to slip back. Usually these apparent regressions are caused by the child's grappling with awareness of another concept or a new aspect of the activity either not encountered before or not attended to before. Marie Clay (1991) calls this the "pebble in the pond" effect because the new addition can cause a reorganization of the knowledge developed to date. A familiar analogy can be made with young children's developing understanding of past tense in speech. A child who has been conventionally using past tense words like *went* and *gave* may suddenly begin using *goed* and *gived*. This apparent regression is caused by the child's new realization of the general pattern of adding *-ed* to form the past tense, and overgeneralizing the principle. Once this new concept is fully understood, *went* and *gave* will return, but the child will understand them differently. The same sort of thing happens as children acquire generalizations about letter-sound relationships. New knowledge about tense vowels, for example, may temporarily disrupt knowledge they already have about lax vowels (Ehri, Wilce, and Taylor 1987).

Another cause of these apparent regressions stems from the fact that the child's attention may be split among many different demands, including some that are not yet automatic. For example, a child for whom analyzing speech and representing it are still very difficult will tend to make trade-offs between composing and representing when writing a story. Deciding which letters are needed for a word, and writing them, can take up the lion's share of the child's attention so that the composition itself takes second place. Another child, however, faced with the same dilemma, will opt to focus on the composition, with some deterioration in spelling and certain other conventions, such as consistent use of upper- and lowercase letters.

Trade-offs occur because of the time-consuming and laborious nature of the translation process, the motor movements required, the complex decisions about which words to use, and the constant need to maintain the construction of the story. These trade-offs also lead to word omissions and the like, as children may reread only one word back to remind themselves where they are, and may not spare the time even for that. The trade-offs do not stop as we get older. Adults hastily writing a letter, for example, will often hesitate to write the word they would like to use because they are unsure of the conventional spelling. Not wishing to appear uneducated, yet not wishing to take the time to consult the dictionary, they choose a word or phrase they know they can spell correctly. Children also use this strategy. Similarly, when writing fiction, a child who focuses on character may spend less effort on the plot, and vice versa (Hansen 1991).

Although literacy development is generally somewhat uneven, there are certain areas of predictability. For example, in a literate environment, children commonly exhibit the surface features of literate activity (what literate people do), followed by an understanding of the *function* of literate activity (why they do it), followed by the details of the *form* of printed language. For example, punctuation marks can come quite early but somewhat randomly, then systematically if not conventionally, and only later conventionally. The period often appears randomly at first in children's writing, and then systematically, to mark word boundaries, revealing an understanding that the period indicates a break in meaning. Children may develop a number of other concepts about print before mastering the use of the period. Similarly, the concept of vowel markers develops before it is regularized as, for example, in the spellings "caek" for *cake* and "yere" for *year* (which themselves show development beyond the earlier spellings "kak" and "yer."

This pattern is reminiscent of the way oral language is learned. Take, for instance, my youngest daughter, Sam. One of her first uses of spoken language was "Dad" (approximately), used mostly around two in the morning. This sounded like a word, but to Sam it was just a use of her voice that worked. Although she soon added three or four more such utterances to her repertoire, she did not find words for a long time. However, she did begin talking to us in sentences. We didn't know what they meant, but they were sentences. They carried all of the intonation patterns typical of adult language: appealing, questioning, asserting, complaining, commenting. Though she attended to some of the smaller parts of speech, she did not notice that words were in there. Thus she would sing "Twinkle, Twinkle, Little Star" with the melody intact, the syllables separated appropriately (one syllable being essentially one musical beat), and the rhyming sounds on the ends of the lines, but no actual words: "Ih hi ih hi ih hi har, Ih hi ih hi hi hi ar." Then she discovered some words, like "juice," and once she had a handful of these words, she could make two-word sentences to convey intentions: "More juice," "I too," "Watch me," "I go," "I do-it." But many ideas just refused to fit into two-word sentences, so Sam continued to give us lengthy unintelligible sentences using the intonation patterns that she knew conveyed intention. Once she discovered words, however, she began to acquire them at an alarming rate. Not all of our children developed speech in this order; indeed, there is considerable individuality even within the one family. However, Sam was a communicative person (and saw herself as one) long before she had the words to be considered truly verbal. At the same time, she had favorite books and would sit and look at them or turn their pages and make reading noises.

Some predictability also comes when we focus on narrow aspects of literacy. For example, we have seen that a child's understanding of the connection between letters and sounds is related to the muscle movements involved in making the sounds in the mouth. The order of acquisition is modified by the sensitivity of muscles in the mouth and by pronunciation differences in dialects. As outlined earlier, the general pattern of development in English is consonants, tense vowels, and lax vowels, but all overlap, and the sequence is complicated by the existence of complex and irregular visual patterns, found particularly in the most common words.

As soon as we step out of a narrow dimension of development, linear sequences evaporate. For example, when my daughter Sam was eight, and had just finished reading *Charlie and the Chocolate Factory* (Dahl 1964), I heard her use "goed" for *went* in a sentence.

If we make up checklists to keep track of students' development, we have to remember that some skills are forever developing and so cannot be checked off on a list. The ability to choose a topic, for example, is an important skill that is developed from kindergarten to graduate school and beyond, as do the skills of providing information, writing conventionally, organizing writing, providing focus, and writing leads and endings. We can't just make the notation "Hears the sounds in language," either. Hearing and using the sounds in language are skills that are developed all the way through college and beyond. In the early stages we might be looking for children's hearing the phonemes in words in order to represent them in print. Later, we look for writers' use of sounds in their choosing exactly the right word to enhance the melody or the power of their language (although even quite young children can show some facility with this more sophisticated use of sound sense, as demonstrated by Emily and her "Mud" story later in this chapter). At what time in our curriculum should we assert that a child should master these skills? Will anyone ever *master* them? And if we cannot put them on a checklist, will they be overlooked?

Dimensions of Development

Obviously, there are so many possible aspects of literacy development that might be described that any simple test will provide a limited reflection at best. Furthermore, placing everything on a checklist is going to make for a very complex list, and selecting the most important aspects of development to write on a list will represent a statement of personal values. Still, we can highlight some of the dimensions of literacy, where general development may be noted.

Quantity, Rate, and Fluency

Sheer quantity of reading and writing is possibly the easiest and most important area to look for literacy development. The amount of time spent reading (or number of pages read) and writing (or number of words or pages written) is an important indicator of how a student is developing in a classroom. A consistent addition of five minutes a day of voluntary reading is far from trivial. A youngster who reads 60 words per minute would be reading an extra 300 words in those five minutes. Over the course of the school year this is about 60,000 extra words. Also, if these five minutes occur outside of school, it can represent a shift of enormous importance (Anderson, Wilson, and Fielding 1988). Apart from anything else, the outside-of-school reading would continue through school vacations, adding almost an extra 50,000 words. Currently, fewer than 70 percent of fifth graders read books for more than ten minutes a day outside of school. The child who is at the 80th percentile in amount of book reading reads twenty times as much as the child reading at the 20th percentile (Stanovich 1992).

As children spend more and more time reading and writing, many routines and common patterns become automatic, picking up speed and actually going through a different part of the brain (Luria 1970), no longer involving conscious effort. Mature word recognition takes only about 200 milliseconds, and it gets that fast with sheer frequency of use. The whole thing is cyclical. The faster you read, the more times you recognize words. So, if readers who increase their reading by five minutes a day end up increasing their rate of reading from 60 words a minute to 80 words a minute, they will read yet another 20,000 words over the course of the school year. This in turn will probably make them even faster readers.

Similarly, the more children write (or type,) the faster they get at it. Indeed, increases in reading rate can indicate development just as extended stability of reading rate can be a possible sign of lack of progress. Reading rate is easily measured and interesting enough; however, without a consideration of the kinds of words, familiarity of the material, and kind of reading being done, it is difficult to know what reading rate means. William James (1899) considered a study by George Romanes in which Romanes had people

> read a paragraph as fast as they could take it in, and then immediately write down all they could reproduce of its contents. He found astonishing differences in the rapidity, some taking four times as long as others to absorb the paragraph, and the swiftest readers being, as a rule, the best immediate recollectors, too. But not,—and this is my point,—not the most *intellectually capable subjects,* as tested by the results of what Mr. Romanes rightly names "genuine" intellectual work; for

he tried the experiment with several highly distinguished men in
science and literature, and most of them turned out to be slow
readers. (p. 136)

Emphasizing the complexity of development is more productive than reducing
it to simplistic scales. Lack of fluency is not always a sign of lack of progress. The
fluency of young readers is often based on their memory of the text and goes
down as they devote greater attention to the details of print, just as accuracy is
often reduced with increased attention to speed. These trade-offs have to be taken
into account whenever we talk about development.

INDEPENDENCE, INVOLVEMENT, AND PERSISTENCE

Indicators of quantity are somewhat related to involvement, or resistance to distraction. In Ann Berthoff's (1978) terms, this might be termed "writer's (or
reader's) compulsion" (as opposed to writer's block). It can take the form of a child
persisting with a single piece of writing until it meets her standards; it can take the
form of a reader's blocking out all other distractions while involved with a book.
This involvement might be measured by the number of decibels of sudden noise
(doorbells, door slams, screams) required to extricate a person from the literate
activity. On two occasions I have encountered children who have been referred for
evaluation of their hearing because they were so immersed in their reading. This
kind of involvement is related to what Don Graves (1983) calls "binging," when a
child reads everything available by a particular author, or spends a month reading
and writing about one particular topic.

Persistence is another indication of literate development. It reflects a number
of things, such as commitment to a goal (to literacy in general or to a particular
topic) and a belief that problems can be solved and that you can solve them.

Children also grow in independence as they develop as literate learners.
Central to independence is the ability to detect and repair one's own errors. Increased ability to self-correct is an important indication of development, as is the
ability to choose materials and activities that are close to the edge of one's
learning.

CONCEPTUAL AND STRATEGIC KNOWLEDGE

Earlier in Part Two of this book I described many of the concepts and strategies
children develop as they become literate. Documenting their development is important. The following example illustrates the potential impact of apparently small
conceptual confusions.

The piece of writing in Figure 16.2 is powerful writing. One way to examine
this piece would be to document the author's command of writing conventions.
For example, the author clearly understands the general function of the exclamation mark, if not the formal rules for its use. But the most useful assessment of
this piece would relate to the writer's feelings about writing and the chance it
would give for conversations about the source of those feelings. The writer appar-

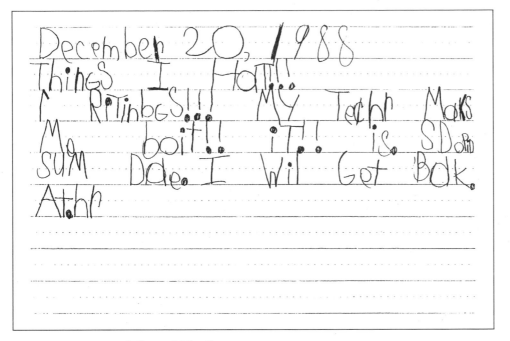

FIGURE 16.2 *"Things I Hate"*

ently hates "writing books" ("RiTinbGS"). This child's teacher has provided many "books" of stapled newsprint for the children to do their writing in. Unfortunately, this child believes, erroneously, that writing means filling the book. He is also unaware that writing can take place over an extended period of time. Being a slow writer, he feels he is never able to complete the task successfully, which makes him frustrated and angry—feelings that he has expressed rather well in this piece of writing. The assessment that matters in this case is one that will reveal problematic conceptions the child has about writing itself and the classroom conditions that underlie those concepts.

COMPLEXITY

Many literate strategies children use will develop in different ways as they gain in skill and confidence. For example, they will begin to use more complex and more numerous cues as the basis for their predictions and self-corrections. Their explanations of characters' motives may become more sophisticated, taking account of a greater number of factors. The complexity of the connections students make when they read will also grow, reflected in the conversations they have about books.

The growing complexity of compositions is manifested in numerous ways. For example, of children's fiction we might ask, "How many characters with dimension are there, and do they interact in meaningful ways?" Composing an original character rather than using one directly from a TV series represents development.

But complexity in itself is not an indicator of development. For example, using simple language to capture complex issues and feelings is deceptively difficult.

FLEXIBILITY AND DIVERSITY

Diversity and flexibility are as important dimensions of development as the quantity of students' reading and writing. Students should be able to flexibly use a range of voices, genres, and vocabularies to accomplish a range of goals with diverse audiences. If a child has only written personal narratives, writing poetry and research reports will be difficult. If he has only written letters to friends, writing a persuasive letter to the principal may be hard work. Similarly, if a child reaches fourth grade and has never read any nonfiction, he will find this lack of experience a considerable disadvantage. In addition to writing fiction and poetry, children should try out a range of nonfiction genres, including essays, letters, directions, travelogues, reports, editorials, and various types of argument.

However, listing all the possible kinds of writing and requiring all students to do one essay on Tuesday and Wednesday, and one letter of request on Thursday and Friday, for example, will defeat the purpose. Students in such a classroom will have attempted a range of genres and will have developed a dislike for writing each. When only children who are interested set out to work on a particular genre, they can be given support, and their enthusiasm will bring some converts. Their sharing of the process of their efforts will provide help in advance for those yet to try. However, teachers need to keep track of the types of writing each student has attempted; otherwise, some students will fall through the cracks and their lack of diversity will not be noticed. Diversity can be documented from writing folders, cumulative folders, portfolios, and activities such as Nancie Atwell's (1987) "status of the class" report, described in Chapter 25. Portfolios can be an excellent way to help students contemplate the range of their work for themselves.

Flexibility comes from having, and exercising, options. For example, when one strategy doesn't work, try another. We might see a student's flexibility in an ability to adopt a variety of different genres to address the same issue, or to shift from one voice to another or one audience to another. Another kind of flexibility might be seen in the range of ways a child can frame, or make connections with, particular books. We look for children to be able to become fully in touch with their own experience, but also to be able to imagine how someone quite different from themselves might feel, speak, and behave.

PREDICTION, RECOGNITION, AND MEMORY

Prediction is central to literate, indeed intelligent, activity, and teachers should see evidence of it in a variety of ways and at a variety of levels in their students. For example, children will anticipate with increasing accuracy the kinds of things that will happen next in a story, or the kinds of feelings that a character might have, and will be able to fill in words omitted in sentences (or anticipate words likely to come next). Patterned language in many early texts will be anticipated too. These are early signs of the attention to language structure that is evident in mature readers. Children will also develop an ability to recognize violations of their expectations, sometimes being amused by them, and to savor surprise more than predictability (which younger children tend to favor).

Knowledge of stories also begins to grow. Initially children ask to have the same story read to them over and over, until they are confident in their expectation of what will happen next. As more and more stories are introduced, fewer repetitions are necessary (except with long, complicated texts), and childrens' knowledge of story structures begins to broaden and become more flexible. Memory for stories and the components of stories increase as children build up a general schema for each genre. Memory for stories is also evident in story retellings. This increased memory is a reflection of pattern recognition and the expectation of meaning from reading. Children develop this memory through lots of successful experiences understanding stories, to the point where they expect to understand them. This expectation is what allows self-correction. Increased memory is what carries children over the decreased fluency they experience as they focus on the details of print, and as they develop word-by-word reading and analyze new words in greater detail.

Along with the predictability of stories comes an increased ability to tell and retell culturally appropriate stories. Awareness of various genres of text, such as lists, instructions, letters, cards, signs, invitations, and advertisements, may be seen in the children's writing and in their pretend reading in role-play situations. For example, they may demonstrate situational use of "book language" and different context-appropriate structures, such as starting pretend letters with "Dear   " and ending them "Love from . . ."

AWARENESS AND REFLECTION

More able readers tend to be more able to talk about how they do things and why they do them that way. This comes about from their learning how to do things and then reflecting on what they are doing. Thus, children's increasing awareness of the whys and wherefores of their literate activity is generally a sign of development.

It is also a sign of a healthy classroom environment that reflection is encouraged, possibly along with an interest in language as an object of study. A good sign of literate development and a healthy literate environment is children's language play. For example, when children make up rhymes, particularly nonsensical ones, they are demonstrating the use of the language as an end in itself. In order to do this, they must separate language from its contextual supports and not use it as a means to an end, but as an object of study in its own right. When we use language simply as a means to an end, we do not attend to the details of the language; as Daniil Elkonin (1971) pointed out, it is rather like the window that we look through to see the world. When we stop and look at the window itself (language) we can gain an awareness of the medium through which we see the world. When we see children looking at language, then, we should take it as an important sign and an indication of their interest in the language. When children laugh at the nonsense they create, it suggests that they understand the conflict inherent in the use of a sense-making tool to produce nonsense.

LANGUAGE USE AND IMAGINATION

Several aspects of oral language development are closely linked to becoming literate. First, there is the growth in vocabulary, much of which comes from books. When we hear a child using "book language," words or phrases out of a story that are not common in everyday speech (such as "Unhand her, you varlet" or "As I live and breathe, you are insufferable" or "Your words show true generosity") we are witnessing an important side of literacy development. The ability to imagine the language a particular character might use is very important both to the composition of believable stories and to the ability to address a variety of audiences.

Imaginative storytelling and role-playing are important signs of the development of the ability to create alternative realities, separate from the here and now, which is central to both reading and writing. In these types of activities children develop and exhibit their ability to identify with various characters, speak in their voices, and notice behavioral evidence of affect and motive. However, imagination is not only related to narrative. It allows us to propose and test hypotheses in our heads, to imagine the consequences of particular actions, and to anticipate the reactions of different audiences.

SOCIAL ENGAGEMENT

Children become increasingly socially competent with respect to literacy. They become more able to engage in productive conversations, to write collaboratively, to provide useful feedback to other authors, and to use their social knowledge to shape their writing and inform their reading.

NOTICING THE COMPLEXITY

To illustrate the complexity of literate development, let us examine a piece of writing. The composition in Figure 16.3, entitled *The Mud*, was written by my daughter Emily. In conventional spelling, the piece reads as follows:

Em 1990, 28 Feb.

THE MUD

To Tina and Peter

It was Sunday, and me and my brother and my friend were riding bikes when we went through some grass and we found some mud and I almost lost my boot in it.

My boot was full with mud. Ew!

Actually, I like it! That oozy mud, so good against the feet. I can't stand without it.

EM ɪpp. 23,Feb.

The mud

To Tino And Pitr

IT was sunday
And me And my druthr
r And my frind
wr rideing diks
wenc we welt
throo sum grass
And we fownd sum
mud And I
almoste lost
my
booT in iT.

FIGURE 16.3 *"The Mud" by Emily*

FIGURE 16.3 *continued*

Then I went back to the mud, and a man came along with a big dog. We ran.

That is the end—until I go back again.

The Mud is interesting to me because my daughter wrote it, of course, but also because of the following features:

- It was written when Emily could have chosen other things to do and under conditions where the noise level and possible distractions were numerous.
- Emily chose her words based on criteria other than on ability to spell them conventionally.
- The words are expressive, and include the use of onomatopoeia (ooze).
- The writing includes a poetic turn of phrase ("so good against the feet") that is not normal spoken language.
- The story has a temporal sequence, two points of narrative tension, and two episodes.
- This is not a "typical" girl's story in that the plot involves a girl, Emily, doing active things with mud. Indeed, this conflict underlies the first narrative tension ("My boot was full with mud. Ew!"—paragraph break—"Actually, I like it!") and is a theme that recurs in her writing and in her life, a point I shall return to presently.
- The story is set up for a sequel (of which there turned out to be two).
- Emily's voice (her "speaking personality"—Bakhtin 1981) is placed in the narrative. We can hear the author telling the story.
- Illustrations are used to support the text rather than the other way around.
- The organization of the book shows a knowledge of title, dedication, authorship, and date.
- Knowledge of print conventions is in evidence (the writing runs left to right across the word, the page, and through the book).
- In Emily's invented spelling, almost all phonemes are represented, including lax vowels.
- The invented spelling suggests that the author is aware of the use of *e* as a marker (rideing, amoste), though it is used inconsistently and is overgeneralized.
- The invented spelling suggests an awareness of some common spelling patterns with double letters (grass, fownd, boot).
- Some words are spelled conventionally rather than phonetically (was, my, along, with).
- The exclamation mark has been used appropriately, as has the period (in the abbreviation "Feb."); the hyphen has been used almost appropriately.

- Spatial orientation of letters is mostly, but not entirely, accurate.
- Upper- and lowercase letters often are used conventionally.

The order of these observations is significant. It is easy for us to get caught up in the details of children's print and to neglect what their writing says about them as writers and readers, and how it relates to their lives. For example, Emily had always been a tomboy, earlier claiming for about a year that she was in fact a boy. However, around the time she wrote this story at school, she went through a stage of trying to be a "girl" (she would squeal "Eeew!" at spiders, and so forth). This lasted about a month before she gave it up. However, the tension continued. Two years later she produced a substantially different story, but with the same underlying tension (see Appendix B).

You might look at the spelling in "The Mud" and make inferences about deficiencies in Emily's knowledge or skill. However, the inference might be premature. The day after she wrote this piece I asked her if she could edit her paper. She did not yet know the term *edit*, but understood what I meant when I described it. That task, she explained, was the role of the teacher's aide in her class. In a flat voice, pointing to each word, she began reading aloud her story, looking for prob-

TABLE 16.1

Spelling Under Different Conditions

Correct Spelling	Spelling While Composing	Spelling on Request
Peter	Pitr	Peater
brother	druthr	deruther
friend	frind	firend
were	wr	were
riding	rideing	riding
bikes	diks	dikes
when	wene	wene
through	throo	throur
some	sum	some
found	fownd	found
almost	amoste	almost
full	fol	foll
actually	aktuleye	acKcholly
liked	like	liked
against	agenst	agenst
can't	cant	can't
without	withot	withont
back	bak	dack
came	cam	came
that	tat	that
until	intil	antill
again	agen	agen

lems, and she found a couple near the beginning: "wr" *(were)* and "throo" *(through)*, which she proceeded to try to correct. After that, her reading became more fluent and expressive, and she detected no more errors. Her involvement in the story made her forget about editing until the end, when she repeated "agen" and commented "Perfect," referring to the spelling. The next morning I asked if she would do some spelling for me. One at a time, I asked her to spell the words I had noted from her misspellings in the story. The words, along with their rendition in her composition and as she wrote them for me on request, are shown in Table 16.1. In her on-request spelling, as opposed to her composition version, she did not mix upper- and lowercase letters. Except for the *K*, all were used appropriately. The next day I asked her to spell my name and she spelled it correctly: "Peter."

Taking Stock

The point I want to make in this chapter is that literacy development is not simple, even, and linear. Although there are some general trends, they appear in complex ways, and somewhat differently in different children. However, the simple fact that keeping track of development can be messy and difficult, involving many consequential decisions, should not stop us from doing it. We must; and we must avoid the temptation to reduce our records to a simple number here and there. Documenting students' development and taking stock regularly are both important responsibilities.

Having learned what literacy looks and sounds like, we can think about ways to document, represent, and reflect on literate learning. In Part Three I examine ways of gathering information, recording it, and generally keeping track of changes in students' literacy. To the extent that there is a technical side to evaluation, this is it. However, viewing assessment only as a set of techniques for collecting data will not get us very far. Many techniques only work in the right conditions, and some techniques can lead to an unhealthy learning environment.

The first item on the agenda is getting children to talk and behave in literate ways and learning to listen to what they have to say. Chapters 18 through 20 provide techniques on how to do this. Next, Chapters 21 and 22, co-authored with Marie

Documenting and Keeping Track

M. Clay, describe how to record and analyze oral reading errors. These chapters are meant to be used with the accompanying tape recording of children reading. Together they will give you practical experience with recording procedures. Chapters 23 through 25 cover checklists and other common, but less time-honored, procedures for recording children's literacy, techniques such as thinking out loud and keeping portfolios.

CHAPTER 17

Opening Conversations

The dictum "Children should be seen and not heard" has been thoroughly applied in schools. Teachers dominate classroom conversation. The delivery, or transmission, model of teaching that we have lived with for so long requires information to flow in only one direction. Teachers have knowledge. Children listen as teachers deliver that knowledge to their waiting minds. In this model the only reason for a teacher to listen would be to check whether the containers were filling up appropriately or whether any was leaking—efficiently detected with a dipstick (test). Within this model, conversation among children not only wastes time, but also might introduce pollutants to the knowledge in the containers.

This way of thinking about learning and classroom organization is thoroughly adultcentric. Julie Tammivaara and Scott Enright (1986) capture this concept nicely as they describe ethnographers studying children:

> In many ways, any adult ethnographer who traipses through a child's world smug in the certainty that the adult world is the highest known form of civilization and a distant goal that young children have just begun to strive for is not unlike the stereotypical "Ugly American" tourist invading the shores of exotic cultures only to find them quaint [in the case of children "cute"] but clearly inferior.
>
> Ethnographers who insist on visiting and studying children from the rigid perspective of adulthood will in the end understand the reality of childhood no better than tourists who visit another land and do their best to bring their "home" along with them. *Respect* for children and their own knowledge about themselves, as well as the same willingness to suspend (adult) judgment and perspective in talking with *children* as in talking with adults are key components of the successful ethnographer's interviews and participant observation. (p. 234)

We can easily substitute "assessor" or "teacher" for "ethnographer" in these comments.

Questions, Questions, Questions

Not only do teachers talk more than students, they also ask lots of questions. Rose-Marie Weber (1985) analyzed over sixty reading lessons and found that although students were asked up to forty questions in a single session, in the entire body of data she collected, not a single student asked a question. James Dillon (1988) reported similar findings: in a study of twenty-seven classrooms, students asked only eleven questions. For assessment purposes, this is a serious loss, because students' questions tell us what they need to know. By contrast, David Yaden and his colleagues (1989) found that children being read to at home, and not being asked questions by an adult, asked literally thousands of questions. The loss of students' questions would be bad enough, but the questions teachers commonly ask compound the problem.

The simple act of asking a question exerts control on the topic of conversation. Worse, most questions teachers ask are ones to which they already know the answer (Durkin 1978; Guszak 1967). The purpose in asking such questions is clearly control rather than information—to check whether the student got the right meaning. There are serious consequences to this practice. In the first place, the lack of talk denies teachers access to information. If we want to understand why our students read and write as they do and how they understand their literacy, we need to have them talking. Second, too many questions from the teacher cause students to stop asking their own questions and learn a controlling form of literacy. Third, it affects motivation both because students feel the loss of ownership of the activity and because some resist the control.

For teachers to begin to listen, then, requires a change of beliefs. It requires believing that children have something important and interesting to say, and that we can become informed by listening to them. This turns out to be difficult for many adults, particularly ones who are in a hurry, who feel they have a lot of knowledge to deliver, who do not trust children, or whose primary interest is control. If we want to know what is going on in our students' minds, we have to arrange conditions in which they will want to speak their minds—to risk revealing themselves and their thinking. Although questioning children may be our first impulse, inviting them to speak or be heard might be more productive.

Getting People Talking—About Literacy

If you can get students engaged in literate talk, all you will have to do is develop skill at recording significant aspects of their conversations. Getting people talking really only requires that they become mutually interested in a topic. In other words, if we can get students interested in what they and others are reading and writing, and in how they go about reading and writing, we are in assessment clover. For example, the following conversation is typical of those to be heard in Mardy Berry's fourth-grade classroom.

BILL: When you're reading a book it's—like you're just reading. When you're reading science or social studies you're spending—you're spending more attention to the words and what it means so you remember.

MATT: When I read a chapter book I can sometimes skip a word if I don't know it or understand it. But in a social studies book I don't do that because—every little word will count more.

TOM: In a chapter book you have a choice. You can stop if you don't like it, but in a science or social studies book you can't.

ELLEN: I agree with Matt that every word counts whenever you read science or social studies. But also when I read a chapter book I seem to read faster, and I like it more than science or social studies. When I read science or social studies I tend to concentrate more and pay more attention to the words. I just kind of pay more attention.

KAREN: I agree with Matt and Ellen in that in a social studies book you should pay more attention and in a chapter book you should also stop if you don't really like it. But . . . in a chapter book you need to pay attention to know what's going on . . .

CHUCK: You don't really learn a lot in a chapter book, but in science or social studies you learn a lot about—something—like how three-quarter hats were made.

JIM: When I read a chapter book or a social studies or science book I pay just about the same attention because in a chapter book if you miss one word it might change the whole course of the book.

DENISE: I agree with Karen that you should pay attention when you're reading a chapter book . . . and I also agree with Chuck that you learn more things in a science or social studies book . . .

BILL: When you read a chapter book you can miss a couple of words and you don't pay as much attention as in a social studies or science book.

JIM: Ellen said that you should pay more attention in social studies or science, and I said that you should *pay equal attention to both.*

MARSHALL: And a chapter book is harder than a minipage because they're *much longer.*

TEACHER:	So you connect harder with being longer?
MARSHALL:	Yes.
DENNIS:	I think it's harder for Marshall to read a chapter book because he's not using his vocabulary real good.
TEACHER:	Could you explain this?
DENNIS:	It's hard to explain this. *He doesn't know what the words mean sometimes and it's longer.*
MATT:	I disagree with Marshall that a book is harder if it's longer. The hardest book in the library might be two pages long but have harder words and more people in it so it might be more complicated. I don't think the harder book is linked with the longer book.
SALLY:	I sometimes think that a chapter book would be harder, but I would say—sometimes reading a chapter book might be harder because you read alone.
TEACHER:	And you don't always read science or social studies alone.
JIM:	I think we got on this topic so long because not everybody is being as specific as they should be.
BRUCE:	I wouldn't fully agree with Jim when he says that you should pay equal attention, but I wouldn't necessarily agree with Ellen that you should pay more attention to social studies books. Knowing that you have to pay more attention with a social studies book, you still have to pay attention to a chapter book also. It's just as important to read a chapter book as a social studies book. A chapter book could be very interesting. A social studies book could be interesting, but in a different way. It's interesting to know about real life and knowing all the facts, but it's also important knowing about a chapter book, but it's more important in a different way . . .
ELLEN:	I said a couple of things to Bill, but in different words. The reason I don't pay as much attention to a chapter book is because in a chapter book you're usually reading for fun or for a hobby. But when you're reading science or social studies—well, actually it depends on what kind of book I'm reading. If I'm just reading it to find out about somebody and I'm reading several books about that person, I might not pay as much attention to a paragraph as I do to another paragraph in a science or social studies book. I tend not to pay as much attention to a chapter book.

BRUCE: Ellen, you said before you read a chapter book for fun, but doesn't reading a chapter book for fun mean that you have to get really interested in it and feel that you have to pay attention to it?

ELLEN: Yeah, but then I don't want to pay as much attention to it like I do in school. If I had to concentrate so much on a chapter book I probably wouldn't read. After concentrating so much it kind of gets annoying and so I do not pay as much attention to a chapter book as to social studies only because I read chapter books for pleasure and usually I don't read a science or social studies book for pleasure. I read it for an assignment.

BRUCE: Don't you ever read a good chapter book and get so into it that you can't put it down and then you end up using your brain as much as you didn't want to?

ELLEN: Well, I'm not saying that I'm not using my brain. I don't want to work it so hard that like—I read a chapter book for pleasure—Like, say, in *The True Confessions of Charlotte Doyle*, sometimes I would pay more attention to some parts than others . . .

MATT: Actually I think what Ellen's trying to say is that she strains her brain all day so when she gets home she wants to relax. She doesn't want to make her brain go insane. She doesn't want to have a nervous breakdown.

ELLEN: Right . . .

BRUCE: Bill, what would happen if Ms. Berry gave everybody the same book, O.K., and you had to go home and read the book, and come back and sit in a medium-sized circle. How would you read? Would you read like a social studies book or like a regular book?

BILL: Well,—if Ms. Berry gave you,—us, the same class the same book to read and then we had to talk about it, I'd pay like as much attention as science or social studies.

BRUCE: So what if you had to go home, and say everybody had a different book, and you had to go home and read it and had to write down on paper? Do you think it would be harder to write it down on a piece of paper or tell it to everybody in the class?

BILL: Tell it to the class . . .

MATT: Actually, Jim, I don't think [skipping a word] could change the whole course of the book. Possibly. I think that the course of the book would still follow the same trail, but you won't understand it because you had a different idea . . . And also I think that when

Bruce and Ellen were having that slight dispute I know what Bruce was saying. You should pay the same, as much, attention to a chapter book and it's because it might be a very interesting book that you want to read. Ellen was saying what I said. It might not matter if you skip a word because you'd still pretty much understand the rest of the book. I know right now I'm disagreeing with what I just said a minute ago. But it's complicated.

(More interchanges follow, and a lunch break. After lunch, the children return to their discussion.)

MARSHALL: Now that I have had more time to think about it—I agree with Matt . . .

KAREN: Somebody said you have to read a science book and it's boring, say you like had to read a book about the Revolutionary War and you like to read about the Revolutionary War, it wouldn't be boring.

To the uninitiated, this might appear to be a conversation among children about minor issues. But this kind of conversation provides an excellent ground for assessment of a classroom as well as individuals' literacy. To begin with, these students clearly respect one another, though they do not necessarily agree with one another. They responded to what they heard, asked for clarification, drew on and analyzed their own experience, supported, extended, and disagreed with one another, and were thoroughly engaged. They demonstrated and extended their awareness that simple dichotomies are not much help; that even deciding how difficult something is depends on many factors, including number of words, size of words, relevant vocabulary knowledge, whether you are reading alone or with someone, and the purpose for which you are reading. They raised the importance of interest and relevance and whether the kind of knowledge to be gained from nonnarrative text is more or less important than that gained from narrative. All of this they did with a display of engagement and respect. In other such conversations children have been able to repeat things that other students have said a month earlier—certainly a mark of respect. In the context of others' comments, and after thinking about it, children can change their understanding. Notice that in this conversation the matter of one child's reading difficulty was raised publicly with respect and without ego-involvement. This is the conversation of democracy— among neighbors who do not necessarily agree, but who are committed to respectful conversations, with the intention of all parties being to reach a more productive understanding. It is a conversation in which neighbors try to understand the topic better, both through their own experience and through understanding and clarifying others' experiences.

Mardy Berry and her colleague Betsy Nolan call these forums "circle discussions." The topics arise from both teacher and students, though more are from the teacher. They are always issues on which there is no right answer. Usually a discussion time is set up to a week in advance to allow time to consider the issues. The rules for discussion are that initially everyone around the circle gets to say something (perhaps twice around the circle—people can pass), and then discussion is open to all. The teacher has similar status to the students, but can ask a student to clarify, perhaps by restating and asking for verification, and can draw students back to the main topic if necessary, although this does not always work if the students have their teeth well into a subtopic.

Circle discussions such as this can be tape-recorded and transcribed (as Mardy and Betsy sometimes do), or they can be used to answer questions about a child's participation or understanding, or to examine patterns of participation, such as gender differences (Nolan 1993). They need not be taped. Some teachers take the role of recording secretary. This requires them to step outside the circle and develop their note-taking ability. Pat McLure does this (Newkirk and McLure 1992). Her first- and second-grade students have book discussions in smaller groups while she takes notes and occasionally steps in to stimulate or clarify. This has an additional benefit in that it forces her to take a listening role, since it is hard to both record and be an active participant in the group. The teacher's stronger listening role allows the students to take greater control of the conversation and the curriculum. It also gives the teacher the details needed to describe students' development clearly and convincingly. More important, it makes it clear that the teacher respects what the students have to say. Tom Newkirk asked Pat McLure once how she could be so patient in allowing the students sometimes to stray far from the topic. Newkirk notes that "she looked at me quizzically and said, 'I don't think of it as patient. I'm interested in what they say'" (p. 149). Rather than viewing their experience as irrelevant or insignificant, she finds her students' connections between the book and their experiences absorbing. Unlike the "good" teacher popularized in the media, heroic and delivering knowledge, McLure "is resolutely anticharismatic" (p. 148). In place of control she offers curiosity and respect. Her opening invitation is "Say something about this book" (p. 51).

There are, of course, less formal situations in which useful conversations take place. For example, Ellen Adams's second-grade students have regular group discussions without Ellen, though the foundation of those conversations is set up in larger classroom conversations as the year progresses. In classes such as Ellen's, students also regularly collaborate in their reading and writing. When students collaborate they make many of their processes and decisions overt as they negotiate, seek help, and share experiences. Often they are struggling with processes that are barely within their reach, which they could not accomplish individually. The value of these engagements is not only that the students' thinking is overt, but that what can only be accomplished at the present by the collective mind is on the way to becoming the thinking of the individual minds.

Cultivating Constructive Conversations

Casual eavesdropping on these engagements can produce a wealth of useful information. However, such conversations do not just happen. As one lower-track high school student commented, "We never talk if she, you know, wants us to say things . . . talk about something, you know? Everyone shuts up" (Jones 1991, p. 80). In spite of her teacher's efforts, this girl and her peers systematically worked against being heard by the teacher, insisting instead that she write down lists of facts for them to learn. Their view of knowledge as facts and teaching as transmission sustained this relationship. And there are other reasons for silence in the classroom. For example, Simone, a college student, felt that the point of classroom conversation is that "it helps to see if the students are doing the reading. There's not much else to grade on" (Belenky et al. 1986, p. 108). If students see the point of discussion in these terms—to produce evidence for judgment—it will be no surprise if they take no risks, or even say nothing at all. In other words, there are conditions under which productive conversations will happen and conditions under which they will not. I described some of these conditions in Chapter 3, but let me review them briefly in a different way.

- There must be a relationship of trust, one that you could say is based on anti-Miranda rights: "Anything you say may be written down but *will not* be used against you" or perhaps "will only be used to your advantage." In other words, students should be encouraged to share incomplete or experimental ideas; the only foolish question will be the unasked one. All contributions will be treated with respect. There will be no put-downs. The classroom will be nonjudgmental.
- Differences in power among participants should be minimized, and the importance of any remaining differences in power also minimized. For example, one of the informal rules of conversation among equals is that they don't ask questions to which they believe there is a single answer they already have, unless one of them would like to be tested. In addition, engagement should generally be invited rather than enforced.
- Conversations should be personally meaningful first and foremost. The view of knowledge that underlies the conversation should be a constructive one. In other words, knowledge is viewed as something made by people in the community using language. Interpretations will often be different because they are based on different experiences. These differences, the controversial issues, will commonly form the basis of discussions.
- Participation in discussions should be based on interest, curiosity, purposefulness, and an expectation that the participant will both learn from and contribute to the community.

These principles are likely to make conversations more inclusive and more expansive, but the teacher also plays a role in opening up the conversational possibilities in the classroom. I think of this as "seeding" the conversation in much the same way that people seed rain clouds, and in the sense that the seed is the beginning of life. We can invite children to make connections with their experiences, to critique, to notice, to extend—all of the things touched on in Part Two. For example, if teachers turn children's attention to the processes of reading and writing and routinely ask such questions as "How can we do this? How else could we do it? How can we check?" not only will they learn a great deal about students' thinking about literacy, but also the students will understand that such conversations are appropriate to have with each other and with themselves. This opens up more strategic possibilities for students. (Of course, if we did the same thing with our teaching, we would reap the same benefits.)

If you ask questions like "Did anyone try any new kinds of writing today?" "Did anyone try any new or surprising words today in their writing?" "Has anyone tried a new . . . ?" students will come to expect that writing normally involves experimentation. As they understand that, they will begin to experiment in their own writing. Similarly, if conversations take for granted that everyone has problems with reading and writing and that there are many ways to overcome them, students will be less daunted by the problems that they encounter and will begin to come up with many more ways to solve them. Such conversations might begin with "I had a problem when I was writing today. Twice I could not think of the right word to use, so I just used a word that wasn't quite right and I underlined it and went on. I will use the thesaurus later. What other problems did people have today? How did you solve that problem? Has anyone else had that problem? How did you solve it?" (For more on this see, Graves 1994.)

In one of my graduate courses for teachers I noticed that the group discussions went as far as participants' coming to grips with the complexity of issues, but people did not seem to be acting on their knowledge. At the end of each session, I began to ask "What are you going to do about it?" At first they found this a difficult question. But by the time we were partway into the semester, they had begun asking the question of themselves and incorporating it into their reading.

CHAPTER 18

CONVERSATIONS IN PRINT

*A*ll this talk about books is terrific, you might say, but speech is gone in a flash and recording it isn't easy. True. In fact it is just this ephemeral quality that literacy was invented to overcome. Why not just get kids to write down their conversation? Sounds silly, but in practice it is far from silly, provided we bear in mind the word *conversation*. Most of us remember having to write book reviews when we were in school; most of us hated it. Many of us are now teachers and continue the tradition. The problem with the book review is that it is not normally part of a conversation. Remember, literacy is a social activity, and literate talk is socially motivated. This is where dialogue journals come in. Dialogue journals are simply journals in which people write first-draft letters to one another. For example, students write notes to the teacher in their journals, and the teacher takes time, usually at the end of the day, to respond to the children's entries. Students can write to each other in dialogue journals too. All that is needed is a sturdy notebook that is large enough to write in easily and to see the continuity from page to page; a box to keep the journals in; and a specific time set aside daily for the writing, although even that is not essential as it can be fitted into the regular reading-writing program. Your main responsibilities as a teacher are to respond to the *content* of the student's entry, *not* to the conventions such as spelling and punctuation; and to respond personally as another literate person, be it friend or mentor, or just a partner in conversation. The topic of conversation can be restricted (to literary works, for example) or relatively unrestricted.

Literary Dialogue Journals

Dialogue journals provide a built-in motive for both writing and making the writing less than cursory. Furthermore, they provide for dialogue, which is the basis of learning to be literate. Nancie Atwell's classic, *In the Middle* (1987), provides a wonderfully readable and practical account of the use of literary dialogue journals. Atwell describes the process and consequences of inviting her middle-school students to engage in written dialogue with her, and each other, about books. These dialogues took place in spiral-bound notebooks that were numbered and filed alphabetically. The tone of the letters was informal, like notes to friends, and the conventions of spelling and grammar were not given overt attention. The idea was to create, in Atwell's words, a "dining room table" atmosphere. The result was literary talk written down. Atwell's requirements were that students spend their reading workshop time reading and writing about their reading. She required at least one literary letter a week to be written to someone in the classroom community, and at least once every two weeks one of the letters should be to her. At least one letter a week was to be analytic, going beyond simple plot descriptions. The letters were considered first-draft writing, with appropriately little concern over convention.

This practice of writing turns out to be habit forming for many students, and has the effect of leaving a paper trail of literary dialogue, which yields volumes of information about students' development. At the same time, the different perspective of the teacher or student colleague prompts students to think of the books they read in ways they might not otherwise have done, and pushes them to develop their thinking. Others' connections with different books, writers, and personal situations expand students' literate experiences. The act of writing about their reading can provoke students to step back from their reading and think more deeply about it than they might if they only spoke about the books. This helps them to become aware of their own knowledge and changes in it and to be able to talk about what they know and have learned—to move away from an inability to talk about what was learned at school. Indeed, if report cards must be done, students could write a good part of them themselves, using their journals as field notes. This would accomplish at once ownership, reflectiveness, and interest in their own development.

Students' literary journal entries tend to move from such statements as:

> I liked Charlotte's Web. It was great.

to

> I cried over Tomie DePaola's *Now One Foot*. The relationship which he
> builds up between Bobby and his grandfather is so strong and the way
> he has him do just what his grandfather did is—wow! Its alot like *A
> Special Trade*, which Mrs. Sims read to us last year.

The journals provide student and teacher with insights about being literate, the kind of strategies and habits readers engage in. For example:

> I've sort of noticed "trends" or "cycles" in my reading. Right now I'm
> in a Paula Danziger "cycle." At the beginning of the year I was in a
> Science Fiction "cycle." (Atwell 1987, p. 173)

Letters also speak of students' emerging literary understanding, and their developing sense of what makes for good literature. For example:

> I think that some of Auel's situations were a bit silly. One thing that bugged me was how Ayla discovered things, like building a fire with flint, riding Whinney, etc. You knew exactly what she was going to do next. When she gets on Whinney you just know that's going to lead to riding her, then using her to chase animals, then to hunt. She makes it so obvious! (Do you understand what I'm trying to say?) (Atwell 1987, p. 173–174)

or

> To me, *Sea Pups* is more of an essay because there are more facts blended in than the number in a normal book. I think that *Sea Pups* is uniqe because I haven't read anything quite like it. I've read my brothers essays, of course, but no real essay like books.

Chapter 10 contains other examples of dialogue journals from Linda Rief's students. Her book, *Seeking Diversity*, from which they came, is a "must read."

Nonliterary Dialogue Journals

The topic of conversation in dialogue journals need not be restricted to the literary. The journals provide a functional, self-motivated context in which students can share personal time and experiences with their teacher while incidentally developing their writing and producing a historical record of their interactions and their writing development. In the process, they also produce a lot of writing. Here is an example from David's journal:

[DAVID:]   I wnt to the grat scap wth my dad and we had iscrem and petsa. it was kul.

[P.J.:]   I bet you had a lot of fun at The Great Escape. Did you go on any rides? I have never been there. Would I have fun if I went? I really liked the toad you brought to school but I am pleased that you let him go again.

[DAVID:]   I went on the stemn demn. it was rel scare. and I went on the wota slid that was neto. you wod love it I bet. I cot a slumndu in the lak.

The sheer quantity of writing produced and the communicative nature of the enterprise ensures that a considerable amount of learning will take place. At the same time, students read the teacher's notes, which provide models of ways of talking, conventional spellings and response structures, more complex language, and indications of the needs of audiences. Dialogue journal writing also helps students move from conversation to essay writing. Indeed, Shirley Brice Heath describes the history of the essay style as emerging from letters to journals to essays (Heath 1987). A central shift which takes place along the way is from the personal audience, or conversation, to the general audience, or what amounts to public speaking. One young student who was being tutored in our lab was quickly able to write in his journal to his tutor, beginning every entry "Dear Sharon," but he would not write stories. He would write the odd line and be unable to continue. He asked if he could start his stories with "Dear Sharon" and, told he could, found story writing no problem (in his final draft he would delete the salutation).

Dialogue journals allow children to engage in a wide variety of functional written language and at the same time leave a record of their competence. Jana Staton (1988) has noted examples in journals of students' asking questions, reporting personal experiences, making promises, evaluating, offering, apologizing, giving directions, complaining, and giving opinions. Staton and Joy Peyton (1988) have also observed changes in students' selection of topics. Toward the beginning of the year, they noted, the topics tended to be closely tied to the classroom community—the shared context. Later in the school year the topics tended to be more personalized, reflecting shared understanding and a deeper relationship between teacher and student. Through journals, children also become more competent with gearing their communication to specific audiences. It is the writer's (or speaker's) job to convey information clearly and coherently, but not to provide so much information that the listener or reader will be bored (Grice 1975). These desiderata of communication are not easily developed in children's writing, but dialogue journals provide a context in which students are motivated to consistently reflect on and develop how they elaborate on topics. As the writing develops, there tends to be changes in such things as the frequency of one-sentence statements, the reporting of specific new information, and the use of comparative and categorizing statements. All of these are documented in the journals, providing as much "hard" data as one could wish for. On many fronts, students' and teachers' writing tends to move closer together over the course of the year (Staton 1988).

In addition to these benefits, dialogue journals can be used as a tool in classroom management. Students and teacher have a context in which they can write about the things that are bothering them in the classroom, and they can communicate their concerns in a reflective way (which writing encourages) and after toning down the emotion with which they might have been charged (the writing can also be a safe means of discharging that emotion). In interviews, students point out that they like dialogue journals for numerous reasons: through them, students are able to share problems, complain, have things explained that they did not understand, and get action taken on class problems (Staton et al. 1988, pp. 33–55). Dialogue journals between teacher and student can also allow students to raise questions they would not ask in a more public forum.

More Advantages

Not only are dialogue journals often habit-forming; they are also community forming. The individual nature of the journals tends to open up personal sides of students (and teachers) that might otherwise not arise. This can form the basis of more understanding relationships.

Because the journals hold a record of the developing interaction between teacher and student, and between others in the community of learners, they are very useful for teachers' self-assessment. For example, the way teachers themselves talk about books will be reflected in the journals. If a teacher is unable to say more about a book than "It was a good book. I liked it," the students are unlikely to talk more insightfully about the books, and even if they did, the teacher would not be likely to notice. In other words, how useful the dialogue journal will be (as with anything else to do with literacy) depends a lot on how much the teacher knows about literature, literacy, and the students. There is no avoiding the fact that, in order to teach literacy and literature, teachers must develop their own knowledge and practice.

Students can help teachers think about their teaching, if that is considered reasonable conversational material in the classroom. Figure 18.1 is an example of the feedback that Trudy Warner, a first-grade teacher, received from her students when she switched from using a basal reader and grouping to organizing her program around children's writing and students' choice of literature. Jeff's letter gives a clear evaluation of the change in classroom procedures. Trudy and her students use both letters and a discussion wall in the classroom for communicating with one another. Trudy's response to Jeff is a good example of the type of response that will maintain extensive, informative dialogue.

Journals also allow students to reflect on their own learning. In interviews about their journals, or in the journals themselves, students often comment on changes in their own writing—for example:

> I use to do real short things but now I write alot because the more I
> tell her about what Im writing the more she understands what Im
> saying. Also the more she likes to read what I write. I think I write
> more stuff about less things than I use to.

Such self-evaluation is encouraged by the simple presence of the continuous record of communication the journals provide. I use dialogue journals in my university teaching, and I ask students to write an analytic memo reflecting on changes in their journal entries.

As mentioned earlier, teachers often dominate classroom interactions, particularly by asking questions. Roger Shuy (1988) found that in the six elementary language arts classrooms he studied, 97 percent of all classroom exchanges were initiated by the teacher. Teachers ask most of the questions and by doing so control the topics of discussion and maintain authority and control. Virtually all of the questions in the classroom are made by teachers, and the majority of them are meant to prompt interactions of the form teacher question—student response—teacher evaluative feedback. Such questions are called "display questions," because

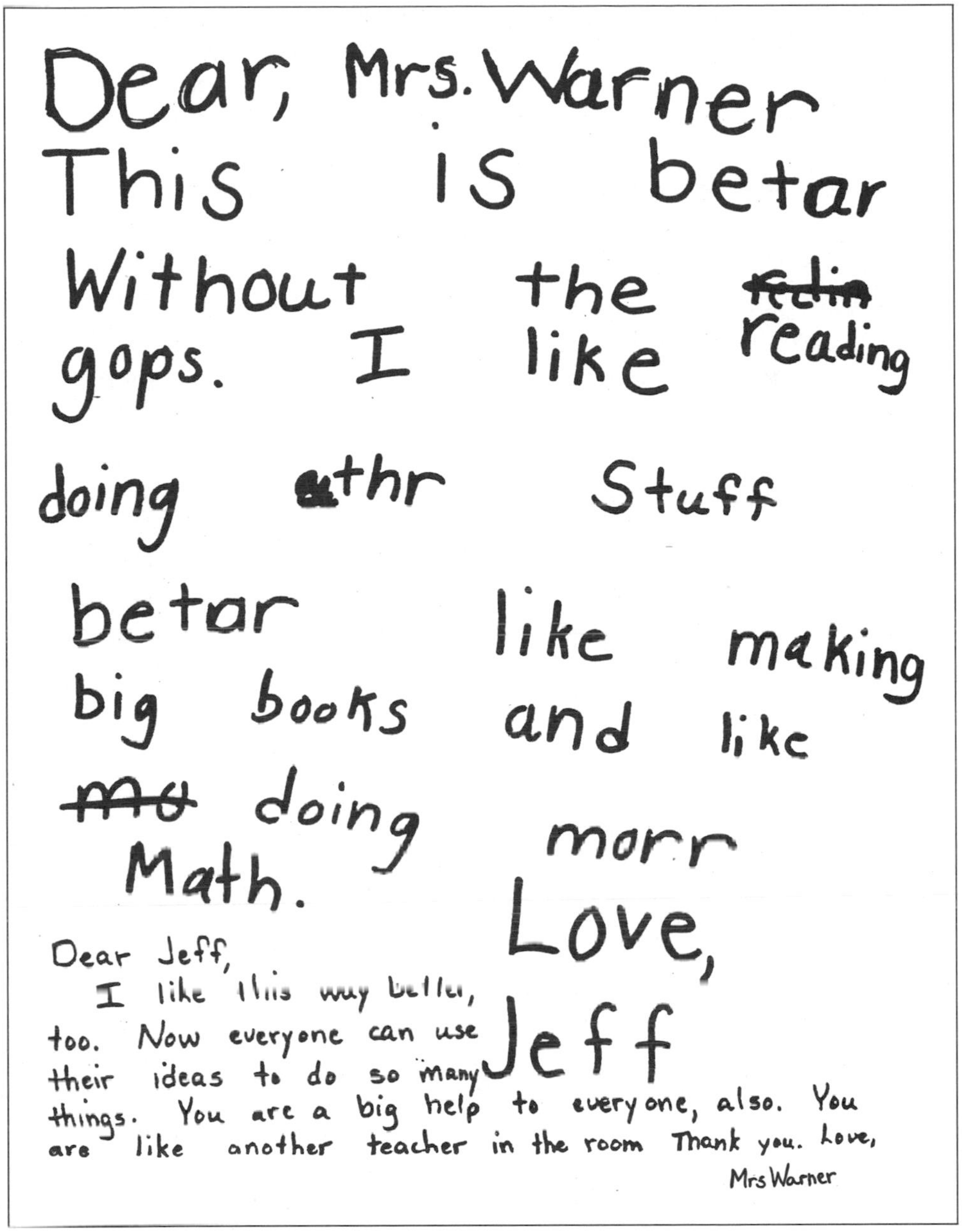

> Dear, Mrs. Warner
> This is betar
> Without the ~~rdin~~ reading
> gops. I like
> doing ~~a~~thr Stuff
> betar like making
> big books and like
> ~~Me~~ doing morr
> Math. Love,
> Jeff
>
> Dear Jeff,
>   I like this way better,
> too. Now everyone can use
> their ideas to do so many
> things. You are a big help to everyone, also. You
> are like another teacher in the room. Thank you. Love,
>   Mrs Warner

FIGURE 18.1   *Student-to-Teacher Feedback*

the object of the exercise is for the student to display his or her knowledge (or lack of it).

The nature of teacher-student interactions tends to be different in dialogue journals. Shuy found that children asked twice as many questions through their journals as they did in the classroom, and their journal questions were more directly related to learning. Teachers spent less time asking questions in journals than they did in their regular classroom talk (15 percent compared with 35 percent), and the questions they did ask were genuine. The most frequently asked questions, about half of all questions, sought an opinion. Questions that solicit opinions do not carry the same power differential as other questions, since an opinion is neither correct nor incorrect, and everyone has one. The second most common type of question teachers asked in journals sought unknown information; display questions were rare. In other words, teachers in journals commonly asked for expansion of the student's topic, thereby showing interest in it and helping to develop the student's writing. The third most common type of question teachers asked in journals was reflective questions, which encourage students' self-evaluation and metacognition. Teachers also used fewer directives in their journal writing than in their regular classroom talk.

There are several reasons for this difference. First, the journal opens up a different form of social interaction, in which one can choose which questions to answer. It is O.K. not to answer questions; this takes away the power imbalance normally produced when teachers ask a question that forces a response. Also, since students ask more questions of their own in journals, they gain greater control of the dialogue and, at the same time, highlight their own concerns. The kind of questions students ask tend to be requests about procedures, requests for information, requests for opinion, and challenges. Through these questions, many instructional and personal issues are resolved, and a greater rapport between teacher and student develops.

Although dialogue journals provide a wealth of information about students' literate development and about their interactions with the teacher, they also serve other functions useful to evaluation. Writing for, or talking with, parents about a student's development in reading and writing with concrete examples of that student's performance in hand is a good deal easier than doing it from test scores. Anecdotal descriptions from such data are compelling and generally more understandable to parents. The teacher can demonstrate a knowledge of the student as a person, and can easily reveal some of the student's interaction with the teacher.

Some How-To's

There are some simple guidelines for responding to students' journals. First, your response to their writing should be a genuine response to the content rather than to its form. Responding to the form would be like someone in a conversation saying, "You mean *is* able, not *ain't* able." Even positive comments on the form of the student's writing can be problematic. Telling them that they did a great job with their writing in their journal changes their understanding of the nature of the interaction and their motivation for participation. Responding to the content is what communication is all about. Second, your response should be friendly and supportive. This does not mean that you cannot express problems that you are having with the student, just that you do it in a friendly, supportive, and nonblaming way, taking into account his or her feelings. Third, your responses should prompt more writing. This hardly needs elaboration. If you write interesting things, students will want to get more, and if you ask questions relevant to them, they will often answer them. Fourth, try not to be forceful and demanding. Asking (rather than telling) students to do something and providing options for responses gives students choice, which (as discussed in Chapter 8) has many advantages. For example, you might say, "Would you mind . . .?" or "Perhaps you could . . .? or "Are there any other ways you could have done that?" or "Have you considered . . .?"

Younger students sometimes have difficulty getting under way, but Leslie Reed's solution is to give the students a sample journal entry at the outset. She allows them to copy it if they want, but encourages them to write their own. At the beginning one or two may copy it and some others will use parts of it and perhaps add to it, but quite quickly they become independent as they discover that they get a real response to their writing. She requires her fifth graders to write a minimum of three sentences per entry. She also gives some direction to her students' journal writing. During the first few weeks of school she puts on the board some made-up examples of journal entries and asks the students which ones they would prefer to read and why. She also points out to them that she is very busy answering so many letters each day, and she appreciates not having to go back to read earlier letters in order to understand what is being talked about that day. In other words, she helps her students gain some sense of audience, and the need for explicitness in writing (Reed 1988).

Journals have a way of informing us about how they are going. A teacher friend of mine began using dialogue journals in his classroom, but after a couple of months found that his students were writing very little in them and doing so reluctantly. While the students wrote in their journals, I went around asking them about what they were doing. I asked what kinds of things they wrote and what kinds of things the teacher wrote. Every student I spoke to said that the teacher wrote questions. Having recently shifted from a basal reader, Tom had essentially transferred the "read the story and see if they got the meaning" format to the journals. When I explained what the students said, he decided to stop asking questions altogether. Instead, he began to write comments about his own reading. Two or three days later, student journal entries began appearing that said "How come you aren't asking any questions? If you're not going to ask them, I guess I will" and "Since you haven't asked me any questions, I guess I'll tell you what I think." Interestingly, toward the end of the year he began asking questions again, some of them the same ones he had been asking before, but the students continued to write a great deal with enthusiasm, and they even answered many (but not all) of his questions.

Remember, there are two sides to asking a question: an attempt at control and a request for information. When we ask a question, we control the topic and essentially force an answer. At the beginning of the year, the students understood Tom's questions principally as attempts at control, which meant that the journals were essentially not theirs, since topic choice and focus were taken away from them. When the questions stopped, they were able to establish their own topics and receive legitimate responses. Within this context, when questions arose again, they were not viewed as controlling, but as genuine requests for information arising naturally out of the dialogue.

Children can sniff out tests at forty paces. A teacher may take it as an insult if students ignore his questions in their journals but it may actually be a compliment if the students feel comfortable enough to offer what they want to talk about and to decide which questions to answer when. Getting students to answer questions is secondary to getting them to reflect on and talk about literature and their reading. The basis of the engagement is a trusting relationship. The important thing in teaching is not to let assessment concerns distract you from the conversation.

In Principle

The principle of dialogue journals is one of mutual involvement in a conversation in print. Journals do not have to be the medium that facilitates such conversations. They can be carried out in letters between classes, or between students and parents, college students, prisoners, or whoever will take children seriously (see especially Hall and Robinson 1994). Furthermore, dialogue journals are not the only useful kind of journals. Ann Berthoff (1981, p. 123) describes the "double-entry" journal, or "dialectical notebook." These do not involve others writing in them. Instead, students (or teachers) transcribe sentences on one side of the page and comment on them on the other. This type of journal encourages deeper, reflective thinking about reading. It also leaves a useful trail. Berthoff points out a secondary audit function of such journals: "Requiring a double-entry notebook is the only way I know to defend yourself against plagiarism, if you want to assign formal term papers" (p. 123).

The principal value of these journals is, of course, the development of reflective inquiry, examination of one's own knowledge and its construction. The double-entry notebook is also useful for teachers' learning about their own practice. On one side of the page may be notes of classroom activities, and on the other, comments about them.

Resources

Nancie Atwell. 1987. *In the Middle: Writing, Reading, and Learning with Adolescents.* Portsmouth, NH: Heinemann.

Kathy Danielson. 1988. *Dialogue Journals: Writing as Conversation*. Bloomington: Phi Delta Kappa Educational Foundation.

Toby Fulwiler, ed. 1987 *The Journal Book*. Portsmouth, NH: Heinemann.

Nigel Hall and Anne Robinson. 1994. *Keeping in Touch: Using Interactive Writing with Young Children*. Portsmouth, NH: Heinemann.

Linda Rief. 1992. *Seeking Diversity: Language Arts with Adolescents*. Portsmouth, NH: Heinemann.

Jana Staton, Roger Shuy, Joy Peyton, and Leslie Reed, eds. 1988. *Dialogue Journal Communication: Classroom, Linguistic, Social, and Cognitive Views*. Norwood, NJ: Ablex.

CHAPTER 19

INTERVIEWS AND CONFERENCES

*A*lthough conversations among class members can be very informative, some students are quieter than others, and teachers cannot be present for all of the classroom conversations. In addition, some information can be gained only in one-to-one engagements. Many different school personnel rely on interviews to understand the nature of children's problems and to figure out where to go next. Classroom teachers spend some time each day with individual students, learning about their reading and writing. School psychologists need to learn about individual students and their families to help solve problems. About 80 percent of the students seen by school psychologists are seen because of difficulties with literacy development (Birman 1981). Sometimes the "presenting problem" is inattention or acting out, but these symptoms are frequently caused by situations of failure in which the student finds himself. Just like the teacher, the school psychologist needs to understand what the student's behavior means.

Building a Relationship

We interview individuals to understand how they understand and organize their world or some domain of knowledge within it; in this case we are interested in literacy. It is easy for us to think that children share our understanding of literacy, particularly when they do not say much. Often, though, as we have seen, children can have very different understandings, some of which only become clear as they talk about what they are doing in a trusting relationship. Trust and respect are important, and are established mostly indirectly. You can say, "Trust me. I want to help you. Think of me as your friend. I really respect you," as much as you like, but children are much more likely to believe actions than speech. They learned language in the first place because they were so adept at making sense of people's actions and then applying it to the patterns of speech sounds. If you are relaxed, supportive, and show that you are interested in what students have to say, especially on topics they are interested in, you convey much more powerfully the message that you respect them and find what they have to say important. The principal message to be conveyed throughout is that the students are the experts from whom you wish to learn, and that you can be trusted with the information they give you. It may help to point out explicitly that you are interested in their opinion, or in how they see it, but these statements are of little use if not backed up with evidence. For example, simply restating parts of what students say in their own words shows your interest in and intention to understand what they have to say. Not allowing other children to interrupt conveys the importance of the individual's message too.

Establishing a trusting relationship will not only be different from student to student, but it will also be different for the principal, the school psychologist, the specialist reading teacher, and the classroom teacher. Classroom teachers have the advantage of extended contact, in that they see the child every day for most of the day; the disadvantage is that they are responsible for lots of children and hence have less opportunity for individual, uninterrupted conversations unless they specifically organize the classroom for them by stressing independent and collaborative problem-solving and self-evaluation.

Classroom teachers also have the considerable advantage of being able to set up a predictable relationship. Within the security of a predictable relationship, children speak more. This security also allows more challenging questions to be asked, including ones that cause a temporary loss of control. A child who struggles with a difficult question, or a process he does not yet control, from a position of confidence develops independence. Don Graves (1983, p. 116) notes that such questions are particularly effective if accompanied by a reason or even a challenge, such as "Do you think you are ready to handle a problem like this?" These questions work best within the security of a trusting relationship based on frequent interactions.

Still, there are times when classroom teachers have to take a controlling role in the classroom, and this can work against establishing a balanced relationship within which a child will be a helpful informant. Furthermore, because of their familiarity with their students, teachers may find it more difficult to establish the need for certain information, and thus for the child to adopt the role of "expert" in which he or she is likely to be most informative.

Specialist teachers and support staff such as reading teachers and school psychologists often meet with smaller groups of children, sometimes one-on-one. However, they have less contact with children than the classroom teacher does and usually meet children in a testing session. It would probably be better for school psychologists, for example, to spend time in classrooms each day so that they could become more familiar with children in a less controlling setting and could do some of their interviewing in the context of the classroom. Indeed, school psychologists assessing children for learning disabilities are required to document the classroom context.

Requesting Information

If an interview is to provide useful information, the student must do most of the talking. Although this may seem obvious, most of us find this difficult. Learning how to keep others talking is certainly not what teachers are usually taught to do. Quite the contrary. Record yourself interviewing a child, and if you find that you are doing all of the talking, consider this: The more you listen, the more you will learn (and often the more the students learn about themselves). Get used to saying, "That's interesting. Could you say more about that?" Showing that you are checking on your own understanding is also useful. For example, you might say, "So let me see if I have this right." However, whenever you do this, make sure your summary includes the key words the *student* used. Otherwise you put words in his or her mouth, and you may get them back without knowing then whether they are the student's or yours.

One of the informal rules of conversation is that you don't ask questions to which you already know the answer unless your conversation partner wishes to be tested. But many teachers feel obliged to have read every book in the classroom before the students read them. Another difficulty for teachers is letting go of the idea that they must check to see whether the student understood each story. If you have trouble with this (as most of us do), I suggest trying interviews in which you and the student have read different books and you have not read the one that the student read. The student really does know more than you then and will likely be able to talk about the book quite readily if you show interest. Try this as an exercise and see how it feels. Once you have a feel for it, try a book that you have both read and strive for the same feel. You could give information first about what you liked or what it reminded you of.

The idea in an interview is to establish a legitimate need for the information or to establish the limits of your knowledge. This will be particularly difficult for a teacher who has construed his or her role as being the provider of information for the children to learn. If students do not accept the premise of the teacher's ignorance, they cannot provide information free of comparison. For example, children are often asked to retell a story that they just read aloud to the teacher. It is impossible for the teacher to establish ignorance under these circumstances. If the child thinks that the teacher is looking for specific correct answers, the student will believe that his or her authority is being questioned, and either the interview will cease or the information the student provides will be only a reflection of what the child thinks the teacher thinks is correct. If we want students to tell us about what it is like for them to be readers, they must feel that they are experts on that topic.

Students may think that the teacher "obviously" knows all that they know. After all, teachers and students spend a lot of time together, so it is easy to assume that they have shared knowledge. One way to get around the problem of presumed shared knowledge is to talk about the problem in class on a regular basis. Another way is to propose "what if" situations. For example, you might ask a student, "Suppose . . . How would you . . ." This kind of question is useful in trying to find out how children understand stories, but it is also useful to find out how they understand being literate. For example, a second grader might be asked "Suppose you had a younger brother who was just going to go into first grade. What things could you tell him about reading [or writing] that would help him to become good at it?" or "If you were giving advice to a first-grade student about this, what do you think would be most important to tell him [or her]?" Of course the usefulness of this kind of question will be negated if it is followed by any suggestion that the student's response is wrong.

Make It Concrete

Young children find it hard to articulate their experience, so it is particularly important that you discuss things as concretely as possible. If you want to find out about their writing, interview them while they are writing. (Actually, the principle holds true of adults being interviewed. I have recently been studying school psychologists and I found it most useful to interview them as they worked.) Having a portfolio of the student's work to leaf through and talk about can also make the interview concrete and specific. Similarly, when the student makes a generalization in an interview, it's a good idea to ask them to give an example. For example, if a child says, "I mostly read nonfiction," getting him or her to give an example or two might clarify what she means by "nonfiction."

Questions about use are another way to make things concrete. For example, I might ask a second-grade student, "If a first-grade student was having trouble knowing when to use a comma, what could you tell him [or her] about how to use a comma?" This kind of interview strategy also removes a question about conventional knowledge from the right-or-wrong framework. In general, questions that have a right or wrong answer should be avoided, although students may be skeptical. For example, a book that has been read can serve well as the focus of an interview about reading and writing generally. However, children whose chief experience with text is in reading lessons that emphasize single right answers are likely to assume that book interviews are reading lessons in disguise. Under that assumption, students will feel that they are not the experts and will be more likely to spend time thinking about what answers the interviewer wants than what they actually understand about the book. In general, interviews strive to open the mind and close the mouth.

Using students' own terminology is especially important in understanding their perspective. In addition to showing that you are listening and trying to understand, it reduces the likelihood of your putting words in their mouth and misconstruing their position, and encourages them to be reflective. Reflectiveness is something you wish to encourage, both because it helps children self-evaluate, reducing your own role in evaluation, and because once children understand their role in your partnership, they will continually be collecting and analyzing information to teach you during your interviews. Reflective children can provide extraordinarily focused, instructionally relevant information for teachers. For example, Jane Hansen (1987) asked some of her young students such questions as "What have you learned most recently about writing?" "What would you like to learn next?" These questions work best over an extended period of time, so that students become used to reflecting on such things (and having the time to do so) and will regularly ask themselves such questions.

Asking Questions

If an interview is to be useful, the child must not construe it as a test. How could this happen? Past history with such one-to-one encounters might lead them to such an assumption. The teacher's body posture and location might suggest it (sitting opposite the student in a higher chair). The teacher's tone of voice and the kind of questions asked might also lead to this conclusion.

We ask questions in order to provoke productive conversations, to get information from students, to focus conversation (and the thinking that goes with it), and to control behavior. Whenever we ask a question, though, we give as much information as we get. Although you intend to learn about the student, the student will be learning from you, and much of what she learns might not be what you intended. Because of our status as adults and teachers, many children will interpret even (to us) quite neutral statements in terms of their usual relationship with teachers in particular and adults in general. Thus, a simple question such as "Is this your classroom?" can be interpreted as a controlling or critical statement, perhaps meaning "You are supposed to be in your classroom."

The kinds of questions we ask also convey information about the kind of knowledge we think the interviewee has and the kind of information we think is important. For example, if we ask how many books a person has published, we are suggesting that that is important. If we ask "What do you think the poet was trying to do with this poem?" we are assuming that the student understands poetry as something that someone writes with a particular goal in mind. In a similar way, the responses we give can also convey unintended information. For example, if we say "Good" or "O.K." or "Right" in particular ways, it can be interpreted as evaluative feedback, which conveys a message about the nature of the activity: that there are right and wrong answers (or at least better and worse answers), and that we already know them.

The way we ask questions conveys a message too. If we use a standardized procedure, we may inadvertently imply that we will be making comparisons, or that we are objectifying students, negating personalization in order to produce quantification. To the extent that we are seen as part of a particular social group, we can also be seen as representing the group's values. Thus, if we ask about the most recent book a reader read and it happened to be the Kama Sutra, we may or may not get an honest response depending in part on the extent to which we appear to be the sort of person who would approve or disapprove of the material. Of course the students' own motives come into play, too. If they suppose that we will not approve but they wish to shock us they will respond differently than if they want to impress us or if they want to participate in honest dialogue. We can never be exactly sure what messages are being conveyed, but we need to be alert to the possibilities.

There are essentially three types of questions that are most useful in gathering information: descriptive questions, structural questions, and contrast questions (Spradley 1979). *Descriptive questions* are the ones of initial concern, since they are the ones most likely to keep students talking, putting them into the role of teacher. Here are some examples:

- Could you tell me what it is like for you to read at school?
- What do *you* do when you read?
- Could you tell me what usually happens in your reading group?
- Could you study the next piece of your textbook just as you would do it at home and explain to me how you do it?
- How do you use the classroom library? When do you use it?
- Can you give me an example of when you might use that kind of strategy in writing?
- If I were to sit in on your reading group, what kind of things would I hear kids say to each other?

Such questions tend to put students into the role of teacher, and put the teacher in the role of listener and learner.

Descriptive questions can also be used to find out about students' reading habits. For example, part of the problem faced by those whose literacy is not well developed is the pattern of habits they have developed to avoid print. Since becoming more fully literate requires that they participate more in literate activity, they may need to restructure the way they go about their daily lives. Descriptive questions that James Spradley calls "tour" questions can be helpful in finding out how the person's day is organized, and which can lead to helping him or her make small adjustments that will allow the inclusion of more frequent literate activities. You could ask "Could you describe the things you usually do in an evening?" or "Could you give me a moment-by-moment description of what you did today?" or "You mentioned that you have to read and write in the log book. Could you tell me everything that you did with the log book today?"

Structural questions can help us understand how aspects of the interviewees' world relate to one another. For example, you might ask "Is it O.K. to write in reading class?" or "Can I say reading is part of writing?" I might ask "Are there different kinds of books?" or "Are there different kinds of writing?" or "Are there different ways to write? Could you tell me what some of them are?" or "Are reading a book and reading a poem different sorts of reading?" Answers to these questions tell us how people structure their world—how they relate literacy concepts to one another.

Contrast questions are used to try to find out how the interviewee understands a domain. For example, I could ask individual students how many different types of books they know of. From the list they produce, I could then ask how two of them—say, folktales and mysteries—are the same and different. I might ask students for a list of authors they have read and then we could play Twenty Questions. From the list of authors, I could choose one, and have the student guess which one I selected by asking questions to which I am allowed to respond only yes or no. The questions the student asks will give a lot of information about the ways in which he or she differentiates the authors. Or I might restrict the kinds of questions asked to ones about writing style. Or I could present three authors and ask "Which one is different from the other two? Is there any way to regroup the authors so that one of the others is different?"

Appendix C consists of a list of questions I have found to produce informative responses in interviews about literacy. You might try some of these as a way to explore what can be learned from different kinds of questions.

Problems with Standardized Interviews

There are many types of interviews, some of which are useful with adults and possibly older children but do not work well with younger children. A structured interview does not work well with younger children generally, especially when the interviewer reads the questions. Adults, with their schedules and time constraints, can better understand such formalities (though they may not always accept them). However, pushing younger children to conform to your schedule and your set of questions makes it clear to them that you are an adult intent on pulling rank. They will then often begin trying to figure out what you (the adult) would like to hear. It is a game they play often enough. If they are good at the game they may leave you satisfied, but ignorant. This is a common problem in structured interviews, such as those used in research studies or large-scale evaluations. Researchers in such studies are usually trying to make comparisons—between children, between programs, or between behavior before and after a procedure or event—and are attempting to quantify responses, standardizing the interviews in order to do so. Even though the written questions might be excellent (Wixson et al. 1984), much is lost in the process of standardizing (as opposed to personalizing) the interview. Fortunately, classroom teachers (and most others concerned with the welfare of children) do not need to compare children with each other, so standardization in interviews is usually not necessary.

A common example of standardization is the "interest inventory," in which children respond to a number of rating scales or multiple-choice questions on a standard form. This is meant to allow the teacher to find out what each child is interested in by looking at the form rather than talking to him or her. Interviewing a child is a far better way to get this information, along with conferring about writing and the books he or she is choosing to read. This would be true even if we used "interest" in the narrow sense of the word meaning "horse riding" or "motorbikes" and the like, but it is so much more true when we are referring to the issues that occupy the child's thoughts such as the birth of a sibling, feelings of failure, an impending plane trip to grandma's, divorce, and so forth.

Resources

An excellent resource on how to talk with children *and* help them manage their behavior is:

Adele Faber and Elaine Mazlish. 1980. *How to Talk So Kids Will Listen and Listen So Kids Will Talk*. New York: Avon Books.

CHAPTER 20

LEARNING FROM LISTENING

One question from a child yields more information than his or her responses to ten questions from an adult. For example, a child asking "If we went in the car all day would we get to the edge of the world?" reveals a great deal about his knowledge of time and the nature of the Earth, among other things. Therefore, we should arrange our classrooms in a way that establishes a trusting, noncompetitive environment in which children are more likely to ask questions. Also, we can directly elicit questions from the questions we ask, such as "What would be a good question to ask the author of this book?"

Sometimes the information we seek is tacit knowledge, which is not consciously available to the student. This is particularly the case with less competent students (Baker and Brown 1984). Thus, the children from whom we need the clearest information are likely to need the most help providing it. We must help them provide it without putting words in their mouths. They are also likely to have the most at stake in terms of defending their self-esteem, and to have suffered the most at the hands of the schooling system. Why should they trust us with what might be sensitive information?

Much of the information that becomes available through interviews with children is embedded in the way things are said, the order in which they are said, and the kinds of words used. For example, the order in which someone describes the features of something often reflects the importance he or she places in those features. Consider Ben's response to the question "Could you describe your classroom to me?"

> Well, I sit at the back behind Betty and next to Gerry, and the teacher's desk is in the middle up the front. All our desks is separated. Um—We on the second floor and we got lots of windows. There's the chalkboard up front, and the wall on that side's got pictures and stuff on it, and that's about it.

What Ben leaves out of his description (the shelves of books under the windows, for example) is just as important as what he describes and the order in which he describes it.

Efficiency and Place of the Interview

Interviews are time-consuming. Your response to that is probably "Fine. When do I find the time for them?" On the face of it, interviewing seems like a highly inefficient way of gathering information. But there are four major reasons why it is actually efficient:

1. Interviewing provides information that often cannot be obtained any other way.
2. The information obtained is often most critical for adjusting instruction.
3. Over the course of the year, many (but not all) students will come to understand their role as a teacher in interviews—about themselves and the literacy culture of their classroom. They will begin to take it upon themselves to observe, reflect on, and analyze their activity in the classroom from their own perspective and to inform the teacher about these things during interviews. In other words, the process becomes increasingly efficient as rapport and roles are developed.
4. The process also becomes increasingly accurate as teacher and student achieve a cooperative arrangement in which they understand each other's needs. Students may begin to correct the teacher's errors of interpretation. They also become more likely to offer more personal (and sometimes more painful) information. As you help students teach you about themselves as literate individuals, they will increasingly understand and be reflective about themselves and their literacy.

What Information Can We Get from an Interview?

Many kinds of information can be gathered from interviews. For example, we can find out how students conceptualize literacy and literature, how they feel about reading and writing, and how they understand themselves. Let us examine some examples of information that can be obtained only through interviews, keeping in mind that often the most important information is tacit information, information that students do not have conscious access to and do not know that they know.

Becoming literate involves the development of complex sets of knowledge that are interrelated. These kinds of knowledge govern not only what we do, but what we see and understand. In other words, what I think I know today in some ways determines what I learn tomorrow. When I read or see something new, I attend to what seems to me to be the most important information, and what I already know or don't know plays a big part in determining that. Sometimes we see a student continually behaving in a way we are tempted to describe as bizarre. However, children behave one way or another for a reason, and our job as teachers is to try to understand the reasons. For example, one adult who worked with me read the word *dwindle* as "windle." I asked him how he knew to pronounce it that way and he told me he thought the *d* in that position would be silent.

Such misconceptions are not uncommon and can make life somewhat difficult for the student. To repeat an earlier example, a student was not enjoying writing at school. His writing was done in booklets the teacher made up ahead of time. He mentioned his dislike to his teacher, and she asked him what he saw as the major problem. He said it was just too much to write; "there are too many pages." Once he learned that he did not have to fill the books, writing was easier, even enjoyable, for him. His teacher also decided not to make up books for the students to draft stories in. Another example, perhaps more common, is children who believe that when taking a test it is cheating to reread the passage after they have looked at the questions.

Tom Nicholson (1984) has provided a number of useful examples of other conceptual confusions that teachers can discover through interviews. He describes from his interviews a junior high school student's understanding of the steps involved in "doing research":

1. Ask your friends for information.
2. Check any magazines or books at home.
3. Ask older siblings or your parents.
4. If necessary, adjust your research topic to fit your resources.
5. If steps 1–4 do not work, check with the teacher, or perhaps even try the school library.

Michael Cole and Peg Griffin (1986) report a student who revealed in an interview the use of what they call the "copy matching" strategy. The student was puzzled when she had to answer a question of the form "Who was John Smith?" when the text contained the name John Smith three times. Her normal strategy of looking for the name and transcribing the sentence in which it occurred had been foiled, since there were three different sentences to choose from. She thus felt that the question was unfair.

We also can learn about students' writing strategies. For example, you might ask "Are there things you wrote in your story to help your audience learn about Chuck [a character]?" to which you might get a response like: "Yeah. Like, here I told how Chuck smells and how his clothes are trashed and, like, here when he pushes the kid off his bike." This suggests the student is aware that physical features and actions can give insight into a character, but that he is perhaps not yet aware of the potential of dialogue.

Many other decisions young readers and writers make can also be topics of discussion. The following questions can elicit such information:

- "Are there any other decisions you made while you were writing this piece where you tried to get the audience to think in a particular way?"
- "How did you come up with this way of writing the story [this plot, this topic, etc.]?"
- "Does this story you have written remind you of any stories you have read?"

These questions lead us, and our students, to understand how their literacy is shaped by their reading and writing and the social interactions in which they are immersed.

In interviews we can learn what being literate means to a student, or what it means to succeed or fail. These concepts are very important, since they tell us a student's criteria for success or failure, and his or her motives for reading and writing. When students say they are not good readers, they are often able to say quite clearly how they know this to be so, and who is a good reader and why. Knowing that Shaquala thinks being a good reader means "getting done quickest" enables her teacher to think about what should be valued and what should be changed in the classroom. If she defines her reading ability normatively, her teacher might want to reduce or eliminate the grounds for simplistic normative comparison in the classroom. If we can change our students' notion that successful reading means getting more words right than the other guy did to having a satisfying interaction with a book, we will change the extent to which various children in the class feel that they were successful or not and how they choose to spend their time.

In interviews we can also learn about the emotional aspects of students' developing literacy. For example, while tutoring an adult and interviewing him along the way, I learned about his feelings of stress. He told me:

> I was getting . . . for some reason something triggered me off before this that I was starting to get tense . . . and I could see, I could feel myself shutting down. Like when I get this way I can feel my whole self tense . . . and I'm not absolutely, not even been . . . I'm not even . . . at one point there I wasn't even being able to . . . I had to force myself to concentrate because everything was going. What it is, it's the old feelings. It's like, y'know, well . . . something will trigger it. Like when I was a kid in school and they would ask me to read, and the teacher didn't know that I couldn't read. Well, those feelings still can come back to me, and it's like feeling . . . never . . . I can't even

begin to explain . . . It's like you completely feel isolated, totally alone.
(Johnston 1985, p. 167)

Many other affective aspects of reading and writing, such as frustration, elation, and depression, may also be revealed in interviews.

Interviews can also reveal people's rationalizations. People tend to try to explain the things that happen to them. For example, students who pass a test can attribute it to luck, simplicity of the test, their own brilliance, the teacher's marking it in their favor, a clever study strategy, or many other possibilities. Similarly, students who define themselves as being unsuccessful can ascribe it to a simple lack of ability. These attributions have consequences for future learning. If students attribute their success to luck, and their failure to lack of ability, there is no reason for them to try harder or to attempt alternative strategies. On the other hand, if they attribute their success to the strategies they used, there is some incentive for them to feel responsible for the success and some motive for them to think strategically in the future. Thus, the definitions students have for success and failure and the explanations they give for their occurrence are important for their learning. For example, one adult who had trouble reading explained to me, "You feel stupid . . . because they're smarter than you. And if you say anything then you're lower than them . . . 'idiot can't read.' "Y'know" (p. 170). Other adults showed a similar pattern of attributions. For instance, Jack commented, "What's wrong with me that I have this problem?" indicating that he felt the source of the problem was within him. After his ability to read had improved considerably, however, he showed a change in this perception, commenting:

> I don't know if I should say this or not, but the last few months I felt
> a little resentment towards my mother because of the instruction, and
> that bothers me. I sort of at some point say, "Well, why didn't she
> intervene or why didn't she do whatever she could have done to make
> this not happen to me?" Because . . . see . . . prior to now I have
> always felt that there is a possibility that something was wrong. You
> know, maybe I was retarded. I think that was always in the back of my
> mind, and that's a hard thing to live with. (p. 170)

These comments suggest a different orientation toward the situation he is in, one which suggests that he has some degree of control.

Some Cautions

Always try to buttress the information students give in interviews with observations of actual literate activity. Interviews are not perfect reflections of the interviewees' thinking, but they can give us a lot to go on. Thinking, to the extent that it is accessible, is described in language, which can be ambiguous even without the factor of participants' many possible motives. For example, I asked one adult how much he wanted to become literate and he held out his arms to me and said,

"Take these." I am sure he believed that. However, it turned out that even though he had the house to himself in the mornings while his children were at school, he could never find the time to read or write anything outside of our sessions. To tease apart his complex motivations and emotions would be very difficult indeed.

Similarly, it should be clear that a single interview will be less informative than multiple interviews or ongoing ones such as can occur in a classroom. Over time, you can notice patterns of consistency or inconsistency in what people say at different times. However, don't pounce on the inconsistencies you notice, or you will get nothing further. Good rapport needs to be established before any difficult issues or discrepancies are raised. With good rapport, such discrepancies can be the perfect situation for learning to take place.

Interviews do not necessarily result in tangible products to which you can return. That may not matter. The things you will learn will tend to stick in your mind as you develop your understanding of the students you interview. Not all evaluation requires tangible records. However, it can be helpful to jot down an occasional interview comment to place in your file or journal, perhaps a comment a student made about a book or some other issue you would like to return to later. These comments can also be useful in illustrating to parents changes that have occurred in their child's understanding. Direct quotes are most helpful for later reflection.

In Appendix C I have listed a variety of questions you might like to explore in order to get a feel for interviewing. But there is simply no magical question or set of questions that will transform children's writing or produce a successful writing conference. The key to good interviewing is listening to what the child has to say and responding to it with genuine interest.

$\mathcal{R}$ECORDING ORAL READING

Co-authored with Marie M. Clay

$\mathcal{M}$ature reading is generally done silently in the privacy of one's own head. This is not a problem for self-evaluation, but it poses a bit of a problem for teachers who wish to assess their students' reading. Fortunately, beginning readers tend to read aloud quite naturally, even when asked to read silently. Oral reading has been used for many years to assess the kind of language processes taking place in the head of the reader. This assessment can be only an estimate of the reader's mental processes, however. Oral reading and silent reading are not the same thing (Leu 1982; Schumm and Baldwin 1989). The two serve quite different functions for adults. Nonetheless, there is sufficient similarity between the two to make analyzing students' oral reading a useful way to understand the way they process language when they read.

Detailed analysis of oral reading errors began seriously with the work of Ken Goodman (Goodman 1965; Goodman, Watson, and Burke 1987) and Rose-Marie Weber (1970), both of whom used the term *miscue* rather than *error*. Analysis of oral reading is a particular example of error analysis (hence my use of "error"). Because errors are not made randomly, and because each is partly right, they suggest the kind of mental processing taking place and allow us to examine the leading edge of a learner's development. An individual error is less informative than a pattern of errors, and the clearer the pattern, the more helpful it is for informing teaching.

Over the years, oral reading has occasionally suffered some bad press because it is not really the same as mature reading (Allington 1983). In addition, oral

---

In this and the following chapter we draw on Marie M. Clay's book *An Observation Survey of Early Literacy Achievement*. Although they are co-authored, we have maintained the first person singular voice for continuity of style. All the examples of running records that appear in these two chapters are recorded on the tape that accompanies this book.

reading as a classroom round-robin activity can be a socially threatening situation for readers who struggle with word recognition. Oral reading is most appropriate in choral or shared reading, or in the context of readers' theater, in which prepared reading can be done as a public performance. However, for purposes of evaluation, oral reading need not be stressful or done so frequently as to suggest that it is the most important or only form of reading.

Ways to Record Oral Reading

An experienced teacher in the early elementary grades can often listen to a reader and get a good idea of the strategies being used and the reader's state of development. However, generally it is not enough simply to listen to oral reading and depend on your memory. Memories are frail and are not much use to present to anyone as a sole source of information. You could tape-record a child's reading; this is useful and certainly has the advantage of fidelity, but in the long run it is inconvenient: you don't have immediate access to a particular reading and you can't focus on the important aspects without listening to the whole thing. It is much better to have a graphic record of the oral reading so you can get the instructionally relevant information at a glance, compare earlier and later performance, and keep the record conveniently filed and accessible.

Many people have devised ways to record oral reading errors; each has its advantages and disadvantages. In this chapter, with the help of Marie Clay, I describe how to record children's oral reading using *running records,* a method she devised and presented in her book *An Observation Survey of Early Literacy Achievement* (Clay 1993a), to which you should refer. (I have taught classes using this book and its earlier editions for the past sixteen years and have yet to encounter a secondhand copy). To use the method, you simply take a blank (or lined) piece of paper or a special record sheet, and use shorthand to write down the child's reading behaviors as he or she reads aloud. An overview of Clay's shorthand recording scheme is presented in Table 21.1. There are other methods of recording, including the commonly used Informal Reading Inventories (IRIs), which I refer to later in the chapter. However, in order to avoid confusion for those who are already familiar with IRIs, I should note that running records are different from IRIs in one important way. To take a running record, you do not need to have a copy of the text to write on; you just need a piece of paper. This makes running records more difficult to learn than informal reading inventory procedures, but it is also a major advantage. It allows you to record oral reading at any time, from any book, without any preparation such as photocopying or dittoing the pages or having extra copies of the book available. This makes the recording system very flexible.

Running records have other advantages too. First, because you don't have to do anything except pick up a pen and paper when a child is reading, you are more likely to actually make them. Second, running records do not establish a "test" environment (although whether the child feels it is a test depends on many factors,

TABLE 21.1

Recording Symbols for Running Records

General format:

	Child's response	Final response
	Word in the text	Teacher prompt

WHAT IS SAID	DURING READING	AFTER READING
Correct response	✓	✓
Omission	—	$\dfrac{—}{\text{text word}}$
Substitution	spoken word	$\dfrac{\text{spoken word}}{\text{text word}}$
Insertion	spoken word	$\dfrac{\text{spoken word}}{—}$
Repetition[1]	R	R
Attempt	attempt | attempt	$\dfrac{\text{attempt} \mid \text{attempt}}{\text{text word}}$
Appeal for help	APP	$\dfrac{\text{attempt} \mid \text{APP}}{\text{text word}}$
Teacher prompt: tells the word	⌐ T	text word | T
asks to try section again[2]	TA	TA

1. Number of repetitions is recorded with a superscript. Size of repetition is recorded with a line from the R to the beginning of the repeated section.
2. The line extends vertically from the beginning to the end of the section to be repeated with TA (for "try again") alongside it.

---

including the child's experiences in the past, the relationship with the person taking the record, and the situation in which the reading is done). Running records can be done frequently on whatever the child happens to be reading. Third, unlike IRIs, which often use texts assumed to be comparable to the level of the basal reader on which the child will ultimately be placed, running records use a variety of children's books taken from the classroom or chosen by the student.

Using the Tape and the Text

The rest of this chapter will show you how to record oral reading errors; the next chapter will help you figure out what they might mean. Each kind of error a beginning reader might make is illustrated in the examples on the tape that accompanies this book. (My use of the audiotape is modeled on the superb Early Reading Inservice Course [ERIC] developed by the New Zealand Department of

Education, which also developed the record-keeping system in greater detail.) The number of each example is announced on the tape. Use a blank piece of paper to make a record of each example. After listening to each example, stop the tape and return to this text to check your record against the one provided here.

Learning now to make running records takes time. The critical ingredient is practice. You wouldn't expect to learn shorthand overnight, so don't expect to learn running records overnight. Your facility will improve with practice. Fortunately, you can easily practice on the sly, and no one is likely to be looking over your shoulder. If you are a teacher practicing running records with your students, you will find your students will be very understanding about your clumsiness. Always explain to them what you are doing at the outset; tell them they can look at the record afterward and you will explain it to them. This makes the process less threatening for the students and a learning experience for all concerned.

Often people learning to record oral reading tape-record the reading so that they can stop the tape to make time for writing, or go back to make sure they got everything right. This tends to make you dependent on the tape recorder, and using a tape recorder makes running records (or IRIs) take at least twice the time they would otherwise. As a result, there is a good chance that you will do fewer of them and eventually none at all. Occasionally using recordings for self-checking and for repeated record-taking in order to build fluency (like repeated readings) can help. However, it becomes a hindrance if you continually stop and start the tape to try to keep up. Patience and practice are what you should rely on.

Beginning the Record

At the top of the page always note the reader's name, the date, the book and page(s) being read, and any special conditions, such as whether or how often the book has been read previously or whether the book has been read to the child.

Words Read Correctly

Each word read correctly is represented by a check mark (✓). Thus the following rendition of a text by a child would be recorded as shown:

TEXT:	Today the class went to the zoo.
	We saw an elephant and a monkey.
READER:	Today the class went to the zoo.
	We saw an elephant and a monkey.
RUNNING RECORD:	✓ ✓ ✓ ✓ ✓ ✓ ✓ ✓
	✓ ✓ ✓ ✓ ✓ ✓ ✓ ✓

Note that there is one check mark for each word, and that they are arranged in exactly the way the words are arranged on the page so that we can tell which check represents which word. Now you try it with Example 1 on the tape. The correct record is shown alongside the text below.

"Go home," ✓ ✓

said the hens. ✓ ✓ ✓

"No," said Little Pig. ✓ ✓ ✓ ✓

"Go home," ✓ ✓

said the ducks. ✓ ✓ ✓

"No," said Little Pig. ✓ ✓ ✓ ✓

"Go home," ✓ ✓

said the cows. ✓ ✓ ✓

"No," said Little Pig. ✓ ✓ ✓ ✓

"Go home," ✓ ✓

said the sheep. ✓ ✓ ✓

"No," said Little Pig. ✓ ✓ ✓ ✓

"Go home," ✓ ✓

said the butcher, ✓ ✓ ✓

"or I'll make you into ✓ ✓ ✓ ✓ ✓

sausages." ✓

"Yes, I will," ✓ ✓ ✓

said Little Pig. ✓ ✓ ✓

Words Omitted

Sometimes, deliberately or accidentally, readers skip over a word. We record this with a dash (—). After we have finished the running record we go back and write the omitted word beneath the dash, separating the two with a horizontal line. This is the standard practice for making the record. Record the reader's behavior and, after the record is complete, return to add the relevant words underneath each recorded deviation from the text. A running record with omissions should be recorded as shown below:

TEXT: There was once a jolly farmer
who had a red tractor.

READER: There was a jolly farmer
had a red tractor.

✓ ✓ — ✓ ✓ ✓

— ✓ ✓ ✓ ✓

✓ ✓ —/*once* ✓ ✓ ✓

—/*who* ✓ ✓ ✓ ✓

Your record of this done while the student was reading would look like the record alongside the student transcript above. After the child finished reading you would add the details from the text so that your record would look like the one below the first.

Now try to record the second example on the tape. The text for it is:

TAPE EXAMPLE 2

"I'm looking for a house,"
said the little brown mouse.

Your first pass at the running record should look something like this:

✓ ✓ ✓ ✓ ✓
✓ – ✓ ✓ ✓

After you have finished taking the running record, add to it the details—the word omitted and a line separating the two. It should look something like this:

✓ ✓ ✓ ✓ ✓
✓ $\frac{-}{the}$ ✓ ✓ ✓

When you are learning to take running records it is very important to wait until the end to add the actual word missed. It only takes a minute to add these finishing touches to the running record. If you try to do it during the reading, you will miss a lot of other details of the reading. When you become fluent, you may be able to add some of these finishing touches on the run, but you will find it a lot easier to learn the method if you do it in two steps to begin with.

Words Substituted

Younger readers commonly substitute a different word for the one on the page. When this happens, simply write down the word the reader says, and later fill in the word that was in the text. For example:

TEXT: Harry was a good boy.
READER: Harry was a nice boy.   ✓ ✓ ✓ $\frac{nice}{good}$ ✓

Now try your hand at recording the example on the tape. The text being read is the following:

TAPE EXAMPLE 3:   *The Dragon's Birthday* by Margaret Mahy (1984a)

At the same time, Richard
and Claire, Henry and Huia and Billy,

were going up the road wearing
their dragon costume.

Your running record for this should look something like this:

✓ ⟋ ✓ ⟋ ✓
✓ ✓ Harry/Henry ✓ ✓ ✓ ✓
✓ coming/going ✓ ✓ ✓
✓ ✓ ✓

Notice that although two words are substituted, the meaning has not been lost, and the substitutions reflect some of the print features of the author's words. The reader is striving to make sense *and* to match what he says with what he sees.

Words Inserted

Sometimes children add words to the reading that are not in the text. To record this, simply write the words into the record just as you record substitutions. Later, add a dash *underneath* the added word to indicate that there was no matching word in the text. An example of an insertion would look like this:

TEXT: I went to the shops.
READER: I went down to the shops.   ✓ ✓ down ✓ ✓ ✓

Now take your turn at this recording with the example on the tape.

TAPE EXAMPLE 4: *Old Tuatara* by Joy Cowley (1984)

Old Tuatara sat in the sun.
He sat and sat and sat.
"Asleep," said the fantail.
"Asleep," said the gull.
"Asleep," said the frog.
"Asleep," said the fly.
"Not asleep," said Old Tuatara.

Each of the animals thinks Old Tuatara (an ancient and almost extinct reptile) is asleep, but the hapless fly finds out he is not). Note the relish with which Samantha reads this passage (even though it has been read to her and by her a number of times before). This book is an excellent example of what a good author can do with a handful of words and a good illustrator. You probably also noticed how easily Sam picked up on a connection to another book, *Fantail, Fantail* (Mahy 1984b), which also ends with the fly being devoured. She actually quotes the final words from the book ("Goodbye, fly"). Would it make sense to ask Sam questions to see whether she understands *Old Tuatara?* I don't think so. Your running record for this fourth tape example should look like this:

✓ ✓ ✓ ✓ ✓ ✓
✓ ✓ ✓ $\frac{he}{-}$ ✓ ✓ $\frac{he}{-}$ ✓
✓ ✓ ✓ ✓
✓ ✓ ✓ ✓
✓ ✓ ✓ ✓
✓ ✓ ✓ ✓
✓ ✓ ✓ ✓ ✓

Made connection to
Fantail Fantail + recited lines

I thought Sam's connection to another book (the next example on the tape) was important enough to note on the record.

Sometimes recording substitutions is not as simple as you might at first think. Remember, the idea is to record deviations from the text, word by word. Try the following example.

TAPE EXAMPLE 5. *Fantail, Fantail* by Margaret Mahy (1984b)

"Fantail, Fantail,
have some cheese."
"No. No. No.
I don't like cheese."
"Fantail, Fantail,
have some peas."
"No. No. No.
I don't like peas."
"Fantail, Fantail,
have some pie."
"No. No. No.
I don't like pie."

Here is the running record for this reading:

$$\checkmark \quad \checkmark$$
$$\checkmark \quad \checkmark \quad \checkmark$$
$$\checkmark \quad \checkmark \quad \checkmark$$
$$\checkmark \quad \frac{do}{don't} \quad \frac{not}{-} \quad \checkmark \quad \checkmark$$
$$\checkmark \quad \checkmark$$
$$\checkmark \quad \checkmark \quad \checkmark$$
$$\checkmark \quad \checkmark \quad \checkmark$$
$$\checkmark \quad \frac{do}{don't} \quad \frac{not}{-} \quad \checkmark \quad \checkmark$$
$$\checkmark \quad \checkmark$$
$$\checkmark \quad \checkmark \quad \checkmark$$
$$\checkmark \quad \checkmark \quad \checkmark$$
$$\checkmark \quad \frac{do}{don't} \quad \frac{not}{-} \quad \checkmark \quad \checkmark$$

The interesting and positive thing about Emily's reading error is that she substitutes book language for the more natural language actually in the text: books are more likely to avoid contractions, using, for example, "do not" rather than "don't." The down side is that she is not as concerned about matching one spoken word to one printed word.

Self-Corrections

When we make an error in our reading, often (though not always) we stop to correct it. This is a very important behavior because it is usually evidence that we are cross-checking one set of cues with another. Every time readers do this they learn something. Self-corrections are recorded by using the letters *SC*, as in the following example:

TEXT:	Once upon a time there lived a dragon.	
SUSAN:	Once upon a time there was [pause] lived a dragon.	$\checkmark \quad \checkmark \quad \checkmark \quad \checkmark \quad \checkmark$ $\frac{WAS/SC}{lived} \quad \checkmark \quad \checkmark$

Susan may have used her knowledge of sentence structure (syntax) and perhaps of other stories to predict that *was* would follow *there*. However, when her eyes reached the actual word she did not see the letters that fit with her prediction. Instead of the letters *w-a-s* she saw the letters *l-i-v-e-d*. In light of this new information, she corrected herself. *This is an indication of healthy reading.* Susan was being efficient in trying to predict what was coming, but she also showed a concern for accurate representation of the text. We call this "self-correcting from print" because the print leads to the self-correction. This interpretation of Susan's mental processes is plausible because her first effort made sense and it fit the structure of the sentence; the only mismatch was with the print. The next example on the tape illustrates this type of self-correction. The following is the text:

TAPE EXAMPLE 6: *Who Took the Farmer's Hat?* by Joan Nodset (1989)

He saw Squirrel.
"Squirrel, did you see
my old brown hat?"

The running record for this would look like this:

✓ ✓ ✓
✓ have/did |sc| ✓ ✓
✓ ✓ ✓ ✓

Self-corrections do not always occur this way. Sometimes incongruities in meaning prompt the correction. Consider the following:

The girl's hair was really quite ornate. Her bows for the audience were received with much applause.

In this passage, you probably read the word *bows* incorrectly and then returned to correct it. You made a plausible reading but discovered later in the sentence that it did not make sense. This is called "self-correcting from meaning." Good readers engage in both types of self-correction as needed, showing their awareness that reading requires a balanced use of the available cues.

Recording self-corrections is the point at which most disagreement will occur among different recorders. Remember that in order to record something as a self-correction we must infer a mental activity that we cannot see, so we rely on little clues like voice inflection to help us. We have to decide whether the reader was just figuring out a word or actually making an error and then going back and correcting it. Such situations occur often enough with self-corrections that they do require some caution in interpretation. We will get more practice at this along the way.

There are also other things that make self-corrections difficult to interpret. First, not all self-corrections are made out loud. As readers mature, they become increasingly able to correct their errors silently. Second, some older readers become overly concerned about relatively trivial errors, such as substituting *a* for *the*. Although this kind of error might be an important place for beginning readers to learn, in a more mature reader it might be too much of a good thing, slowing the reader unnecessarily and diverting attention from the bigger picture.

Repetitions

Sometimes readers, having read a word, a sentence, or some other segment of text, decide to go back and reread it. There are numerous reasons for this. They might reread because what they read the first time did not seem to make sense, or they might reread to savor what the writer said or to help figure out a difficult word, or they might reread to get a better flow if there were several difficult words in the sentence. Repetitions are recorded with the letter *R* and a line, as in the following example:

TEXT: The spider grabbed the fly
and wrapped it up.

READER: The spider grabbed grabbed the fly
the spider grabbed the fly
and wrapped wrapped wrapped it up.

$$\checkmark \ \checkmark \ \checkmark R \quad \checkmark \ \checkmark R$$
$$\checkmark \ \checkmark R^2 \ \checkmark \ \checkmark$$

As shown in this example, a numerical superscript is used to indicate more than one repetition. Also, notice how the notation is used for either a single word or larger sections of text. The repetition of a larger section is indicated by drawing a line from the *R* back to the beginning of the repeated segment.

Try recording repetitions from the following text.

TAPE EXAMPLE 7: *My Bike* by Craig Martin (1982)

On Tuesday I rode my bike
around the tree,
over the bridge,
under the branches
and through the puddle.

The running record should resemble this one:

$$\checkmark \ \checkmark \ \checkmark \ \checkmark \ \checkmark \ \checkmark$$
$$\checkmark \ \checkmark R \ \checkmark .$$
$$\checkmark \ \checkmark \ \checkmark$$
$$\checkmark \ \checkmark \ \checkmark$$
$$\checkmark \ \checkmark \ \checkmark \ \checkmark$$

Now try the next example:

TAPE EXAMPLE 8: *Saturday Morning* by Lesley Moyes (1983)

"Dad, the car is clean,
and so are we," said Mark.

Here's how the running record should look:

Problem-Solving

Often when a reader does not recognize a word right away, he will try to figure it out, possibly making several attempts. These attempts are frequently made out loud, especially by younger readers. Each attempt should be recorded, because they tell us a lot about the reader's strategies for figuring out words. Consider the examples of readers reading the following sentence.

TEXT:	She could see people swimming in the water.
READER 1:	She could see people s/sw/swim/swimming in the water.
READER 2:	She could see people sing in the water—swimming in the water.
READER 3:	She could see people swing/ing/swim/swimming in the water.
READER 4:	She could see people—in the water—swimming in the water.

Each reader was successful in figuring out the unknown word, and each tackled the word in a different manner. Even a single example of problem-solving gives us some useful information, but a pattern of several examples gives us more dependable information.

Students' problem-solving on words is recorded using vertical rules, as shown below:

TEXT:	We all went to the fair.
READER:	We all went to the f/fire/far/fair. ✓ ✓ ✓ ✓ ✓ f/fire/far/✓ fair

Try your hand at recording problem-solving using the next taped example.

TAPE EXAMPLE 9: *The Dragon's Birthday* by Margaret Mahy (1984a)

The next morning, a boy named Richard
said to his sister Claire,

"Today's the dragon's birthday."
"Everyone knows that," said Claire.
"Poor dragon. No one is brave enough
to go up to his cave and say,
'Happy birthday.'"
"Perhaps we could go," said Richard.
"It's too dangerous," said their mother.
"He might frizzle you up."

Your running record should resemble this one:

Recording problem-solving is not easy. In fact, it may be the hardest part of taking running records. However, the information that it provides about the strategies the reader used to figure out unfamiliar words is very important and well worth the effort. You will notice in the reading in Tape Example 9 that Nick was very consistent in his attempts to figure out the words. One part of your record may have been different from mine. I recorded Nick's figuring out of the word *brave* as a self-correction rather than as a word that he finally figured out: I wrote "SC" at the end instead of a check mark. I interpreted his intonation on "braf" as an indication that he was satisfied that he had made a word. His voice had an air of finality about it. But then, having said it, he changed his mind. It sounded to me as though it was a self-correction. You may differ. Our difference on the matter is not particularly important unless we have hardly any other examples of Nick's reading. If this were the only example of self-correction and it was doubtful, we might seek some more data. Multiple examples are important for establishing patterns.

Sometimes rather than sounding out words, readers will spell them. This is recorded with capital letters instead of lowercase ones.

Sometimes we witness very complex strategies for figuring out words, and great persistence in doing so. Listen to the next example on the tape, in which Nick figures out the word *midnight*.

---

for his midnight swim.

The running record for this reading looks like this:

Readings as complicated as this one may outfox you in the beginning, but you can simply make a side note later of some of the strategies that you heard. In this example, Nick first tried to figure the word out left to right, then he backed out to get the context and have another go, then he recognized a word he knew within the word, which finally allowed the whole thing to come together. I recorded the outcome as a self-correction rather than as simply correctly figured out because he said "midingth" with a tone of "Got it!" and then returned to a puzzling-out tone before finally reading the phrase correctly

Time to Take Stock

If you normally write in small print, you might have found yourself cramped for space when the reader repeated a section and corrected an earlier error. You will probably find it easier if you allow yourself to be a little more expansive in your recording. The next example on the tape should help you begin to get the feel of putting together what you have learned so far. Nick is reading.

TAPE EXAMPLE 11: *Busy Beavers* by M. Barbara Brownell (1988)

Page 2:
Beside a pond, a beaver snacks on tall grass and weeds.
On land, beavers find trees to use for making their homes,
called lodges. They build the lodges in deep water.
A beaver swims back and forth from its home to the land.

Page 4:
This beaver is busy building
a dam to hold water back

in a pond. Soon the water will be
deep and will be a safe place
for the beaver to build its lodge.

With its sharp front teeth,
the beaver cuts a branch in two.
A hard orange coating on the
teeth keeps them from chipping
as the beaver bites through wood.

The running record should look something like this:

Notice how the page numbers are recorded at the left.

You might have found yourself at or beyond your limit in attempting to take this record. This should not be surprising. You are essentially in the process of learning shorthand and should not expect to become comfortable with it in only a few minutes. Fortunately, like reading, the more you do it, the easier it becomes. Indeed, you might like to rewind the tape and try Example 11 again. Just as beginning readers find rereading helpful for developing fluency, teachers beginning to take running records can develop fluency from repeating a record. Just be careful not to become addicted to tape recorders.

In recording Example 11, you might also have found that your running record was not the same as mine. Actually, there is more than one way to record this reading, depending on how you interpret certain reading behaviors. For example, Nick read one part as follows:

TEXT: Soon the water will be deep
          and will be a safe place . . .
NICK: Soon water will be deep
          and will be s—a safe place . . .

When I was making my record, I felt that Nick predicted the word *safe* and began to say it, but then encountered the actual word, *a*, noticed the discrepancy, and corrected his error. You might have interpreted it as suggesting that he skipped over *a* to *safe*, but then noticed the *a*. This would be recorded as follows:

Again, some differences in interpretation are to be expected, but in the long run should not have serious consequences. One way to determine the correct interpretation is simply to ask the reader. For example, after he or she has finished reading you might ask, "How did you know to . . .?" or "I noticed that you . . . What were you thinking when you did that?" Provided these questions are not interpreted as calls to justify errors, you will often learn something about the reader's thinking. However, some children (and adults) are more able to recall their strategies than others.

One final reader behavior is worth recording. Sometimes readers realize they are stuck and ask for help. We record this with the letters *APP,* for "appeal." If the child attempts the word first, a record might look like this.

p | panded | pandled | APP

In the next example on the tape Sam appeals to me for help, unnecessarily it turns out. You will have to listen carefully as she whispers her appeal. Try to record it now.

TAPE EXAMPLE 12:   *Harry Goes to Funland* by Harriet Ziefert (1989)

          Harry even rode
          the roller coaster.

Your record should look like this:

Notice that I used a check mark at the end of the record because she finally figured the word out correctly. She did not make an error and then correct it, so it is not a self-correction.

An appeal to another person is a useful strategy for figuring things out and is important to note. However, if it occurs with any regularity on text that is not that difficult for the reader, it suggests a lack of independence and confidence. In such a case, teaching interactions should be examined to see what is producing the situation.

Sometimes children realize there is a problem, but neither appeal for help nor fix it themselves. In this case, I use a question mark to indicate the questioning inflection in the reader's voice.

Intervention

In general, when you are taking running records, you should intervene as little as possible because you are interested in learning how readers manage things themselves. However, occasionally there are times when it is appropriate to intervene, particularly when the usefulness of your subsequent records or your rapport with the reader is at risk. Sometimes children make a series of errors that compound themselves and stall their reading. When this happens, they either cease to read altogether or cease to read in a manner that is typical of their normal performance. The sensible thing for the teacher to do in this case is to help them get back on track and restart themselves by giving them a prompt to reread. Usually you would say, "Why don't you try that again?" and direct them to the beginning of the sentence, paragraph, page, or other meaning unit. This allows readers to approach the problematic section with greater momentum. It amounts to a prompted rereading. If they are successful at rectifying the problem, we have modeled a repair strategy (which we might later point out to them), and their subsequent reading tells us something about what they can do when given some strategic support.

However, interventions must be recorded so that they can be taken into account in our later interpretations. A prompted rereading can be recorded simply with the letters *TA* (try again), as in the following example:

TEXT: Once upon a time,
an old man planted
a little turnip.
He said to the little turnip,
"Grow, little turnip!"

BOB: Once upon a time,
an old man p/panded/pandled?
a little t/trip/trinip—turnip.
   [Try that again.]
Once upon a time,
an old man p/planted
a little turnip.
He said to the little turnip,
"Grow, little turnip!"

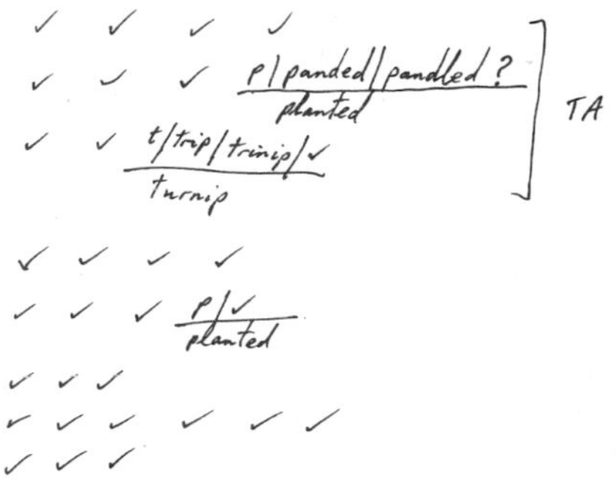

(Handwritten running record with checkmarks beside each line; notations read:)
✓ ✓ ✓ ✓
✓ ✓ ✓ p/panded/pandled? — planted
✓ ✓ t/trip/trinip/✓ — turnip   ] TA
✓ ✓ ✓ ✓
✓ ✓ ✓ p/✓ — planted
✓ ✓ ✓
✓ ✓ ✓ ✓ ✓
✓ ✓ ✓

Notice that the whole repeated section is bracketed and marked "TA" for "try again." Basically this record tells you, "This section was not typical of Bob's reading, so I got him to take another run at it."

Try to record the next example on the tape. Sam is reading the text:

TAPE EXAMPLE 13: *I Can Read* by Margaret Malcolm (1983)

I read to my mother.
I read to my father.
I read to my nana.

Your record should look something like this:

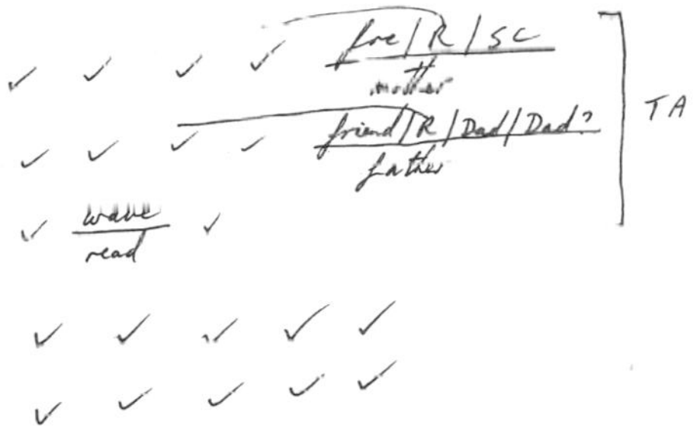

(Handwritten running record with checkmarks; notations read:)
✓ ✓ ✓ ✓ love/R/sc — mother
✓ ✓ ✓ friend/R/Dad/Dad? — father   ] TA
✓ wave/read ✓
✓ ✓ ✓ ✓ ✓
✓ ✓ ✓ ✓ ✓

The reason Sam had trouble with this book is because she had just read the book *Going to School* (Cowley 1983a) and still had the melody of that book in her head. She noticed that the words and letters on the page did not match that melody, and her voice shows her confusion. Suddenly she realized exactly what had happened and she is able to read it the way it is supposed to be.

The second type of intervention you can make is actually telling the student the word. You should try to minimize the likelihood of having to do this—by introducing stories well (including any particularly awkward words) and by knowing the student well enough to predict how he or she will manage the book.

However, sometimes it is clear that introducing the context will give little or no support, or you know from your experience with the student that a particular word is out of her range. So you tell the child the word. When you do this, it is recorded by writing *T* in the bottom right corner of the record, as in the following example:

TEXT: We cannot go back to
         the old quarry.

READER: We cannot go back to
         the old [Teacher tells *quarry*].

Now try the next example on the tape.

TAPE EXAMPLE 14:   *Indian Two Feet and His Horse* by Margaret Friskey (1959)

He could sing.
He could dance.

Your record should look like this:

Other Observations

Other types of reading behavior may be important for different children. For example, pauses can be recorded as ⌴. Pauses, however, do not usually provide much information, although some children do a lot of figuring out silently, and the pauses can represent a child who otherwise appears not to be using many strategies.

You might find it useful to code teacher assistance besides "try again." For example, for a particular child you might say, "What word would make sense there?" or "Do you know another word that starts that way?" and you may want to devise a code for these kinds of support. However, normally when you take a running record you want to see what the child can do independently, so you will have chosen a book and introduced it so that assistance will not be necessary. The more you intervene, the less reliable your record. In general, it is more helpful to make a record of what the child reads, with you simply noting irregularities or providing additional context to help with later interpretation. For example, I often find it helpful to comment on fluency, pace, any relevant student comments or nervousness, and expression.

Instructionally, the point of running records is to answer these two questions:

- Does the record suggest that the reader is trying to make sense?
- What kind of strategies and sources of information are being used to make meaning?

I also make annotations to record other significant behavior or comments. For example, if a child points to the words for some or all of the text, I would note that. Comments the child makes can also be very revealing about the child's ongoing understanding of the text.

Other Observations

211

*I*NTERPRETING ORAL READING RECORDS

CO-AUTHORED WITH MARIE M. CLAY

*T*his chapter is primarily about the interpretation of the overall running record. It might seem as though this is where the interpretive part begins, but I want to remind you that even when we are making the running record we are necessarily interpreting. We had to decide which behaviors to record (for example, repetitions but not hesitations) and we had to decide whether a reader was self-correcting or just figuring out a word. In this chapter we add a further layer of interpretation as we make sense of our running records (for more on this see Clay 1993a; for an alternative approach see Goodman, Watson, and Burke 1987).

Error Rate

Whatever the recording system used, teachers want to assess how the student is doing. Whether students choose their own books or we choose books for them, we want to make sure they are reading materials they can manage. But what is manageable? The first thing to consider in the running record is the error rate: the proportion of words read incorrectly (although in the long run it is probably more important to ask the students how difficult a book is because doing so gets them to begin thinking about the matter for themselves).

The error rate is simply the ratio of the number of words read incorrectly to the total number of words read. This seems like a reasonable way of estimating how difficult a text is for a child, but it is not perfect for a number of reasons. For

In this and the preceding chapter we draw on Marie M. Clay's book *An Observation Survey of Early Literacy Achievement*. Although they are co-authored, we have maintained the first person singular voice for continuity of style. All the examples of running records that appear in these two chapters are recorded on the tape that accompanies this book.

many years researchers have argued over which error rate indicates that a text is too difficult ("frustration level"), which indicates that it is very easy ("independent level"), and which indicates that the text is just right. Actually, these arguments are futile, for two reasons. First, all errors are not created equal. Some suggest difficulty with the text whereas others do not. Many substitutions of *a* for *the* and *shouted* for *said* and the like are not the same as substitutions of *jump* for *joker*. Self-corrections may take a lot of mental effort and disrupt reading substantially, or they may not. Hesitations may suggest increased mental effort. Second, some children seem to have a higher tolerance for different kinds of word level errors than do others. Some children's reading processes seem to fall apart when they reach an error rate of about one in twenty (5 percent). Other children seem to feel comfortable, showing healthy reading processes, even in material they read with an error rate of one in eight (12.5 percent). There also appear to be developmental differences in manageable error rate.

Nonetheless, error rate is not a bad indicator of difficulty if we use it cautiously. Marie Clay suggests that an error rate of up to one in twenty (5 percent) indicates that the text is generally easy enough to be read independently. She calls this *easy text*. Text read with an error rate greater than one in ten is considered *hard text*. An error rate of between one in twenty and one in ten is at the edge of what a student can manage without assistance. This is often called *instructional level text*, but let's call it *learning text*. While it provides information that is useful for instruction, it is most important because children actually *learn* from it, provided they are self-correcting appropriately.

In general, running records are of most value when the text is in the learning range because with this kind of text there are not enough errors to disrupt meaning, but it is difficult enough so that many of the strategies used by the reader are overt and able to be recorded.

What Counts as an Error?

Words are easy to count, but errors are less straightforward. Researchers have argued back and forth about what counts as an error, and this is reflected in the various oral reading tests on the market. Table 22.1 shows the differences between researchers when it comes to counting errors. In a way it depends on what we think we are counting. If we are counting "errors," it hardly seems "fair" to count repetitions, words laboriously figured out, and self-corrections. However, if we are counting "indicators of difficulty," which is, after all, the main reason for counting them at all, it is easier to argue for counting these, and even extensive hesitations. Unfortunately, there is no sensible formula for doing this. There is no way to weight different types of errors. Is an omission as serious as a prolonged hesitation? Is a substitution as serious as an insertion? Is substituting *smell* for *small* the same as substituting *little*?

TABLE 22.1

*Oral Reading Behaviors Counted as "Errors" by Various Authors of
Diagnostic Tests*

Behavior	Gray 1915	Gates 1927	Durrell 1937	Gilmore 1951	Spache 1963	Clay 1975
Omission of sound and/or word	x	x	x	x	x	x
Addition of sound and/or word	x	x	x	x	x	x
Substitution or mispronunciation	x	x	x	x	x	x
Repetition	x	x	x	x	x	
Self-correction	x		x	x	x	
Word aided	x	x	x	x	x	x
Hesitation		x	x	x		
Punctuation ignored	x		x	x		

Source: From Allington 1984, p. 836. One-word repetitions not counted. The table originally indicated that Clay counted repetitions, which was not accurate. It also indicated as a source Clay 1975. The correct reference is Clay 1972.

I do not see an immediate solution to this, and I don't think one is necessary in most cases. It is probably enough to have a consistent method for counting and a way of making a reasonable explanation when our knowledge tells us that the counting method has failed us in a particular instance. A consistent method of counting allows us to make certain comparisons while being on the lookout for qualitative changes. Since I have used Marie Clay's (1993a) method of recording oral reading behaviors, I also use her method for counting errors, with minor adjustments. Here are the guidelines:

- Omissions count as one error each.
- Insertions count as one error each.
- A word repeatedly read inaccurately counts as an error every time, except when it is a proper noun. Proper nouns count only the first time. For example, if a child continually reads *went* for *want* it counts as an error each time. But if he or she continually reads *Roger* incorrectly, it only counts as an error the first time.
- Words that are pronounced differently because of a child's dialect (for example, *frigeator* for *refrigerator*) do not count as errors.
- Self-corrected words do not count as errors.

- If a page (or two) is omitted, count it as one error but do not count the words in the word count. But if a line is omitted, count each word in that line as an error.
- An intervention in which you tell the child the word counts as one error.
- An intervention with "Try that again" counts as one error. Any other errors in the bracketed section are not counted. Errors made in the second reading of that section are counted. For example, in the following record, the error count is two, one for the TA, and one for the substitution of *a* for *the*. The five errors within the bracketed section do not count.

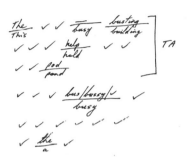

- If there are several ways to record a section, choose the one that fits with your interpretation of the pattern of errors (or the one that fits the child's explanation of it). If that is not possible, choose the one that produces the lowest error count.
- Sometimes you will end up with more errors on a given line than there are words on it, but on any given page, do not count more errors than there are words. Usually in this situation, the reader is creating his or her own text from memory or from the pictures, and there is little point in continuing the running record. Simply note the picture-story match, the quality of the constructed story, and any concepts the child demonstrates about print (see Chapter 12 for explanations of the concepts about print).

To calculate error rate, divide the number of errors by the number of words in the text, and multiply that figure by 100. For example, if a child makes 15 errors in a 192-word text, the error rate is 15 divided by 192 (which equals about .08) times 100, which equals 8 percent. This can be written as:

$$\text{Error rate} = \frac{\text{Number of errors} \times 100}{\text{Number of words}}$$
$$= \frac{15 \times 100}{192}$$
$$= 8$$

Accuracy is simply this percentage subtracted from 100 percent; in this case it would be 100 percent − 8 percent = 92 percent accuracy.

For practice, calculate the accuracy for the running record of *Busy Beavers* in Tape Example 11 in Chapter 21 (page 206). The correct calculations are at the bottom of this page.[1]

Self-Correction

At the beginning of the book I explained the importance of self-correction. If children do not correct their own errors, they learn nothing from their mistakes, run the risk of not understanding the text, and may even get to the point of automatically identifying certain words incorrectly. If they do self-correct, there is a good chance that in a literate environment they will teach themselves to read with relatively little help. Thus, it is helpful to have a measurement of how often children correct their own errors. The self-correction rate is the proportion of times a reader corrected her own errors in relation to the number of errors initially made (that is, the number of errors plus the number of self-corrected errors). As a formula, the self-correction rate is the ratio:

Self-corrections : (Errors + Self-corrections)

which is symbolized:

SC : (E + SC)

Calculate the self-correction ratio for the *Busy Beavers* reading (Tape Example 11). The correct calculation is shown at the bottom of this page.[2]

Within the learning range of text difficulty, the self-correction rate can indicate the extent to which readers are monitoring their use of the different sources of information available to them. It is not a perfect indicator, since some readers will monitor their reading and find problems but not correct them overtly. Self-corrections are evidence of the reader comparing different sources of information, finding them discrepant, *and* doing something about correcting the discrepancy. However, as I have mentioned before, some readers go through the process silently.

---

[1]There are 105 words and 1 error. so the error rate is 1 percent:

$$\frac{Errors \times 100}{Words} = \frac{1 \times 100}{105} = 1\%$$

The accuracy, then, is 99 percent (100 percent − 1 percent).

[2]There is 1 error (E) and 6 self-corrections (SC) in Tape Example 11.

SC ratio = SC : (E + SC)
          = 6 : (1 + 6)
          = 6 : 7
          = 1: 7/6
          = 1: 1.2

The self-correction rate, then, is approximately 1 : 1.

Not all self-corrections are equal. It is important to examine which sources of information the reader sees as discrepant. For example, Susan might make substitutions that do not make sense but that would, if written down, look a lot like the word on the page. However, she immediately notices when what she says does not make sense, and she tries again, using both the meaning and the print. We can interpret Susan's running record as suggesting that she is attending most strongly to the print detail but comparing it with a strong internal notion of the meaning of the text. We call this *self-correcting from meaning*. It is as if she says to herself, "That doesn't make sense."

On the other hand, Jane goes about her reading in the opposite manner. She concentrates on meaning, producing substitutions that make sense but that do not fit well with the print. She corrects herself from the print. It is as if she says to herself, "No. That doesn't look right." We call this *self-correcting from print*.

When the text is very easy for readers, they will usually use all the sources of information necessary to get things right the first time. However, as things become harder, they will tend to abandon one or another source of information for a first attempt and then use the neglected source as a check. As things become harder still, they may totally neglect information that they are quite capable of using under normal conditions. Thus, running records taken on material that is too difficult can be quite misleading. They will tell us relatively little of any importance about the reader's strategies, except how they break down.

Prediction

Prediction is at the heart of efficient reading mainly because it is hard to know how to interpret letters or words without knowing the context in which they appear (Bruner 1985). For example, the sound associated with the letter *e* can vary depending on its location in the word, the letters next to it, the letters next-but-one to it, the root of the word, and so forth (consider the sound of *e* in *bed, bead, readmit, give, baker, revere* . . .). In addition, the pronunciation of words depends on their location in the surrounding text. For example, consider the pronunciation of the word *read* in the following contexts:

- I have *Read Along with Mother.*
- I have read that book several times.
- She screamed, "I *have* read along with mother, and I told her she read too fast."

This complexity is partly why predicting is an important aspect of effective reading. Oral reading errors can give some insight into whether or not children are, or are not, predicting. Prediction is an extension of meaning or patterns into the future. Thus, if a reader, without hesitation, makes, or begins to make, a substitution that would make good sense up to that point, but does not fit entirely with the print detail, then he or she is likely to have been predicting. For example, consider the following:

TEXT:	One day the teeny tiny woman
	put on her teeny tiny bonnet
READER:	One day the teeny tiny woman
	wen—put on her teeny tiny bonnet

In this case the reader predicted that the word *went* would begin the next line, but got there and did not find the letters expected. There might be other explanations for this reading, but prediction fits best with our own experience: as mature readers, we do it all the time.

The next two examples on the tape illustrate prediction. They do not require any new recording techniques.

TAPE EXAMPLE 15: *Indian Two Feet and His Horse* by Margaret Friskey (1959)

There was
a little Indian.
He wished
he had a horse.

The running record should look like this:

TAPE EXAMPLE 16: *Saturday Morning* by Lesley Moyes (1983)

Mum hosed the garden.
"Please will you hose me?"
said Helen.
"Please will you hose me?"
said Mark.
Mum hosed Helen and Mark.

The running record is the following:

✓ ✓ ✓ ✓
✓ we/sc ✓ ✓ ✓
   will
✓ ✓
✓ ✓ ✓ ✓ ✓
ask/sc ✓
said
✓ ✓ ✓ ✓ ✓

In the first example, Emily predicted that the story would begin "There once was . . ." but she looked and either saw some letters there that disagreed (*once* does start with the same sound as *was,* but *was* does not have an *n*), or she went on to the next line and saw *a* and realized that you can't say "There once a," so she corrected herself.

In the second example, we heard Nick predicting on two levels. Using normal conversation, Mark *asks* a question, so the text should say, "asked Mark," but it doesn't, so Nick corrected himself. Then, when he got to the bottom of the page, he began to predict where the story would go next, and looked for verification when he turned the page. In contrast to this is the child who substitutes nonsense words or words that do not fit the context. It is unlikely that such a reader is predicting.

It is always helpful to have several examples of a particular type of error in order to be comfortable with what you are inferring. However, sometimes you see a single example of an error that is almost certainly a result of prediction and you can say with reasonable certainty that the student does predict while reading. Although we all spend our lives predicting what will be said next when we converse with others, what will happen in traffic when we are driving, and so forth, it is still important to be able to say that a child predicts when reading because it means that the child understands at some level that the point of reading is to make sense.

Prediction produces words that make sense up to that point, although they do not necessarily fit the letters that are on the page or the words that follow. In other words, substitutions that make sense in context often suggest that the child has predicted. However, there are exceptions. For example, if a reader comes to a word with which he has difficulty, pauses, and then says a word that makes sense up to that point and fits with some of the print detail, it is evidence that he is trying to make sense and to integrate cues, but not that he is predicting. Prediction takes place *before* you get there, not after.

The Balance and Method of Information Use

When I study children's oral reading, I am most interested in the information they use and how they use it. In a book that is not too easy and not too hard for them,

I want to know whether they use the available information from their language, from their experience, and from the page in a flexible and active manner. I want to know whether they try to stay a little ahead of what they are reading, and whether they check one source of information against another. Sometimes problems occur. For example, some children rely on one source of information to the exclusion of another. They may rely on their knowledge of the alphabetic system, for example, without checking against their knowledge of the language or their own experience. An oral reading such as the following might occur:

TEXT: I cannot go out to play with you today.
READER: I cannot go oot to play with you todda.

There are, of course, a number of possible reasons for this kind of pattern. The readers might not have the relevant experience, or their language pattern may be substantially different from that of the text, or they may not have learned "book language." They may have come to doubt the relevance or adequacy of their own knowledge or language. Their interpretation of reading instruction might have convinced them that reading has nothing to do with making sense. Whatever the cause, we should try to encourage these readers to make more use of these other sources of information in conjunction with what they already use. At the same time, we will certainly be interested in seeing whether something in the classroom (or at home) is contributing to the problem. For example, if the books such readers have in class are too difficult, their error rate may make it impossible for them to construct meaning from the text. Consistently deprived of meaningfulness in activities designated as reading, they may have developed unfortunate reading habits and misconceptions about reading itself.

Similarly, we may see imbalances in the use of information sources in the opposite direction. Some children depend too heavily on their own knowledge and language patterns, and more or less ignore what is on the page. For example:

TEXT: Down came the biscuits
         and the book
         and the bucket
READER: Down came cookies
         down came the pails
         down came the books

It is true that readers must construct meaning using their own knowledge. Some reading situations (such as reading a paperback novel) do not require much concern over the use of exactly those words the author used. However, other types of reading (such as instructions for running expensive or dangerous machines) require detailed attention to the words the author used. Good readers are flexible in their use of the different sources of information, and we teachers should encourage readers who ignore too much of what is on the page to attend more to print detail, particularly when checking predictions. Such readers usually are predicting, but they do not verify their predictions. They may lack the knowledge of print conventions or of alphabetic relationships, or they may have such knowledge but fail to use it.

It is very common for children to pay too much attention to one cue source or another for brief periods of time and in particular situations (Biemiller 1970, 1979); and it is quite common for children who are just getting the hang of letter-sound relationships to devote too much effort to them, even to the extent that they lose meaning as they read. Rereading at such times can substantially improve performance. Similarly, children who overpredict will perform better when asked to follow the text with a finger.

Although readers should show a balanced use of sources of information, they should also use the information flexibly and strategically in the service of meaning. If one strategy fails, are other strategies used? Are the strategies efficient? These are important questions to ask of running records. For example, we might see children rereading sentences, parts of sentences, or paragraphs. This can be an effective strategy, but if it is used as the major method for figuring out unfamiliar words, it is inefficient. We might observe children repeatedly rereading parts of a sentence to help figure out a word in a situation where rereading from the beginning of the sentence would give better contextual support. Sometimes we see readers who simply give up after one attempt at each problematic word. There are no hard and fast guidelines as to what constitutes efficient reading strategies, except to say that flexible use of strategies and information sources is likely to be most efficient, provided that readers clearly direct their efforts toward the goal of constructing meaning.

Analyzing running records this way leads us to examine each deviation from the print to see what type of cues readers have used: *meaning* (M), *structure* (S), or *visual* (V) cues. We can then make a record of the analysis down the side of the page.

Here is an example:

TEXT: Danny ran to his house
         and went to his room.
READER: Danny ran to his hus
         and ran to his room.

The completed running record would look like this:

NAME:				DATE:		E	SC	E	SC
BOOK:								MSV	MSV
✓	✓	✓	✓	$\frac{hus}{house}$		1		✓	
✓	$\frac{ran}{went}$	✓	✓	✓		1		ms	

Analyzing running records in this way allows us to check our intuition about the reader's use of the available cues and later to see at a glance changes in these patterns.

Cues can be used both to identify a word and to correct an error. For example, a reader can predict (M and possibly S) and then self-correct from print (V). This is different from first trying the word from visual cues (V), then self-correcting because it doesn't make sense (M) or because it doesn't sound right (S).

One way to simplify the recording is to print running record sheets that have columns down the right-hand side specifically for analysis, as shown in the example above and in the remainder of the examples in this chapter (a blank form is provided in Appendix D). One column can be made for the analysis of errors (E) and one for analysis of self-corrections (SC). You might also have a column for tallying the number of errors and another column for self-corrections, as in the form in Appendix D.

Since the letters *M, S, V* are always written in the same order, we can simply write

```
M   S   V
M       V
    S   V
```

and so forth for each error or self-correction. The absence of an *M* in the third sequence above shows the failure to use meaning as a cue. Thus,

TEXT: He went down the street
READER: He went down the road—street

would be recorded as follows:

NAME:	DATE:		E	SC	E	SC
BOOK:					MSV	MSV
✓ ✓ ✓ ✓ read /sc ̲ street /				1	ms	✓

Alternatively, you may write MSV for every line and circle the cues that were used.

The MSV analysis is not as simple as it might appear. You will certainly encounter differences of opinion over whether particular cues were used. For instance, if the text word has only two out of eight letters in common with the word the child said, does that count as use of visual cues? What about two out of four? You must use your judgment on such matters, keeping in mind that ultimately it is the *pattern* you should be concerned about, not each individual error. You will not be able to say for sure that a reader used a particular cue system. All you can do is say that what the reader did was or was not consistent with some cue systems and that your hypothesis fits the data. For example, suppose a child reads as follows:

TEXT: Once there were

READER: Once upon—once there were

One possible cause of this self-correction is that the child predicted "upon" but when his eyes got to the word he noticed that the wrong letters were there (visual cues), so he corrected himself. Another possibility is that he predicted "upon" with such confidence that he paid little attention to the letters there and proceeded to the next word, "were," which he recognized. Realizing that "Once upon were" doesn't sound right (structure cues), he corrected himself. We can ask the child how he managed to correct himself, but we will never know for sure. In short, do not get caught up too much worrying over individual examples unless there are larger disagreements over patterns.

All Together Now

To pull it all together, try taking a running record of *Owl Babies,* an excellent children's book. It is the last example on side A of the tape.

TAPE EXAMPLE 17:   *Owl Babies* by Martin Waddell; illustrated by
                       Patrick Benson (1992)

Once there were three baby owls:
Sarah and Percy and Bill.

They lived in a hole
in the trunk of a tree
with their Owl Mother.
The hole had twigs and
leaves and owl feathers in it.
It was their house.

One night they woke up and
their Owl Mother was GONE.
"Where's mommy?" asked Sarah.
"Oh my goodness!" said Percy.
"I want my mommy!" said Bill.

The baby owls *thought*
(all owls think a lot)—
"I think she's gone hunting," said Sarah.
"To get us our food!" said Percy.
"I want my mommy!" said Bill.

But their Owl Mother didn't come.
The baby owls came out of
their house, and they sat
on the tree and waited.

A big branch for Sarah,
a small branch for Percy,
and an old piece of ivy for Bill.
"She'll be back," said Sarah.
"Back *soon!*" said Percy.
"I want my mommy!" said Bill.

It was dark in the woods and
they had to be brave, for things
moved all around them.
"She'll bring us mice and
things that are nice," said Sarah.
"I suppose so!" said Percy.
"I want my mommy!" said Bill.

They sat and they thought
(all owls think a lot)—
"I think we should *all*
sit on *my* branch," said Sarah.
And they did, all three together.

"Suppose she got lost," said Sarah.
"Or a fox got her!" said Percy.
"I want my mommy!" said Bill.
And the baby owls closed
their owl eyes and wished their
Owl Mother would come.

AND SHE CAME.

Soft and silent, she swooped
through the trees
to Sarah and Percy
and Bill.

"Mommy!" they cried,
and they flapped and they danced,
and they bounced up and down
on their branch.

"WHAT'S ALL THE FUSS?"
their Owl Mother asked.
"You knew I'd come back."
The baby owls thought
(all owls think a lot)—
"I knew it," said Sarah.
"And I knew it!" said Percy.
"I love my mommy!" said Bill.

The analyzed running record can be found on pages 226–229. Notice the consistent pattern of cues used in the reading. For Sam, words had to make sense and sound right first. They also had to look right, but that was a secondary concern (by a small margin).

Educators may want to ask, "Did she comprehend what she read?" I think we could easily answer in the affirmative just from listening to the expressiveness in Sam's voice. Better questions might be "Is Sam reading to make sense?" and "What sort of engagement did Sam have with this text?" To answer the first of these two questions, aside from her expression, Sam's use of cues reveals an emphasis on meaning, as does her use of strategies. Viewing her reading this way makes it unnecessary for us to examine it on every occasion, as her focus on meaning and her strategic efforts in the service of meaning suggest that Sam understands that meaning is what reading is about. She is unlikely to change her mind on her next reading. The answer to the second question—what sort of engagement Sam had with the text—draws our attention to other features, such as her persistence in

NAME: Sam J.	DATE: 1/24/96	E	SC	E	SC
BOOK: Owl Babies	P.①			MSV	MSV

	E	SC	E	SC
✓ ✓ was/were ✓ ✓ ow/R/✓ owls	1		msv	
✓ ✓ ✓ ✓				
✓ ✓ ✓ ✓				
✓ ✓ ✓ ✓ ✓				
✓R² ✓ ✓ ✓				
✓ ✓ ✓ twig/tig/trig/t/tig/✓ ✓ Twigs				
l/✓ ✓ ✓ ✓ ✓ leaves				
✓ ✓ ✓ home/house	1		ms ✓	
✓ ✓ ✓ ✓ ✓				
✓ ✓ ✓ ✓ ✓				
✓ m/✓/mom/sc s/sc ✓ mommy asked		1 1	msv ms	✓ ✓
w/wha/how/sc ✓ god/R what goodness T		1 1	ms✓ ✓	ms
✓ ✓ ✓ ✓ ✓ ✓				
They/sc babies/sc ow/R/✓ ✓ The baby owls		1 1	ms✓ ms✓	✓ ms
✓ ✓ ✓		1	msv	
✓ ✓ she/R got/R/good/sc/R ✓ ✓ ✓ she's gone		1	msv	✓
✓ ✓ ✓ w/✓ ✓ ✓ ✓ our				
✓ ✓ ✓ ✓ ✓	④	⑥		

Words (W) =   Error Rate (ER) = E/W x 100 =
Self-corrections (SC) =   Accuracy = 100 - ER =
Errors (E) =   Self-correction rate = SC : SC + E =

figuring out words and in reading a lengthy text, and particularly her commentary along the way. Her comments suggest not merely that she understood, but the ways in which she understood—the qualities of her engagement. The following are her comments while she read, and what they suggest to me:

SAM: "Twigs" is a hard word. [She reflects on the process and estimates difficulty. I could have asked her what made it hard which might have led to some focused and timely instruction].

SAM: They just said that they lived in it up here. Why do they say it again? [Critical reading of author's style.]

NAME: SAM J.	DATE: 1/24/94	E	SC	E MSV	SC MSV

BOOK: Owl Babies continued P.(2)

```
✓  ✓  ✓    ✓  ✓  ✓
✓  babies      ✓  ✓  ✓               1    m s ✓    ✓
   baby
✓  ✓  ✓  W/R/W/R/SC  ✓                1    m s      ✓
              They
✓  their/sc   ✓  ✓  watched           1    m s ✓    ✓
   the              waited                 m s ✓
_____
   ✓  ✓  ✓  ✓  ✓
   ✓  ✓  ✓  ✓  ✓
   ✓  ✓  ✓  ✓  ✓  ✓  ✓
she/sc   ✓   soon/sc/R²   ✓            1    m s ✓    ✓
she'll          said
✓  ✓  ✓  ✓                            1    m s ✓    ✓
✓  ✓  ✓  ✓  ✓  ✓
✓  ✓  ✓  ✓  ✓  fores/R/SC  ✓          1    m s      ✓
                 woods
✓  ✓  ✓  ✓  ✓  ✓
✓  ✓  ✓  ✓
✓  be/sc  ✓R  ✓  ✓                    1    m s ✓    ✓
   being
✓  ✓  ✓  ✓  ✓  ✓
✓  ✓  ✓  S/R/✓/R   sarah/R/sc          1    m s      ✓
          said       Percy
✓  ✓  ✓  ✓  ✓  ✓
_____
                                    (1)  (8)
```

All Together Now

227

Words (W) =   Error Rate (ER) = E/W x 100 =
Self-corrections (SC) =   Accuracy = 100 - ER =
Errors (E) =   Self-correction rate = SC : SC + E =

SAM: I feel sad for Bill. He must miss his Mommy a lot. [Connection to own experience and empathy for character.]

SAM: These are good pictures! Look at the leaves and the branches. See the little lines? Isn't that good? . . . And isn't it good that he did, like, blue on the sides? . . . I can't even do those black lines on there. [Appreciation for the craft of the illustrator in the use of detail and color. She is also viewing herself as a possible illustrator but one who currently lacks the particular skills possessed by the book illustrator.]

SAM: He might think he messed . . . Who's this from again? . . . Is that a boy

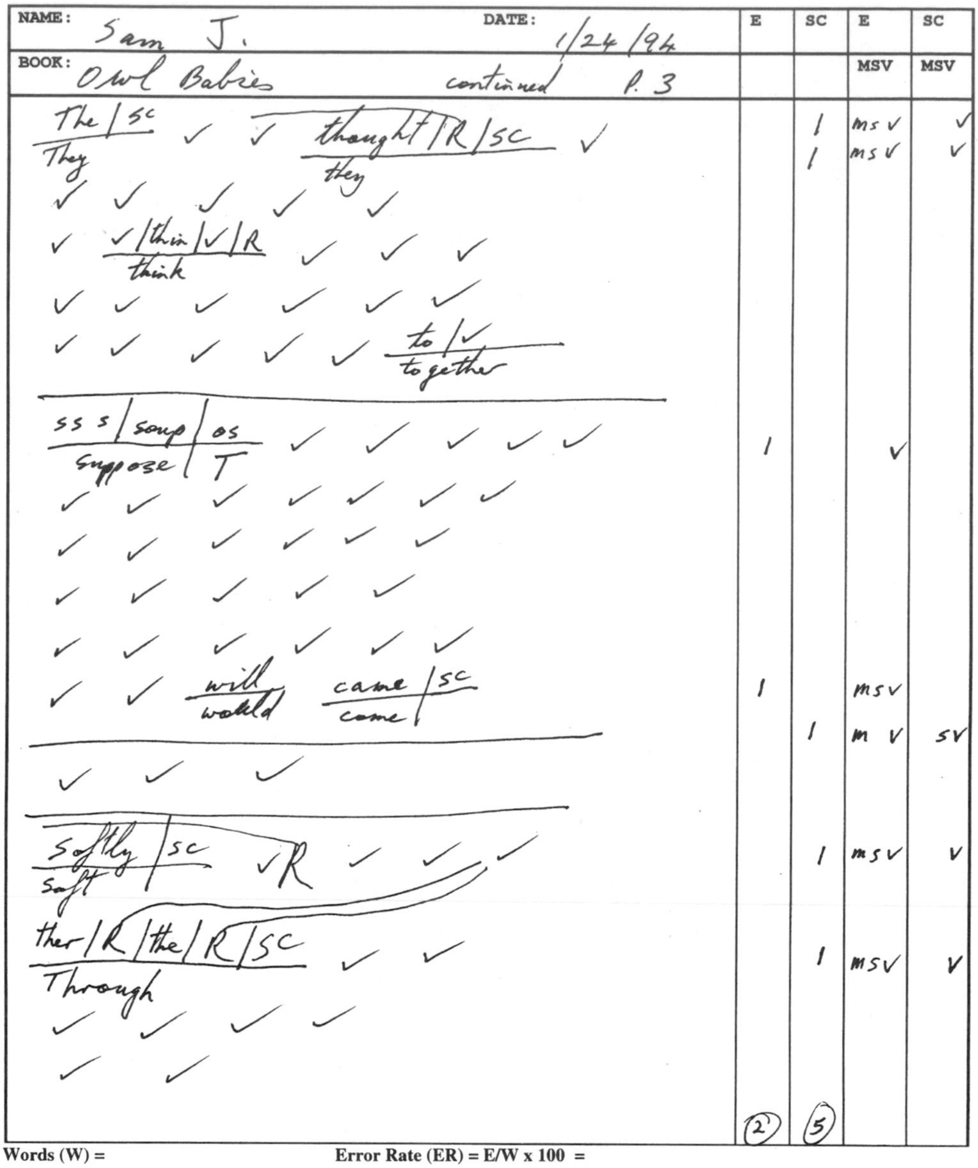

		E	SC	E	SC
NAME: Sam J.	**DATE:** 1/24/94			**MSV**	**MSV**
BOOK: Owl Babies	continued P. 3				

The form contains a handwritten running record with check marks and notations:

Line 1: The/sc ✓ ✓ thought/R/sc ✓ — E: 1, MSV: m s ✓ / SC: ✓
Line: They (they) — E: 1, MSV: m s ✓ / SC: ✓

✓ ✓ ✓ ✓ ✓
✓ ✓/thin/✓/R think ✓ ✓ ✓
✓ ✓ ✓ ✓ ✓ ✓
✓ ✓ ✓ ✓ ✓ to/✓ together

ss s/soup/os suppose/T ✓ ✓ ✓ ✓ ✓ — E: 1, SC: ✓
✓ ✓ ✓ ✓ ✓ ✓ ✓
✓ ✓ ✓ ✓ ✓ ✓
✓ ✓ ✓ ✓ ✓ ✓
✓ ✓ will/would came/sc come — E: 1, MSV: m s ✓
— SC: 1, m ✓ / s ✓

✓ ✓ ✓

Softly/sc Soft ✓R ✓ ✓ ✓ — E: 1, MSV: m s ✓ / SC: ✓

ther/R/the/R/sc Through ✓ ✓ — E: 1, MSV: m s ✓ / SC: ✓
✓ ✓ ✓

Totals: E: (2) SC: (5)

Words (W) =

Self-corrections (SC) =

Errors (E) =

Error Rate (ER) = E/W x 100 =

Accuracy = 100 - ER =

Self-correction rate = SC : SC + E =

or a girl? . . . He thinks he messed up, but it really looks good. Or maybe he thought that it looked good, but then first he thought that it looked bad and then he said, "Oh, I think it looks good." [Awareness of authorship—in this case that of the illustrator—and that authors are ordinary people who have feelings and evaluate their own work.]

SAM: Wait a minute, Dad! There's a problem. How can Bill get down to his Ivy? Baby owls can't fly.

ME: Maybe they hop.

NAME: Sam J.	DATE: 1/24/96	E	SC	E	SC
BOOK: Owl Babies	continued P.4			MSV	MSV

✓ ✓ all/R/sc ✓

I/sc ✓/R/th/R/✓ ✓ ✓ ✓ ✓ TA | 1
and they

— — — — — —

✓ ✓ ✓

✓ ✓ ✓ ✓

✓ ✓ ✓ ✓ ✓ p/b/APP/da/dankd/✓
danced

✓ ✓ jumped ✓ ✓ ✓ | 1 | | ms
bounced

✓ ✓ ✓

———————————

✓ ✓ ✓ ✓

✓ ✓ ✓ cried | 1 | | ms
asked

✓ ✓ ✓ ✓ ✓

✓ ✓ ✓ ✓

✓ ✓ ✓ ✓ ✓

✓ ✓ ✓ ✓ ✓

I/sc n/R/sc ✓ ✓ ✓ ✓ | | | 1 | ms | ✓
and I | | | 1 | ms | V

✓ ✓ ✓ ✓ ✓ ✓

③ ② | 3 | 2

Words (W) = 323   Error Rate (ER) = E/W x 100 = 3%
Self-corrections (SC) = 21   Accuracy = 100 - ER = 97%
Errors (E) = 10   Self-correction rate = SC : SC + E = 2:3
= 1:1·5

SAM: How can they hop? They would be scared . . . [Goes on to discuss how it would be possible to get from one point to another on the tree.] [This is a critical reading of the logic of the story as portrayed in the text and illustrations. Her analysis includes the physical probability and the emotional probability, and the consideration of alternative possibilities.]

SAM: I like how he said that. [Appreciation for author style and character development.]

SAM: Sarah always says stuff like that. [Reflecting, accurately or not, on character development.]

SAM: They'll do it one more time and that'll be three times they say that. In one of the first parts they said it, and they said it right here, and they're going to say it at the end. [Analyzing structure of the text.]

SAM: [Can't figure it out.] And that one doesn't give you any pictures. [Considering strategy options.]

SAM: She has pretty eyes.

SAM: I like Bill. Bill's plump. Plump. And Sarah is big. She's a big owl. I think that's Sarah. [Connecting text image to illustration.]

SAM: Is that a *B* or a *D*? [Awareness of the source of a problem.]

SAM: I didn't read that one . . . I just goed straight to "on their branch." [Analyzing her own error.]

Sam's comments help us to understand her understanding. If you want children to have such conversations, remember that they are most common:

- After multiple readings.
- In contexts that maintain reading as a social activity.
- When the texts being read are engaging, manageable, and relevant.
- When other people they know engage in commenting on what they read.

It shouldn't be too difficult to remember these conditions if you consider your own experiences as a reader.

Some Caveats

Running records are not perfect reflections of children's oral reading, let alone perfect reflections of their reading in general. However, they do provide some extremely useful data that can both document change and direct instruction. They provide indirect evidence of how children are going about understanding what they are reading. A number of studies have shown that particular patterns of errors are strongly related to other measures of understanding: cloze tests and retellings, both of which will be discussed in later chapters. Increases in self-correction alone, given a comparable error rate, suggest a greater degree of understanding. However, more consistent indicators of competence can be produced by adding together different oral reading behaviors (Sadoski and Lee 1986). In general, it is unnecessary to engage in mathematical exercises to show change, but studies do show a strong relationship between healthy patterns of oral reading behavior and other indicators of healthy reading.

When talking about change over time we can look at changes in readers' cue use and integration, range and flexibility of strategy use, persistence, fluency, book difficulty, expression, and confidence. Some of these are not recorded in the running record per se, but can be important annotations on the record. For example, fluency can range from fluent to finger-pointing (when children point with their finger at each word as they read) to voice-pointing (when children do not use their finger, but separate each word orally as if they were using their finger). Expression is also an area to consider, and is an indicator of the sense that the reader is making, as are comments made during and after the reading. Annotations describing the context are also important, both for understanding the particular reading and for comparing records over time. For example, a tenth reading is not the same as a first exposure to a book.

Running records have some bonuses. In my experience, when I begin to take running records, students generally want to know what I am doing. I explain what I am doing and that I will show them the record and explain it when they have finished reading. Students find this interesting, and it gets them thinking about their reading through the records. Also, it is easy with running records to highlight the positive. To begin with, you have a page of check marks with only a few other marks, with the check marks visual evidence of all the words the student read correctly. You can also highlight the value of the strategies the student used. Sharing the records with the student is important. Sometimes it leads them to record each other's reading, which provokes further discussion of the process.

When you are beginning to learn how to take and analyze running records, you will need to skip sections occasionally when you fall behind the reader. Just draw a double line and pick up again on the next page or paragraph. But every now and then it is O.K. to ask a student to stop for a moment while you catch up because you are just learning and she is reading so fast. This is good news for less competent readers—they are doing well and you are a novice. Very good for the confidence, this!

Some students in the beginning may be a bit anxious about the records, especially if they can hear you taking them. For example, if you use a pencil on a piece of paper on a wooden desk, it is often quite easy to hear the difference between a check mark and some other record. If a student is nervous and starts focusing on the sounds of your record rather than her inner monitor, self-monitoring goes out the window, replaced by the monitoring of your pencil. A student who is thus concerned can be helped if you discuss the records and share them, but you may also reduce the problem simply by substituting a ball-point pen on a pad of paper for the pencil and single sheet. Also, if you are right-handed, try to sit on the right-hand side of the student; otherwise the recording paper will be too close to the student and you may find yourself poking her in the eye with your elbow.

Remember, Appendix E contains further practice examples of running records to help you become more automatic in your recording.

*T*ELLING THINKING: EVALUATION THROUGH THINKING OUT LOUD

*I*f you have ever watched young children writing you will have noticed that they write with their mouths. Their hands are holding their pencils, but their mouths are doing all the work, exaggerating the sounds of their words so that they can know how to represent them on paper. In fact, if you prevent them from using their mouths by having them bite or hold their tongues, many of them have great difficulty writing (Clay 1991). Similarly, when reading "silently" young readers often make quite a racket.

Thinking out loud is common in the early stages of many kinds of learning, and early efforts at literacy are no exception. The Russian psychologist Lev Vygotsky (1962) pointed out that this talking out loud often reflects the conversations the child has had with others, as the social conversation becomes part of the child's use of language in thinking.

Thinking aloud diminishes as people get more able at the activity or as the task becomes easier. Our brains automate frequently used actions and we lose conscious access to them. However, thinking out loud does not simply go away as people get older. Indeed, when younger (and less verbal) students are asked to think aloud, they tend to produce less complete reports than older (and more verbal) students. Alexandr Sokolov's (1972) studies of inner speech show that when people are novices at a task, their processing is less automatic and more available in their working memory. Ake Edfeldt (1960) made three related observations from his work. First, more able readers engage in less silent speech than do less able readers. Second, less silent speech occurs when people read easy texts than hard texts. Third, the more the print in a piece of text is blurred, the more readers engage in silent speech. Thus, not just young children, but all of us, tend to read out loud, or at least subvocalize (activate the vocal chords without actually speaking), when the reading becomes difficult or when we are trying to spell a difficult word.

Try, for example, to read the following real but uncommon words, and watch yourself doing so: *resipiscence, internecine, onychophora.* For most people, the strategies they use to figure out these uncommon words will be available to them consciously, at least in part, unlike their reading of common words, such as *the, some,* and *happy.*

For assessment purposes, this externalized thinking is very helpful. It allows a window into the learner's mind, letting us glimpse, even if briefly and incompletely, how he or she is going about the task of reading and making sense of the language, and sometimes why. Thinking aloud has been studied at least since the turn of the century, when Edmund Huey (1908) and Karl Marbe (1901) explored its use in certain areas of psychology, including reading. Though its use in research has been sporadic, recently it has undergone a revival in the study of reading and writing (see Afflerbach 1990a, 1990b; Bereiter and Bird 1985).

Thinking aloud can occur accidentally, as an unconscious by-product of a difficult activity, or it can occur as a conscious attempt to make silent speech no longer silent. A classic example of unconscious thinking aloud occurs in oral reading. When a student makes several attempts at a word he or she is stuck on, it is reasonable to assume that the nature of these attempts actually reflects the kind of problem-solving being done. Similarly, when a student reads a piece of writing out loud and makes corrections and comments along the way, these are probably reasonable reflections of the thinking activity going on. Sometimes, then, asking students to think out loud can provide useful information about how they plan or write a piece, for example, or read a book.

Increasing the Quality of Think-Alouds

Just asking people to think out loud does not guarantee that the talk they produce has anything to do with their thinking. When people are worried about looking foolish they are not likely to make their unedited thinking public unless they are enormously self-confident. Students in such a situation are more likely to report what they think the teacher wants to hear rather than what actually occurred. Verbal reporting requires students to some extent to bare their minds, letting someone else be privy to their thought processes. When reading and writing are difficult, students may not feel secure enough to give an unadorned and unedited version of their thinking. For most people, having listeners to their thinking out loud requires a trusting, supportive context.

Getting people used to noticing how they do things makes them more able to report their thinking. In studies my colleagues and I have asked people to "watch themselves reading" whenever they can in the week preceding a think-aloud session. This is a habit of mind that can readily be developed in classrooms—taking one's own thinking as an object of study. The more people think out loud, or attend to their private speech, the more they are likely to be able to do it without thinking about it. That is, they become more able, and more likely, to take their own problem-solving strategies as an object of study with a view to improving them. This type of awareness has recently been called *metacognitive awareness*. As people become aware of the effective strategies they use they become more able to apply them in new and different situations.

There are many different ways of eliciting think-alouds. The basic principle is to have the student actually involved in doing whatever it is you are interested in learning about. People talking about what they *think* they do provide different information from when they think out loud *while actually doing the activity*. For example, I asked children how they choose the books they read and how they know whether the books are right for them. Several of the children from one teacher's class said they used "the five-finger rule" to determine suitability, which involved reading a page of the book and keeping track of the difficult words on their fingers. However, when they explained what they were thinking as they actually chose books, none of them actually used the five-finger rule. They used far more diverse and complex strategies.

When people think out loud, they occasionally fall silent as they become completely absorbed in the task and forget that they are supposed to be thinking out loud. Sometimes it is necessary to prompt them with "What are you doing now?" or even a cough or something to remind them of your presence. Some researchers have used red dots at the end of each sentence to prompt readers to say something. Nonverbal cues are often useful points for discussion. Smirks, frowns, changes in eye movements, and changes in reading rate can all relate to understandings or puzzlements. You might use prompts, such as:

- "You look puzzled. What's up?"
- "Did you just realize something?"
- "Wait a minute. I'm lost. How did you get from thinking about Chicago to thinking about potatoes?"
- "I think I got something wrong here. I wrote down ———, but I don't think that's quite what you said."

You must always make it clear that *you* are the one responsible for the misunderstanding. Once children understand that you often have this kind of problem, they will begin to explain things for you even before you ask them to do so. At the same time, they will begin to attend in more detail to how they are going about the things they are doing. This kind of evaluation pays dividends to all concerned.

Generally it helps if the child has confidence in his or her ability to read or write, so a history of successful reading will help the child continue through the more difficult reading material that produces more thinking out loud. You would do well to ensure that the student is comfortable and succeeds in reading at least at the start and end of a think-aloud collaboration. Sometimes when children cannot find the words to describe the strategies they used, they can be helped to do so by observing someone else, such as the teacher, modeling the same activity, though not necessarily the same way. Provided the situation is not threatening, children can often describe how their strategies differ from those that were demonstrated.

There is always some trade-off with prompting. It increases the quantity of reports but runs the risk of changing the way the learners engage in the activity. Furthermore, if they do not actually have access to what they were thinking, they may feel obliged to make up something, thus reducing the quality of the information they provide.

There are even more complicated techniques for prompting think-alouds such as Charles Fillmore's (1981) technique of blocking off part of the text and asking questions systematically. For example, the child opens the page and sees:

> Once upon a time xxxxxxxxxxxxxxxxxxxxxxxxxxxxx
> xxxxxxxxxxxxxxxxxxxxxxxxxxxxxxxxxxxxxxxxxxxxxxxx

or possibly:

> Dear Sir or Madam:
> xxxxxxxxxxxxxxxxxxxxxxxxxxxxxxxxxxxxxxxxxxxxxxxx

The child is then asked, "What can you tell me about this piece so far? . . . How do you know that?" then "What do you think we might see in the next part of the story? [Some of the text is then read.] Do you want to stick to your guess about . . .?"

Such complex techniques are useful only in rare situations. Judith Langer has used them effectively to study how children negotiate their way though reading tests (Langer 1987) The time and effort involved make such techniques impractical for classroom teachers and most others involved in educational settings. In addition, there are other reasons to be cautious of such techniques. The questioning involved in this type of think-aloud procedure produces an additional text for the student to "read": the dialogue of the activity itself. Furthermore, such techniques are very invasive and change drastically the nature of the activity the student is engaged in. For example, spreading a ten-minute story over half an hour does serious damage to the story. In the interests of learning how children comprehend, we may obliterate their understanding. Having the student read the story first, and then using the prompting as a stimulated recall ("What were you thinking when . . .") can help with this problem but introduces another, in that the talk concerns a *re*reading, not a first reading.

What We Get from Think-Alouds

Despite these cautions, much interesting information about how readers read and how writers write can be obtained from think-alouds. The extent that students monitor their understanding becomes evident, and their responses to their realizations become apparent. Readers report skipping ahead, rereading, rethinking the logic of an argument, changing their expectations about how much they expect to get out of the reading, picturing things in their minds, and many other strategies. They reveal their predictions about where the text is going and how they use such text features as signal words ("next," "first, . . . second . . .," "because," and so forth). They report feelings about authors and connections they make with other books, authors, and personal experiences as they read. Here is part of a think-aloud from an eleventh-grade student.

> I'm not quite sure of this reference . . . so I need to go back to . . . to where I remember seeing the sentence on academic requirements . . . I'm rereading that sentence . . . and it is the one . . . the reference . . . so it seems that the author is winding up his argument . . . for the importance of having academic standards for student athletes . . . and I expect that the final paragraph will restate the author's thesis and perhaps give a strong example to back it up . . . that's what I expect.

We can also gain access, through thinking out loud, to some of the difficulties readers experience in understanding the written word. For example, failure to use their own experience or lack of previous relevant experience will become apparent, as will overuse of their experience. Some readers expect a particular meaning and, in spite of the text, insist on clinging to that meaning. Readers often embellish and elaborate on the story they are reading. These elaborations (or lack of them) often become obvious in think-alouds and sometimes point to areas of difficulty in children's attempts to construct meaning from print. As a consequence of think-aloud reading and writing, both students and teachers tend to focus more on the processes of reading and writing than they had previously, a consequence that has many advantages.

Writers can also provide helpful information about their writing process through thinking aloud (Flower and Hayes 1981, 1983). They can provide reasons for their choice of words, punctuation, topics, style, plot, character, and the like, and can discuss various other decisions they make along the way. Also revealed in the think-alouds of writers are their assumptions about audiences and about the goals of the writing activity.

Not only can readers' and writers' strategies become accessible, but also their attributions for the apparent success or failure of their performance can be revealed. For example, you might hear such statements as "I'm losing it—shouldn't have partied so late last night." or "I knew it. I knew I'd screw it up—Idiot." Students also often engage in self-instructions, at least more able readers and writers do ("No—wait—slow down. You're rushing this and losing it. Start over"). Most students also engage in self-congratulation and accusation, cheering themselves on or criticizing themselves mercilessly ("All right, now we're getting somewhere. O.K., we know where that fits" or "Damn—you always do that, you fool"). Students can be helped to become more inclined to cheer themselves on, as more successful students do, and within that context become more constructively analytical. Remember, though, that students' inner conversations are transformed reflections of the conversations they have had with others.

Remember, too, that some of the decisions, strategies, and judgments students make as they read and write are not made consciously and so will not appear in their think-alouds. Sometimes these decisions, strategies, and judgments are erroneous, inefficient, or based on incorrect knowledge or assumptions. Knowing the source of the problem is instructionally useful. Often, simply raising a problem to consciousness is sufficient to allow the student to see that it needs to be solved. Students must first become aware of a problem before they can solve it. Indeed, problem strategies that have become automatic generally must first be brought to consciousness in order to be changed.

Pat Edmiston (1990) has been using an interesting technique to help children externalize their reading processes. After a student has read a book, he then draws pictures of the characters in the book and himself and cuts them out. Next he rereads the book, paragraph by paragraph, moving the figures around as if in a play. But there is also a figure for the reader, who can move in and out of the performance as either a spectator or a participant. If the reader becomes one of the players in the story, the two cutout figures are attached to each other. This technique thus offers the possibility of understanding point of view and involvement in reading, and in general offers considerable promise for teachers' understanding children's reading and for children's becoming more reflective about their own reading. I have found this both informative and instructionally powerful, even when used in the initial reading.

For Teaching Too

Aspects of teaching, too, are accessible through thinking out loud. For example, when you are grading papers or writing report cards, you can think out loud into a tape recorder and go back later to try to understand that particular evaluation process. This kind of review can have a profound effect on one's teaching practice. I sometimes find that just turning on the tape recorder and thinking out loud make me so aware of the process that I do not always need to go back and listen to the tape. The activity itself has made me sufficiently reflective that I have already learned enough to make some useful change.

Many of us do not think of what we do when we ourselves write—what it is for us to be readers and writers. Just as children do not think about the language they use as an object worthy of study, teachers often do not take their roles as readers, writers, editors, and researchers as objects of study. Thus these activities remain unanalyzed and it is harder for them to help children figure out difficulties they might have, or to do so in an empathic manner. This is why it is useful for teachers themselves to think aloud while reading and writing. It makes them aware of the strategies they themselves use, and hence makes them more aware of writing and reading as strategic, constructive activities. It also helps teachers to think of their instruction in different terms. For example, when engaging in a think-aloud about a particular reading, you will find it easier to manage if the text is not very easy for you to read, or if the goal of the reading is novel to you. To examine the possibilities for the think-aloud approach to learning about reading and writing, try thinking out loud into a tape recorder while reading a book, particularly a difficult one, and try thinking out loud while trying to write a letter, research paper, report card, or whatever.

Think-alouds also provide excellent grounds for discussion among school faculty. For example, some middle-school faculty studying student think-alouds together with some upper elementary school faculty would provide excellent grounds for discussion of goals and instructional techniques. Such a collaborative activity would be rewarding for college and high school teachers as well, since it would help them think more clearly about the nature of the academic community and its expectations. These efforts seem desperately needed given analyses done by Linda Flower of the confusion of university freshmen as they make a transition from one discourse community to another (Flower 1989). Such efforts would help high school and college teachers line up their instructional and evaluative practices and expectations.

QUESTIONING, CLOZES, RETELLING, AND TRANSLATING

*L*ouise Rosenblatt (1978) distinguishes two types of reading, aesthetic and efferent. *Aesthetic reading* is the kind of reading you do when you read a novel for pleasure; it is done for the feeling you get while you are reading it. *Efferent reading* is done to learn—to remember what you read (the word *efferent* is from the Latin *effere*, meaning "to carry away from"). Both types of reading are worthwhile activities that literate adults engage in. Unfortunately, schooling discourages many students from aesthetic reading by ignoring it or by forcing students into only efferent reading by making them answer recall questions about the novels and short stories they read. It is not that literate people, having read a text aesthetically, do not remember what they have read, and talk about it with other literate people. Rather, their reading of the book focused on their emotional involvement first. In efferent reading the reader's focus is on the content of the text. In both types of reading one may ask questions about what the reader remembers. Literate people do that. However, with efferent reading *the reader* expects to remember particular things about the text and might be concerned if he or she didn't, whereas in aesthetic reading, recall of the text is incidental. The two kinds of reading are not restricted to particular kinds of texts. For example, I often read aesthetically theoretical papers, cookbooks, and other texts written as exposition, not as narrative.

How can we as teachers evaluate a student's understanding of a text so that we might be instructionally helpful? In order to evaluate a child's understanding of a text, we need some sort of response from the child. The kinds of possible responses are many, and most have been used as evaluation by someone at some point. Tests have had students respond to both "open" and multiple-choice (including true-false) questions, provide verbatim and free recall, summarize, restore deleted words, reorder pictures, draw pictures, and select pictures (Moore 1983;

Readence and Moore 1983). Each of these responses tells us something different, and each is influenced by performance factors, such as writing or artistic skill.

Every response is also a response to something, and we can never be sure of what that something is. The student may have read a book, and we might think that the book prompts the response. But the response is to a social situation, which includes the book but might not feature the child's understanding of it. For example, the student might suspect that the situation calls for guessing the evaluator's interpretation of the book. Any response is to a perceived audience, and we do not know how the person being tested perceives that audience. For all these reasons, we can never be certain about what information we are getting from different responses.

There is always the problem of the frame of reference for the interpretation of the text. A child might understand the text on his or her own terms, yet we judge the interpretation within the context of our own frame of reference. The same book can mean different things to different people. Robert Munsch's book *Love You Forever* tends to be accepted by young children as a melodic, cyclical story that appeals to their desire for predictability. Older children appreciate the book as a comedy. Many adults cry uncontrollably over it; other adults are left unmoved. Even writers change over time in their interpretation of what they have written. Our job as teachers is to understand children's understanding rather than to measure it. The question is not "How much did she understand it?" but "How did she experience it?" Note that the *how* in the latter question can—and, I believe, should—be interpreted as "How was it accomplished?" and "What is the nature of the outcome?" I mean it in both senses.

Questioning (Again!)

When we are trying to determine how children understand what they read, we often use questions. Legitimate questions can result in our gaining insight into children's understandings and at the same time help them to view themselves as more fully literate. In Chapters 17 through 20 I described some of the types of questions and contexts for questioning that are likely to be productive. Unfortunately, these are not generally the kinds of questions that have been asked in schools. The more frequent types of questions have been described by Dolores Durkin (1978–79), Frank Guszak (1967), and others, and a quick review of a basal reader or a standardized test will provide plenty of examples. The questions generally elicit information the teacher already knows, and they do not foster dialogue. In other words, too often we have asked questions that would not be part of normal social interactions between literate people, and that address not *how* children understand, but *whether* they understand the text the way we think they should. The questions call not for reflection, but correction. Furthermore, they are often extraordinarily numerous. In one basal reader I counted one question for every seventeen words in the story the children were to read (and that wasn't even the part called the "test"). Such questioning techniques run the risk of being destructive. Rather like medical experiments in which the rat must be killed in order to find out what physiological changes it has undergone, children's interest and natural curiosity must be slaughtered to find out how much they understood the text. Asking questions to which the asker already knows the answer can be done without these consequences if all parties clearly understand that recalling information in the particular text is important and that the intention is to help the students develop a review strategy. In other words, this technique can be justified when the agreed-upon reason for reading the text is efferent. In addition, if the situation is not competitive, problems are less likely to arise.

Questions are commonly classified in ways that are presumed to indicate underlying differences in the mental processes being tapped by the questions. A common distinction is that between *literal* and *inferential* questions. For example, consider the following text and questions:

> The camping trip did not turn out as John had planned. The trip to
> the mountains that Friday was not bad, and they set up the tent easily.
> But on that first night the rain was so hard that the tent pegs pulled
> out of the soft earth. It didn't get better. In the morning the wind
> came up, and he and Bill sat shivering in their damp clothes trying to
> hold up the tent. To make matters worse, their matches had not
> survived the night, and they could not light a fire. They had plenty of
> food, but most of it needed to be cooked. They were cold, tired, and
> hungry. At about two o'clock they began to face the facts. If they
> stayed another night, they might not be alive in the morning. If they
> went home, how would they feel? They had boasted about this trip for
> weeks and even called Steve a chicken for not coming.

> 1. On which night did it rain hard?
> 2. Why could the campers not light a fire?
> 3. How would they feel if they went home?

The first question would generally be classified as literal, meaning that the answer is "right there in the text" (Raphael 1986), even in the same sentence as the words of the question (this is not actually true, but we shall return to that matter presently). The second and third questions would be classified as inferential, meaning that an inference must be made from information provided in the text in order to answer them. This classification implies that students reading and responding to the three questions will perform a predictably different mental process in answering question 1 than they will in answering questions 2 and 3. The assumption is that an inference must be made to answer the latter questions and is not needed to answer the former. But inferences must *always* be made. We cannot escape them. Even the most bluntly "literal" question requires inferences to be made about the type of response expected, how the language is being used, why the question is being asked, and so forth.

David Pearson and Dale Johnson (1978) propose an alternative classification system, which takes into account both the question and the response given to it. For example, they propose that responses A and B to question 1 are both correct, but involve a different mental process.

1. On which night did it rain hard?
   A. On the first night of their trip.
   B. On the Friday night.

The combination of question 1 and response A is classified as *text explicit,* meaning that the question and response are both explicit in the same part of the text. The combination of question 1 and response B is classified as *text implicit* because the reader had to put together different pieces of information from across parts of the text. When a reader uses information from outside the text to answer the question, that combination is termed *scriptally implicit,* meaning that information from the reader's general knowledge, or "script," about the particular topic has been used.

It has also been popular to talk about "higher-level questions"; many references to these can be found in the professional literature. The problem is, what counts as higher level for whom, and under which circumstances? Take, for example, a supposedly literal question about a particularly small detail in a story. Such a question can be very hard to answer when the text is unavailable to refer to, but easy enough if the text can be referred back to. In some types of texts, these small details are nonessential but in other types, detective novels, for example, these details are important and potentially "higher level." Children who have been read to a great deal or who have been told many stories will develop a good sense of the structure of stories; for children such as this, inferential questions may be easier to answer than literal questions about details that are not central to the plot. A child whose Sunday revolves around going to church will not need the word *Sunday* mentioned in the text to make the question "On which day every week did the family go to church?" a lower-level question. The same question might be categorized as higher order if the child knows virtually no one who goes to church on Sunday.

In short, what counts as higher- and lower-level questions depends a great deal on what you know, what you are used to, how you conceive of the question, and under what conditions you are answering. A classic example of this is shown in the following anecdote about the great mathematician J. von Neumann (Ceci and McNellis 1987). Von Neumann was asked by one of his friends the following question:

> There are two cyclists a mile apart, cycling toward each other, each going at 10 miles per hour. A fly flies from the nose of one cyclist to the nose of the other, backwards and forwards between them, until the cyclists meet. The fly flies at 15 miles per hour. How far has the fly flown when it gets squashed by the cyclists' noses meeting?

Von Neumann is reported to have thought for several minutes before answering the question. In order to answer, he computed the distance that the fly traveled as the limit of a mathematical series. He did this mentally, which is a stunning feat well beyond the capabilities of even the most accomplished mathematicians. Had he conceived of the problem differently, all he needed to do was to calculate how long it would take the two cyclists' noses to meet traveling a mile toward each other at ten miles an hour; or, how long does it take a cyclist traveling ten miles an hour to cover half a mile (half the distance)? The answer is three minutes. In three minutes, or 3/60ths of an hour, traveling at 15 miles per hour, the fly would travel three quarters of a mile. Was the question a higher-level one or a lower-level one? It depends on what one knows and how one goes about answering it.

Questions are currently the main means of attempting to evaluate children's reading comprehension. Many different classifications of questions have been attempted, and it is possible that asking such questions is helpful. In general, though, it is probably more helpful simply to ask the reader how he or she went about reading the text and what the experience was like; at the least, it certainly seems less risky than to ask questions without knowing how the reader is going to understand what the question means. Asking questions in various classifications may be of some use, but the questions should be considered within the social context of which they are part. This context includes the text and the reading of it, but also includes the relationship between teacher and student, the nature of the question, and the background of the student. Often children will tell you more if you actually tell them something about your own experience than if you ask them for information.

Cloze

Cloze is a commonly used procedure for assessing comprehension. The technique is derived from Gestalt psychology, and involves the ability to complete incomplete wholes (ideas, images, sentences, and so forth). For example:

> Once upon a ———— there was a little ———— called David who had
> ———— pet dog. David loved his dog ———— than anything in the
> ————.

A person who is making sense out of mutilated text such as this is performing many of the processes used by a person reading a complete text. It is perhaps similar to reading text containing a number of difficult words. Still, reading a cloze passage is not the same as reading a normal text and thus, like all other means of studying the sense readers make of text, it is limited. The best way to use the cloze procedure is to have children talk about the reading as they go along. This commentary provides information on how they arrive at their responses, which is, after all, what we need to know in order to provide instructional support. Unfortunately, cloze procedure is seldom used this way. The most common use is in standardized tests, in tests designed to prepare children for such tests, in basal end-of-unit tests and workbooks, and perhaps in certain kinds of detective work in which some of the words in a letter have been deleted. Actually, if we were to use cloze techniques in the context of reader commentary, we might as well use unmutilated text in the first place.

Cloze activities can take a variety of forms. There can be letters missing from words (for example, r_ma_n_ng), there can be blanks of various lengths, and there can be possible responses for the reader to choose among. The difficulty of the task can be controlled somewhat by controlling the difficulty of the alternatives. For example:

Jack and Jill went up the _____.
(a) car		(a) hell
(b) at	or	(b) rope
(c) in		(c) house
(d) hill		(d) hilt

When a cloze procedure is used as a test without providing response options, usually the only correct response is the precise word used in the original text. For example, take the sentence

Their car was now rolling down the hill and the brakes appeared useless. They were terrified of what was about to _____.

If you wrote "unfold" you were correct. Increase your score by one point and your percentile rank by five. If you wrote "happen" or "occur" or "ensue," go directly to jail, do not pass go, and do not collect $200. Exact replacement is required simply in order to obtain agreement among scorers, rather than from a belief that synonyms are an inaccurate or unreasonable response. In other words, if we allowed "explode" or "appear," some scorers would mark it correct and others would not. Enough of these scoring problems and pretty soon different scorers would get quite different scores for the same student. We can't have that. What would the scores mean?

Researchers have debated whether the cloze procedure can provide information about a reader's understanding of anything more than a single sentence at a time (McKenna and Layton, 1990; Shanahan, Kamil, and Tobin 1982). Some claim that by careful selection of the words to be deleted, the procedure can require students to know the whole meaning of the text (assuming that only a single meaning can be acceptable). Of course, in order to feel a need to engage in these arguments you have to feel that it is necessary to obtain some numerical indicator of a child's "ability to comprehend." If you do not feel such a need, then the cloze procedure simply remains a useful instructional technique for helping some children to attend more to the use of context to figure out unknown words.

Retelling

One common comprehension assessment practice for some time now has been to ask children to retell what they have read. Various reading tests have required written reproductions of text since around 1914, when testing was really getting under way in this country. Some currently popular individual oral reading evaluations still require a child who has just read a story out loud to a teacher (or evaluator) to retell it to the very person who just listened to it being read aloud. This practice has always seemed odd to me. It is certainly an unusual social situation. It is like two people coming out of a movie theater and one turning to the other and asking her to give an oral rendition of the movie they both just saw. This might be a reasonable request if the person asking for the retelling had slept through the movie, or had been involved in intense romantic activities and needed to be able to give a coherent story to inquiring parents, but otherwise it would most likely be thought of as odd.

More and less capable readers retell stories differently. As Connie Bridge and her colleagues (Bridge, Ciera, and Tierney 1978–79) discovered, more able readers are likely to retell the whole story in sequence, whereas less able readers give a fairly truncated version of the story and nearly half of what they do tell has to be dragged out of them with questions. There are several ways to interpret this finding. We could argue that less able readers are less able to attend to the coherence of the plot, or that they are unable to organize oral responses well, or several other possible causal arguments. My interpretation is that more able readers tend to interpret the retelling situation as the test situation it is and thus give the kind of retelling that is appropriate to such a situation. These readers are more likely to come from middle-class homes (as are their teachers) in which known-answer questions are routinely asked as part of their socialization into literacy (Heath 1983). The less successful readers, not sharing the same socialization, tend to interpret the retelling as a normal social situation and give a socially appropriate (less redundant) response to an audience who they know just heard the story. (Alternatively, they may talk about the most interesting or memorable event or character.) These students are also less likely to have been read many stories and are thus less likely to be familiar with the more common story structure in Anglo-American culture. Also, different cultures have different kinds of predictable structures to their stories, so students may be more or less prepared for the kind of stories they read in school. Students who do not do well on the retelling may simply be shy in performance situations. It is also possible that some readers in some situations interpret the request to retell as an attempt at control (see Chapters 18 and 19), since it is clearly not an honest request for information, and may simply refuse to acquiesce such control.

However, as I have suggested, there are situations in which retellings do make sense. For example, it makes sense for a person who has read a book to explain it to a person who has not, and to explain it in some detail and in sequence. Indeed, if you have not read a book that a child has read, you will likely find that they youngster is happy to regale you with considerable detail. When a child can tell a teacher about a book he has read and the teacher has not, the child has the luxury of being the expert and the teacher the novice. The teacher gets to ask (and model) legitimate questions about the book that would otherwise quite blatantly be controlling questions. If a teacher cannot determine from such a retelling how a child understood the story (this is rare), the teacher can decide to read the story on the basis of the child's recommendation. This allows some closer evaluation of the child's understanding, but at the same time provides the possibility of subsequent dialogue and possible legitimate rereading as part of the dialogue. This scenario also compliments the student who was able to influence the teacher's reading, reflecting a level of trust and respect, along with the possibility of sustained intellectual engagement.

There is another socially appropriate retelling situation that can be useful for getting information. Storytelling in the oral tradition is a kind of retelling that is perfectly legitimate and has other social functions at the same time. In many cultures storytelling has been, and is, a means of handing down culture and learning, as well as a form of entertainment. However, there is a difference between the oral tradition and the text tradition. One of the advantages of text is that it is, at least on the surface, linguistically (if not interpretively) the same each time. Indeed, children learn this quite early and will correct adults who misread their favorite stories. In the oral tradition, by contrast, personalization and transformation of the story are expected in the process of retelling. There are two points at which these traditions overlap. In oral cultures, certain ritualized stories are repeated in absolute detail (Chafe 1982). These usually occur in formal situations. In addition, some written stories were originally traditional oral stories. For example, there are many written versions of "The Three Little Pigs," "The Teeny Tiny Woman," "In the Dark Dark Woods," and other such classic stories. Children who have examined such books can come to understand how they can vary, and written retellings of stories can be done within this context, so that a cumulative record of students' retellings can be made over time. Something like this view of retellings is used by Hazel Brown and Brian Cambourne (1989) in their book *Read and Retell,* which provides numerous examples of children's written retellings and the changes therein. Actually, "the folk process" easily extends to the use of the same plot with different characters; and even when there is only one version of a modern story—for example, Tomie de Paola's *Now One Foot, Now the Other*—children can transfer it to the oral tradition, making it their own, by changing some of the characters, details of the plot, and so forth. In the process students will not only demonstrate their learning, but will also develop new talents.

Oral retellings need not be restricted to stories. They can also be used with expository text that is part of students' efferent reading. An interesting example of this can be seen in a cooperative studying procedure described by Donald Dansereau (1987). Students pair off and divide their reading assignment in half, with each student responsible for retelling his or her portion of the reading to the partner. They then switch and read the other part. In the process of preparing for the retelling, they are likely to find that they cannot retell, which signals a need to return to the text. At the same time, one student's retelling to the other student prepares the listener for his or her own reading of the text and leaves open the possibility of the partners discovering discrepancies between their versions.

Retellings done routinely in useful contexts can help children take greater control of the schematic structures of stories. Thus, the texts chosen for retellings can be selected from diverse genres so that children can explore types of texts and their functions with which they might otherwise not become comfortable. Biographies, fables, mysteries, exposition, essays, all can be used in some way in retelling. At the same time, these activities provide students with a self-checking of their own learning. In other words, they can help develop self-evaluation.

Translating

Translating texts into a variety of different modes and media can also be used to help us get a sense of children's understandings of particular texts. For example, arranging pictures to represent the story and then talking about the arrangement is useful but requires that there be appropriate pictures available or that the teacher be a reasonably good artist. Perhaps a more fruitful activity is for children to dramatize stories as moviemakers do when they make a book into a movie. Dramatizations can be done with others and acted out, or alone with small props. Pat Edmiston (1990) cut out shapes and colors to represent aspects of the book and the children's reading of it. After first reading the story, students made some small paper figures to represent their favorite character, themselves as reader, and any other props they needed to portray the story. Some provided a setting, some made images to represent the ideas "I like to read," "I don't like to read," "Remembering things," "I'm in the book," and "I have feelings." While rereading the text, these readers moved the pieces around, paragraph by paragraph, to represent the story, their involvement in the action, their stance, and aspects of their reading process. Some of the students became involved in role-playing ("If I were him I would . . ."), and some would compose dialogue and thoughts for the characters ("She's thinking 'Boy, he's a nerd'"). This approach at once gives an indication of how the story is being understood, and at the same time suggests some of the processes involved.

The advantages of dramatization are that the process of evaluating prompts a reflectiveness about the reading process on the part of the student, thus developing self-evaluation. The down side of such a procedure is that it disrupts the normal reading process and takes a substantial amount of time. It does not seem like something one would do often, since the time it takes would drastically cut down the amount of text students would have time to read. Still, it offers the possibility of intensive and instructional discussion in and about the process of reading. Indeed, children can study the process of translation through the writings of authors whose works have been dramatized, such as Patricia MacLachlan's revision of *Sarah, Plain and Tall* for television (MacLachlan 1990). The strategy is well worth exploring for its instructional and evaluative properties, especially for students who appear to be having some difficulty with understanding.

Translating stories into different media can be helpful. Indeed, young children commonly draw a picture first, then write a story about the picture. The picture helps them maintain coherence in the story as they struggle with phonetic representations of words. Visual representations can include paintings, collage, montage, charts, graphs, time lines, outlines, flowcharts, and the like. These are simply different symbolic representations of the concepts represented by print. For example, Linda Rief's (1992) students' collaborative art projects, which they undertook to represent books they had read, were discussed in Chapter 10.

Educators and psychologists have disagreed about the usefulness of these various measures for a long time. The arguments against them focus on the notion that they confuse the things being measured. When a child does a bad job of a written retelling, for example, you can't tell whether it was because of inadequate writing ability or because of inadequate comprehension. In general, these arguments are made by people involved in constructing standardized diagnostic tests to identify subskill deficits and who don't want their deficits muddled. Such tests cannot allow interviews, or information on normal writing performance in the classroom, as part of the evaluative procedure, as they would ruin the standardization aspect of tests. They can't allow writing either, because it would both make scoring difficult and "confound" reading with writing. Confounding of reading with writing ability may be less of a problem in classrooms in which children regularly write about their reading. It is also less of a problem if we concentrate on students' being literate rather than specifically how well they read or write. If students spent equal time reading, writing, and exploring artistic expression and interpretation, and each pursuit was valued as much as another, I doubt that this entanglement would be seen as such a problem in assessment situations. We should encourage students to see the various symbol systems as having the same aims: to understand the world and construct representations of it. In a way it is a matter of being multirepresentational (which is like being multilingual, but *lingual* refers only to verbal language). The instructionally interesting information is centered on the process of making meaning and representing it symbolically.

The making of meaning from someone else's representation has been termed "comprehension," but people forget that comprehension is something humans *do*, not something they *have*. They also forget that human beings are *always* interpreting representations. The human eye does not simply make an actual world in the human mind. It *represents* the world electrochemically, and the brain takes these representations and constructs yet another representation. The ear, too, translates a mechanical representation into an electrochemical representation from which the mind, in turn, constructs another representation. Each time we try to represent a mental representation or intention in speech, it comes out differently.

We could construe a good deal of children's literate activity as translation. We could, for example, think about the activity of transforming sound into print in this way. Dictation is a form of translation. Indeed, moving from any symbolic system to a different form of representation may be viewed as a translation. Following instructions (translating print into action) can provide a good demonstration of understanding in a socially appropriate context. Not long ago, I was asked to evaluate a student who was about to start school and had been labeled "speech delayed." She was nonetheless reading quite well before going into kindergarten. The question I was to answer was "Does she understand what she reads?" Her expressive language was not particularly well developed, but when she was presented with simple directions in print (for example, "Put the doll on the table") or sequences of such directions to follow, she was able to perform as the directions required. Still, this evidence of her language competence did not prevent her from being classified as learning disabled and her being placed (counterproductively) in a class of children who were classified as speech delayed. Because speech and language are developed through interactions with other, more competent users, these children would be better placed in classrooms where they would routinely interact with more competent peers.

OBSERVATION RECORDS AND CHECKLISTS

I am a list maker. I make lists of things I need to do over the long term, and I often make daily lists of things I want to accomplish. That way I don't let important things slip by, and by organizing my list I can fit things together in the most efficient sort of way (not that I always accomplish this, but it's a start). There is also something satisfying about crossing off the things that I finish. Sometimes, when it seems that I am accomplishing nothing, I can see from looking at a list that I have in fact managed to make some progress. Even young children like to take inventory of such things as what they know or what they have read. It gives them a sense of competence and externalizes their expertise. When children keep track of their own developing writing skills they at once can admire and be admired for their knowledge, and be more consistent and responsible in its use.

Within the literacy folders they maintain, students can list things they contemplate working on. Such lists are useful for the students in their writing and incidentally provide information on the students' interests and the diversity of topics they contemplate. Special topics, the ones on which the student would like to become particularly expert, might be underlined in color or kept on a separate list. These topics might involve some form of ongoing research. Some students use a prompting format for listing their writing topics: places I have been, things I have done, things I would like to know more about, interesting people, people I would like to interview, word play, memorable moments, and so forth. These prompts might be kept on the classroom wall instead of in the folder, leaving the possibility of greater diversity in the folder. Indeed, the list on the wall can grow as the class discusses different books and how authors got their ideas for those books.

It is easy to see the appeal of lists; easy, too, to see how checklists might be a way of keeping track of children's learning—taking inventory to prevent oversights and to remind ourselves (and others) that we are accomplishing something. A checklist provides a framework for the answers to various yes-or-no questions, such as "Did you get butter?" "Did you get coffee?" or "Can Mary write her name?" "Does Mary understand the concept of 'word' in print?" Checklists can be very helpful for automating repetitive procedures, for taking the burden off human memory, and for freeing us from constant worry. Pilots of commercial airplanes have a safety checklist that they run through before they take off—and I am glad they do. People who go camping regularly have a checklist to make sure that they don't arrive in the wilderness with no matches or water, and to ensure that their trip is not spoiled by constant worrying about whether or not they turned off the gas before they left. For a teacher to keep track of classroom routines, and to ensure that some students' development is not overlooked, checklists can be helpful.

However, checklists have their limitations. For example, few campers would use a checklist to summarize their experience of camping. Checklists require that everything be reduced to a yes-or-no format; this is easier with some things than with others. For example, we might ask whether or not a child edits his or her work, but it would be more interesting to know *how* a student goes about doing it. In the end, students must continue to develop their editing skill, they never get to just cross it off their list, though they might be able to cross it off their list of "things to do with this paper." Also, not everything can be put on a checklist. One has to select items, otherwise the list gets too long to be manageable. Do we list every letter of the alphabet, every kind of connection children might make with a book, every kind of strategy they might use? Probably not. We will make selections depending on our purpose, what we value, and our theory of literacy learning. Of course, as we select items we run the risk of neglecting important items not on the list. Remember, things that cannot be reduced to a yes-or-no answer will be systematically excluded. Also, checklists are by nature rather cryptic. They often reflect assumptions about what the person reading the checklist already knows. For example, a pilot might have an item on his or her checklist that says, simply, "ailerons." This assumes that the person reading the list knows what an aileron is, how it is tested, what it will look like when the test is successful (or not), and possibly what to do if the test fails.

When teachers use checklists as part of their reporting to parents or to each other, there is some likelihood of miscommunication. Stripped of the richer context the classroom teacher has available, misinterpretation is common. This problem can be exaggerated when people are short of time because they tend to simply scan the list, looking for missing check marks, for abnormalities or negatives, and tend to skip over the things that the child *can* do. This makes it likely that they will form a negative impression of those students who most need to be viewed positively. The more stress those reviewing the list are under and the higher the stakes, the more this will happen.

Checklists and Communication

When checklists are used for self-checking, they can be very helpful. They can help us overcome the frailties of our memory and our constantly shifting focus of attention in opportunistic teaching. However, when more than one person is to use the same checklist, those people must share some common assumptions and interpretations—they must be part of the same conversation. The best way to make this happen is to have the checklist constructed collaboratively by the people who will use it. Constructing checklists produces useful discussions. When a group of teachers (and parents and administrators) get together to come up with a workable list, they have to deal with the following facts:

- The possible list can be extremely long.
- A workable list must be reasonably brief.
- Everyone will have different priorities among the items listed.
- Items are not necessarily of the same order. For example, "recognizes letter *A*" is very different from "enjoys reading."

The production of a working checklist is thus likely to produce lively discussion about constructs, categories, and values. It encourages some important theorizing about literacy and learning. In fact, having negotiated to the point of agreement on the final form of the checklist, the participants could almost throw the checklist away. The process of negotiation will have caused them to internalize the checklist and, at the same time, will have helped each participant develop his or her view of literacy and learning. Although the checklist will still be a shorthand version of complex ideas, the participants in the discussion will at least be part of the same conversation. If the checklist is always viewed as a working draft, the conversations are likely to be returned to, thus further reducing the danger of misinterpretation. But in the end, no checklist will suit everyone. As teachers transform their knowledge, they come to view children in different ways, and they need to be able to change the structure of their record-keeping too.

Beyond Yes and No

The checklist is the most reductive form of record-keeping because it is dichotomous: check or no check. This problem is easy to overcome, though. For example, we can move from the "got it/ain't got it" or "did it/didn't do it" kind of entry to a notation of dates rather than check marks to show when a behavior was observed. Dates provide more information than simple check marks, can show whether development is taking place, and can suggest the need for closer observation. Similarly, codes can be used to represent the nature of the event being recorded. Nancie Atwell (1987) describes a procedure she uses to keep track of students' progress. At the beginning of each class she conducts a "status-of-the-class" conference in which she calls each student's name and the students each respond with what they will be working on that day. For example, Bill might be working on the third draft of a poem about dirt bikes. JoBeth might be planning to work on a draft of a letter to the editor of the local newspaper. Samantha might be going to have a conference with herself about her short story, "Pimples." Atwell devised simple abbreviations for the possible things the students could be doing including drafts ("D1," "D2," etc.), self-editing, conferring with self, revising, re-writing for final copy, and conferring with the teacher with a focus on editing ("ed. con.") or content ("response"). She also codes when a person is scheduled for sharing a piece with the group. The recording sheet is simply a chart with the students' names down the side and five columns, one for each day of the week.

This kind of approach helps the students set their own goals and results in a verbal contract with the teacher. It helps develop students' commitment, focus, and planning. Rather than starting something and hopping around to other things, students are inclined to persist in solving the problems they need to solve. At the same time, it allows at-a-glance checking of students' progress and balance. For example, it will be easy for the teacher to spot a student who never gets a piece to the point of editing, or who simply produces first drafts, or who writes only fantasy stories. In addition, because of the predictability of the status-of-the-class conference, students prepare in advance in order to be able to respond; thus, they start the class ready to begin.

Students can also keep a list entitled "Skills I can use in writing" on the inside cover of their journal. This works especially well if children are encouraged to reflect on their writing and on their folders so that they become able to notice differences in the ways they go about their writing. An extra benefit is that when it comes to reporting to parents, children are able to describe the state of their learning. Similarly, students can keep track of their reading in a simple reading log, set up with the following headings:

| Book title | Date started (S), finished (F), quit (Q) | Easy (E) or challenging (C) |

A list like this might be made more elaborate, showing the author's name and perhaps the genre of the text. These additions would draw children's attention to the range of their reading, or at least provide data for analysis of their reading. The list could also include space for brief comments or observations about the book—reminders for discussion. Even unadorned book lists provide history and the possibility for discussion. However, there are two major cautions with such lists. How long the list is should not become a preoccupation, and the lists should never be made public. An interesting phenomenon takes place when the number of books read becomes the focus of public attention. Our baby-sitter once asked me to sign up for a "readathon" our school district was having. The more books read, the more money would be made for the school or charity. I asked Jenny what she was going to read. Her response? "A lot of short books."

A checklist can be designed with space for topics down the side and checkpoints across the top for planning, writing the lead, composing the draft (this can have a number, rather than a check), reviewing, revising, conferring, editing, and publishing. Many pieces will not go through all, or even many, of these steps, and the order might be different for different pieces. However, having a place holder for "reviewing," for example, may well prompt students to read a piece over to themselves before sharing it with a different audience. But unless the function of such a checklist is made quite clear, some children may feel pressure to go through all the steps with everything they do.

The humble checklist, then, can be stretched to accommodate more than yes-or-no data. It can easily be stretched to accommodate "sometimes" or "maybe," simply by expanding the code from two options to three. In my experience, though, if the answer to "Does the student . . .?" is "Sometimes," I will want to know the answer to the question "Under what circumstances?" Space for a brief comment to that effect would solve the problem. Even space at the bottom of the list could be used, with the comments connected to specific items in the checklist with asterisks or some other key.

Observational Records

The basic value of a checklist is that it makes a process systematic and reduces the burden on human memory. But we can also be systematic without limiting our records to simple checklists. It is also important to record notes about events significant for individuals or the class. Often our best information on children's literate activity comes at the most unplanned time and in the most unexpected way. If we do not make a record of it, we will likely forget some important information.

Particular observations will often be very important for one student and not as important for others. For example, some students do not contribute a great deal to discussions in teacher-directed groups. This is too often true of certain minority children. These students are often much more vocal and involved during peer-group activities (Cazden 1990; Philips 1983). Thus, it can be useful to keep track of when these children contribute to discussions.

Some teachers find it helpful to carry around a journal with a section for each student and one for general observations. With this journal, they can record their observations on the spot. For example, these records might include such shorthand observations as the following:

- Nick—Indep rding chose Mr McGee & My Cat—*Very* easy—consistently choosing well below what he can manage.
- Tracy—asking Sam & Chuck for lots of help on writing—too much interruption for them.
- Sarah—rejected by group—no one conferencing with her.
- Andre—shared his writing with the group today—first time—big smile.

- Eric wrote hate letter to Franklin: U R SUPED I HAT U.
- Science corner unpopular.

Some of these observations will be transcribed in the student's file, and others will be placed in a general class file, to be used in planning. For example, the apparent failure of the science corner might suggest that the teacher take some immediate action after school, or during school the next day, or perhaps that the teacher conduct some interviews with the children, or form a student committee to find out how it might be improved.

Recording immediate observations in a journal can be useful. If the notes are only on one side of the journal, the facing page can be used for analytic comments and questions. An example of this is shown in Figure 25.1. It is important, however, to set aside a regular time to review and make use of these observations. For example, you might reflect on your notes and add some facing-page observations at the end of each day, and then have another look over those at the end of the week or month.

With such record-keeping, you might find yourself noting surprising, puzzling, disturbing, or exciting events and breakthroughs for particular children. The observations that you accumulate, and the reflection they encourage, are powerful means of rethinking your classroom practice. With the hectic pace of the normal day it is hard to take the time to analyze the significance of classroom events and their associated feelings. The records allow you the luxury of more careful analysis after the fact. For example, the reflective notes in Figure 25.1 might lead to an examination of Chaquila's reversals or math, and perhaps to some conversations with colleagues or some reading in professional journals.

The open-endedness of these observations allows you to make records less constrained by what will fit in a particular category. It allows you to question your own practice and expand your theorizing. The down side is that you will fairly systematically miss certain children and certain areas that you think are important but that are more subdued or otherwise easily lost in the activity of the classroom. This is where a more systematic checklist can come in handy. For example, you might have a clipboard carrying a list of the students' names, with spaces to record observations. This makes it possible to see when you are not attending to particular students. A set of index cards, each with a child's name, fastened together as a concertina file (/ \ / \ / \ / \ /) and attached to a clipboard makes it possible to record more observations about individual students while providing a sufficient reminder to prevent students being lost in the shuffle. To explore observational notetaking in more detail, read Brenda Power's (1996) excellent book *Taking Note*.

In Chapter 12, I gave two examples of print awareness checklists (Figures 12.3 and 12.4). I arranged those lists with space for brief comments or examples to illustrate or define the acquisition. For example, for the entry "Identifies 5–6 words consistently" I might record "I, am, in, the, and, to, Steven." Alternatively, by

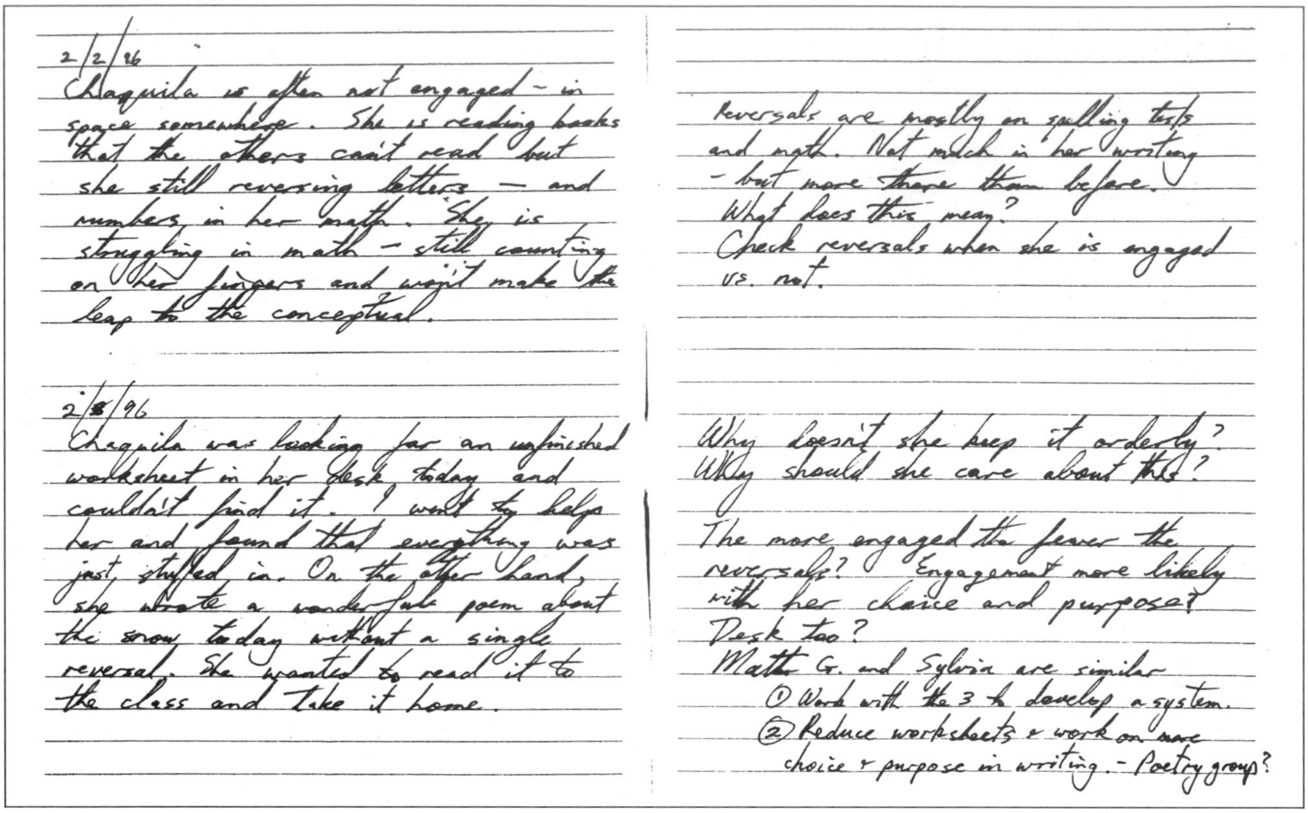
2/2/96
Chaquila is often not engaged — in space somewhere. She is reading books that the others can't read but she still reversing letters — and numbers in her math. She is struggling in math — still counting on her fingers and won't make the leap to the conceptual.

Reversals are mostly on spelling tests and math. Not much in her writing — but more there than before. What does this mean?
Check reversals when she is engaged vs. not.

2/8/96
Chaquila was looking for an unfinished worksheet in her desk today and couldn't find it. I went to help her and found that everything was just stuffed in. On the other hand, she wrote a wonderful poem about the snow today without a single reversal. She wanted to read it to the class and take it home.

Why doesn't she keep it orderly? Why should she care about this?

The more engaged the fewer the reversals? Engagement more likely with her choice and purpose? Desk too?
Math G. and Sylvia are similar
① Work with the 3 to develop a system.
② Reduce worksheets & work on more choice & purpose in writing. – Poetry group?

FIGURE 25.1 *Example of a Double-Entry Notebook*

changing the form a bit, we could make the form a record for specific check-point dates. With a list like this, a code could be used to provide more detail about degree of acquisition of the skills, with 0 to indicate the skill is not acquired at all, 1 to indicate that the child shows the skill sometimes or with assistance, and 2 to signify independent, flexible use.

Of course many of the items in this list could be broken down further. For example, for children to be able to match a spoken word to a printed word they must be able to match one item (blocks, etc.) to another. Similarly, "Developing a social imagination" could be broken down by observing where that knowledge is applied. For example, although a child might be able to imagine the information an audience would need to understand her writing, she might not be able to apply the awareness to her critical reading, or to the creation of plausible characters in her fiction writing. Of course, somewhere we have to draw the line in our written inventory.

Notice, too, that some of the items are applicable over a broader spectrum of development than are others. For some children the more specific skills will be mastered quite early. For example, alphabet knowledge, word-word matching, and acquisition of a set of recognized words, once acquired, do not generally go away.

On a computer this is easy to deal with. We simply close that branch in the file structure. There is no reason why each child's checklist needs to be identical. We could close one branch and open another to more detail, if desired. If we begin with a more expansive list that is applicable over a larger spectrum of development, we could maintain the same basic format and simply vary the details.

An approach to record-keeping that is between the checklist and an open-ended system is to use a set of valued categories to focus observation. For example, Figure 25.2 shows a set of questions that can be turned into an observation system such as that in Figure 25.3. Because the categories in Figure 25.2 are more expansive than those in the early literacy checklist, they do not convert to a checklist so readily. For example, we never finish expanding the range of complexity of the patterns we notice and the domains in which we notice them. An observation sheet like the one in Figure 25.3 would lend itself more to the documenting of examples and situations. Teachers can also use it as a self-evaluation tool, selecting one more and one less competent student as representatives, and keeping track of each for a day. It can also be used to sample classroom conversations without reference to particular students. A school psychologist might also use an observation sheet such as this to observe a referred child in the classroom setting.

There are other ways to represent similar concepts and record what you wish to observe. For example, the following list would provide a reasonably comprehensive set of values to consider when analyzing students' literacy:

- Initiates reading and writing—in and out of school.
- Recognizes what reading and writing can do.
- Has a sense of history and of the future of literacy learning
- Has a social imagination—a sense of audience and social implications.
- Has a sense of the variety of possible genres to read and write
- Takes control of problem-solving and problem-posing.
- Takes an interest in the conventions of literacy.
- Values own experience.
- Values others' experience.

Whichever checklists or organizing frameworks you choose for keeping track, it is best to start with what is manageable and what suits your needs—the purpose you have, what you know, and the ways you think at the present time. Choosing an "off the rack" checklist that you don't understand will simply provide clutter and be a waste of time. Furthermore, if others (children, other teachers, parents) also use it, the form may cause confusion or conflict.

A. Classroom Conditions

- What materials are available and how accessible are they? (range of genre, difficulty, theme, etc., of books; appropriate writing materials; sufficient time to engage with them)
- What reasons are there to read and write (such as a range of audiences for reading and performing own and other's works)? Are reading and writing construed as social and purposeful? Is student work visibly valued?
- Under what circumstances are classroom relationships respectful and nonjudgmental?
- In what ways are assessment responses focused, positive, and reflective?
- In what ways do classroom conversations reveal the processes of reading and writing?
- How do classroom conversations emphasize engagement?

B. Engagements

In what ways and under which conditions:

- is the student seeking to make sense?
  Is (s)he predicting, making meaning-based errors and self-corrections?
  What kind of connections is (s)he seeking (experiences, books, authors) to expand sense?
  Is (s)he seeking conversations to help expand the literacy experience?
- does the student value his/her own experience and the experience of others?
  Is (s)he actively listening to others' perspectives and feelings, to his/her own, to those of characters in books, and can (s)he imagine herself into those ways of thinking?
  Does (s)he represent others' perspectives in essays, characters, etc.?
- is the student reading and writing critically?
  Is (s)he imagining the intentions of writers and responses of audiences and considering their social significance?
- is the student seeking patterns? What kinds is (s)he noticing (for example, patterns among letters, sounds, words, text structures, plots, author styles, his/her own responses)?
- is the student's reading influencing his/her writing?
  Is (s)he making use of the patterns (s)he notices in his/her reading and writing, such as author's use of language, spelling, choice of verbs, use of metaphors, onomatopoeia, dialogue, punctuation, character development, relationship of character to plot?
- is the student cross-checking sources of information (for example: meaning, language structure, and print cues; text and experience; audience response with his/her intentions as authors)?
- is the student engaged and persistent?
  Is (s)he spending extended amounts of time reading and writing? Does (s)he resist distraction? Does (s)he return to books and unfinished writing pieces? Does (s)he have favorite authors, genres, or books?
- is (s)he thinking strategically (and flexibly)?
  When (s)he encounters a problem does (s)he try to solve it? Does (s)he try a range of strategies?
- does (s)he take control of his/her own learning?
  Is (s)he reflecting on his/her learning, keeping useful records, setting goals and planning means of reaching those goals, self-correcting?
- is (s)he making productive choices?
  Is (s)he selecting books, resources, tasks, and situations to maximize learning?
- does (s)he collaborate productively?

FIGURE 25.2   *Observing Children's Literate Learning*

Name. _____

CONCEPT	EXAMPLES/COUNTEREXAMPLES, CONDITIONS, DATES

A. Classroom Conditions

Range and accessibility of materials (range of genre, difficulty, theme, etc., of books; appropriate writing materials; time to use them)

Reasons to read and write. Reading and writing seen as social and purposeful (including a range of audiences)? Is student work visibly valued?

Respectful and nonjudgmental classroom relationships

Focused, positive, and reflective assessment responses

Literate processes made visible—demonstration, think-aloud, process talk

Conversations draw attention to meaning, choice, and engagement (vs. relative competence.)

B. Engagements

Seeking to make sense (seeks connections with experience, books, authors …)

Valuing own experience; writes and responds with authority

Valuing others' experiences; listens and represents others' perspectives

Reading and writing critically; imagines authors' intentions and readers' responses

Seeking patterns (letter, sound and word patterns, text structures, functions)

Reading affects writing (noticing writers' language and applying to own writing: conventions, word choice, sounds, dialogue …)

Cross checking sources of information—meaning, language structure, print; text/experience; different authors; audience response/intention

Engaged and persistent (sustains reading and writing over time, resists distraction)

Strategic and flexible thinking (tries to solve problems using a range of different strategies—e.g., letters/sounds, read ahead, reread …)

Controlling own learning (reflecting on learning, setting goals, planning, self-correcting)

Selecting books, resources, tasks, and situations well

Collaborating productively

FIGURE 25.3 *Observing Literate Learning*

"Watch your language!" my mother told us. It was good advice. In this part I explore our assessment conversations about children with an eye toward making them more constructive. I argue that specific, contextualized statements about what a student did under which conditions are more instructionally useful than the generalized, context-free statements of ability typical of standardized assessment practices.

Readers familiar with concepts of educational measurement will find issues of reliability in Chapters 27, 29, and 30, though it is addressed as a matter of synchronizing conversations, the subject of Chapter 30. Validity is also an issue as we consider the implications of our conversations and the contexts within which they occur. It turns out that my mother's advice "Sticks and stones may break your bones, but names will never hurt you" missed the mark, as many children named "learning disabled" will attest. Words, it turns out, are not just words, but ways of constructing realities—the measurement people call them "constructs." Words are put together to make stories about children's literate lives, though sometimes we tell these stories as if they are not stories but "scientific facts."

TALKING ABOUT CHILDREN'S LITERACY DEVELOPMENT

BEGINNING PORTFOLIOS

A photographer seeking a wedding assignment is likely to have a portfolio of work for a prospective customer to look through. She might also have a second portfolio of abstract photography, her passion, that she keeps just for herself—a way to assert her identity as an abstract photographer. An architect, a designer, an engineer, a teacher, an artist are all likely to have portfolios to show who they are for particular purposes. Very few professionals present test scores as primary indicators of their credentials.

Portfolios have also been used as an assessment device in some countries for decades, particularly in the arts, and in the last few years they have featured in most conversations about educational assessment in the United States. Hopes are high for portfolios. They are often viewed as the penicillin that will cure what ails education. Although this portrayal is overly optimistic, portfolios do offer some wonderful possibilities that other approaches to assessment cannot.

Conversations about portfolios can be confusing because there are different ways of thinking about what portfolios are, what they should look like, what should go into them (and who says so), what they can be used for, and how they should be judged. They have been used as a vehicle for students to reflect on their learning, as a tool for holding teachers accountable, and everything in between, sometimes at the same time. Here are two contrasting examples to suggest the range of ways portfolios are used.

Mary Wilson's fourth-grade students use portfolios to think about and keep track of their learning and to explain their learning to others, including their teacher, their peers, and their parents. The fact that some of the portfolios have similar containers or other features is purely incidental; this reflects their owners' normal appropriation and elaboration of good ideas by other community members. In fact, the most obvious feature of the portfolios is their diversity. The children alone are responsible for including and removing material (Mary also keeps a portfolio of her own). Although each member of the class keeps a portfolio, to do so is not a requirement; it is merely one way of "going public" about one's learning and having conversations about the nature of that learning. Mary and her students feel that the portfolios are exciting, though often difficult, to put together and to share, and that their learning improves because of them. This makes them feel good about themselves as learners. Mary also believes that the portfolios have led to valuable conversations with parents and other teachers. For example, the class has made several attempts to agree on sets of criteria for evaluating their literacy and their work in science. These criteria have been preserved in class record books, along with notes they have made from their class discussions about books and science. The record books have been shared with parents.

Students in Jim Vesper's sixth-grade class on the other side of town also keep portfolios of their work. Students have separate portfolios for writing and for science. The portfolios are used to provide end-of-year report card grades and as part of a school "quality control" program. The portfolios are all identical in format. Each writing folder contains three items: two "best pieces" selected from the students' classroom writing; and a timed, standardized piece. Although Jim does not keep a portfolio himself, in individual conferences he helps the students choose their best pieces. The criteria used for scoring the portfolios are posted on the wall, and Jim has shown students how the criteria are used to judge their work by a company that has contracted to provide evaluation services to the school district. Students have mixed feelings about the portfolios. Some are very proud of them and others are not. Parents get to see the final, scored portfolio by request at the end of the year. The portfolios are kept in the school and are passed on to the child's next teacher with the child's standardized test scores and other data written on the inside cover.

These two kinds of portfolio share little more than the name. Their functions are different, the roles of teacher and student are different, their relationship to classroom learning is different and, most important, how they are put together is radically different. Teachers who are interested in using portfolios in their classroom or school need to understand the nature of these differences. The best way to learn about portfolios, of course, is to experience them yourself—to get together with colleagues or parents and put together your own portfolios to share. In the meantime, in the remainder of this chapter I will try to convey a sense of what to expect from portfolios and some ideas for working together.

On a number of occasions I have worked with groups of teachers interested in developing portfolios. At the outset, I ask them to put together their own portfolios as a way of representing themselves to each other as a teacher or a learner or a literate person. I suggest that they represent themselves with no more than ten artifacts. Then, when we get together, we share our portfolios with one another in small groups and talk about why we selected the various items. While the experi-

The Process
- Write down some of the process you went through in putting together the portfolio.
- What criteria did you use to decide what went in and what didn't?
- Describe some important feelings you experienced in the process of putting together the portfolio.
- Write down something you learned about yourself while putting together the portfolio.

Sharing
- Write down something you learned as people shared their portfolios.
- In what ways did people's selection and presentation of portfolio material differ?
- What do these differences reflect, and where do they come from?
- Look through your portfolio and describe how you have portrayed the dimensions of literacy (or teaching and learning).
- Did other people's portfolios influence the way you viewed your own so that you might do it differently next time?

FIGURE 26.1   *Exploring the Portfolio Experience*

ence is fresh in our minds, we individually reflect on the twin experiences of composing and sharing the portfolios. The prompt sheet in Figure 26.1 helps participants notice details on which to base the discussion of their experiences.

Portfolio Experiences

Most of us have a schooling history of other people telling us exactly what and how much to do, so the initial request to make a portfolio, which is very open, makes some people nervous. They want to know exactly what should be in the portfolio, what it should look like, how big it should be, what is meant by "literate person," and so forth. Others relish the freedom and expand the possibilities as much as they can. The openness of the task produces a wide range of portfolios and thus a rich discussion of the possibilities.

As they consider what to include in their portfolios, people frame themselves quite differently from one another. Some view themselves historically, while some focus only on their current practices. Some find that, like the items in Mem Fox's book *Wilfred Gordon McDonald Partridge*, the items they choose stir powerful memories. Some find threads of experience running through their lives that, like a loose tooth, they can't help pulling at. The selection experience for these people is generally positive and generative, and can become a powerful journey of self-discovery. People often report spontaneously setting or resetting goals for themselves. Perhaps they realize that their reading has become restricted to one genre (or virtually none), and they resolve to expand their horizons or change their priorities. Perhaps they realize that they haven't written more than a shopping list since college, and resolve to return to the poetry they once enjoy composing.

If people think of portfolios as a one-shot judgmental event, their conception is quite different from those who see portfolios as ongoing, to be shared and shaped over a period of time. Those with the former view approach portfolios much as they might approach an essay in a final exam. Those who take the latter view commonly take greater risks in selection and presentation. Some people construe the situation as competitive and, rather than examining their own learning or teaching, try to ensure that they will look good when compared to others, or at least will not look bad (some going so far as to "forget" to bring in their portfolio on the preappointed day). The number of those who view portfolios this way will depend, among other things, on the nature of the teaching community. Some people begin with this comparative framework but accidentally find themselves caught up in the process, and their experience changes accordingly.

Sharing Portfolios

Sharing portfolios sparks remarkable conversations. An artifact is produced and explained, and people ask questions, report related experiences (similar or contrasting), want to know more, and comment on specific features (virtually always positively). In the process, participants' ways of viewing themselves and their literacy expand, as does their thinking about literacy, learning, teaching, or whatever domain they choose to consider. The greater the range of artifacts and criteria, the livelier the conversations.

Because literacy, learning, and teaching are parts of our lives, of who we are, the conversations are engaging and often personal. People are often shown a side of their colleagues they had never anticipated. They learn that others have parents at home with Alzheimer's disease, have experienced recent deaths in the family, have unusual talents and hobbies, or have surprising community commitments. The two-dimensional stereotypes teachers sometimes hold of each other begin to break down as they see dimensions they had never imagined. This tends to result in greater trust and respect among the group, creating the basis of a productive learning community. It becomes possible to have previously unimaginable conversations about learning and teaching. People who edited certain items out of their portfolios because of the audience they expected find their audience is different, and they take the risk to share the more complex or personal parts of themselves.

In our sessions I ask participants to list the criteria they used for deciding what to include and exclude in their portfolios. Their lists are always extensive and diverse, provoking complex discussions about criteria and standards—about what matters. This discussion alone might be worth the effort of putting together the portfolio. However, composing and sharing portfolios can foster many things:

- An understanding and control of one's own learning.
- A commitment to exploring and expanding one's own learning.
- A development of self-identity based on engagement and connectedness (with others and among domains of experience).

- A trusting, supportive, more caring community based in diversity, commonality, and connection, rather than uniformity.
- The expansion of individual consciousness and empathy.
- Productive conversations about what matters in learning.
- A heightened awareness of the processes of learning.

These outcomes seem likely not only to improve learning, but also to sustain a democratic way of life. On the basis of my experiences in adult sessions, and similar experiences in classrooms, I believe that portfolios have enormous potential for schooling in a democracy. At the same time, however, I have seen that circumstances can drastically alter the potential of portfolios, making these valued outcomes more or less likely.

Getting Started

The important place to begin with portfolios is with attitude—yours. Here are three ideas to keep in mind as you introduce portfolios in your classroom. First, it is not the portfolio itself, the material collection of work, but the processes of putting together the portfolio and sharing it that are most important. The compilation process asks students to take their own learning seriously—to assert:

- Here is what I did that is significant.
- Here is why it is significant.
- Here is the process I went through.
- And here is what I've learned from that process. (Romano 1992, p. 157)

Second, a portfolio should be ongoing: each version of the portfolio is a draft that we expect to change as we learn. Third, diversity in portfolios is to be valued. The more diverse the portfolios, the more interesting and productive will be the conversations that take place around them and the more supportive will be the relationships among the members of the learning community. If you keep these three ideas in mind, your experience with portfolios will be a productive one.

Mark Milliken (1992) introduced his fifth graders to portfolios by asking them to find out what thoughts their parents had on the subject. This produced a list of potential features and an offer by a parent (an interior decorator) who routinely used a portfolio to share it with the class. After the presentation and lots of discussion, the students produced a new list of features. Mark asked his students how they thought portfolios might work in school. They brainstormed and set to work with only a few details of what their portfolios might be like. Along the way he asked them what was going well and what was not, which stimulated discussion of how to show progress and how to represent less tangible experiences.

Another way to start is simply to ask your students to put together a portfolio—a collection of things—that shows who they are as literate people (or as learners), a sort of self-portrait using objects. Tell them that you will make one too and that you will all spend time sharing them when you are done. The students will have lots of questions, but tell them that you don't have many answers, that the idea is new to you, too, and you are keen to see the different portfolios they come up with. Be sure you actually do show an interest. Remember, it is the process that counts, and each version is a draft.

Place an upper limit on the number of items to go in the portfolio. Somewhere between three and ten artifacts is about right to start, with younger students having fewer items and older students more. This at once makes the portfolio itself more manageable, and requires students to consider their learning more carefully. Ask students to write a comment about each artifact describing why it was selected. These can be written on regular paper or stick-on slips and attached to the items. Older children might also write a piece commenting on the portfolio as a whole. Kindergartners and some first graders might dictate their comments. Like other pieces of writing, these can be worked on through drafts and revisions until the writers are satisfied with them. This commentary adds to the portfolio's worth in instructional value.

Examining your own portfolio with your students is very important, primarily because it shows your commitment. It also incidentally provides them with a model. But one model often produces copies. If you use a cereal box as a container, you will soon see a lot of cereal boxes in your classroom. If you include a copy of your favorite book in your portfolio, so will many of the students. There are a couple of ways to counter this. One is to invite other community members to the class to present their portfolios. Artists, writers, architects, designers, advertisers, stockbrokers, and other teachers are all people who might have professional portfolios. These should provide both a range of examples and grounds for fruitful discussion. It is especially useful if these portfolios are not meant to represent literacy specifically; their applicability must be through metaphor. You might even try such a portfolio yourself. If you have a hobby, such as watercolor painting, remodeling houses, or gardening, you could put together a portfolio for that activity and ask your students how they could apply the ideas to literacy or learning. Or you could present students with a range of options and encourage diversity. For example, you could make three different kinds of portfolios of your own and talk about each, or bring in friends or colleagues.

Managing Portfolios

At this point you may be wondering how you will manage portfolios given the fact that the school day is already full. I think it is probably better to ask how *the students* will manage them. Better still, ask yourself why they would bother. If they can see a real benefit then, with help, they will take care of most of the management themselves. Having your own portfolio and working through it with the children will increase the likelihood that they will consider portfolios important enough to maintain their own, particularly if you maintain the portfolio for yourself rather than just for teaching purposes. This is really no different from reading and writing. If you do not show that you enjoy reading and writing yourself, or if your students' experiences with reading or writing are consistently unsatisfying, you will find that you have to manage the activities for them and that it will consume a great deal of energy.

It can be easier to start small. Perhaps begin with a handful of volunteers or a small group. Aim for interest and diversity first and sort out the details as you go along, with the students fully involved in the problem-solving. The more authority they have, the more engaged they will be.

If the children are already keeping folders of their accumulated work, portfolio preparation will be simpler than if they do not have such folders. A good way for students to arrange their work is to have an archive or source file, a working file, and a portfolio. This way, all of the material is readily available for review and selection.

What Should a Portfolio Look Like?

The actual form of a portfolio is relatively unimportant. It could be a three-ring binder with plastic container sheets or photograph-album sheets, a cereal box, hanging files, pocket folders, accordion files, a computer file, or a time line or wall display. Although the form is relatively unimportant, it does have implications. For example, if a flat folder is used, then chunky things such as videotapes or models obviously won't fit (although photographs of models can). Similarly, computer files have both advantages and limitations. Technically, it is possible to scan writing samples, photographs, and so forth, and annotate them. Multiple drafts of documents are easily stored in computers, and it is possible to store video and audio data. With a computer, physical storage space is minimized and archiving becomes possible. However, technical expertise and resources are essential, and at first computer users find it easy to be sidetracked by the technical possibilities rather than focusing on the content of their composition. Also, unless the classroom is amply supplied with powerful computers, using them will prove unmanageable.

Having some consistency in the physical shape of the portfolios can have storage advantages, and accessibility is very important if children are expected to consider constant revision. It is always possible for children to personalize their portfolios with artwork. Using a pocket folder, a portfolio can be divided into a writing side and a reading side. But if literacy learning is going well it should become difficult to tell which side is which. Similar division could be made for school and outside-of-school pieces. But again, if things are going well, the dichotomy should break down. Indeed, its breakdown would be a useful indicator of development.

The main thing is not to be distracted by the form but to find something that works for your class and to keep the possibilities open for renegotiation.

Where Should Portfolios Be Kept?

Maintaining portfolios does require some space. Hanging files are very convenient; they can be hung in a range of containers from elaborate cabinets to simple (and cheap) milk crates. Even kindergarten children can manage a milk-crate source file. If you have ample shelf space, perhaps the idea of cereal boxes that can be stacked next to each other will appeal. The important considerations are access and functionality. If the portfolios are not readily accessible, it will be hard for children to manage them. It will also be hard for children to consider them ongoing. The more flexible the system (like hanging files), the greater the possible variety of contents.

What Goes into a Portfolio?

A portfolio is composed from available material. A classroom in which there is little writing, or little range of writing, will be reflected in the portfolios. If personal narratives are all that gets written in the classroom, that's all there will be in students' portfolios. If all writing in the class is assigned, the portfolios in the class will look very much alike. They will be less interesting than a more varied collection of pieces, there will be fewer opportunities for learning, and it will be much easier for children to be drawn into unfortunate interpersonal comparisons.

The best way to work out what might go into portfolios is to get students to brainstorm the possibilities. Their ideas will come from what they do in the classroom and what they can imagine. That said, a literacy portfolio *might* include some of the following:

- Any piece of writing (whole or part, book to sentence) from any genre at any stage of development, and perhaps more than one version of the same piece (for example, there might be a published piece with two earlier revisions or a piece of prose that has been transformed into a poem).
- Genres, such as parodies; letters to the editor, to a politician, to a friend, etc. (for a range of purposes); poems; mysteries; research papers; journal entries; essays; articles for magazines; different types of dictionaries; instructions; expository pieces; humorous pieces; and more.
- Writing that others have done that was inspiring, with notes on what it inspired.
- Collaborative pieces of writing—committee proposals, plays, books, and so forth.
- Videotapes or audiotapes of plays and other performances (whatever the role of the individual) or of oral reading.
- A running record or two, showing change over time, or tape-recorded readings showing expression or change over time.

- Notecards on books read or simply a record of books and other works read (or attempted), including works by classmates. Book lists might include ratings of difficulty, classifications of genre, and reason for reading.
- Book reviews, critiques (perhaps marginalia on a text).
- Illustration, dance, music, or sculpture to represent a piece of literature or as a response to some literate activity.
- A résumé.
- A piece of writing formatted for maximum impact.
- Summary of a group discussion of a book.
- A comparison of authors' styles, perhaps with a piece of writing imitating a particular author's style.
- Hard copy of e-mails.
- A collection of sports cards.
- A record of change in words per minute typed or read.
- A record of change in words spelled correctly (list from draft writing at beginning of the year and from middle or end of year).
- A journal or sections of a journal (a reading journal, a writing journal, a science journal, a learning log, etc.).
- Work that reflects on literate decisions, changes, processes, etc. This could take the form of an essay, a narrative, a list of qualities with examples, an annotated piece highlighting certain qualities, and could be written on index cards, stick-on slips, or whatever.
- Records of conferences on reading or writing.
- A classroom newspaper (itself potentially a class portfolio) with a description of the child's role in its production or marketing.
- Expanded topic lists.
- Evidence of increasing skill at having conferences with other writers, perhaps evidence of ability to sustain and make productive use of critique, or evidence that a conference was helpful to another writer.
- Reflective commentaries on individual pieces and the overall collection.

This already large list could be expanded considerably given the breadth of activities in which literate people engage.

Selecting Work

A critical part of the portfolio process is what Geof Hewitt (1995) calls "weight control," or the selection of which items should go into the portfolio. The items mentioned above are the kinds of things that might go into a portfolio, but the actual selections students make will be based on criteria that come from the conversations they engage in and from the situation as they see it. For example, selections will be influenced by:

- Whether activities inside school and outside of school are both seen as possible sources of works.
- Who is considered the audience for the portfolio—self, peers, parents, respected practitioners; and whether students are allowed to choose their audience.
- What is seen as the purpose of the portfolio (to be judged, to learn).
- The stakes involved (graduation, self-knowledge, grades, public recognition).
- How much value is placed on the portfolio. If portfolios are seen as good enough for the teacher to do, then they are more likely to be valued. Similarly, if past experience with portfolios has proved satisfying, it is more likely to be valued.
- The criteria by which the student thinks their portfolio is to be judged.
- The criteria implicit in the conversations of the classroom.

In other words, children's selections do not occur in a vacuum. If you grade children's work and then they select pieces for their portfolio, it is likely that they will choose the pieces with good grades rather than the one that was less polished but most personally meaningful or the unfinished one that had such a great lead. Creating a portfolio is like writing. When we write we compose with a particular audience and purpose in mind. If I were making a portfolio to apply for a job at an elementary school, I would put together a different portfolio from one I would prepare for promotion at a university or one to share with colleagues as part of an ongoing effort to collaboratively improve our teaching. A teacher preparing a portfolio for discussion with her peers about her classroom practice, as part of setting and monitoring her own goals, will produce a different portfolio than the one she would produce for a principal if her next year's salary or job security depended on it. Children will sometimes put together a different portfolio to represent themselves to their next year's teacher than to represent themselves to their peers or their present teacher. If the audience is not (yet) to be trusted, chances are the personal (often the most meaningful) and the tentative (often the most engaging) will be edited out. The same thing can happen if students are asked to represent themselves as learners in their portfolios and they view learning as separate from their personal experience.

Children's selections for their portfolio thus have as much to say about the circumstances in which they learn as about their learning. As children present their portfolios, you (and the rest of their audience) will learn about their selection criteria. This can lead to useful discussions. Ask them why they did not choose particular items as well as why they did. Their reasons for the items left out will be just as revealing as their reasons for the material selected. As students make their criteria clear, they can begin to select bad examples of writing as well as good ones and thus open the way for setting goals for themselves. It also helps students see progress, since there are poorly written pieces in every writer's history.

If a purpose of the portfolio is to show change, some material will be selected for historical comparison. This is the advantage of having an archive or cumulative file from which a student can draw such examples. Seeing one's progress in this manner can be very satisfying and motivating. It also provides a productive antidote to normative comparisons of competence.

Another way to help students develop productive criteria for judging their writing is through conversations about what good writers (or readers) do. These conversations can be used to produce lists of criteria. For example, students might learn that good writers notice details, take notes, read a lot, think about their audience, write a lot, listen carefully, choose words carefully, and write drafts. These lists can form a trail of class learning that can be returned to after a new list is made, especially if they are made on transparencies. They can be particularly helpful if sent home so that parents get a feel for the kind of behavior and competence they can help their children develop.

Linda Rief distinguishes between internal and external criteria for including items in a portfolio. External criteria are the ones she sets as a teacher. For example, a teacher might require that the portfolios for this semester or term contain at least one poem and at least one book review. Internal criteria, by contrast, are those applied by the students themselves. As you can imagine, this internal-external distinction is not a simple one. Criteria that begin as external frequently become internal. For example, requiring both a reading and a writing example from outside of school may motivate some students to continue to pursue these activities voluntarily.

Who Gets to Choose?

The previous section is based on the assumption that students will be making the decisions about what goes into their portfolios. Sometimes students choose pieces for their portfolios that their teacher would not have chosen, or omit pieces that the teacher might have included for reasons they might not yet understand. Whether or not this is a problem depends on the function of the portfolio. If its major function is to help students become reflective about their learning, whether you agree with their choice may not matter much, since student reflection has been accomplished. However, if the students' portfolios are going to be used to assess the quality of your instruction, perhaps publicly, the students' selections will matter more to you. Even if the portfolios are simply part of parent conferences, if you feel they do not do justice to the students' learning, you might want a way to present what you think does. But bear in mind that the more you take over the choosing of portfolio contents and criteria, the less the students will be engaged in the process and the more likely it is that they will neglect their portfolios, forget them, dump them, or not pick them up when the year is done.

One way to solve this problem is to "rent" space in the student's portfolio. This keeps the portfolio in the student's hands, but allows you to add selections. A second solution is to simply keep your own records of important items and, with the student's permission, take the items from the student's source file as the occasion arises. Some teachers solve the problem by requiring that both teacher and student have to agree on one or two of the selections. This, too, can lead to productive conversations. Another solution that can open useful conversations is to create a showcase portfolio that contains selections by the student, the teacher, and the parents, each with its own justification.

The selections made depend on the criteria used to make judgments about the portfolio. These criteria can be under the control of students or others. The same principles used to select specific pieces apply in decisions about criteria. Criteria chosen democratically, or individually, are more likely to be embraced by students than are criteria imposed by someone else, such as the teacher or the state. (We will come back to this topic again in the next chapter.)

Should Portfolios Go Home or Stay at School?

Where to keep portfolios is a dilemma that many teachers struggle over. If the portfolios belong to the students, how can we justify keeping them at school? But if they are to provide some sort of consistent assessment, how can we justify letting them go home and risk their getting lost? Particularly when portfolios are used to bridge the gap between grade levels or years at school, if students take them home and then lose them, their function of helping to inform the next year's classroom teacher is lost.

There are several ways to handle this dilemma. First, if the process of putting together the portfolio is seen as the most important part of keeping portfolios, then it is less serious if a portfolio does not return at the beginning of the school year. Second, if children find their portfolios valuable (and there is every indication that they do when they have control of what goes into their portfolios and know that their work is valued by others), the possibility of loss is sufficiently small to risk their being taken home. Third, perhaps photocopying can be put to good use. Fourth, a balance might be struck; perhaps portfolios could be checked out of the classroom for brief periods, say, two days at a time.

Finding the Time

Unless there are parts of the day in which you are doing nothing, adding portfolios to the classroom means that something else must go. Before you decide that it is the portfolio that must go, let's consider some ideas. For one thing, the contents of the portfolio require no extra time to produce. The pieces are what students normally do in class (and at home). Remember, too, that there are efficiencies to be gained through the use of portfolios. As children become more competent at self-assessment, their independence will allow you to have more time for other things.

Reviewing, commenting on, and organizing the material does, however, require extra time from students, and portfolio conferences and presentations (perhaps one to three per year) also require extra time. With older students you might want to take even more time to review the portfolio yourself and take notes before a conference. The key is to develop a manageable schedule for putting together and presenting portfolios. The teacher and/or peers are probably the students' best first audiences. Remember, not everyone has to present a portfolio at once. You can schedule perhaps ten minutes each day for a student to work through their portfolio with you. You can also have presentations in groups, perhaps one group a week. Set aside around thirty minutes for a small group to share their work. As students become more familiar with responding to portfolios, the groups will become more self-sustaining.

Some teachers use the portfolios as public celebrations of learning—parties at which all students present their portfolios to peers, friends, parents, grandparents, and neighbors. Portfolios can also be put on display for a period of time in a particular location. Doing this means that the portfolio must be able to stand on its own; the student will not be there to explain the significance of the selections and in the process perhaps rethink them.

Children can be videotaped presenting their portfolio to the teacher. The tape can then be presented to parents, grandparents, or other relatives who cannot come to meetings. Videos also make possible cumulative portfolio presentations, enabling children to review their own development. And tape doesn't take up much room.

After keeping their work in folders until they had quite a lot of material, Lois Brandts's (1993) first graders developed showcase portfolios to display their best work. Lois discussed with the children who their audience might be (friends, teacher, parents, other family members and neighbors, etc.) and asked the children to write a letter to the reader of their portfolio. She modeled presenting a portfolio and had the children take home their portfolio with a request for family members to look at the portfolio and write a response to the student. She followed up with a letter of thanks to the parents and student.

In short, the possibilities for portfolios are great, but they do take time. I once apologized to my cousin for my failure to keep in touch with her. I had a list of all the things I had to do that vied for my time. She responded that if it was important enough I would find the time. Similarly, if you are having trouble finding time for portfolios in your busy classroom schedule, either you are unconvinced of their value or you do not value them more highly than you do the other activities of the classroom. Another possibility is that you are reluctant to disturb your routines. You have to decide what is the bottom line in your literacy instruction. Construct a brief list of what this consists of (such as "enjoyment of reading and writing"). Next, decide which events in your classroom accomplish these goals most effectively—independent reading, literature discussion groups, book reviews, the core basal reader program, whatever. As you consider each activity, ask whether it makes an important contribution to your bottom line goals. Drop whatever does not contribute. Then, consider how different domains (reading, writing, social studies, and so on) might be integrated (as they are in life outside the classroom). This is a way of making time available so that you can expand your classroom practice to include portfolios. But in the end you and your students must be convinced of their value, and the benefits I described earlier must become part of the bottom line for your classroom.

$\mathcal{T}$ALKING ABOUT PORTFOLIOS

$\mathcal{A}$s with any conversation about your students' work, let the students lead the conversation about their portfolios. Active listening is the center of the portfolio conference. You will of course be asking questions, particularly reflective ones, but making your responses to what student say honest and nonjudgmental is central. It sets the stage for a productive conversation in which challenging questions can be asked.

Laurie Mansfield, a first-grade teacher, had this conversation with a student who was putting together a portfolio:

LAURIE: Why did you choose that one?

STEVE: It's exciting.

LAURIE: Will everything in your portfolio be exciting?

STEVE: No, but so is "My Award in Soccer."

LAURIE: You plan to put that in?

STEVE: Yes.

They continue to look through Steve's cumulative folder, and Laurie asks if there is anything else that shows he is a good writer. Steve rejects one piece that he had difficulty reading, noting its messiness and its excess of periods, but Laurie points out its positive points, that he was experimenting with periods for the first time and that he had used uppercase letters. Steve chooses another piece because "the illustrations are better."

LAURIE: So one is in here because it's exciting—

STEVE: Yes, exciting and good.

LAURIE: Good in what way?

STEVE: I writed better and drew pictures better.

LAURIE: When you say you wrote "better," do you mean spelled better or used words better?

STEVE: Both.

In this conversation, although Steve has little to say about the qualities of his work, a seed has been planted that he will return to. From now on, he will have different conversations with himself about his work, and he will listen differently to other conversations in class. Talk about good writing will have greater significance for him and will sharpen his observations of his own work.

Students in the beginning are likely to have difficulty articulating the reasons they value certain pieces over others. Ask them to think out loud about their choices. Ask, "Why not this piece?" As students walk you through their portfolios they will explain what they see as reasonable criteria for judging something valuable or significant. Sometimes students' criteria are not necessarily ones that you might have chosen or even thought of. Accept their criteria as a way to help you understand their conception of literacy and learning, and themselves as literate individuals. One first grader was asked why he had chosen a piece of writing in which he had expressed his wish for his divorced parents to get back together. He explained that when he wrote it, "I opened my heart" (Peter Winograd, personal communication). His criterion was not focused on a quality of the writing itself, but rather on the quality of his experience of writing the piece. Conversations about pieces that were not chosen for the portfolio can be equally revealing. You might say, "I notice that you decided not to include your piece on the Navajo. How did you decide this?"

After discussing the significance of the selected pieces, the conversation can move to what the student learned in the process and where to go from there. For example, Dennie Palmer Wolf (1989) quotes one student who observed:

> When I look back, I see my poems were very basic in the beginning, they were all rhymed haiku because that was all I knew about. Then I experimented with going with the feelings or ideas . . . don't kill yourself over the rhymes, go with what you feel. I did that for two months. Then I started compacting them, shortening them to make deeper meaning. I could see that it would make more of a point if I washed out the *the*'s and *and*'s and *if*'s. Now I am working on something different—the morals. If one day my mom's car broke down, I might write that night about how a fish got caught, or the feeling of not being able to swim. I am not trying to write how I feel only, but metaphors. (p. 38)

This is the kind of talk about learning that is most productive. It is a historical narrative that projects into the future with no sense of finality but rather of emergence.

Experiment with the kinds of questions you ask students about their portfolios as a whole. You will find for yourself what sort of conversation is most productive. Try some of these questions (but try them on yourself first):

- What did you notice [about your learning] as you put the portfolio together?
- What does your portfolio show about you as a reader [writer, learner]?
- What do you do well as a reader [writer, learner]?
- How have you changed as a learner [reader, writer] this year? [In what way is this portfolio different from the beginning of the year? What do you do differently now as a reader/writer/learner?] How come?
- What has changed most about your reading [writing]? Why do you think that happened?
- What change would you like to see next? What could you do to help you make that change?
- What surprised you as you put the portfolio together? Is there anything about your portfolio that you think will surprise someone else who views it?
- What was difficult in putting together your portfolio?
- Were there any things that you wanted to put in but decided not to? How did you decide?
- Did other portfolios influence your selections?

These questions need not wait until the student is standing in front of you with his or her portfolio. You can suggest students ask themselves these questions as they put together their portfolios. Indeed, part of the students' portfolios can (perhaps *should*) be a piece of writing that provides a statement of what they do well or what they learned, and what they want to learn next or what they want to do better, or what they want to change. Some of these questions can be used as prompts.

Once children have identified goals, they can begin to think about how to attain them (what they will do next). This is a lot to think about at once, so it is often better to begin the simpler questions of what they do well and what they would like to do better, introducing the goal-setting and planning aspects after affirmation and analysis. Notice how these conversations around the portfolio make students think historically. They reflect on the past and project into the future. They form a narrative about learning.

Many of the conferences that take place while portfolios are being composed are brief, perhaps less than a minute. They are designed for teachers to keep reading, writing, and learning moving along while not taking control of it. Remember, instruction should improve the quality of the students' reading and writing in the portfolio, not just by their selecting better material from the cumulative folder, but because the material to be selected from is better. Conferences about the final portfolio are longer, maybe up to ten minutes, and should be grounded firmly in the work that was selected. "What does this show about your learning?" you might ask. "You observed that you have improved in your use of dialogue. Read me the piece that shows that best." Sometimes these conversations lead to students' discovery of a mismatch between what they believe is in the writing and what they see is actually there. This makes them reevaluate their learning for themselves.

Enlarging the Audience

Conversations between teacher and student are not the only ones to think about. It is not helpful if a child presents a portfolio to peers or parents only to face relentless negative commentary. Getting potential audiences involved in discussions of the most productive ways to respond to portfolios is important. Involving parents in producing their own portfolios, even fantasy ones, will help. The idea is to cultivate a community for portfolios. Help students understand that they can have portfolio conferences with others in the class and that these conferences are a lot like writing conferences. They must be sure the person gets to hear or read what they have written, and to think about it. Careful listening is the most important concept to stress.

You might seek students' permission for parents other than their own to examine their portfolios. That way, a parent can examine several children's portfolios and get a sense of the range of possibilities. You may want to write a letter to parents to accompany each portfolio, explaining what you see as the student's strengths and goals. Actively seeking parents' feedback can be illuminating. Generally parents are impressed by the portfolios and the children's knowledge of their own work. However, they sometimes have concerns about things they see or don't see but expected to. For example, they might raise concerns about spelling, grammar, or other skills, or about the kinds of books read. These concerns can be reduced somewhat by doing the following:

- Increase contact with the parents prior to the arrival of the portfolio, making clear the nature and logic of the program. Explanations could be made at the "meet the teacher" night at the beginning of the year, or at special workshops, or in a letter. The greater parents' understanding of the portfolios prior to viewing them, the fewer the questions.
- Ensure that at the initial presentation the parents' questions about the portfolio are discussed fully. At least at these early sessions the teacher might be part of the child's presentation of the portfolio to the parents.

However, when the concerns of parents (or other audiences) remain, it is a good idea to bring these concerns back to the students and to have them think about how these problems might be addressed. All concerns should be taken seriously. A letter explaining the solutions to the problems might then be sent home as a follow-up. This would be a good opportunity for the class to collaborate on a letter—a great chance for modeling.

Recording Portfolio Conferences

Portfolios that are in transition (as I think they should always be) do not necessarily leave a trace or have a clear history. We have already mentioned some ways of creating a record, such as videotaping conferences or simply returning superseded works to the source folder with the selection letter attached. For documenting change, it is a good idea to date all the items in the source file. The simplest way to accomplish this is with a date stamp.

It can also be helpful to have a written record of the portfolio conference to return to later (for example, at a later conference). Mark Milliken (1992) uses a three-column record sheet: in one column he records student responses; in another, new learning goals; and in a third, his own responses. Goal-setting thus becomes a collaborative matter, but with the student taking the lead. The teacher's role is to point to items in the portfolio and ask the student to talk about it. Milliken asked one of his students, Ryan, what the reading lists in his portfolio suggested to him. Ryan had finished only one book each term. Ryan's response was "I've found tons of good books this year. Like *Hatchet*—it's a great adventure. I'm not a very fast reader, but I understand what I read. They [some friends who read a great deal] read a lot faster, but I bet they can't tell as much about what they read as I can" (p. 41) As they talked, Mark learned that Ryan often forgets his book at school and has none at home, and that he mostly reads in the morning lying in bed, which does not work well, because he falls asleep. These are both problems that can be addressed. The conversation also helped balance Mark's concern for quantity of reading with Ryan's actual interest and reminded Mark that before entering the class Ryan had a history of difficulty with reading.

Judging Portfolios

One of my children's Saturday chores is to clean their rooms, but every now and then their constructions and artwork and dismantled machinery, their hoarding and gathering, and even their schoolwork threaten to make their rooms uninhabitable. On these occasions we have assisted cleanups: one adult, one child, and a roomful of stuff to be reduced to manageable proportions. The task might take an entire morning but results in a tidy room, a happy and more thoughtful child, and a happy and more understanding parent. What makes it worthwhile is the conversations and reflections we share as items are evaluated and their stories told, and they are saved or discarded. This is essentially the portfolio process with the room as the portfolio. The owner of the portfolio (the room) makes decisions about its contents and their significance, the process of composing the portfolio (reassembling the room) is educative for its owner (and for the teacher or parent), and the process fosters self-assessment and a better understanding of oneself.

The everydayness of this example is appropriate, and the emphasis on conversation is critical. Teachers who use portfolios this way emphasize the benefits of students systematically and collaboratively reflecting on their learning. They talk with students about how to generate criteria for evaluating their work and set manageable and productive goals for themselves. The teachers consider how to capitalize on the diversity of the portfolios their students are producing. The important outcome in the long run is not the tidiness, which will only last a short while, but the reflective disposition of the owner and his relationship to the other occupants of the house (or classroom). It would be counterproductive to be judgmental or make comparisons to the others.

This is not, however, how portfolios are often viewed and used. In its application pamphlet, the Pacific Northwest College of Art defines an application portfolio as "a visual representation of who you are as an artist, your history as well as what you are currently doing" (Paulson, Paulson, and Meyer 1991, p. 61). Another definition is "a purposeful collection of student work that exhibits the student's efforts, progress, and achievements" (p. 60). Both of these conceptions are reasonable enough, but the function of these portfolios is very different. Their audience has more judgmental purposes in mind, and these purposes will change the nature of the portfolio experience. One way to think of portfolios is as a product to be used to make summary judgments about students for the purposes of school graduation, selection, report card grades, and so forth, or to make judgments about schools, programs, or teachers. This view suggests the richness of the portfolio contents (by comparison with standardized tests) and the fact that the contents tend to be more direct evidence of achievement than that provided by tests. From this perspective, the important considerations are how to increase the reliability of judgments, how to ensure that the work was actually done by the student, how to devise better scoring rubrics (sets of criteria with which to score the work), and how to standardize the portfolios for easier comparison.

These different stances are not mutually exclusive, but there are compromises to be made as the function of the portfolio becomes more judgmental and the stakes become higher. In the examples given earlier, the students have control of the criteria for selection and hence the criteria by which the portfolio should be judged. However, when it comes to deciding on the basis of portfolios who should be admitted into a school and who should not, or how well a school system is serving its students' development, a different approach is taken.

The standard impulse under these circumstances is to standardize portfolios so that comparisons can be made, to clearly specify the criteria and make them available in advance so that they might be applied fairly. To this end, people develop "rubrics"—formalized, explicit statements of criteria, the intention being that students should have no surprises when their work is judged by another party. But making these criteria explicit and available does not mean that they have to be generated by the teachers or other professionals. Neither does it mean that they must be the same for each student. Students could generate their own criteria, and they could be different from one class to the next.

Indeed, Linda Rief's (1992) eighth-grade students do just that. She provides them with a range of writing examples from past students. Each student in the class selects four different pieces, which they rank order; they then describe the criteria they used to order their pieces the way they did. In small groups they discuss their criteria and try to reach consensus on which are most useful. The class thus negotiates a uniform set of reasonable criteria to be applied to their writing. These criteria can cover such things as leads, style, flow, choice of words, adherence to conventions, and use of details. Because the students themselves have negotiated them, these are criteria in which they have an investment, and at the same time they learn a great deal about writing as they work through the process. The selection criteria will not be the same from class to class, but they will be consistent within a class. Geof Hewitt (1995) suggests that having students produce their own deliberately bad examples is a productive way to extend their knowledge of these criteria.

Nancy Green's fifth graders also negotiate what will be valued in their efforts (Green 1993). Whereas Linda Rief's students negotiated what would count as good writing, Nancy Green kept that decision for herself, but encouraged the students to develop further criteria. Her students selected as one of their criteria sheer volume of writing.

Of course it would be difficult to have students negotiate statewide assessment procedures. Furthermore, the wider the range of materials found in a portfolio, the more difficult it is to apply standard criteria to them. Even in Linda Rief's classroom there are some parts of the portfolio that are open to student negotiation and some that are closed. She herself specifies domains that must be represented in the portfolio based on the instructional emphases during the semester. If they have spent several weeks on poetry, for example, she asks to see poetry represented.

In Vermont, portfolios are used as a statewide assessment device. The following dimensions are used there to guide judgments of adequacy: purpose, organization, details, language mechanics, and voice (or tone). The state also has a scale for judging how often the student is successful on these dimensions: extensively, frequently, sometimes, or rarely (Hewitt 1995). Examples of previously rated portfolios are given to teachers in an attempt to ensure consistency.

The possible rubrics used to evaluate portfolios are numerous, of course, depending on what is valued, and how literacy is viewed. For example, take the dimensions range and focus. On the one hand, we want children to read and write widely; a wide range of ways of representing the world opens more possibilities both for individuals and for the community. On the other hand, a deeper understanding or a more refined performance requires focus on specific areas. For example, to become a good poet, one needs to read and write a lot of poetry. There is a balance to be struck, then, between range and focus—a constant tension.

No matter which dimensions we choose, how to judge their adequacy must also be decided. If we decide that range is a criterion in evaluating portfolios, we still need to specify what is considered a "good" range. Would reading four different genres be "good" or "excellent"? Would "excellent" require a certain number of genres from a certain number of cultures and subject areas? In the end we will still be stuck with decisions about what trade-offs are acceptable between range and depth. For example, in the context of a student reading everything ever written by Roald Dahl and writing pieces in the style of Dahl, would a more modest range of writing count as "good"?

We can reduce this ambiguity, but only at a cost. The cost is in the loss of students' control of their own learning and literacy, and in the tendency to trivialize much of the learning that takes place. Teachers faced the same conflict with objectives-based assessment. The more trivial the objective, the easier it was to make it explicit. Similarly, the more we standardize portfolios, the fewer surprises we will have and the more judges will agree on the quality of the product, but the less creative and engaging will be the portfolios and the less grounds there will be for productive conversations. Standardized tests are the logical end of the path to standardization.

When one of the purposes of portfolios is to pass judgment on the student's work—for a grade, graduation, or whatever—the criteria take on increasing significance. The higher the stakes involved, the greater the significance, and the greater the mistrust and anxiety. Why should an African-American student sensitive to the material inequities of society trust a white middle-class teacher to provide a fair, unbiased judgment of his or her portfolio? Although on average perhaps less prejudiced than the general population, teachers do have their biases; ask students. Students and their parents have theirs too; ask teachers. We all have different perspectives and experiences, and we are all afflicted with the tendency to frame differences as deficits—a tendency exacerbated by pressure. When a child hands in a portfolio with a rap piece in it, or something else that is not adult mainstream culture, how is it judged? Should we exclude such works at the outset to avoid the dilemma?

Standardizing Portfolios

The more open the definition of a portfolio, the greater the diversity you will get, and in a democracy diversity is an important tool for social and personal development. However, the greater the diversity of material in the portfolios, the less likely it is that two different judges will agree on the relative quality of portfolios. As explained earlier, people reduce the diversity by standardizing in the interests of facilitating comparative judgments. For example, the following dimensions might be standardized:

- Domain (for example, all students are to compile a portfolio to represent themselves as writers rather than as readers, learners, or literate people).
- Form (for example, all are issued the same commercially produced folder with two pockets. This implicitly restricts the dimensions of the contents).
- Allowable or required contents—for example,
    - Three pieces of writing, one of which must be a book report.
    - Must be done in school, specifically in English class (not social studies or science).
    - Must be written in the English language.
    - Must be done within a given time frame.
    - Must be done entirely by the portfolio owner, rather than by someone else or in collaboration with someone else.
- Evaluative criteria (dimensions of content, grammar, spelling, or style).
- Time frame (all portfolios must be completed at the same time).

Some restrictions can be implicit. For example, children often think of reading and writing as referring only to school activities. Even learning can be construed this way so that experiences beyond school do not count as learning.

Restricting the range of possibilities has drawbacks. First, the greater the restriction, the more it invites direct comparisons, competitiveness, and concern over ability as capacity, with consequent ego-involvement. This in itself reduces the range of artifacts the portfolio compiler will choose from in order not to look different. It also increases the possibility that some students will disengage from the process. Second, reducing the range reduces the development of more complex self-evaluation by limiting the criteria available for adoption. Third, restricting the range also reduces the grounds for conversation about values, the very stuff of democracy. It can also restrict the metaphors available for people to make sense of their own lives and learning.

However, I do not want to give the impression that restricting the range in a portfolio is inherently bad. Restricting the domain and narrowing the evaluative criteria can make for more tightly focused conversations. For example, my wife paints watercolors. She spent months working almost entirely on flowers, concentrating on fluidness, shade, and detail selection. The restriction was her choice. Others in her group emphasized different criteria.

Why Bother?

Given all the complications, you may ask, why bother with portfolios? The reasons are many and various. For example, I can think of no better way for teachers to get to know their new students at the beginning of the year than for individual students to bring in a portfolio to describe themselves as learners—perhaps one produced at the end of the previous school year. Taking ten minutes per student and perhaps two students a day would accomplish several goals. First, the teacher would learn about each new student in a personal way that focuses primarily on how the student would like to be known and what criteria the student values. In general, this first conference should focus on what students can do, the positive, rather than dwelling on what they cannot do. Second, the process itself would send the message to the students that their self-evaluation is important. Third, it would ensure that students do not slip through the cracks for the first half of the year. All in all, not a bad harvest for a simple procedure. It certainly beats the report cards that teachers often use to get to know students.

There are, of course, problems to be solved and dilemmas to be faced with portfolios. For example, what about the children who lose their portfolio over the summer? First, as mentioned earlier, the more commitment students have to their portfolio, the less this will happen. Students can leave their portfolios in school over the summer, though this would deprive them of the possibility of using the portfolio over summer. It would also reduce their attachment to it. Another way to look at this possibility is to say simply "So what?" If a student were to lose his or her portfolio over the summer, he or she could put together a new one over the first two or three weeks of school, just as new students would do, and carry on from there.

Some advantages to portfolios are easy to overlook. For example, buried in paperwork, professional people must constantly make decisions about what to keep and what to throw, what to file and what to show. Student portfolios acknowledge this part of being a literate person. Indeed, Mark Milliken (1992) found that his students' organizational habits improved with portfolio use. But portfolios have benefits well beyond the mundane. They offer increased investment in learning (writing, reading), and a changed sense of self as learner or literate person. For example, when portfolios play a central part in high school graduation ceremonies, students seem to value the portfolio over the diploma (Hewitt 1995). Compiling a portfolio gives students a goal and a time limit for putting together what amounts to a performance, a normal part of children's learning (Holdaway 1986), but gives control of the nature of the performance to the student. Having control of the performance reduces unproductive stress (productive tension remains) and gives a clear purpose to the daily record-keeping for which students are responsible. These records provide the basis for researching their own literate development.

There are also important reasons for establishing a portfolio approach to assessment. A portfolio generates ongoing reflective attention to development in one's own work. As children become aware of the course of their learning, that over time their work changes, they become more observant of their own development and more interested in setting goals and taking control of the course of their learning. Portfolios raise for public discussion the concept of what it means for an individual to "achieve." This helps develop the independence of judgment necessary for democratic living. At the same time, portfolios make students think historically, in the sense that they come to realize that their concerns now, the insecurities of growing up and the level of skill with which they sometimes become frustrated, do in fact pass. This encourages personal growth and the development of a more grounded personal identity. In the social domain, portfolios, viewed as a collective project of a learning community, can contribute to a trusting, supportive, more caring community based in diversity and connection.

Portfolios also provide a fertile ground for teacher self-evaluation. For example, in a classroom in which there is very little reading and writing, the portfolios will reflect this. If classroom writing is formulaic and focused on convention, the portfolios will reflect this, too. If the teacher does not generate and value discussion of reading and writing, students' evaluations of their own development will remain general and simplistic. After all is said and done, it is not the portfolio itself, the material entity, that accomplishes all these feats, but the conversations that revolve around the portfolio. In short, the portfolio is a great catalyst for productive conversations.

CHAPTER 28

*W*RITING
CASE STUDIES

*A person does not have to be a professional writer to tell a case-history with
authority and power. He has only to know his journey intimately and carry
some attitude toward it which enables something more than a bad list of
names and dates.*

KEN MACRORIE, 1970

*S*ome of what teachers learn is privileged information given by students
with the understanding that it remain confidential. However, teachers
have responsibilities to others as well. Students' parents are interested in their
children's progress. Every year teachers write millions of report cards to anxious
parents (and their children). Others in the school system (such as specialist teachers, next year's teachers, and administrators) are also interested in students'
progress. This means that part of our responsibility as teachers is to communicate
useful information clearly to the appropriate audience. Often this cannot be
accomplished without educating the other party (and ourselves). For example,
many parents and administrators currently are most persuaded by test scores. They
were not born with this interest in test scores, and if they are ever to become interested in more important and relevant assessment information, they will need to
learn other ways. Therefore, writing about, and otherwise reporting, students'
literacy development should not be taken lightly.

Language

Once, while I was traveling, a flight attendant announced on our arrival at the
airport, "All unaccompanied minors please remain seated until other passengers
have deplaned." The eight-year-old next to me got up to leave. Writing a report
about a child's development and making an announcement to a planeload of

passengers have the same general goal: to communicate with others. Choice of words is important, as demonstrated by the flight attendant who mistakenly expected all "unaccompanied minors" to understand the words used to describe them. A case study requires clear language with carefully chosen examples and enough detail for the reader to understand the student and make good decisions as needed. When we write or speak about children we commonly use abstractions. For example, a teacher might say "Jack has an improved attention span" instead of saying "Jack has been attending to his work for longer periods of time" or even "Yesterday, Jack wrote for an hour without leaving his chair or even talking to anyone." Abstract words have two distinct disadvantages. In the first place they do not invoke memorable mental images. Second, they tend to carry an implicit permanence. Being "learning disabled" is not seen as something that will go away quickly, if ever.

Most professions have their own specialized language, which allows them to talk with colleagues in such a way that those outside the profession feel unable to participate. This makes the client feel helpless and the professional feel powerful. Medical doctors speak of hemorrhaging or exsanguinating rather than simply bleeding. School psychologists, speech therapists, and others have developed their own terminology. Such jargon may, in part, be a sign of a lack of confidence that respect can be earned any other way, and in part a lack of consideration for their audience. Educators must avoid this trap. Some specialized terms may be unavoidable, perhaps when referring to a completely new or specific phenomenon, but we should aim for no jargon. Even terms such as *syntax* may be replaced by *sentence structure*. *Semantics* is probably better spelled *m-e-a-n-i-n-g* or called "sense." Consider the difference between the following two versions of the same report:

> Lucy's text processing skills are very weak in the decoding area,
> particularly in decoding polysyllabic words. She decodes accurately the
> initial and terminal elements of monosyllabic and bisyllabic words but
> cannot adequately process the medial elements, particularly
> diphthongs, and does not integrate syntactic and semantic contextual
> information with the graphic cues. Whereas processing textual
> information is weak, auditory comprehension is strong.

versus

> Lucy understands stories very well when they are read to her.
> However, when she reads them for herself she sometimes has trouble,
> particularly in figuring out longer words. She can generally determine
> how the beginning and end of the word might sound, but is often
> confused by the middle of the word, particularly when there are two
> vowels. She has not yet learned to use the meaning of the other words
> to help her figure out confusing words.

Try to use plain English as much as possible. Pretentious, thoughtless language, usually used to establish a power difference, has more consequences than people think. Melissa, a seven-year-old, came to our reading lab with a report from the director of a medical center. The report contained the following segment:

> The root of Melissa's academic difficulties appears to be a developmental language disorder of a mixed semantic pragmatic/phonologic syntactic deficits *(sic)*. These have been translated into more academic difficulties as it relates to the pragmatic use of language in the verbal setting that academics generally require.

Never, never do this. It may inflate your ego (errors notwithstanding), but to parents who care deeply about their child's welfare, such a report is devastating. One way or another the negative evaluation is passed on to the child. Physicians can be the worst when it comes to mystifying and terrifying their patients with abstract technical terms. But this behavior has its consequences. As Neil Postman (1976) put it, the field of iatrogenics is the study of "how doctor-talk can intensify and even induce illness" (p. 228). Children's literacy development might well produce a similar field of study. Indeed, it has in the field of special education (Coles 1987; Mehan 1993; McDermott and Varenne 1995).

Framing

In "clinical" reports it is common practice to present background information at the beginning, to provide the reader with a context, or frame, within which to interpret the evaluation information. This is meant as recognition that the child's reading and writing activity is influenced by the current and the historical context. Sometimes, however, contexts that are less than helpful for one reason or another are inadvertently presented. Consider this beginning of a report we received:

> Bruce is a nine-year-old fourth grader who is about to enter the Riverside School remedial reading program. He has a central auditory processing deficit, significant language, reading and writing deficits, and visual perceptual difficulty. The City Hospital has determined that Bruce has moderately low receptive and expressive language skills, moderately severe delays in syntax development, decreased language processing abilities and pragmatic skills (ability to label categories, sequence, follow more than a 3-step directive, continue a conversation, and think imaginatively), and a moderate articulation disorder. He has been referred to the school speech therapist but the parents have refused this help.

There are several points worth commenting on in this excerpt. First, the choice of words is critical. For example, it would be better to say "his parents have declined this help" or "have decided against this course of action" than to say "refused this help." "Refused" has a negative connotation, which unnecessarily tilts the reader against the parents. Second, no matter what information is presented after this introduction, the reader is likely to respond, "Well, this is only to be expected, given the student's disabilities."

One way of preventing the problem of readers giving up on the student before even finishing the report is to avoid attributing to the student such permanent-sounding traits as a "central auditory processing deficit" and to save any such information, if relevant, until somewhere near the end. It could be included in a section of, say, "instructional history," which should emphasize what the child *does* and the nature of the instructional environment, thus deflecting blame from the child. At the very least, the opening might be rewritten as follows:

> Bruce is a nine-year-old fourth grader at Maplehill school who is about to enter the reading support program. He receives speech/language therapy at Hillside Hospital three times per week. The school has offered the services of the school speech therapist. However, Mr. and Mrs. Green have declined this service as they feel that with his reading support program as well, Bruce would be away from his regular class too much and would fall behind in other areas. There is some discrepancy between the evaluations of his reading performance made by the school and by the hospital.

Filed under "Additional Information" at the end might be the following:

> David's speech therapist, John Morton, reports that David has been later than most children in developing mature speech patterns. In test situations he appears not to speak or listen as well as his peers. Sometimes Bruce's speech is not easy to understand as he does not articulate L's and R's very clearly. In a test situation he does not participate well in discussions with adults, and he has trouble repeating exactly sentences of more than four words which are read to him. He tends to alter them to his own language patterns. Greater detail on this aspect of David's development can be found in the hospital's report. However, it is not yet clear that this is the source of any difficulties with David's reading or writing.

There are other problems related to framing. Children who are least able are most likely to be described in negative terms because:

1. Schools are structured normatively, and those below the norm are generally seen through what they do not know and cannot do, rather than through what they know and can do.
2. Tests (and I include basal readers in this term) enforce and make consequential a normative view of children, particularly when the tests are used for teacher accountability.
3. Less able children are most likely to be given material that is too difficult for them, which makes them exhibit even more negative behavior.

When people observe a child's performance, particularly if the child has already been determined to "have a problem," they tend to see and report a lot of negative information. In the same way, readers of a report who assume at the outset that the child has a problem (otherwise why would there be a report?) tend to scan the report looking for the problems. If the student's activities are divided into "strengths" and "weaknesses," these readers often bypass the strengths and go directly to the weaknesses, especially if they are short on time. One way around this is not to organize the report around such simplistic categories. A second way is to ensure that the recipients of the report are not novices. Steps should be taken to educate the audience. For example, to keep parents informed, you could send them regular explanations of what is being done in school and why, what changes they should expect to see, and why invented spelling is important, and you could give examples of children's development in newsletters, at parent nights, and on local TV channels.

The sheer weight of information can present a serious framing problem too. Take, for example, a test like the Diagnostic Reading Scales (Spache 1981). This test provides three "text level" scores (an instructional reading level, an independent reading level, and a potential reading level) and twelve test scores at or below the word level (syllables, manipulation of sounds and letters, and so forth). Once all those details have been reported, it is hard to write instructional suggestions that focus on the less easily measured and less frequently mentioned aspects of reading, such as enjoyment and frequency. Unfortunately, the resulting instructional suggestions intended to accomplish one goal are often antithetical to another. For example, overattention to children's spelling or decoding can easily make writing or reading even less enjoyable by distracting them from the meaningfulness of the activity.

Voice and Style

Throughout this book I have tried to make it clear that teachers assessing children's literacy are simply people describing the activity of people. We cannot avoid interpreting what we observe, so it is proper for us to write reports that sound like an involved person wrote them. It is dishonest to pretend that our assessments are statements of "fact" that are independent of human judgment. It is easier for educators to assume objectivity when they use group tests, which depersonalize the situation and make it seem as though the group is not made up of individuals; but reports are often written about individuals in the same way, as if the writers were simply passive recorders of *truth*. These writers fear that if a strong, active voice is heard in the writing, the subjectivity of the process will be obvious. This stance is unfortunate and should be discontinued. First, such an attitude is dishonest: it pretends to have an objectivity that is not possible. Second, such writing is usually cast in the passive voice, which tends to be boring and eminently forgettable. Third, the style depersonalizes the individual being written about and discourages the reader from attempting to know the person whose activity is being described. Indeed, such writing is an attempt to disguise the fact that there is a person to know. Mikhail Bakhtin (Todorov 1984) has called this *thingification* (as opposed to *personification*).

Writers favoring the "objective" approach to report writing avoid narrative writing in favor of more expository styles. They feel that narrative style connotes "stories" with their implicit subjectivity. After all, stories are based on motives and goals and feelings and other such "soft" stuff, and they are associated with fiction. But when I have read a report of a child's writing and reading development, I want to have the feeling that I have come to know the student and will remember him or her. It is not enough for me to have lots of data, no matter how good the data may be. I must relate the information to the person who was responsible for the activity, not to the behavior per se. Although reports are functional (and often legal) documents, they need not be boring and unreadable.

When you write about students, always remember that the children are your clients. There should be nothing in the report that you would not be able to say in front of them. Indeed, normally it makes sense to go over the report with the student before sending it. This does not mean that you should expect a six-year-old to be able to understand all that you might have written, but you should weigh carefully the consequences of what you have to say. Do not send a report such as that suggested in the manual for the Reading Test for New York State Elementary Schools (The University of the State of New York, the State Education Department 1986) test. The writers of this manual suggest sending the following form letter to parents:

> This test score indicates that [David] cannot read many of the books commonly used in school, and that [he] is not reading as well as most other third grade students.
>
> In order to help [David] improve [his] reading ability, we are placing [him] in a special reading program called _____. A description of the program is enclosed with this letter. (p. 55)

Please!

When you are reporting the results of a test, you should identify it in full, including the name of the publisher, the copyright date, the form (A, B, C, etc.), and any deviations from standard procedure. Reporting the source and date of information should really be routine for all sorts of data. Annotated, dated photocopies of samples of a student's writing make a report about that student much more meaningful.

Important Information

It is not especially helpful to know that "Sarah is a cute little girl with sparkling green eyes." When I read a report I want to learn how the student goes about literate activity and in what context he or she normally does so. (Other report readers may have different goals, which I discuss later in this chapter.) I want to know what aspects of literate activity the student controls, and I want to know under what circumstances he or she actually engages productively in reading and writing and what that engagement looks like. (The questions I seek answers to are those outlined in Part Two of this book.) Describing the context of a student's activity can, however, be difficult for a teacher who is in the middle of it.

The immediate context can be simple enough. For example, you might make notes such as the following:

> Running record of *There's a Nightmare in My Closet* (M. Mayer 1968). Record taken on 4/3/96. This book has been read to the class twice in the two weeks preceding this running record. However, Tony has never read it himself before.

Similarly, a writing sample might have the following information appended:

> This is the first draft of a story by Paul Simpson written on 2/24/96 during a free choice period. He chose the topic himself, and the piece was completed in less than thirty minutes. He did not return to it.

It makes a big difference if a piece of writing is an example of reflex writing in a five-minute period, or the result of four drafts and three hours of work. It makes a difference if the piece was copied, or if the topic or activity was selected by the author.

Sometimes broader contextual information is important. It might be helpful to know about the relevant school curriculum and organization. If, for example, Jennifer is taken out of her regular classroom for reading and for speech, we would want to know what she misses while she's away from the classroom. If a child has been retained, or has changed schools recently (or frequently), these facts are important. Some aspects of the context are more easily noticed by those outside the classroom than by those who live with them. If, for example, a visitor notes that the classroom walls display a clock, two pictures of birds, and a Santa Claus, but no children's work, the teacher might be surprised, not having noticed this before, and might reflect on its possible significance. Describing the classroom as "drab and uninteresting," however, is likely to make the teacher defensive rather than reflective.

Using shorthand jargon such as "whole language" or "direct instruction" or "traditional" to describe classroom contexts should be avoided. Readers' assumptions about those terms can be problematic. They have become "red flag" words for many people, and so can distract readers from useful observations. Simply providing accurate detail is more helpful. For example:

> I observed Michael during his language arts period. He spent a total of 2 minutes, 36 seconds reading. The story was *My Dog Al* in his reading book. He read it with a word-level accuracy of 85 percent. He read it out loud for the teacher. He spent a total of 1 minute, 20 seconds composing a piece of writing. He completed four worksheets, which required filling in the blanks in sentences and drawing lines between words and pictures. Of the 31 items on the worksheets he completed 7

accurately. These 7 involved matching a word with a picture. Michael participated in one whole-class lesson on the subject of capitalization. In an interview he had the following responses:

Q: What does a good reader do?

A: Says all the words right.

Q: I have a friend who will probably be in this class next year. Do you have any advice for him about how to do well in reading?

A: Sit quietly and have a sharp pencil.

The order in which observations are made, their emphasis, and the extent to which the information is memorable will influence the effectiveness of a report. Clear, concrete examples help readers to know the students better and to remember and use the information during instruction.

Instructional Suggestions

In most reports there should be clear instructional or support suggestions. This is often what teachers and parents find most important, but is usually the aspect of the report most poorly handled by specialists who lack classroom experience teaching reading and writing. Often the parents of children who are failing to become literate feel powerless in the face of a severe threat to their child's well-being (teachers can feel this way too). This feeling of helplessness can complicate interactions with the child. Often, parents can be helped as much as children if they can be shown how to develop a supportive role at home through such things as: reading to and with their child, providing study space and study time free of television and other distractions, and discussing world events in the newspaper or on television.

When making written suggestions, be sure to make them practical and clear, and preferably with a rationale. The following actual example would probably not be accepted well by a teacher looking for help:

> William needs to develop print skill strategies. He has a limited sight vocabulary that needs to be addressed. In addition, William needs to progress beyond blending of initial consonant sounds. He would improve his reading fluency and accuracy if he understood variations made by vowels including the *r*-controlled vowel. William's word analysis and phonics test showed a weakness in identifying common consonant digraphs such as *ch* and *th*. Include in the lessons writing samples using sight words and other phonetic skills. Once William has mastered some of these print skill strategies, comprehension based on visual modes of instruction will reflect an understanding of the author's intended meaning.

A more helpful recommendation regarding this student would be:

> William's reading program should focus on two areas. First, he needs to read a great deal of easy material in order to develop his fluency. Many books could be reread, and some books could be made easy

enough for him to read himself by first reading them to him. I have added to this report a list of books that will be appropriate and that match some of his interests.

In order to help William figure out words using letter-sound relationships, involve him in writing, helping him to say the words slowly as he writes them. Also, find opportunities in his writing to highlight words containing *th, ch,* and *sh,* as these are difficult for him. Since he already is comfortable with the words *the* and *she* in both reading and writing, I would use these as keys to help him work out related words. His use of vowels will be helped by attention to rhyming, particularly in his writing, and to the feelings in his mouth when he says them.

When you are writing a case study, be aware that you are creating a representation that can have serious consequences for the student. Introduce the student as a person rather than as an object. Draw readers' attention to the things students can do and the circumstances under which they can, and will do them. The value of case studies hinges on your careful selection of concrete observations and the appropriateness of the story you weave to explain their significance. If your efforts are to be of value, your audience (which almost always includes parents) must understand and remember what you have to say.

OPENING PANDORA'S GRADE BOX

*T*he moment our first child was born my wife, who could not see him yet, was frantically asking, "Is he all right? Is he all right?" Most parents don't get over this completely. One of the major functions of a report card for some parents is to allay their fears. They want to know "Is he all right?" and surely, if there is genuine reason for concern, teachers would be remiss if they did not explain the nature of the problem. Report cards are meant to perform the simple function of reporting a child's state of learning to his or her parents. Seems simple and innocuous enough. But I have yet to meet the teacher who enjoys the activity. Furthermore, since reports of child abuse skyrocket around report card time (and that's counting only physical abuse) it is unlikely that most students look forward to them either (Valentine 1990).

The business of report cards is often highly contentious for all parties. It certainly is for teachers. Peter Afflerbach and I asked some teachers to think out loud with a tape recorder running while they wrote their report cards (Afflerbach and Johnston 1993). These tapes revealed the complex decision-making demanded of teachers. Most found the activity very stressful. In fact, the more a teacher knew about a child, the more stressful it was to reduce that knowledge to the categories and grades on the report card. Aside from the complexity of their knowledge of the child's current performance (transcriptions of their comments on literacy alone filled several pages), teachers would try to take into account growth over the year ("he's come so far . . ."), relative performance ("but when you compare him with Ricky . . ."), and the consequences for the child of receiving a particular grade ("his parents would kill him"). The only teachers who did not find the process stressful were two whose students did lots of basal reader tests and worksheets. For them the report card involved a few minutes with a calculator. Their method of instruction also kept them at sufficient emotional distance from their students to simplify the process even further.

In one local school district virtually all of the parents turn up for the first parent-teacher conference of the year. At these conferences the teacher uses the child's work and running records to show the parent what the child knows and can do, tying these to categories on the report card. These categories—actually, descriptive statements of literate behavior—are qualified on a four-point scale: "not yet," "sometimes," "often," and "almost always." The parents take the report card home; it serves as a summary of their conversation with the teacher. This system is in place for kindergarten through grade three. At grade four it changes dramatically. Starting with that grade, the system requires teachers to give number grades—89, 75, and so forth. The conversations that these numbers evoke are quite different from those in the earlier grade, and the teachers' attention becomes directed toward strategies for defending against questions about grades. The easiest way to do this is to assign multiple-choice tests and work sheets, which at once provides easily countable (and accountable) data and trivializes the classroom experience of the students.

Middle school often provides a sharp contrast with elementary school when it comes to evaluation. Both teachers and parents shift their stance. Children begin to be shuffled among teachers, and each teacher interacts with a larger number of students. The relationship between teacher and student changes, and teachers and parents begin to take a different view of the purpose of schooling. Competitive college and job markets begin to loom on the horizon. At one middle school parent night I attended, each teacher opened his or her comments with a statement on grading policy, making clear that the grade was entirely dependent on the student and an objective, rule-governed system. Parents responded with questions about grades. One asked, "What is the range for an A?" The teacher responded, "Basically in the 90s," and parents nodded. They did not feel the need to ask the meaning of the numbers that were used to explain the letter, yet if everyone in the room wrote down the meaning of an 83 in this grading system, they would notice that the meanings differed substantially from one another, particularly if they were asked to note the expected instructional response. If the number is meant to refer to an average percentage of accurate responses to questions, one might ask what the questions were, and whether they were interesting questions. But if we begin this line of conversation the whole enterprise will unravel because the interesting questions don't have known answers. They are difficult to mark right or wrong, and they are easily contested (and who wants that?). That is why the little grade box is really Pandora's box. If we open, it serious things start to happen.

Coming to Terms with Report Cards

Report cards are often the lightning rods for highly charged curricular conflicts. People who try to change them are often seriously burned. For example, consider the Riverland school district. There has been considerable conflict over elementary school report cards in that district. The conflict revolves around several issues: grades and grading, dimensions of learning, and the nature of the process that produced the report card. Here is the story as I see it.

The district has always had a progressive bent, and most of the teachers are deeply committed to their work. Many can be found in their classrooms well into the evening and in the summer months. For many years the district has had a process of shared decision-making that involves a set of committees of parents, teachers, and administrators who develop and direct the curriculum for the district. The district also supports teachers' professional development through conference participation and local study groups. As teachers developed their teaching practice they began to realize that the report card they had to fill out did not reflect what they worked for in their classrooms. Indeed, for many of the teachers, filling out the report card was highly stressful, since it involved reducing a complex, personal, narrative understanding of a child into simple, impersonal, comparative judgments. The more knowledgeable and caring the teacher, the more stressful the activity was. So the curriculum groups worked on the matter and set up a report card committee of teachers and parents. The committee came to the conclusion that the report card should no longer have grades, but should instead provide space in each subject area for a description of the child's development.

This new report card suited some of the teachers who were good observers and had a lot to say about each child, although some felt there was too little space; they had to write small and use extra sheets of paper. The report cards also took more time to fill out, so teachers with families and other commitments were forced to begin filling out the February report cards in December, making some thoroughly out of date by the time parents got them. In addition, some of the parents on the committee were unhappy that there were no grades on the report cards. As a compromise, teachers were required to embed somewhere in their narrative the words "excellent," "good," "fair," or "having difficulty." In short, this new report card still had the old shortcomings and introduced a new problem, especially for the less observant teachers, who were faced with relatively large spaces to fill with relatively little information to fill them with—an uncomfortable experience. They responded by writing in large letters comments that were not specific enough to be of any help to parents and by expressing their frustration to the teachers' union, which reacted by demanding that the report card be replaced.

A new committee was formed to develop a successor to this report card. The committee worked very hard and produced a new compromise form that generated even more frustration, anger, and resentment than the previous one. Nobody but the committee, it was argued, could understand it. Descriptive details were to be conveyed through a complex checklist-rating system. Those on the committee had worked out this compromise through lengthy conversations. It made sense to them because they had been present at the negotiations, but those who had not been part of the conversations could not understand the report card. Some of the teachers who were not on the committee made disparaging comments about the report card to parents when the reports were distributed.

This report card also lasted one year. Setting up yet another report card committee was not easy. Who wants to put in that sort of effort only to get grief in return? Some parents got together and set up a committee to insist on having grades. The situation reached the polls at budget-voting time.

Conflicts

What is going on? Here we have a lot of people dedicated to children's education, putting in a great deal of work with the best of intentions, yet failing to find sustainable reporting practices. Several conflicts are embedded in this problem, which, at the risk of oversimplifying, may be summarized as follows:

- Different groups use different language to represent children's learning (for example, "emerging," "B," "sometimes," "87%").
- Different groups value different aspects or kinds of learning (spelling versus composition or view of self as learner, engagement versus relative competence, ability versus effort).
- Different groups have different theories of how children learn and why (reward/punishment versus interest, linear stage-by-stage development versus development on a broader and more complex front).
- Different groups hold different beliefs about the goal of education (preparation for the workforce versus engagement in a democracy, membership in a homogeneous society versus individual development as a contemplative person).

These are serious differences that can never be completely resolved, but that deserve ongoing discussion. The earlier this discussion begins, and the better and the more sustained the contact among the parties, the better.

Taking Things for Granted

Although these are issues that divide, there are others that might make for more productive negotiations. Report cards are meant to inform parents and students of the progress that the students are making in school. For many parents they are the principal source of information on their child's development. However, report cards also give teachers time to take stock of each child's progress, so that no one falls through the cracks. These two functions can be served in many different ways. Habit and unexamined assumptions frequently limit us unnecessarily. I have often seen committees struggle to come up with a new report card only to produce something that looks like the old one with more categories and a few different labels because they failed to examine basic assumptions.

For example, the report does not have to be on a single side of a single sheet of paper. It could be a book with a page for each domain. It could be a portfolio, as discussed in Chapters 26 and 27. It could include a videotape or audiotape. The form and medium can be whatever we want, provided people understand it. This means engaging in ongoing discussion so that everyone using the report card understands it in the same way. Also, the form chosen this year (or for this school, grade, or teacher) does not have to be the same for the next ten years, or even the next year. Report cards really should be viewed as drafts. Computers have made it possible to change formats at will. The major catch is that each change involves a change in the conversation and must involve all parties.

Reports of a student's progress do not have to be composed entirely by the teacher. Certainly the teacher should have a considerable amount of knowledge about the student's development. But so should the student. The more we can involve students in the reporting of their own development, the more reflective and involved they will become in their learning. Indeed, the less they are involved, the more they come to believe that evaluation is something that is done to them, rather than something for which they are responsible. In many schools the reporting is done as a three-way process with parent(s), child, and teacher involved either in the entire interaction or in parts of the reporting. In some schools both teacher and student contribute to the writing of the report card either individually or collaboratively. Involving students in writing their own report cards is not without its problems, of course, especially when students are involved in their own grading. On the one hand, getting students so involved gives them a chance to influence their grades, which may make the system less controlling. In addition, students involved in deciding their own grades rarely disagree with their teachers' assessment (Atwell 1987; Austin 1994; Rief 1992). Some many find this comforting, but I am not sure what it means when students agree with their teachers' judgment about grades. There are difficult power issues involved. I am somewhat less uneasy when the criteria for judgment are generated mutually by students and teacher and when both use concrete examples to justify their judgment.

In some schools, where evaluation is based on portfolios, the reporting often begins with the child taking his or her parent through the portfolio and ends with the teacher meeting with the parent. If parents' comments on portfolios, for example, will go into the students' permanent file, the parents will very likely respond and consider their comments very carefully. Sessions in which all three parties meet can help keep the assessment process open and reduce students' fears about what people might say. Like teachers, parents may need some help in learning how to observe and respond to children's work.

The report form does not have to be divided into categories that are the same for each child. Although it may be useful for teachers to refer to a checklist in order to make sure they do not leave important aspects of particular children's development unexamined, I would just as soon see a report card that was essentially a blank page. Of course, such a report card demands of a teacher a great deal of knowledge. A teacher who cannot write such a report probably needs help organizing the classroom, setting up ways of keeping track, or learning about the various patterns of development. There is no reason for us to assume that all teachers are equally competent at observing and documenting children's learning, or that any one teacher is equally competent at this in every domain of learning. Workshops and study groups are often critical.

Documentary reporting demands a fair amount of time. But all reports do not have to go out on the same day. Once we get rid of this habit, we can consider different possibilities. For example, if teachers are given a month within which to send out reports, they can select a child or two each day to meet with, discussing the child's reading and writing and generally taking stock, then writing up the record at the end of the day and sending it out or meeting with parents. Indeed, reporting need not be constrained to a designated month. Continuous reporting with, say, three or four children per week throughout the year is also possible (Woodward 1994). Such procedures would ensure up-to-date, detailed descriptions of children's development. They might also prevent such problems as all of the children opening their report cards on the school bus, showing them around and making destructive comparisons. Many aspects of reporting can be distributed over time. For example, Riverland's descriptive form could have been phased in over a period of time, beginning with those teachers who were most comfortable with it. This would have allowed any problems to be solved along the way, and conversations to be built slowly.

Distributing the reporting over time can help a lot, but the report does not have to carry the entire burden of informing students or parents of the student's progress. The more we can shift this burden from the report card, the better. For example, reports can be timed to coincide with parent-teacher conferences, perhaps being summaries of those conferences. At that point, the teacher's understanding of the student will be at its freshest, and potential misunderstandings can be addressed face-to-face. Indeed, according to a survey in Riverland, most of the parents found conferences with teachers much more helpful than report cards. These conferences offer the possibility of attending to parents' particular concerns, especially if they focus on parents' concerns. To facilitate this, a letter can be sent in advance of the conference asking parents if they have any specific concerns they would like addressed in the conference. In addition, the first thing a teacher must do in the conference is listen to the parent's concerns in a nondefensive manner. If a parent has a particular concern it is often hard to listen to someone else spouting until the concern has been addressed.

Some of the burden of communication can be spread out over time. For example, each day you might choose two or three students and send them home with an envelope of their work (with sticky notes commenting on specific features that show growth). Involving children in this process would also be productive. This could coincide with your ongoing systematic review of students' learning. A form letter inviting parental response will also facilitate communication. An initial letter explaining that you will be doing this and possibly providing some description of likely developments in the children's learning would also be helpful. Follow up your announcement of the process at the initial meet-the-teacher night. Once the system is in place it need not take large amounts of time.

Standardizing forms, times, and the like is very difficult for people, particularly administrators, to give up. But standardization is often not necessary. Just because some parents want their children graded does not imply that all children must be. Although some may argue that grading facilitates communication, if all parties are not involved in the same conversation, it does not.

Reporting does not have to include grades or ratings of any kind. Grades do not serve children well. It would be better—more accurate and humane—to replace grades with descriptive details of the child's development.

Also, reporting does not have to be done by the teacher. Children are quite capable of taking on this responsibility.

Detecting the taken-for-granted parts of the process, like unnecessarily standardizing reporting times and not involving students in the reporting process, is hard enough. But getting people who take them for granted to change the way they think is considerably harder. Often, contemplating change requires examining deep cultural and personal values that are hard to face.

Degrading Students Through Report Cards

There is always the problem of grades. And they are a problem. Aside from the issues of motivation and self-worth they raise, they often drive a wedge into the relationship between teacher and student. As Nel Noddings (1984) put it:

> The teacher does not grade to inform the student. She has far better, more personal ways to do this. She grades to inform others about the student's progress. Others establish standards, explicitly or implicitly, and they charge her to report faithfully in observance of these standards. Now the teacher is torn between obligation to the employing community and faithfulness to the student. After a relationship with the student as a subject, grading requires us to treat the student as an object. (p. 194)

But grades make so much sense to so many people, often for different reasons. Some parents argue, as one did in our local paper, that "a lot of parenting is about giving rewards and punishments." I would not like to think of parenting that way, but I imagine most of us would confess to some use of rewards and punishments. I would prefer to spend my time with my children in more interesting conversations than such controlling ones. Most parents would prefer not to have to use rewards and punishments. Parents would much rather have their children clear the table because they care about the family and want to do their part to contribute than because if they don't they don't get to watch TV or if they do they get some pocket money. Parents would much prefer that if there is homework to be done the children do it because they find it engaging. Most parents do not enjoy spending their time meting out rewards and punishments to ensure that homework is done. I think this is true simply because constant controlling and adversarial relationships with one's children do not result in a happy home life. Neither contributes to children's love of learning, nor to their caring for others or for themselves.

John Dewey observed in 1913 that we should spend less time looking for reasons *for* learning activities and more time looking for reasons *in* them (Dewey 1913). Outcomes like grades are too remote from the actual activity to sustain one over a period of struggle. Worse, when people get external rewards for things they previously did for enjoyment, or for the thrill of engagement, they often cease doing them as soon as the external rewards stop. This is not something we want to see happen with children's reading and writing. There are so many serious motivation problems associated with grades and grading that I have barely scratched the surface here; they are well documented in Alfie Kohn's (1993) book *Punished by Rewards*.

If we are to have grades, we have to decide what they should represent. Should an A represent a given level of achievement? If so, some children will constantly get A's without any effort. Some children will constantly get D's in spite of maximum effort. What children take from such grades will depend on their understanding of learning, ability, and the social situation, but it will generally not be what we hope they would learn. Should all children have exactly the same learning material? For example, should all eight-year-olds be reading the same book? If we concede that there is a range of competence and "native ability" (and I would be surprised if people expected otherwise), the same instruction for all students would be inappropriate, because some already will know the material and others will find it too far beyond their current understanding (and we haven't even mentioned personal interest). Organizing instruction so uniformly would be unfair because it would result in differential motivation. But if we differentiate so that each student has optimal instruction, some will be judged against standards that they might not have had instruction on. If rewards and punishments are at stake, this would be unfair.

Perhaps the grade should represent effort. Certainly parents who desire grades so that they might know whether to reward or punish their child would want to know whether lack of effort is the source of the problem. However, if a child is constantly faced with problems that are too difficult to solve, and is given inadequate instruction on how to solve them, all the effort in the world won't help. Indeed, ultimately these children will be convinced only of their own stupidity. Furthermore, how will we know whether the student's performance is due to effort or ability or some other factor? How do we know how hard a student worked—or why? Grading on effort is particularly problematic once children develop a notion of ability as capacity and when they are in a comparative, ego-involving situation. Children in this situation decide that trying hard means they are not able. To them, ability is inversely related to effort. Even if they work hard, they will try to conceal the fact. Also, if we manage to convince children that their achievement does relate to a lack of effort, it is easier to justify paying people with greater achievement substantially larger amounts of money by convincing others of their relative worthlessness. Grades are often referred to as "earned," just as a line worker earns $10,000 a year while a CEO earns two hundred times more.

Grades are also problematic because it is not clear who should get them. Indeed, there are often arguments about this. Is it the child's fault that he didn't learn? The teacher's? The lack of parental support? Who should get that D? Arguments will likely go different ways with an A or an F.

How should reporting between home and school be arranged so that it is not complicated by motivational matters? Perhaps the first thing is to understand why parents and administrators want grades. Some want them because it is what they experienced and thus what they feel they understand. Some want them because they feel that they are a common metric. Some simply feel they do not have the time to try to make sense of more complex reporting—"Just cut to the bottom line." Sorting out these reasons can help. For example, if some sort of uniform summary is what's sought, then something like the Primary Language Record (Barrs et al. 1988) might provide what's needed without the problems of grading (see Chapter 30). If people seek a source of motivation, then exploring the reasons why people engage in literate activity and how those factors might be made present in the classroom might help.

As long as we fail to help parents think through the costs and benefits and the alternatives, we will be stuck with grading. But even if we continue to grade, developing a common understanding is important. For example, even if we use a scale of 1 = almost always, 2 = mostly, 3 = sometimes, 4 = never, many parents, because of their own schooling, will immediately convert these numbers into A, B, C, and D or F because that is what they know.

Grades mean different things to everybody. In our studies of teachers writing report cards mentioned at the beginning of this chapter, teachers themselves differed in their assignment of grades. Some gave weight to effort, some to normative achievement, some to amount of improvement, and some took into account probable parental response (perhaps fearing physical abuse of the child). Others balanced these and other factors differently for each child (Afflerbach and Johnston 1993).

If teachers are grading for report cards, the students should know where they stand, what the grade means, and what produced it well before the report card goes home with the grades.

Changing the Conversation

Probably the best way to make changes in the reporting system is to start with the early grades and follow those students and parents through into the upper grades, constantly involving parents, administrators, teachers, board members, and students in the process. Having a good relationship among the parties involved is very important. Some conversations are only possible within a trusting relationship. Extending this relationship and expanding the understanding of all parties is easier if begun early. In the early grades, parents are fascinated by the new and interesting things that their children are accomplishing. It is also easier to make these accomplishments evident to them. Betty Shockley and her colleagues have used home journals to assist in this function (Shockley 1993; Shockley, Michalove, and Allen 1995). These are journals that travel between home and school as a sort of ongoing mail system. Students write to parents about what they are learning and parents respond, or teachers and parents write back and forth, or all three correspond. Terri Austin (1994) uses two kinds of letters. One is a general purpose letter, which the teacher writes by hand on brightly colored paper, that goes home to all parents. The second is a personal letter the teacher writes in the student's take-home journal some time during the week, documenting the highlights of the student's week and raising any concerns or asking for advice. The students also write a letter in this journal on Fridays and take it home to their parents.

What makes these journals so important? First, they build trusting relationships and a sharing of responsibility. Second, they build parents' interest in, and knowledge about, the development of literacy. Third, writing them models for children both the significance and the everydayness of literacy. Fourth, the journals provide a pressure relief valve. The frequency of the communication prevents small misunderstandings from developing a serious head of steam. Fifth, parents and teachers begin to develop a common language based on connections between common experiences, making misunderstandings increasingly unlikely.

Systemic change starts with conversations like this. If you want to make changes in the way assessment is done in your school system, involving a wide range of people in the discussions from the outset is critical. The more diverse the perspectives, the less likely it is to miss alternative options. Furthermore, the wider the direct and indirect conversational network, the lower the chance of subsequent outbursts from groups left out of the discussion. The conversations need to be wide-ranging, multipartisan, and as concrete as possible. Diverse groups often make for slower but more lasting progress. Remember, when you are trying to develop new ways of reporting to parents you are trying to change ongoing conversations that have deep roots. It takes time. It is a bit like dealing with silly putty. If you move it slowly, over time it will flow into a new form. Move it too quickly and it snaps.

Start with the idea that the enterprise will evolve. Printing out revisions of forms is easy to do nowadays. Make it clear that you are not in the business of producing the final version so that you can then leave it, but rather that you mean to project where you would like the process to evolve and what it will take along the way. For example, you might want to develop a self-evaluation system. In your realistic moments you realize it won't happen in the next two years. Consider what changes might be possible this year and how you might use the conversations those changes generate to move to where you would like to be. And remember that by the time you get there your thinking might have evolved beyond your original goals.

Early in discussions about change you might establish what you want a report card to accomplish. In any group, most will agree that the primary function is to communicate with parents, but other functions will also come up for discussion. You might end up with a list that includes:

- Communicate with parents.
- Initiate and change conversations about learning.
- Communicate with the next teacher.
- Communicate with students.
- Motivate students.
- Take stock of students' learning.

You might then brainstorm the possible ways of accomplishing these ends. Report cards might be one of them, but many functions may be best accomplished other ways. You might want to list the potential "pros and cons" of each approach.

Imagining Possibilities

Often members of report card committees cannot imagine how different reporting systems might be set up. One way to overcome this hurdle is to set up pilot programs. For example, three or four teachers might try portfolios. A couple might try using portfolios in three-way meetings with parents and students, while others might have children take the portfolios home to explain them to the parents, with the parents then returning it to the teacher as part of a conference. Two or three teachers might try documentary report cards, some doing three or four reports per week and others doing them all at once. In some classes students might take on half of the reporting. Some teachers could try a version of the Primary Language Record (described more fully in the next chapter). Some options might take a couple of years just to pilot, since learning how to do them well can take time. Cooperative piloting with other schools is also a possibility. Students and parents could become involved in researching the methods and gathering data for the committee. For example, collecting and analyzing data, particularly on student opinions, might be a good project for high school students; or students in pilot and nonpilot classes might work together to compare experiences.

Researching our own reporting practices can provide grounds for productive conversations. Kim Young (1995) reports how Rochester Elementary School did just this. Over a five-year period the teachers and parents worked together to design, pilot, and refine their reporting system. They began by writing desired outcomes for each grade level, which were then translated into report cards. With the school board's permission, they then ran a pilot program with the draft report card. The program involved two students in each classroom, selected to represent a range of competence. School board members had been involved in the discussions and the reading of relevant articles, so they were sufficiently informed about the issues to engage concerned parents in constructive, informative conversations.

At a meeting of participating parents and teachers, the principal discussed the nature and purpose of the new report card. After the report cards were sent, a meeting of relevant parents and teachers was held and a survey sent to the parents to get their feedback. The feedback was positive, so the board authorized a one-year schoolwide pilot. The school newsletter provided information and articles about issues related to reporting, such as grades, alternative assessment, and competition.

The following year modifications were made, again based on feedback, and teachers developed folders of students' work to illustrate aspects of the students' development to parents. Students chose one piece of work each week to represent their learning and wrote a reflective statement about its significance. Even as late as the third year, different teachers and parents were interpreting the coding system on the report card differently, but the differences were less pronounced. Although there remained some disagreement about the value of the system, the board authorized another year of the pilot. Discussions about the reporting system were ongoing, and a public meeting with board members, administrators, teachers, and parents was held in the spring along with another survey. Further revisions were made for the fifth year; at that point the form was computerized.

The changes made in Rochester Elementary required all classrooms to use the same reporting system. Students were only marginally involved in the process. Parents, although involved in the negotiation of the form of the reporting, were not involved in the actual assessment process. Of course, there are alternatives to this approach. For example, Lisa Bietau (1995) describes a process that involves greater participation of students and parents in the actual data gathering and reporting. Parents are provided the district outcomes at a parent orientation session two weeks into the year. They are invited to consider and record on a form their child's strengths, challenges, "giggles" (things the child enjoys in school), and "worries." The children also fill out the form in school in preparation for a goal-setting conference the next week. The object of this conference is to develop two personal goals, one to expand a strength and the other to identify a challenge.

Involvement in goal-setting clarifies the goals for the students and gives them a sense of ownership.

The district outcome criteria involve dimensions of communication (writing, reading, listening, speaking); independence (initiative, time use, resource use, self-evaluation, self-management); complexity of thinking (observation, scientific and logical thinking); production (craftsmanship, creativity); and community contribution and participation. The reporting system uses a five-point scale ranging from "not yet met" (1), through "met" (3), to "met and exceeded" (5). Projects are the basis of classroom learning, and students set project goals and regularly evaluate their performance within this framework.

After the initial meeting, quarterly conferences are set up at which parents, students, and teachers confer. The teacher's role is primarily to facilitate discussion between parent and child of what growth has occurred and to help set new goals. Students are encouraged to rehearse with other students prior to the meeting. The second quarter conference is more expansive. The class sets up centers so that students can introduce parents to as many areas of learning as seem reasonable within the time frame. The required part of the session is a portfolio sharing and a ten-minute period of goal-setting with the teacher, when student, teacher, and parent assess progress and adjust goals. The thirty-minute third-quarter conference, again with all three parties, revolves around the progress reports that parents have received the week previously. If there are concerns or issues that are not raised in these conferences for whatever reason, subsequent phone conferences or additional personal conferences are arranged. The final conference is a celebration involving the whole group (a four-classroom team). Group projects and portfolios are displayed; often, there is a group performance of some sort. If parents desire individual conferences, they can sign up for a thirty-minute period for the following Saturday morning (the chalkboard lists the times). The students' celebration portfolios, made up of works carefully selected from throughout the year, are kept for the following year's teacher.

Successful student-run conferences require careful preparation. If they work well the first time, parents will trust the student's authority and not say, "That's nice," and then go to the teacher for the "real" story. Terri Austin (1994) takes these conferences very seriously. She makes sure that students have ample material for their portfolios and that they are practiced at reflecting on their learning. But having good data is not enough because the portfolio conference is a performance in itself. So she role-plays with another adult a bad portfolio conference in which she (the student) is inattentive, thoughtless, uninformative, and disorganized. She then role-plays a second conference in which she is organized, attentive, thoughtful about parents' needs, and specific in her descriptive comments. Discussion of these skits prepares students for a practice conference with an adult (not Terri and not the student's parent), after which students reflect (in writing and in conversation) on the role of the conference leader. Rehearsing the presentation not only ensures a more productive experience when the parents arrive, but it also gives students another opportunity to reflect on their work. As a result, Terri's students are in control of both the contents of their portfolio and how they are represented.

You might ask, "Where do I find the time for this?" There are certainly trade-offs to be made. Lisa Bietau admits that she and her colleagues had to make adjustments to accommodate the process. They cover fewer topics but in greater depth, delegating such things as book club orders (and perhaps class newsletter management) to parent volunteers. They have found that having clear ground rules facilitates the flow and timing of the conferences. But there are other savings too. Getting all interested parties involved in assessment makes animosity and miscommunication less likely because there is increased contact between parent and teacher, and a greater chance for learning-related conversations between parent and child. Teachers are also likely to have more classroom volunteers (making the home-school connection even stronger).

There are dividends in students' and parents' commitment—teachers' too. In addition, students in this kind of system learn to know their own learning with a security and sensitivity that few of their parents experienced. As Melissa, one of Terri Austin's students, observed: "I think parents understand things better when their child answers their questions. Also, we know the answers to all the questions. Maybe a teacher-parent conference wouldn't answer all their questions" (1994, p. 28).

CHAPTER 30

SYNCHRONIZING OUR CONVERSATIONS: MODERATION IN ASSESSMENT

*H*ave you ever had a conversation in which both you and the other person were talking past each other—apparently talking about the same thing but not understanding what the other was saying? Most teachers have had this experience with a parent, a colleague, or an administrator. Parents, of course, also have this experience with teachers. Indeed, as I described in the previous chapter, parents often have to learn a new language to talk to their child's new teacher. Sometimes the language changes each year with each new teacher. Reducing misunderstanding helps to increase trust. So let's consider some ways to synchronize our conversations.

In the past educators have tried to gain consistency in assessment conversations by controlling what students do: standardizing tasks (everyone takes the same test, writes in the same genre on the same topic, etc.) and requiring narrow and closed responses, such those on multiple-choice tests of "factual" information stated explicitly in a text. These techniques certainly reduce arguments about grades; the numbers are difficult to dispute. However, they achieve consistency at the cost of narrowing the curriculum and taking control away from students, and often from teachers.

Specifying domains and criteria in detail certainly produces greater consistency in judgments than leaving domains and criteria open. However, getting agreement on the specific domains and criteria to be valued in the first place is very difficult. Furthermore, precise definition and specification turns out to be easier to accomplish with more trivial aspects of literacy. But even though agreement is hard to come by, the discussions involved in making values explicit are productive. At the least, they help us teachers examine our practice.

Another way to achieve consistency is to have more than one person judge the same performance, as they do at the Olympic games. Disagreements are resolved by ignoring the reasons for them and simply averaging the ratings. However, the disagreements occur because one judge notices something another doesn't, or values something differently—exactly the kinds of things where discussion among the judges would produce valuable learning (outside of the pressure of the Olympics) and would lead to greater consistency in judgment in the long run. In education we call this process of negotiating agreement among judges *moderation*.

Moderation

In 1989, Vermont, one of the last states to move to some form of accountability assessment, cautiously began a statewide assessment program using portfolios. The idea was to have students put together portfolios of their work, which could be judged and which could provide an overall picture of literacy development. I won't go into the detail of the nature of these portfolios (for more information, see Hewitt 1995); suffice it to say that they are "best piece" portfolios with additional, on-demand pieces of writing. The most interesting part of the enterprise to me is the process through which they generated criteria for evaluation and consistent conversations about these portfolios.

The problem the state Writing Assessment Committee faced was wanting to allow diverse language engagements in classrooms, yet at the same time having some sort of reliable and common metric to describe overall competence to the public and to the schools. To begin with, the state brought together a group of teachers to negotiate the best dimensions to use for judging the portfolios. Next, a large group of teachers sat in a big hall with mounds of portfolios and haggled over their various qualities to reach a consensus on judgments. After that, when students produced a crop of portfolios groups of teachers would collectively analyze the portfolios to increase the consistency of their ratings—in short, to synchronize their conversations. Although initially reliability (consistency) was not high, it gradually improved. More important, however, is the fact that teachers left these meetings saying how much they had learned from the process. Since the ultimate reason for instituting the state assessment program was to improve teaching, if there is an active ingredient in the process, the collective conversations is it.

Let me give you a second example of moderating. The Primary Language Record (PLR) is a record-keeping and reporting procedure that was developed in the multilingual inner-city schools of London, England (Barrs et al. 1988). The form provides space for descriptive documentation of each child's development in reading, writing, speaking, and listening in different contexts, along with space for information from parent conferences. Besides the descriptive documentation, the Record also uses two continua to summarize children's reading development for parents and other interested parties. The first continuum is *from dependence to independence.* The categories used on this continuum are beginning reader, non-fluent reader, moderately fluent reader, fluent reader, and exceptionally fluent reader. The second continuum is *from experienced to inexperienced* and spans the categories inexperienced, less experienced, moderately experienced, experienced, and exceptionally experienced.

Teachers are able to reliably rate students on these categories even the first year they begin to use the procedure (Klausner 1995). This means, for example, that a child can be rated reliably as a "moderately experienced, fluent reader" and that people within the community—teachers, parents, administrators—have a reasonably consistent understanding of what that means. Furthermore, teachers become increasingly reliable with their ratings because of the moderation procedure. PLR moderation involves a group of teachers, parents, and administrators getting together and working through a sample of specific case studies to reach a consensus on each.

Agreement among raters is easier to obtain because there are detailed descriptions of each category. For example, a "less experienced reader" is one who is:

> Developing fluency as a reader and reading certain kinds of material
> with confidence. Usually chooses short books with simple narrative
> shapes and with illustrations and may read these silently; often re-reads
> favorite books. Reading for pleasure often includes comics and
> magazines. Needs help with the reading demands of the classroom and
> especially with using reference and information books. (Barrs et al.
> 1988, p. 46)

The clarity of communication of the PLR is also improved by specific documentary comments and examples of the child's efforts. The form requires the teacher to document the strategies a child uses when reading aloud. For example, a teacher might note the following about a student:

> In a familiar book, *Owl Babies*, read for meaning, errors made sense,
> and she self-corrected mostly from print, e.g., read "going" for "gone"
> and then corrected.

These concrete examples make all the difference to both the reliability and the communicative properties of the Record (though it is difficult to distinguish between reliability and communication in this situation). The bottom line is, the more concrete examples available and the greater the ongoing discussion about these examples, the more people will arrive at common understandings. Lack of specific data is the main reason teachers disagree on their ratings and fail to reach a consensus. In the end, consistency requires good observers, and the moderating procedure helps produce them.

Moderating can make a real difference in a school community. It can also be used to synchronize conversations within a district or even beyond. For example, it is common enough to want diplomas to mean the same thing across schools. The usual means of ensuring this involves having common tests and standards, which unfortunately have a way of becoming the curriculum. But moderation can be used instead, leaving the curriculum more open while maintaining consistency. In New Zealand moderation allows schools to use their internal assessments to grant diplomas. The work of random samples of students from each school is judged anonymously by a common group of trained raters. The ratings are used to decide what proportion of students a particular school should be allowed to award diplomas on the basis of their internal assessments. Students who do not get a diploma on the basis of their school's internal assessment can take a test. Because the test need be taken by only a small number of students, educators can make the test more sophisticated, with more labor-intensive scoring than they could afford to do if larger numbers of students were taking the test to graduate.

Criteria and Values

As we consider synchronizing our conversations, we need to consider questions around which to synchronize. Discussions of individual children's report cards can revolve around many different questions. People ask:

- How capable is this child by comparison with others?
- Is this child growing within "normal limits"? (And is that fast enough?)
- What is the problem with this child?
- What can this child accomplish?
- How hard has this child worked?
- Is this child working at a level appropriate to his (or her) grade?

The range of possible questions is broad, and concentrating on different questions has different consequences.

We might consider organizing our conversations around the question "Under what circumstances is this child intellectually engaged?" and "What plans do I have to expand that engagement?" The same question might also be applied to both teacher and parent. A report card that reflects these concerns might look like that in Figure 30.1. Such a report card is based on understanding literacy in situational terms. It would locate responsibility for instruction clearly in the teacher's court and focus attention on situations that can be changed. This report card would not arise in, or tend to produce, conversation about a child's relative incompetence.

In other words, report cards could be seen as a way of beginning a productive conversation with parents—a conversation that is perhaps not one they could imagine given their own school experiences. A portfolio could do the same. Teachers could generate a nonrestrictive list of questions that parents (and teachers) might ask of a child and her portfolio. This would help synchronize the conversations by helping parents understand the context. It might also prevent

LEARNING AREA	CONDITIONS UNDER WHICH [Name of Student] IS SUCCESSFUL	OBSERVED SUCCESSFUL BEHAVIORS	HOW I WILL ADJUST INSTRUCTION TO EXPAND THE RANGE OF BEHAVIORS AND CONDITIONS
Reading			
Engagement			
Functions			
Book selection			
Connections			
Self-correction			
Problem-solving			
Critical Analysis			
Conventions			
Range			
Writing			
Engagement			
Functions			
Topic selection			
Problem-solving			
Audiences			
Conventions			
Range			

FIGURE 30.1 *An Uncommon Report Card Format*

teachers from skipping over things, since it tends to force them to make explicit some of the things they may not normally reveal.

Specifying Criteria and Stages

As the example of the Primary Language Record shows, one way to establish clearer communication in reporting is to specify in more detail what categories and indicators mean. Whether you are using an A–B–C system, a not yet–sometimes– always scale, or an early–emerging–maturing–expanding scale, specifying what you mean by these categories can help a great deal. For example, you might specify what the categories mean through "anchor" behaviors, or examples. For example, Figure 30.2 shows some aspects of development in early writing that can give an idea of what to focus on. The idea is that, although development is not simple and linear, there are some trends that can be capitalized on. Even though there will be

WRITING EXAMPLE	WHAT CHILD KNOWS AND DOES
[child's scribble/mark-making] Child intends "Keep out."	Writing is what people do, and it has certain forms. Has an idea of the functionality of writing.
p u t o o/n s c D x Child intends "Dear Mary, I went to the hospital with my brother."	Writing has consistent forms, and it goes from left to right. It is used to represent what you want to say. There are conventions ("Dear Mary") that are used in some kinds of writing.
Wd patm dLad JASON Child intends "Once upon a time there lived a dragon."	Stories have conventions, and book language is different from normal language. Words are made up of parts, and letters are used to represent parts. Notices one sound in a word and represents it (not necessarily conventionally). Can perhaps write a word (often name). Words and letters in print not clearly distinguished.
I P. W. my. MSD Hc. I WD. #L FOVDM, Child reads "I played with my monster trucks. I rammed all four of them."	Clear separation of words. Some represented conventionally without being analyzed by sounds. Some words have more than one sound represented ("MSD" = monster). Sounds are represented with one letter, sometimes using the name of the letter (e.g., H can be used to represent ch because H = *ach*. Here "truck," pronounced "chuck" is written "Hc"). Beginning to explore punctuation.
TADA is my BRATH BRShDA it is cabin to Be AtSDing for him. Child reads "Today is my brother's birthday. It is going to be exciting for him."	Shows social imagination. Beginning to revise/edit. Words and sounds are not the same. Most sounds are represented. Knows that the letter-sound relationship is not simply one-to-one (*th*) and that there are some predictable sets of letters (*ing*). Knows that words have conventional spellings (and some are spelled conventionally) but chooses the best for the composition rather than those that can be spelled conventionally.
Nevember is cold not warm. it has no leavs and flowers to smell no sun so warm and hot, Days as short as time go's by. air so sweat and cold mountains so big and wise So free that I think I can fly.	Investigating a range of genres (here poetry). Many words can be spelled conventionally without analysis. Predictable conventions are used in words that are not conventionally spelled. Detailed observation of the world and personal experience, and valuing of that experience. Beginning sense of new punctuation.

FIGURE 30.2 *Anchor Examples of Early Writing*

some overlap in categories, if not viewed too rigidly, such scales might convey the necessary information without having an adverse effect on instruction.

Anchor examples can be used in more interactive situations too. One way to begin to have common conversations with parents is to walk them through the stories of several children's development. For example, if you collect two students' writing samples over a period of two or three years, on the "meet the teacher" night early in the school year you could walk the parents through the development that took place for those students. It helps if the students are very different from each other in their development and if it looked from their early work as though there might be cause for concern. Such an exercise helps parents learn what to notice, and at the same time shows that development is not the same for all students.

Providing examples to anchor judgments is often done when judging writing tests—for example, when students are asked to write a persuasive essay on whether or not homework is a good idea. Judges are given examples as "benchmarks"—two different examples of what a "1" might look like, two examples of a "2," and so on. This procedure is simple enough with narrow domains, but much harder as we talk more generally about development. Providing more than one example opens up the possibilities, and the process of deciding on the benchmark examples makes for very productive discussions.

A second way to establish clearer communication is to provide an accompanying handbook or explanation with report cards, such as that in Figure 30.3. Perhaps, with some modification, you will find the "beginning" to "expanding" scale in Figure 30.3 useful in your school. Alternatively, you may want to build your own scales or use the Primary Language Record (Barrs et al. 1988).

Trade-offs

There is no one "best" way to synchronize conversations in reporting. What works well in one place may not work at all in another. Also, each approach involves trade-offs. The more we specify assessment criteria, the more agreement we will get, but the more we are likely to reduce learning to elements that are easily specified. When we dissect something organic, in the end it loses life. If we understand that literacy learning takes place on many dimensions at once, greater specificity will produce a more mountainous list of items, but less specificity invites the complaint that our assessments are abstract and "fuzzy." A detailed and specific documentary process is time-consuming to do, but produces less miscommunication (except when people decline the invitation to read it because of its length).

Moderating is not problem-free, either. Negotiating the most valuable criteria is productive, but it takes time. Besides, taking complex development and forcing it into a linear hierarchy misrepresents the nature of development. When we forget this compromise, the linearity of the process can take on a life of its own, particu-

We encourage our teaching faculty to be descriptive rather than judgmental in their assessments of children's development because it helps them to be more focused on their teaching. However, the detailed knowledge that the teachers have to their students can be very time-consuming to write down, and possibly more than some parents might want to know. To be efficient, we have developed some categories as shorthand for describing students' literacy development. These categories are: *early*, *emergent*, *maturing*, and *expanding*. Reducing children's development to these single words means trading detailed documentation for ease of reporting, which opens the possibility of misinterpretation. So the following table describes the ways we are using these terms.

READING DEVELOPMENT IN THE PRIMARY GRADES

BEGINNING	EARLY	EMERGENT	MATURING	EXPANDING
• Participates in story reading activities • Curious about print • Has memory for book language • Retells story to match the illustrations • Knows how books work but not how words work • Recognizes own name • Relies on being read to	• Has favorite books • Consistently recognizes 5 or 6 words • Independently engages with books for around five minutes at a time • Makes connections with other books and experiences • Views self as a reader • Tries to match each spoken word to a written one in familiar books with one sentence per page, and tries again if the numbers don't match	• Consistently recognizes 20 or more words out of context • Initiates independent reading of favorite books • Chooses books of appropriate difficulty • Makes connections with own writing • Uses initial letters along with meaning and other cues to figure out words and correct errors • Still needs some support with unfamiliar texts • Beginning to understand what reading can do for him/her • Beginning to recognize different authors' styles	• Familiar with a range of genres • Attempts challenging books • Thinking critically, speculating on why the author used particular words, characters, etc. • Reads for learning and entertainment • Mostly reads silently • Beginning to use reference texts • Comfortable using all letters and some groups of letters and some analogies to figure out words • Initiates conversations with others about books	• Can think about own response to reading and speculate about others' responses • Expects texts to have more than one meaning, and notices subtleties • Reads independently for at least 45 minutes—cannot be easily distracted when in a good book • Uses library independently • Self-motivated, confident reader • Figures out most new words

You might notice that your child's literacy development has been described as "emergent," yet you find that he or she also does things that are found in the "expanding" column. That is common, and reflects the fact that children are different in the ways they develop. The term used to describe your child's development is where the *balance* of his or her literacy is represented. Additional comments by the teacher will help put a little more detail into the picture.

If this report does not provide you with sufficient information about your child's learning, we encourage you to schedule a conference with his or her teacher in which you might seek more detailed information. In such conferences we expect teachers to provide clear examples to illustrate the nature of your child's development. Alternatively you might wish to check out our more detailed booklet describing children's literacy development or our video on the subject. Contact the principal's office at your child's school.

"Normal Development"
When we assess students' reading and writing, we do not emphasize comparisons between students' different degrees of competence. Research shows that such comparisons interfere with students' efforts to seek assistance in their learning and with their motivation for learning. We do, however, watch for children whose rate of development is not within what we view as a normal range

so that we might prevent serious problems from developing. If your child is not developing within a normal range, his or her teacher will contact you before December to discuss what steps might be taken at school and at home to reduce the problem.

Remember, the report card is not a statement of your child's worth. It is a statement of what he or she knows and can do *at this point*.

FIGURE 30.3 *Report Card Handbook Entry Specifying Categories*

larly when pressure is applied to achieve "higher levels." On balance, though, provided we understand the compromises we make, moderation is particularly helpful. Although its main goal is to help participants obtain reliable judgments and a common language, it can achieve a great deal more. When people are regularly engaged in moderating, they get a greater sense of what observations are necessary and how others think about the defining features of the assessment process, thus further increasing their agreement. The participants then also become better at collecting appropriate data. At the same time, the process builds trustworthiness and the observation skills of all parties. These benefits offset the time it takes to engage in the process, *and they more than offset it.* Moderation allows for much more open and diverse classroom performances and practices while allowing for consistency in judgments about competence and provides the basis for trusting relationships in the community.

But the benefits don't stop there. Provided the stakes are kept low, the moderation process provides a forum within which to explore the differences between teachers' observations, based on data. As mentioned earlier, places of disagreement are sites for people to expand their understanding of a topic—in this case, children's literacy learning. Indeed, there is a point at which having everyone agree is not very helpful. Within a trusting relationship, we learn from places of tension. In other words, rather than striving for conversations that are synchronized because we all agree, perhaps we should value conversations in which we all *learn*— conversations in which we work through productive agreement and dissent.

CHAPTER 31

*K*EEPING TRACK WITHOUT LOSING OUR WAY

*T*erri Austin (1994) opened an important conversation with her sixth graders' parents when she met them at the school's open house. She asked them to imagine their child at the end of twelfth grade. "How will that child be? Not what will they be, but how will they be?" (p. 30). She introduced them to the idea of a "fast-write" (first-draft writing in a brief time frame, maybe five minutes) and got them to write down their vision of their child. These parents, it turned out, were more interested in the quality of the person than in specific academic skills. Their responses—how they wanted their children to be—included the following: "solid learning foundation," "learned how to study," "confident," "independent," "caring," "creative," "not afraid to take risks," and "respond responsively to world situations" (p. 31). Terri used the list as the basis for classroom discussion the following day. Her students found the matter engaging, and their conversations and explorations (including interviews of teachers and other students) led to a set of class values in which both they and their parents had a stake. This is a strong foundation on which to build conversations about literacy development. Happily, it is also a strong foundation on which to build a democracy.

I wonder if any of those parents could imagine what Michelle Fine (1981) found in her study of "successful" high school students and school dropouts. She found that the successful students (judged as such by current assessment standards) were more conformist, less critical of social injustice, more depressed, and less willing to take the initiative than were the dropouts. This is not the success Terri Austin's parents want for their children. Neither is it what I want for mine.

In Linda Rief's classroom, in Terri Austin's, and in many others' across the country, students represent their literate learning through portfolios. In collaboration with the teacher and their classmates, students negotiate the grounds of their assessment and select the works that will be used to represent their learning. In many cases, relevant works include the fruits of collaborative effort and reflective commentary on the significance of the works and experiences selected. Not only do the portfolios provide a place for students to reflect on their literate learning and on themselves as literate learners, but they also provide grounds for productive conversations about what matters in their lives. This seems to me to be democratic. It encourages independent judgment and collaborative action, and it values diversity. The process incidentally fosters social commitment as students come to better understand one another's lives, realize the value of diversity for their own development, and recognize that intelligence is a property of communities more than individuals, though each contributes to the whole. The openness of this evaluative practice and its emphasis on individual goal-setting turns attention away from comparative or competitive judgments of ability—judgments that are not only undemocratic but unjust because they result in some students judging themselves as incompetent, thus reducing their commitment to learning.

A just, caring democracy demands this kind of assessment because such a society cannot exist without social commitment, collaborative action, and independent judgment (Barber 1984; Dewey 1966). It must demand this kind of assessment because its very existence depends on it. It must demand assessment that values diversity too because, as John Dewey (1966) pointed out, a democratic society:

> counts individual variations as precious since it finds in them the
> means of its own growth. Hence a democratic society must . . . allow
> for intellectual freedom and the play of diverse gifts and interests in its
> educational measures. (p. 305)

Assessment practices that result in a narrow and standardized curriculum will stifle democracy, as will practices that stem from, or result in, a stunted conception of life and human achievement.

The approach to literacy and assessment that I have advocated, then, is not just nice, it is necessary. So although I have suggested synchronizing our conversations, I want to be quite clear that not just any conversation will do. Current conversations emphasize standardized, norm-referenced, multiple-choice testing, usually associated with high stakes, such as public comparisons, teaching salaries, placement in different ability tracks, and so forth. These conversations have led to serious constriction of the curriculum, a reduction of diversity in the classroom, and a preoccupation with ego-involving notions of ability (Johnston in press; Smith 1991). Can democracy thrive in such a climate? I don't think so. Can learning flourish in such an environment? Not the learning I value. Do the experiences of these assessment practices foster caring? Quite the contrary.

My goal in writing this book has been to change our assessment practices: to change the ways we talk about students, teachers, learning, and literacy in ways that will more likely lead to a democratic society. But making real change in assessment will not happen overnight because changing our conversations is not just a matter of changing our words. When people talk about improving teaching and some begin with the word "accountability" and others start with "teacher learning," they are not merely words apart, they are worlds apart. But changing our words can lead to rethinking. For example, what if, rather than having our conversations focus on "instructional level" or "ability level," they revolved around "engagement level"? "Disengaged" would become the problem category—a category that could apply to teachers, parents, and administrators as well as to students. What if, instead of talking of students being "smart," "brilliant," "intelligent," and "quick," we spoke of students being "involved," "thoughtful," "caring," and "reflective"? Being quick is not the same as being reflective, and you don't teach it the same way. Changing words can help because we see the world through our words.

But changing our words can be slow because we live inside them. They form an invisible prison. How often, as teachers, we refer to our classroom data, no matter how systematically collected, as "informal," "subjective," or "anecdotal." We use these terms disparagingly, with uniform, "objective" tests being the standard by which our data are judged. If we continue to think this way we cannot participate equally in democratic negotiations of the meaning of our work. As Jerome Bruner (1985) points out,

> the language of education, if it is to be an invitation to reflection and
> culture creating, cannot be the so-called uncontaminated language of
> fact and "objectivity." It must express stance and must invite
> counter-stance and in the process leave place for reflection. (p. 129)

Unequal authority is built into our language. It would be more productive, and more accurate, to refer to classroom observations as direct assessment, or documentation, and tests as indirect assessment. We might also refer to tests as invasive assessment and classroom evaluation as noninvasive assessment. These communicate different relationships and invite different conversations. If we do not take our own assessment practices seriously, others will find it difficult to take them seriously too. Assessment conversations will be more productive and democratic if no one is talking down to anyone else.

Although changing conversations is difficult, we can start with little things. For example, if you send home a card for parents to sign showing that their child read a book, ask for a comment instead. And when you get a comment, give one back. This simple adjustment changes the nature of the relationship and changes the potential for conversation. The more parents are involved in writing and reading, too (even fast-writes), the easier it will be for us to have productive conversations about literacy learning, about the connection between our hopes and dreams for our students and children, and about the kind of literacy experience we want them to have. Indeed, the very act of engaging students and parents in responsible negotiation of the values and means of organizing our collective lives in school is the stuff of democracy. With the pressures and busyness of school and home and the battering of the media, it is easy to lose sight of our guiding values. The more we have colleagues, students, and parents helping us keep them in sight, the better. I do not want to suggest that these conversations will always be easy. I would hope they would not be. If we are all in agreement, there is little room for learning.

Keeping Track
Without Losing
Our Way

Alphabet Knowledge Record Sheet

Name: _____ Date: _____

F	S	z	j
W	L	y	e
T	A	g	r
D	M	k	q
H	I	n	b
X	C	v	u
G	J	o	p
Y	E	f	s
Z	R	w	l
K	Q	t	a
N	B	d	m
V	U	h	i
O	P	x	c
		a	g

Confusions: _____

Comments: _____

_____

_____

Record correct identification with a check mark; when there is no response, leave the space blank; and record errors the child says. Count as a correct response the letter name, an appropriate sound, or a word beginning with the appropriate sound.

F	S	z	j
W	L	y	e
T	A	g	r
D	M	k	q
H	I	n	b
X	C	v	u
G	J	o	p
Y	E	f	s
Z	R	w	l
K	Q	t	a
N	B	d	m
V	U	h	i
O	P	x	c
		a	g

Why Do Boys Say Girls Are Afraid of Creepy-Crawlers?

by Emily Johnston

One hot summer day me and my friends were walking in the pine bush. Suddenly, we saw a bush moving. David asked, "What, what, what was that?"

Just then a snake popped out of the bush. David shrieked, "Heeelp." Then he ran.

I picked up the snake and put him off to the side of the road and said, "Let's go see if he still wants to play."

My friends said, "O.K."

So we went over to his house and knocked on the door. David answered. We asked if he could play. He said, "Yeah. Why don't you come in."

We said, "Sure."

We went into his dark and mildewy basement to ask his mom if we could play Nintendo. She said, "No." So we started up the stairs.

Amelia screamed, "Aaaaah!"

I asked, "What is it?"

She yelled, "A spider!" and sped out the door. I ran after her and caught up and suggested that we go to my house.

Amelia said, "If there's no spiders."

I answered, "There's no spiders."

So we went over to my house and my mom asked us if we could plant some flowers for her. We agreed to. We started planting and David found a worm. He put it up to Stephanie's face. She screamed and ducked. David fell on her leg. She screamed again, yelled, "Get off me," popped up and ran.

I called her back and told David to apologize. He did. She said, "I accept." We finished planting and went inside and started playing air hockey.

My mom said, "You know, I have a lot of work to do. Could you play somewhere else?" So we went out on a bike ride. On the bike ride Ted fell off his ten-speed in front of a big mud puddle. He started squealing for he saw something squirming in it. I went over to see if I could help him. I picked up the squirming thing. It was a tadpole. I dropped it back in the puddle and we started back to my house.

All of a sudden David asked, "Emily, are you afraid of anything? I mean, you are not afraid of snakes, spiders, worms, or tadpoles."

"I am not afraid of tadpoles," Ted said quickly. "I didn't know what it was."

I said, "Well, I am afraid of poisonous stuff like cobras and corals or tarantulas, but they're poisonous. Just then a bird swooped down and dropped a plop on me. I yelled and hopped three feet! But it was too late. The plop splattered on my face. "Eeehhhhuuu!" I exclaimed.

"Sick" whined Amelia. Ted covered his mouth trying to hide his upchuck, but it came out on the ground. David stooped, looking from me to Ted. I ran home with my friends close behind. I jumped inside the house, washed my face off, and feeling much better I stepped outside where my friends were waiting.

After that we had a pretty normal day.

The moral of this story is: Not only girls are afraid of creepy-crawlers and slimy stuff like that.

Some Interview Questions

*T*he following questions are provided as suggestions to get you started thinking about the kinds of things you might learn from students. You might try out some of these questions in a colleague's class. Coming in as a visitor makes it easier for you to establish a position as sincere knowledge seeker. The power difference between you and the students will not be as great, and you will be less distracted by other classroom activities. The idea is just to be curious about how the students understand reading and writing. Most of these questions can be asked about either reading or writing—just substitute words as needed.

- How would you describe yourself as a reader?
- Do you have any favorite books or authors? Do you know what kinds of books any of the other kids like best?
- Are any of the kids you know especially good readers? What does he [she] do that makes him [her] a good reader?
- Suppose you had a pen pal in the same grade in a different school and you wanted to find out about him [or her] as a reader. What questions would you ask?
- Do you find some reading harder than others? Can you give me some examples? What makes the one harder than the other?
- Are there ways a writer can make a story more interesting or easier to read?
- Are you really good at some types of reading? What is it that makes you good at that?
- Have you read any hard books lately? What was it that made it hard?
- What kinds of reading do you like best? Can you give me some examples?
- Do you discuss books with the other kids?
- What did you do in your reading time today? What other reading do you do?
- How did you choose this book you are reading?
- If I were listening in on kids' discussions about this book you are reading, what kinds of comments do you think I might hear?
- Could you describe how you wrote this piece, starting from when you were deciding what to write about?
- You mentioned [x] writing and [y] writing. How are they different from each other? When you are writing these two kinds of pieces, what would you do differently? Are there other types of writing?

- What would you like to learn so you can become a better writer?
- What is something new you have learned to do in writing?
- Do you ever write with someone else?
- What is the best part about writing?

Appendix C

Sheet for Running Record Analysis

NAME:	DATE:	E	SC	E	SC
BOOK:				MSV	MSV

Words (W) =   Error Rate (ER) = E/W x 100 =

Self-corrections (SC) =   Accuracy = 100 - ER =

Errors (E) =   Self-correction rate = SC : SC + E =

Practice Running Records

Here are examples of running records that appear on side B of the audiotape accompanying this book.

TAPE EXAMPLE 18:   *Oops!* by Fran Hunia (1984)

(The completed running records are on pages 336–337.)

Page 4:
Billy wanted a biscuit . . .

Page 5:
but
he
couldn't
reach.

Page 6:
He stood on a chair . . .

Page 7:
but
he
couldn't
reach.

Page 8:
He put a box
on the chair . . .

Page 9:
but
he
couldn't
reach.

Page 10:
He put a bucket
on the box
on the chair . . .

Page 11:
but
he
couldn't
reach.

Page 12:
He put a book
on the bucket
on the box
on the chair
but

Page 13:
OOPS!

Page 14:
Down came the biscuits
and the book
and the bucket
and the box
and the chair . . .

Page 15:
and Billy.

Page 16:
Silly Billy!

TAPE EXAMPLE 19: *Greedy Cat* by Joy Cowley (1983b)

(The completed running records are on pages 338–339.)
Page 3:
Mum went shopping
and got some sausages.
Along came Greedy Cat.
He looked in the shopping bag.
Gobble, gobble, gobble,
and that was the end of that.

Page 5:
Mum went shopping
and got some sticky buns.

Along came Greedy Cat.
He looked in the shopping bag.
Gobble, gobble, gobble,
and that was the end of that.

Page 7:
Mum went shopping
and got some potato chips.
Along came Greedy Cat.
He looked in the shopping bag.
Gobble, gobble, gobble,
and that was the end of that.

Page 8:
Mum went shopping
and got some bananas.

Page 9:
Along came Greedy Cat.
He looked in the shopping bag.
Gobble, gobble, gobble,
and that was the end of that.

Page 10:
Mum went shopping
and got some chocolate.

Page 11:
Along came Greedy Cat.
He looked in the shopping bag.
Gobble, gobble, gobble,
and that was the end of that.

Page 13:
Mum went shopping
and got a pot of pepper.

Page 14:
Along came Greedy Cat.
He looked in the shopping bag.
Gobble, gobble—

Page 15:
YOW!

Page 16:
and that was the end of that!

TAPE EXAMPLE 20: *The Terrible Days of My Cat Cali* by William Haggerty (1990)

(The completed running record is on page 340.)
Once my cat bit me on the nose when I was
asleep. And once she came back on Friday
and did nothing, just sit down in some shed.
Then she came home.

Page 2:
Once my cat climbed on the screen. After my
cat climbed on the screen, she went upstairs
and got under the covers in my mother's bed
and slept for one hour.

Page 3:
After she came out of the covers, she ran
downstairs and purred at the basement door.
Instead of going in the basement door, she
cried at the front door and ran around the
house two times. Then she chased after a
motorcycle. She came back home and she was
hungry.

Page 4:
And today she ran away, but my brother found
her. She made us late for Reading!

NAME: Amanda	①	DATE: 9/12/96	E	SC	E MSV	SC MSV
BOOK: Oops!						

✓ ✓ ✓ ✓

5. ✓
✓
✓
✓

6. ✓ ✓ ✓ ✓ ✓

7. ✓
✓
✓
✓
✓

8. ✓ | st / SC | ✓ ✓ → 1 ms ✓
| pnt |
✓ ✓ ✓

9. ✓
✓
✓
✓

10. ✓ ✓ ✓ box / bucket   1 msv
✓ ✓ ✓
✓ ✓ ✓

Words (W) =   **Error Rate (ER) = E/W x 100 =**
Self-corrections (SC) =   **Accuracy = 100 - ER =**
Errors (E) =   **Self-correction rate = SC : SC + E =**

Running record for Oops! *by Fran Hunia*

NAME: Amanda ② DATE: 9/12/96	E	SC	E MSV	SC MSV
BOOK: Oops!				

11.
✓
✓
✓
✓

12.
✓ ✓ ✓ box / book | 1 | | msv |

✓ ✓ R ✓

an / sc / on | | 1 | ms | ✓
✓ ✓
✓

13.
✓

14.
✓ ✓ ✓ ✓
✓ ✓ ✓
✓ ✓ pa / sc / bucket | | 1 | ms | ✓
✓ ✓ ✓
✓ ✓ ✓

15.
on / an / SC ✓ | | 1 | ms | ✓
and

16.
✓ ✓

| 2 | 4 | | |

Words (W) = 77

Self-corrections (SC) = 4

Errors (E) = 2

Error Rate (ER) = E/W x 100 = 2/77 × 100 = 3

Accuracy = 100 - ER = 97%

Self-correction rate = SC : SC + E = 4:6
= 1:1.5

Running record for Oops! (continued)

NAME: Amanda ① DATE: 9/23/96		E	SC	E MSV	SC MSV
BOOK: Greedy Cat					
3. ✓ ✓ ✓					
✓ ✓ ✓ ✓					
✓ ✓ ✓ ✓					
✓ ✓ ✓ ✓ —shopping ✓		1			
and̲ he̲ —gobble̲|T ✓ ✓		1 / 1		ms / ms	
✓ ✓ ✓ ✓ ✓ ✓ ✓		1		—	
5. momma̲ ✓ ✓ Mum		1		m s V	
✓ ✓ ✓ ✓ biscuits̲ buns		1		m s V	
✓R ✓ ✓ ✓					
✓ ✓ ✓ —shopping ✓		1			
✓ ✓ ✓					
✓ ✓ ✓ ✓ ✓ ✓					
7. momma̲ ✓ ✓ Mum		1 / 1 / 1 / 1		m s V	
✓ —got̲ —some̲ —potato̲ —chips̲					
al̲|✓ ✓ ✓ ✓ along					
✓ ✓ ✓ ✓ —shopping		1		ms	
✓ ✓ ✓					
✓ ✓ ✓ ✓ ✓ ✓					

Words (W) =   **Error Rate (ER) = E/W x 100 =**
Self-corrections (SC) =   **Accuracy = 100 - ER =**
Errors (E) =   **Self-correction rate = SC : SC + E =**

Running record for Greedy Cat *by Joy Cowley*

NAME: Amanda ② DATE: 9/23/96	E	SC	E MSV	SC MSV
BOOK: Greedy Cat				

8.
<u>Momma</u> ✓ ✓ | 1 | | MSV |
Mum
✓ ✓ ✓

9. <u>and / at / SC</u> ✓ ✓ ✓ | | 1 | ms | V
along
✓ ✓ ✓ ✓ s̄hopping | 1 | | ms
✓ ✓ ✓
✓ ✓ ✓ ✓ ✓ ✓

10. ✓ ✓ ✓
✓ ✓ ✓ ✓

11. ✓ ✓ ✓ ✓
<u>and</u> ✓ ✓ ✓ s̄hopping ✓ | 1 | | ms
he | 1 |
✓ ✓ ✓
✓ ✓ ✓ ✓ ✓ ✓

13. <u>Momma</u> ✓ ✓ | 1 | | MSV
Mum
✓ ✓ ✓ ✓

14. ✓ ✓ ✓ | 1 |
✓ ✓ ✓ ✓ shopping ✓
✓

15. <u>on</u> | 1 | | MSV
your

16.
✓ ✓ ✓ ✓ ✓ ✓ ✓ | 20 | 1 |

Words (W) = 166   Error Rate (ER) = E/W x 100 = 20/166 × 100 = 12
Self-corrections (SC) = 1   Accuracy = 100 - ER = 88%
Errors (E) = 20   Self-correction rate = SC : SC + E = 1:21

Running record for Greedy Cat *(continued)*

NAME: Billy	DATE: 6/6/96	E	SC	E MSV	SC MSV

The running record check marks and annotations:

1. ✓✓✓ ✓✓✓✓ ✓✓ ✓✓
   ✓✓ ✓✓ ✓✓ ✓✓
   ✓✓✓ ✓ ✓ and/SC ✓✓ | 1 | ms | V |
                        in
   ✓✓✓✓

2. ✓✓ ✓✓ ✓✓ ✓✓
    ✓✓ ✓✓ ✓ ✓✓
    ✓✓ ✓✓ ✓✓✓✓ ✓R
    ✓✓ ✓✓✓

3. ✓✓ ✓✓ ✓✓ ✓✓ ✓✓
    ✓✓ ✓✓ ✓✓ ✓
    and/R²/SC ✓✓ ✓✓ ✓✓ | 1 | ms | V |
    instead
    ✓✓ ✓✓ ✓✓ ✓✓
    ✓✓ ✓ and/the/SC ✓ do/SC ✓ | 1 | ms | V |
            then   chased | 1 | ms | V |
    ✓✓ ✓✓ ✓✓ ✓✓
    ✓

4. ✓✓✓✓ ✓ ✓ cat/R ✓
   ✓R sh/✓ ✓✓✓✓✓
       she

Words (W) = 129   **Error Rate (ER)** = E/W x 100 = 0
Self-corrections (SC) = 4   **Accuracy** = 100 - ER = 100%
Errors (E) = 0   **Self-correction rate** = SC : SC + E = 4:4
                                1:1

Running record for The Terrible Days of My Cat Cali *by William Haggerty*

REFERENCES

Children's Books

Ahlberg, Allan. 1983. *Ten in a Bed*. New York: Viking.

Browne, Anthony. 1986. *The Piggybook*. New York: Knopf.

Brownell, M. Barbara. 1988. *Busy Beavers*. Washington, DC: National Geographic Society.

Cassidy, Nancy, and John Cassidy. 1986. *The Book of Kids' Songs: A Holler-Along Handbook*. Palo Alto, CA: Klutz Press.

Cowley, Joy. 1983a. *Going to School*. Auckland, New Zealand: Shortland.

———. 1983b. *Greedy Cat*. Wellington, New Zealand: Learning Media Limited.

———. 1984. *Old Tuatara*. Wellington, New Zealand: Department of Education.

Dahl, Roald. 1964. *Charlie and the Chocolate Factory*. New York: Knopf.

de Paola, Tomie. 1992. *Now One Foot, Now the Other*. New York: Putman.

Fox, Mem. 1985. *Wilfred Gordon McDonald Partridge*. Brooklyn, NY: Kane/Miller.

Friskey, Margaret. 1959. *Indian Two Feet and His Horse*. Illustrated by Katherine Evans. Chicago: Children's Press.

Haggerty, William. 1990. *The Terrible Days of My Cat Cali*. Self published.

Hall, Donald. 1984. *The Man Who Lived Alone*. Boston: D. R. Godine.

Hunia, Fran. 1984. *Oops!* Auckland, New Zealand: Ashton Scholastic.

Kent, Jack. 1971. *The Fat Cat: A Danish Folktale*. Harmondsworth, UK: Picture Puffins.

MacLachlan, Patricia. 1980. *Arthur for the Very First Time*. New York: HarperCollins.

———. 1990. *Sarah, Plain and Tall*. New York: HarperCollins.

Mahy, Margaret. 1975. *The Boy Who Was Followed Home*. Illustrated by Steven Kellog. New York: Dial Books.

———. 1984a. *The Dragon's Birthday*. Illustrated by Philip Webb. Auckland, New Zealand: Shortland Educational Publications.

———. 1984b. *Fantail, Fantail*. Illustrated by Bruce Phillips. Wellington, New Zealand: Department of Education.

————. 1985. *The Man Whose Mother Was a Pirate.* Illustrated by Margaret Chamberlain. New York: Viking Kestrel.

Mailot, Hector. 1879/1984. *The Foundling.* Trans. Douglas Munro. New York: Harmony Books.

Malcolm, Margaret. 1983. *I Can Read.* Wellington, New Zealand: Department of Education.

Martin, Craig. 1982. *My Bike.* Wellington, New Zealand: Department of Education.

Mayer, Mercer. 1968. *There's a Nightmare in My Closet.* New York: E. P. Dutton.

Melser, June. 1981. *Little Pig.* Illustrated by Isabel Lowe. San Diego: The Wright Group.

Moyes, Lesley. 1983. *Saturday Morning.* Wellington, New Zealand: Department of Education.

Munsch, Robert. 1986. *Love You Forever.* Scarborough, ON: Firefly Books.

Nodset, Joan. 1989. *Who Took the Farmer's Hat?* Illustrated by Fritz Siebel. Lexington, MA: D.C. Heath and Co.

Parish, Peggy. 1977. *Teach Us Amelia Bedelia.* New York: Scholastic.

Paterson, Katherine. 1978. *The Great Gilly Hopkins.* New York: HarperCollins.

Peet, Bill. 1979. *Cowardly Clyde.* Boston: Houghton Mifflin.

Rylant, Cynthia. 1990. *A Couple of Kooks and Other Stories About Love.* New York: Dell.

————. 1992. *Missing May.* New York: Orchard Books.

Scieszka, Jon. 1992. *The Stinky Cheese Man and Other Fairly Stupid Tales.* New York: Viking/Penguin.

Slepian, Jan, and Ann Seidler. 1967a. *The Cat Who Wore a Pot on Her Head.* New York: Scholastic.

————. 1967b. *The Hungry Thing.* New York: Scholastic.

Tsuchiya, Yukio. 1988. *Faithful Elephants.* Boston: Houghton Mifflin.

Voigt, Cynthia. 1985. *The Runner.* New York: Fawcett-Juniper.

Waddell, Martin. 1992. *Owl Babies.* Cambridge, MA: Candlewick Press.

Wiesel, Elie. 1986. *Night.* New York: Bantam.

Ziefert, Harriet. 1989. *Harry Goes to Funland.* Illustrated by Mavis Smith. New York: Penguin.

Professional Resources

Adams, Ellen. 1995. A Descriptive Study of Second Graders' Conversations About Books. Ph.D. diss., State University of New York at Albany.

Afflerbach, Peter. 1990a. The Influence of Prior Knowledge on Expert Readers' Main Idea Construction Strategies. *Reading Research Quarterly* 25: 31–46.

————. 1990b. The Influence of Prior Knowledge and Text Genre on Readers' Prediction Strategies. *Journal of Reading Behavior* 22: 131–148.

Afflerbach, Peter, and Peter Johnston. 1993. Writing Language Arts Report Cards: Eleven Teachers' Conflicts of Knowing and Communicating. *Elementary School Journal* 94: 73–86.

Allington, Richard. 1983. The Reading Instruction Provided Readers of Differing Reading Abilities. *Elementary School Journal* 83: 255–265.

————. 1984. Oral Reading. In P. David Pearson, ed., *Handbook of Reading Research,* pp. 829–864. White Plains, NY: Longman.

Ames, Carole, and Russell Ames. 1984. Goal Structures and Motivation. *Elementary School Journal* 85: 39–52.

Anderson, Richard, Paul Wilson, and Linda Fielding. 1988. Growth in Reading and How Children Spend Their Time Outside of School. *Reading Research Quarterly* 23: 285–303.

Anyon, Jeanne. 1981. Social Class and School Knowledge. *Curriculum Inquiry* 11: 3–41.

Argyris, Chris. 1970. *Intervention Theory and Method*. Reading, MA: Addison-Wesley.

Argyris, Chris, and Donald Schon. 1974. *Theory in Practice: Increasing Professional Effectiveness*. London: Jossey-Bass.

Atwell, Nancie. 1987. *In the Middle: Writing, Learning, and Reading with Adolescents*. Portsmouth, NH: Heinemann.

Austin, Terri. 1994. *Changing the View: Student-Led Parent Conferences*. Portsmouth, NH: Heinemann.

Baker, Linda, and Ann Brown. 1984. Metacognitive Skills and Reading. In P. David Pearson, ed., *Handbook of Reading Research*, pp. 353–394. White Plains, NY: Longman.

Bakhtin, Mikhail M. 1981. *The Dialogic Imagination: Four Essays by M. M. Bakhtin*. Ed. Michael Holquist; trans. Caryl Emerson and Michael Holquist. Austin: University of Texas Press.

Barber, Benjamin. 1984. *Strong Democracy: Participatory Democracy for a New Age*. Berkeley: University of California Press.

Barrs, Myra, Sue Ellis, Hilary Hester, and Anne Thomas. 1988. *The Primary Language Record: Handbook for Teachers*. Portsmouth, NH: Heinemann.

Bartlett, Elsa Jaffe. 1979. Curriculum, Concepts of Literacy and Social Class. In Lauren Resnick and Phyllis Weaver, eds., *Theory and Practice of Early Reading*, vol. 2, pp. 229–242. Hillsdale, NJ: Erlbaum.

Belenky, Mary, Blythe Clinchy, Nancy Goldberger, and Jill Tarule. 1986. *Women's Ways of Knowing: The Development of Self, Voice, and Mind*. New York: Basic Books.

Bereiter, Carl, and Marlene Bird. 1985. Use of Thinking Aloud in Identification and Teaching of Reading Comprehension Strategies. *Cognition and Instruction* 2: 131–156.

Berthoff, Ann. 1978. *Forming Thinking Writing: The Composing Imagination*. Rochelle Park, NJ: Hayden Book Co.

——— . 1981. *The Making of Meaning: Metaphors, Models, and Maxims for Writing Teachers*. Portsmouth, NH: Boynton/Cook–Heinemann.

Biemiller, Andrew. 1970. The Development of the Use of Graphic and Contextual Information as Children Learn to Read. *Reading Research Quarterly* 6: 75–96.

———. 1979. Changes in the Use of Graphic and Contextual Information as Functions of Passage Difficulty and Reading Achievement Level. *Journal of Reading Behavior* 11: 308–318.

Bietau, Lisa. 1995. Student, Parent, Teacher Collaboration. In Tara Azwell and Elizabeth Schmar, eds., *Report Card on Report Cards: Alternatives to Consider*, pp. 131–153, Portsmouth, NH: Heinemann.

Birman, Beatrice. 1981. Problems of Overlap Between Title I and P.L. 94–142: Implications for the Federal Role in Education. *Educational Evaluation and Policy Analysis* 3: 5–19.

Blachman, Benita, Eileen Ball, Roger Black, and Darlene Tangel. 1994. Kindergarten Teachers Develop Phoneme Awareness in Low-Income, Inner-City Classrooms. *Reading and Writing: An International Journal* 6: 1–18.

Bondy, Elizabeth. 1985. Children's Definitions of Reading: Products of an Interactive Process. Paper presented at the annual meeting of the American Educational Research Association, Chicago, Illinois. April.

Bower, Gordon. 1978. Experiments on Story Comprehension and Recall. *Discourse Processes* 1: 211–231.

Brandts, Lois. 1993. A First Grade Perspective. In Mary Ann Smith and Miriam Ylvisaker, eds., *Teachers' Voices: Portfolios in the Classroom*, pp. 107–118. Berkeley, CA: National Writing Project.

Bridge, Connie, Mary Jane Ciera, and Robert Tierney. 1978/79. The Discourse Processing Operations of Children. *Reading Research Quarterly* 14: 539–573.

Broikou, Kathy. 1992. Understanding Primary Grade Classroom Teachers' Special Education Referral Practices. Ph.D. diss., State University of New York at Albany.

Bronfenbrenner, Uri. 1979. *The Ecology of Human Development: Experiments by Nature and Design.* Cambridge, MA: Harvard University Press.

Brown, Hazel, and Brian Cambourne. 1989. *Read and Retell: A Strategy for the Whole-Language/Natural Learning Classroom.* Portsmouth, NH: Heinemann.

Bruner, Jerome. 1985. Models of the Learner. *Educational Researcher* 14(6): 5–8.

———. 1986. *Actual Minds, Possible Worlds.* Cambridge, MA: Harvard University Press.

Carver, Ronald. 1989. Silent Reading Rates in Grade Equivalents. *Journal of Reading Behavior* 21(2): 155–166.

Cazden, Courtney. 1990. Differential Treatment in New Zealand: Reflections on Research in Minority Education. *Teaching and Teacher Education* 6: 291–303.

Ceci, Stephen, and Kathleen McNellis. 1987. Entangling Knowledge and Process. Paper presented at the Annual Meeting of the American Educational Research Association, Washington, DC. April.

Chafe, Wallace. 1982. Integration and Involvement in Speaking, Writing, and Oral Literature. In Deborah Tannen, ed., *Spoken and Written Language: Exploring Orality and Literacy.* Norwood, NJ: Ablex.

Chase, William, and Herbert Simon. 1973. Perception in Chess. *Cognitive Psychology* 4: 55–81.

Chukovsky, Kornei. 1963. *From Two to Five.* Trans. and ed. Miriam Morton. Berkeley: University of California Press.

Clay, Marie M. 1966. Emergent Reading Behavior. Ph.D. diss. University of Auckland, New Zealand.

———. 1972. *The Early Detection of Reading Difficulties: A Diagnostic Survey.* Auckland, New Zealand: Heinemann.

———. 1975. *What Did I Write?* Portsmouth, NH: Heinemann.

———. 1991. *Becoming Literate: The Construction of Inner Control.* Portsmouth, NH: Heinemann.

———. 1993a. *An Observation Survey of Early Literacy Achievement.* Portsmouth, NH: Heinemann.

———. 1993b. *Reading Recovery: A Guidebook for Teachers in Training.* Portsmouth, NH: Heinemann.

Cole, Michael, and Peg Griffin. 1986. A Sociohistorical Approach to Remediation. In Susan DeCastell, Alan Luke, and Kieran Egan, eds., *Literacy, Society, and Schooling: A Reader,* pp. 110–131. New York: Cambridge University Press.

Coles, Gerald. 1987. *The Learning Mystique: A Critical Look at Learning Disabilities.* New York: Pantheon.

Crooks, Terrence. 1988. The Impact of Classroom Evaluation Practices on Students. *Review of Educational Research* 58(4): 438–481.

Csikszentmihalyi, Mihalyi. 1981. Some Paradoxes in the Definition of Play. In Alyce Cheska, ed., *Play as Context: 1979 Proceedings of the Association for the Antrhopological Study of Play,* pp. 13–25. West Point, NY: Leisure Press.

Dahl, Karen L., and Penny Freppon. 1995. A Comparison of Inner-city Children's Interpretations of Reading and Writing Instruction in the Early Grades in Skills-Based and Whole Language Classrooms. *Reading Research Quarterly* 30: 50–75.

Danielson, Kathy. 1988. *Dialogue Journals: Writing as Conversation.* Bloomington, IN: Phi Delta Kappa Educational Foundation.

Danner, Fred, Elfrieda Hiebert, and Peter Winograd. 1983. Children's Understanding of Text Difficulty. Paper presented at the annual meeting of the American Educational Research Association. New Orleans. April.

Dansereau, Donald. 1987. Transfer from Cooperative to Individual Study. *Journal of Reading* 30: 614–619.

Davison, Alice, and Robert Kantor. 1982. On the Failure of Readability Formulas to Define Readable Texts: A Case Study from Adaptations. *Reading Research Quarterly* 17: 187–209.

Dewey, John. 1913. *Interest and Effort in Education*. New York: Augustus M. Kelly.

———. 1966. *Democracy and Education*. New York: Free Press (original ed., 1916).

Dillon, James. 1988. *Questioning and Teaching: A Manual of Practice*. New York: Teachers College Press.

Durkin, Dolores. 1978. *Teaching Them to Read*. 3rd ed. Boston: Allyn & Bacon.

———. 1978–79. What Classroom Observations Reveal About Reading Comprehension Instruction. *Reading Research Quarterly* 14: 481–533.

Durrell, Donald. 1937. *Durrell Analysis of Reading Difficulties*. New York: Harcourt Brace Jovanovich.

Easley, Jack, and Russell Zwoyer. 1975. Teaching by Listening: Toward a New Day in Math Classes. *Contemporary Education* 14: 19–25.

Eckhoff, Barbara. 1983. How Reading Affects Children's Writing. *Language Arts* 60: 607–616.

Edfelt, Ake. 1960. *Silent Speech and Silent Reading*. Chicago: University of Chicago Press.

Edmiston, Patricia. 1990. From Onlooker to Activist: The Nature of Readers' Participation in Stories. Paper presented at the annual meeting of the National Reading Conference, Miami, FL. December.

Ehri, Linnea, Lee Wilce, and Brenda Taylor. 1987. Children's Categorization of Short Vowels in Words and the Influence of Spelling. *Merrill Palmer Quarterly* 33: 393–421.

Elkonin, Daniil. 1971. Development of Speech. In Aleksandr V. Zaporozhets and Daniil Elkonin, eds., *The Psychology of Preschool Children*. Trans. John Schybut and Seymore Simon. Cambridge, MA: MIT Press.

Ferdman, Bernardo. 1990. Literacy and Cultural Identity. *Harvard Educational Review* 60(2): 181–204.

Feuerstein, Reuven. 1979. *The Dynamic Assessment of Retarded Performers: The Learning Potential Assessment Device, Theory, Instrument and Techniques*. Baltimore, MD: University Park Press.

Fillmore, Charles. 1981. Ideal Readers and Real Readers. In *Proceedings of the 32nd Georgetown Roundtable on Languages and Linguistics*. Washington, DC: Georgetown University Press.

Fine, Michelle. 1981. Perspectives on Inequity: Voices from Urban Schools. In L. Bickman, ed. *Applied Social Psychology Annual IV*, pp. 217–246. Beverly Hills: Sage.

Flower, Linda. 1989. The Undercover Work of Task Representation in Reading-to-Write Tasks. Paper presented at the annual meeting of the National Reading Conference, Austin, TX. December.

Flower, Linda, and John Hayes. 1981. The Pregnant Pause: An Inquiry into the Nature of Planning. *Research in the Teaching of English* 15: 229–243.

———. 1983. Uncovering Cognitive Processes in Writing: An Introduction to Protocol Analysis. In Peter Mosenthal, Lynne Tamor, and Sean Walmsley, eds., *Research on Written Language: Principles and Methods*, pp. 206–219. New York: Guilford Press.

Fox, Helen. 1994. *Listening to the World: Cultural Issues in Academic Writing*. Urbana, IL: National Council of Teachers of English.

Fulwiler, Toby, ed. 1987. *The Journal Book*. Portsmouth, NH: Heinemann.

Gambrell, Linda, Robert Wilson, and Walter Gantt. 1981. Classroom Observations of Task-Attending Behaviors of Good and Poor Readers. *Journal of Educational Research* 74: 400–404.

Gates, Arthur, and Anne McKillop. 1927. *Gates-McKillop Reading Diagnostic Tests*. New York: Teachers College.

Gesell, Arnold. 1925. *The Mental Growth of the Preschool Child*. New York: Macmillan.

Gilmore, James. 1951. *Gilmore Oral Reading Test*. New York: Harcourt Brace Jovanovich.

Gilyard, Keith. 1991. *Voices of the Self: A Study of Language Competence*. Detroit: Wayne State Press.

Glaser, Robert. 1988. Cognitive and Environmental Perspectives on Assessing Achievement. In *Assessment in the Service of Learning: Proceedings of the 1987 ETS Invitational Conference*. Princeton, NJ: Educational Testing Service.

Goatley, Virginia. 1996. The Participation of a Student Identified as Learning Disabled in a Regular Education Book Club: The Case of Stark. *Reading and Writing Quarterly: Overcoming Learning Difficulties* 12: 195–214.

Goodman, Kenneth. 1965. A Linguistic Study of Cues and Miscues in Reading. *Elementary English* 42: 639–643.

Goodman, Kenneth, Dorothy Watson, and Carolyn Burke. 1987. *Reading Miscue Analysis.* New York: Richard C. Owen.

Graves, Donald. 1983. *Writing: Teachers and Children at Work.* Portsmouth, NH: Heinemann.

———. 1991. *Build a Literate Classroom.* Portsmouth, NH: Heinemann.

———. 1994. *A Fresh Look at Writing.* Portsmouth, NH: Heinemann.

Gray, William S. 1915. *Standardized Oral Reading Paragraphs.* Bloomington, IL: Public School Publishing Co.

Green, Georgia. 1981. Competence for Implicit Text Analysis: Literary Style Discrimination in Five-Year-Olds. In Deborah Tannen, ed., *Analyzing Discourse: Text and Talk.* Washington, DC: Georgetown University Press.

Green, Nancy. 1993. Portfolios in a Fifth Grade Classroom. In Mary Ann Smith and Miriam Ylvisaker, eds., *Teachers' Voices: Portfolios in the Classroom.* Berkeley, CA: National Writing Project.

Grice, H. Paul. 1975. Logic and Conversation. In P. Cole and J. Morgan, eds., *Syntax and Semantics.* vol. 3, *Speech Acts.* New York: Seminar Press.

Guszak, Frank. 1967. Teacher Questioning and Reading. *The Reading Teacher* 21: 227–234.

Hall, Nigel, and Anne Robinson. 1994. *Keeping in Touch: Using Interactive Writing with Young Children.* Portsmouth, NH: Heinemann.

Hansen, Jane. 1987. *When Writers Read.* Portsmouth, NH: Heinemann.

———. 1991. I Wonder What Kind of Person He'll Be. *The New Advocate* 4(2): 89–100.

Hanson, Vicki L. 1989. Phonology and Reading: Evidence from Profoundly Deaf Readers. In D. Shankweiler and I. Y. Liberman, eds., *Phonology and Reading Disability: Solving the Reading Puzzle,* pp. 69–89. Ann Arbor: University of Michigan Press.

Heath, Shirley Brice. 1983. Ways with Words: Language, Life, and Work in Communities and Classroom. Cambridge: Cambridge University Press.

———. 1987. The Literate Essay: Myths and Ethnography. In Judith Langer, ed., *Language, Literacy and Culture.* Norwood, NJ: Ablex.

———. 1991. The Sense of Being Literate: Historical and Cross-Cultural Features. In P. David Pearson, ed., *Handbook of Reading Research,* vol. 2, pp. 3–25. White Plains, NH: Longman.

Hewitt, Geof. 1995. *A Portfolio Primer: Teaching, Collecting, and Assessing Student Writing.* Portsmouth, NH: Heinemann.

Holdaway, Don. 1979. *The Foundations of Literacy.* Sydney: Scholastic.

———. 1986. The Structure of Natural Learning as a Basis for Literacy Instruction. In Michael Sampson, ed., *The Pursuit of Literacy: Early Reading and Writing.* Dubuque, IA: Kendall/Hunt.

Huey, Edmund. 1908. *The Psychology and Pedagogy of Reading.* New York: Plenum.

Hull, Glynda. 1986. Acts of Wonderment. In David Bartholomae and Anthony Petrosky, eds., *Facts, Artifacts and Counterfacts,* pp. 199–226. Portsmouth, NH: Boynton/Cook–Heinemann.

Jacoby, Russell. 1994. *Dogmatic Wisdom.* New York: Doubleday.

James, William. 1899. *Talks to Teachers on Psychology.* New York: Henry Holt & Co.

Johnston, Peter. 1985. Understanding Reading Disability. *Harvard Educational Review* 55: 153–177.

———. In press. The Consequences of the Use of Standardized Tests. In Sharon Murphy, ed., *The Evidentiary Basis for Reading.* Mahwah, NJ: Lawrence Erlbaum.

Johnston, Peter, and Peter Afflerbach. 1985. The Process of Constructing Main Ideas from Text. *Cognition and Instruction* 2: 207–232.

Johnston, Peter, and Peter Winograd. 1985. Passive Failure in Reading. *Journal of Reading Behavior* 4: 279–301.

Johnston, Peter, Peter Afflerbach, and Paula Weiss. 1993. Teachers' Evaluation of Teaching and Learning of Literacy. *Educational Assessment* 1(2): 91–117.

Jones, Alison. 1991. *"At School I've Got a Chance." Culture/Privilege: Pacific Islands and Pakeha Girls at School.* Palmerston North, New Zealand: Dunmore Press.

Juel, Connie. 1988. Learning to Read and Write: A Longitudinal Study of 54 Children from First Through Fourth Grades. *Journal of Educational Psychology* 80: 437–447.

Klare, George. 1984. Readability. In P. David Pearson, ed., *The Handbook of Reading Research*, pp. 681–744. White Plains, NY: Longman.

Klausner, Edith. 1995. The Primary Language Record as a Reliable Option for Assessing Children's Literacy: Report of the Initial Phase of Development of a Process for Moderation. Paper presented at the International Seminar on the Primary Language Record/California Learning Record, New York, NY. October.

Knoblauch, Cy, and Lil Brannon. 1988. Knowing Our Knowledge: A Phenomenological Basis for Teacher Research. In Louise Z. Smith, ed., *Audits of Meaning: A Festschrift in Honor of Ann E. Berthoff*, pp. 17–28. Portsmouth, NH: Boynton/Cook–Heinemann.

Kohn, Alfie. 1993. *Punished by Rewards: The Trouble with Gold Stars, Incentive Plans, A's, Praise, and Other Bribes.* Boston: Houghton Mifflin.

Langer, Judith. 1987. The Construction of Meaning and the Assessment of Comprehension: An Analysis of Reader Performance on Standardized Test Items. In Roy Freedle and Richard Duran, eds., *Cognitive and Linguistic Analyses of Test Performance*, pp. 103–124. Norwood, NJ: Ablex.

Leu, Don. 1982. Oral Reading Error Analysis: A Critical Review of Research and Application. *Reading Research Quarterly* 17: 420–437.

Luria, Alexander. 1970. The Functional Organization of the Brain. *Scientific American* 222(3): 66–79.

Lyons, Carol, Gay Su Pinnell, and Dianne DeFord. 1993. *Partners in Learning: Teachers and Children in Reading Recovery.* New York: Teachers College Press.

MacLachlan, Patricia. 1990. Painting the Air. *The New Advocate* 3(4): 219–226.

Macrorie, Ken. 1970. *Telling Writing.* Rochelle Park, NJ: Hayden Book Co.

Marbe, Karl. 1901. Experimentell-Psychologische: Untersuchungen Über das Urteil. Leipzig: Engelmann. Reprinted and translated in Jean Mandler and George Mandler, eds., *Thinking: From Association to Gestalt*, pp. 143–148. New York: Wiley, 1964.

March, James. 1971. Model Bias in Social Action. *Review of Educational Research* 42: 413–429.

McDermott, Ray, and Herve Varenne. 1995. Culture *as* Disability. *Anthropology and Education Quarterly* 26: 324–348.

McGill-Franzen, Anne, and Richard Allington. 1991. The Gridlock of Low Reading Achievement: Perspectives on Practice and Policy. *Remedial and Special Education* 12: 20–30.

McKenna, Michael, and Kent Layton. 1990. Concurrent Validity of Cloze as a Measure of Intersentential Comprehension. *Journal of Educational Psychology* 82(2): 372–377.

McNaughton, Stuart. 1981. The Influence of Immediate Teacher Correction on Self-Corrections and Proficient Oral Reading. *Journal of Reading Behavior* 13: 367–371.

McNeil, Linda. 1987. *Contradictions of Control. School Structure and School Knowledge.* London: Routledge and Kegan Paul.

Mehan, Hugh. 1993. Beneath the Skin and Between the Ears: A Case Study in the Politics of

Representation. In Seth Chaiklin and Jean Lave, eds., *Understanding Practice: Perspectives on Activity and Contexts,* pp. 241–268. Cambridge: Cambridge University Press.

Miller, Arden. 1987. Changes in Academic Self-Concept in Early School Years: The Role of Conceptions of Ability. *Journal of Social Behavior and Personality* 3: 551–558.

Miller, Arden T. 1985. A Developmental Study of the Cognitive Basis of Performance Impairment After Failure. *Journal of Personality and Social Psychology* 49: 529–538.

Milliken, Mark. 1992. A Fifth-Grade Class Uses Portfolios. In Donald H. Graves and Bonnie S. Sunstein, eds., *Portfolio Portraits,* pp. 34–44. Portsmouth, NH: Heinemann.

Moore, David. 1983. A Case for Naturalistic Assessment of Reading Comprehension. *Language Arts* 60: 957–969.

Morphett, Mabel, and Carleton Washburne. 1931. When Should Children Begin to Read? *Elementary School Journal* 31: 496–503.

Morris, Darrel. 1980. Beginning Readers' Concept of Word. In Edmund Henderson and James Beers, eds., *Developmental and Cognitive Aspects of Learning to Spell: A Reflection of Word Knowledge,* pp. 97–111. Newark, DE: International Reading Association.

Newkirk, Thomas. 1986. Young Writers as Critical Readers. In Thomas Newkirk and Nancie Atwell. eds., *Understanding Writing: Ways of Observing, Learning and Teaching K-8,* pp. 106–113. Portsmouth, NH: Heinemann.

Newkirk, Thomas, and Pat McLure. 1992. *Listening in: Children Talk About Books (and Other Things).* Portsmouth, NH: Heinemann.

New Zealand Department of Education. 1980. *Early Reading Inservice Course.* Wellington: P.D. Hasselberg Government Printer.

Nicholls, John G. 1978. The Development of the Concepts of Effort and Ability, Perception of Own Attainment, and the Understanding That Difficult Tasks Require More Ability. *Child Development* 49: 800–814.

————. 1989. *The Competitive Ethos and Democratic Education.* Cambridge, MA: Harvard University Press.

Nicholls, John G., and Susan P. Hazzard. 1993. *Education as Adventure: Lessons from the Second Grade.* New York: Teachers College Press.

Nicholls, John G., and J. Ron Nelson. 1992. Students' Conceptions of Controversial Knowledge. *Journal of Educational Psychology* 84: 224–230.

Nicholls, John G., Marlene McKenzie, and Julianne Shufro. (1995). Schoolwork, Homework, Life's Work: The Experience of Students with and Without Learning Disabilities. *Journal of Learning Disabilities* 27: 562–569.

Nicholls, John G., Ping Cheung, Janice Lauer, and Michael Patashnick. 1989. Individual Differences in Academic Motivation: Perceived Ability, Goals, Beliefs, and Values. *Learning and Individual Differences* 1: 63–84.

Nicholson, Tom. 1984. Experts and Novices: A Study of Reading in the High School Classroom. *Reading Research Quarterly* 19: 436–451.

Nicholson, Tom, Christine Lillas, and M. Anne Rzoska. 1988. Have We Been Mislead by Miscues? *The Reading Teacher* 42(1): 6–10.

Noddings, Nel. 1984. *Caring: A Feminine Approach to Ethics and Moral Education.* Berkeley, CA: University of California Press.

Nolan, Elizabeth. 1993. Learning to Listen. *The Reading Teacher* 46(7): 606–608.

Nolen, Susan B. 1988. Reasons for Studying: Motivational Orientations and Study Strategies. *Cognition and Instruction* 5: 269–288.

Page, R. N. 1991. *Lower Track Classrooms: A Curricular and Cultural Perspective.* New York: Teachers College Press.

Paulson, F. Leon, Pearl R. Paulson, Carol A. Meyer. 1991. What Makes a Portfolio a Portfolio? *Educational Leadership* (February): 60–63.

Pearson, P. David, and Dale Johnson. 1978. *Teaching Reading Comprehension.* New York: Holt, Rinehart and Winston.

Peterson, Barbara. 1988. *Characteristics of Texts That Support Beginning Readers.* Ann Arbor: University Microfilms International.

Philips, Susan. 1983. *The Invisible Culture: Communication in Classroom and Community on the Warm Springs Indian Reservation.* White Plains, NY: Longman.

Postman, Neil. 1976. *Crazy Talk, Stupid Talk.* New York: Delacorte Press.

Power, Brenda Miller. 1996. *Taking Note: Improving Your Observational Notetaking.* York, ME: Stenhouse.

Raphael, Taffy. 1986. Teaching Questions-Answers Relationships, Revisited. *The Reading Teacher* 39: 516–522.

Read, Charles, Zhang Yun-Fei, Nie Hong-Kin, Ding Bao-Qing. 1986. The Ability to Manipulate Speech Sounds Depends on Knowing Alphabetic Writing. *Cognition* 24: 31–44.

Readence, John, and David Moore. 1983. Why Questions? A Historical Perspective on Standardized Reading Comprehension Tests. *Journal of Reading* 26: 306–312.

Reading Test for New York State Elementary Schools Manual for Administrators and Teachers. 1986. Albany: The University of the State of New York, The State Education Department.

Reed, Leslie. 1988. Dialogue Journals Make My Whole Year Flow. In Jana Staton, Roger Shuy, Joy Peyton, and Leslie Reed, eds., *Dialogue Journal Communication: Classroom, Linguistic, Social and Cognitive Views*, pp. 56–72. Norwood, NJ: Ablex.

Renshaw, Peter, and Rae Gardener. 1987. Parental Goals and Strategies in Teaching Contexts: An Exploration of "Activity Theory" with Mothers and Fathers of Preschool Children. Paper presented at the annual meeting of the Society for Research in Child Development, Baltimore, MD.

Resnick, Daniel. 1982. History of Educational Testing. In Alexandra Wigdor and Wendell Garner, eds., *Ability Testing: Uses, Consequences, and Controversies (Part 2)*, Documentation Section, pp. 173–194. Washington, DC: National Academy Press.

Richardson, Elwyn. 1964. *In the Early World.* New York: Pantheon.

Rief, Linda. 1992. *Seeking Diversity: Language Arts with Adolescents.* Portsmouth, NH: Heinemann.

Romano, Tom. 1992. Multigenre Research: One College Senior. In Donald H. Graves and Bonnie S. Sunstein, eds., *Portfolio Portraits*, pp. 146–157. Portsmouth, NH: Heinemann.

Rose, Mike. 1980. Rigid Rules, Inflexible Plans, and the Stifling of Language: A Cognitivist Analysis of Writer's Block. *College Composition and Communication* 31(4): 389–401.

Rosenblatt, Louise. 1978. *The Reader, the Text, the Poem: The Transactional Theory of the Literary Work.* Carbondale, IL: Southern Illinois University Press.

Sadoski, Mark, and Sharon Lee. 1986. Reading Comprehension and Miscue Combination Scores: Further Analysis and Comparison. *Reading Research and Instruction* 25: 160–167.

Schon, Donald. 1963. *Displacement of Concepts.* London: Tavistock.

———. 1983. *The Reflective Practitioner: How Professionals Think in Action.* New York: Basic Books.

Schumm, Jeanne, and R. Scott Baldwin. 1989. Cue System Usage in Oral and Silent Reading. *Journal of Reading Behavior* 21(2): 141–154.

Senge, Peter. 1990. *The Fifth Discipline: The Art and Practice of the Learning Organization.* New York: Doubleday.

Shanahan, Timothy, Michael Kamil, and Aileen Tobin. 1982. Cloze as a Measure of Intersentential Comprehension. *Reading Research Quarterly* 17(2): 229–255.

Shany, Michael, and Andrew Biemiller. 1995. Assisted Reading Practice: Effects on Performance for Poor Readers in Grades 3 and 4. *Reading Research Quarterly* 30(3): 382–395.

Shockley, Betty. 1993. Extending the Literate Community: Reading and Writing with Families. *The New Advocate* 6(11): 11–24.

Shockley, Betty, Barbara Michalove, and JoBeth Allen. 1995. *Engaging Families: Connecting Home and School Literacy Communities.* Portsmouth, NH: Heinemann.

Shuy, Roger. 1988. The Oral Language Basis for Dialogue Journals. In Jana Staton, Roger Shuy, Joy Peyton, and Leslie Reed, eds., *Dialogue Journal Communication: Classroom, Linguistic, Social and Cognitive Views,* pp. 73–87. Norwood, NJ: Ablex.

Sirotnik, Kenneth. 1987. Evaluation in the Ecology of Schooling: The Process of School Renewal. In John Goodlad, ed., *The Ecology of School Renewal: Eighty-Sixth Yearbook of the National Society for the Study of Education, Part I,* pp. 41–62. Chicago: University of Chicago Press.

Smith, John W., and Warwick B. Elley. 1994. *Learning to Read in New Zealand Schools.* Auckland, New Zealand: Longman Paul.

Smith, Mary Lee. 1991. Put to the Test: The Effects of External Testing on Teachers. *Educational Researcher* 20(5): 8–11.

Smith, Mary Lee, Carole Edelsky, K. Draper, C. Rottenberg, and M. Cherland. 1991. *The Role of Testing in Elementary Schools.* CSE technical report 321. Los Angeles: Center for the Study of Evaluation.

Sokolov, Alexandr. 1972. *Inner Speech and Thought.* New York: Plenum.

Spache, George. 1981. *The Diagnostic Reading Scales.* Monterey, CA: McGraw-Hill.

Spiro, Rhoda, and Peter Johnston. 1989. Children's Choices of, and Placement in, Books. Paper presented at the annual meeting of the National Reading Conference, Austin, TX. December.

Spradley, James. 1979. *The Ethnographic Interview.* New York: Holt, Rinehart, and Winston.

Stanovich, Keith. 1992. Are We Overselling Literacy? In Charles Temple and Patrick Collins, eds., *Stories and Readers: New Perspectives on Literature in the Elementary School,* pp. 209–231. Norwood, MA: Christopher Gordon Publishers.

Staton, Jana. 1988. Dialogue Journals in the Classroom Context. In Jana Staton, Roger Shuy, Joy Peyton, and Leslie Reed, eds., *Dialogue Journal Communication: Classroom, Linguistic, Social and Cognitive Views,* pp. 33–55. Norwood, NJ: Ablex.

Staton, Jana, and Joy Peyton. 1988. Topics: A Window on the Construction of Knowledge. In Jana Staton, Roger Shuy, Joy Peyton, and Leslie Reed, eds., *Dialogue Journal Communication: Classroom, Linguistic, Social and Cognitive Views,* pp. 245–276. Norwood, NJ: Ablex.

Staton, Jana, Roger Shuy, Joy Peyton, and Leslie Reed. 1988. *Dialogue Journal Communication: Classroom, Linguistics, Social and Cognitive Views.* Norwood, NJ: Ablex.

Stipek, Deborah J., and John Daniels. 1987. Declining Perceptions of Competence: A Consequence of Changes in the Child or in the Educational Environment. Paper presented at the meeting of the American Educational Research Association, Washington, DC. April.

Stipek, Deborah J., Susan Recchia, and Susan McClintic. 1992. *Self-Evaluation in Young Children.* Monographs of the Society for Research in Child Development no. 226. Chicago: University of Chicago Press.

Tammivaara, Julie, and Scott Enright. 1986. On Eliciting Information: Dialogues with Child Informants. *Anthropology and Education Quarterly* 17: 218–238.

Teale, William, and Elizabeth Sulzby, eds. 1986. *Emergent Literacy: Writing and Reading.* Norwood, NJ: Ablex.

Thorkildsen, Theresa. 1988. Theories of Education Among Academically Able Adolescents. *Contemporary Educational Psychology* 13: 323–330.

Todorov, Tzvetan. 1984. *Mikhail Bakhtin: The Dialogical Principle.* Trans. Wlad Godzich. Minneapolis: University of Minnesota Press.

Valentine, P. V. 1990. Baltimore Tries to Stop Abuse Over Grades. *Washington Post,* Sect. B, p. 4. November 16.

Vellutino, Frank, Donna Scanlon, Edward Sipay, Sheila Small, Alice Pratt, RuSan Chen, and Martha Denckla. 1996. Cognitive Profiles of Difficult-to-Remediate and Readily Remediated Poor Readers: Early Intervention as a Vehicle for Distinguishing Between Cognitive and Experimental Deficits as Basic Causes of Specific Reading Disability. *Journal of Educational Psychology* 88: 601–638.

Vygotsky, Lev. 1962. *Thought and Language.* Ed. Eugenia Hanfmann. Trans. Gertrude Vakar. Cambridge, MA: MIT Press.

———. 1978. *Mind in Society: The Development of Higher Psychological Processes.* Ed. and trans. M. Cole, V. John-Steiner, S. Scribner, and E. Souberman. Cambridge, MA: Harvard University Press.

Weber, Rose Marie. 1970. A Linguistic Analysis of First-Grade Reading Errors. *Reading Research Quarterly* 5: 427–451.

———. 1985. Questions During Reading Lessons. Paper presented at the American Educational Research Association, San Francisco, CA. April.

Wilde, Sandra. 1991. *You Kan Red This! Spelling and Punctuation for Whole Language Classrooms.* Portsmouth, NH: Heinemann.

Wixson, Karen, Margory Lipson, Anita Bosky, and Nina Yokum. 1984. An Interview for Assessing Students' Perceptions of Classroom Reading Tasks. *The Reading Teacher* 37: 354–359.

Wolf, Dennie Palmer. 1989. Portfolio Assessment: Sampling Student Work. *Educational Leadership* (April): 35–39.

Wolf, Dennie Palmer, and Martha Perry. 1988. Becoming Literate: Beyond Scribes and Clerks. *Theory into Practice* 27(1): 44–52.

Woodcock, R. 1973. *Woodcock Reading Mastery Tests.* Circle Pines, MN: American Guidance Service.

Woodward, Helen. 1994. *Negotiated Evaluation: Involving Children and Parents in the Process.* Portsmouth, NH: Heinemann.

Yaden, David, Laura Smolkin, and A. Conlon. 1989. Preschoolers' Questions About Pictures, Print Conventions and Story Text During Reading Aloud at Home. *Reading Research Quarterly* 24(2): 189–214.

Young, Kim. 1995. An Alternative to Letter Grades. In Tara Azwell and Elizabeth Schmar, eds., *Report Card on Report Cards: Alternatives to Consider,* pp. 110–130. Portsmouth, NH: Heinemann.

CREDITS

The author and publishers would like to thank Marie M. Clay and her publisher, Heinemann Education, a division of Reed Publishing (NZ) Ltd., Private Bag 34901, Birkenhead, Auckland, New Zealand, for their cooperation in the preparation of Chapters 21 and 22.

Page 13: Peter H. Johnston. 1987. "Teachers as Evaluation Experts," *Reading Teacher* 40 (8), pp. 744–48. Copyright © by the International Reading Association. Reprinted by permission.

Pages 76, 78, 81, 82: Linda Rief. Copyright © 1992. *Seeking Diversity: Language Arts with Adolescents.* Published by Heinemann, a division of Reed Elsevier Inc., Portsmouth, NH. Reprinted by permission.

Pages 134–135: Ellen Adams. Copyright © 1995. "A Descriptive Study of Second Graders' Conversations About Books," unpublished Ph.D. diss., State University of New York at Albany. Reprinted by permission.

Page 196: *Little Pig* by June Melser. Copyright © 1981. In the series The Story Box, published by The Wright Group, San Diego, CA.

Pages 197–198, 203–204: *The Dragon's Birthday* by Margaret Mahy. Copyright © 1984. Published by Shortland Publications, Auckland, New Zealand. Reprinted by permission.

Page 198: *Old Tuatara* by Joy Cowley. Copyright © 1984. Published by Learning Media Limited, P. O. Box 3293, Wellington, New Zealand. Reprinted by permission.

Page 199: *Fantail, Fantail* by Margaret Mahy. Copyright © 1984. Published by Learning Media Limited, P. O. Box 3293, Wellington, New Zealand. Reprinted by permission.

Pages 205–206: *Busy Beavers* by M. Barbara Brownell. Copyright © 1988. Published by the National Geographic Society, Washington, DC. Reprinted by permission.

Page 207: *Harry Goes to Funland* by Harriet Ziefert, illustrated by Mavis Smith. Copyright © 1989 by Harriet Ziefert; Illustrations Copyright © 1989 by Mavis Smith. Used by permission of Viking Penguin, a division of Penguin Books USA Inc.

Pages 223–225: *Owl Babies* by Martin Waddell. Text © 1992 Martin Waddell. Illustrations © 1992 Patrick Benson. Permission granted by the publishers Walker Books Limited.

Pages 332–333: *Oops!* by Fran Hunia. Copyright © 1984. Published by Ashton Scholastic Ltd., Auckland, New Zealand. Reprinted by permission.

Pages 333–335: *Greedy Cat* by Joy Cowley. Copyright © 1983. Published by Learning Media Limited, P. O. Box 3293, Wellington, New Zealand. Reprinted by permission.

INDEX

ability
  children's concepts of, 131–133
    motivation and, 134
    sense of control and, 136–137
  grading and, 304 305
accountability, 7
active listening, 9, 25
  in portfolio conferences, 277
Adams, Ellen, 84, 87, 134, 135, 165
adversarial relationships, physical posture
    and, 21
aesthetic reading, 239
Afflerbach, Peter, 297
Alphabet Knowledge Record Sheet,
  325–326
appeals, in oral reading, 207
assessment, See also grading; report
    cards; testing
  consistency in, 311–312
  constructive, 11–16
  focus of, 23–24
  future of, 321–323
  involving children in, 5–6, 309–310
  language of, 14–15
  moderation in, 312–314
  objectivity and distance, 25
  as a people problem, 3
  physical posture and orientation, 21
  of portfolios, 281–284, 320–321
  via portfolios, 40–41, 283–284, 307, 312
  power and control and, 20–22
  of process vs. product, 39–40
  productive, 5–6

  self-assessment and, 28
  skills, 9–10
  social interactions and, 6–7, 17–25
  specifying criteria and stages in,
    315–317
  stakes involved, 24 25
  synchronizing conversations in,
    313–319
  time and timing of, 22–23
  trust and, 19 20
  use of term, 2
assessment questions
  competence, 137
  concepts about print, 112
  constructive literacy, 83
  literacy concepts, 97
  meaningful literacy, 75
  strategies, 129
  word visual and sound analysis, 118,
    121
assets, emphasis on, 36–39
Atwell, Nancie, 59, 148, 168–169, 252–253
audience
  knowledge of, 79
  presenting portfolios to, 280–281
  self-evaluation through, 30, 31
auditory analysis, 118
Austin, Terri, 306, 309–310, 320
authors
  children's concepts of, 92
  recognizing, 74
awareness, See also print awareness
  conscious, 30–32, 33

  development of, 149–150
  of genres, 149
  metacognitive, 234

"baby books," 58, 96
Bakhtin, Mikhail, 293
Barber, Benjamin, 9
Barham, Richard, 27
basal readers, 44, 55–56
Belenky, Mary, 77, 80–81, 90, 92, 93
benchmarks, 317
Berry, Mardy, 161, 164–165
Berthoff, Ann, 125, 146, 176
Bietau, Lisa, 308, 310
"binging," 146
body orientation
  conveying adversarial relationship
    through, 21
  conveying power and control through,
    20
Bondy, Elizabeth, 88
*Book of Kids' Songs: A Holler-Along
    Handbook* (Cassidy and Cassidy),
  115
"book language," 150, 220
book reviews, 168
books
  "baby," 58, 96
  chapter, 96
  children's concepts about, 96, 108–110
  choosing, 234
  easy texts, 213
  hard texts, 213

books *(continued)*
    learning texts, 213
    "low-risk," 59
Brandts, Lois, 275
Bridge, Connie, 245
Bronfenbrenner, Uri, 25
Brow, Anthony, 70
Brown, Hazel, 246
Brownell, M. Barbara, 205
Bruner, Jerome, 42, 322
buddy reading, 55–56
Busy Beavers (Brownell), 205–206, 216

Cambourne, Brian, 246
CAP (Concepts About Print) test, 20–21,
    101–102
Carle, Eric, 72
case studies, 288–296
    framing in, 290–292
    information included in, 293–295
    instructional suggestions in, 295–296
    language use in, 288–290
    negative terms in, 291–292
    voice and style in, 292–293
Cat Who Wore a Pot on Her Head, The
    (Slepian and Seidler), 115
chapter books, children's concepts of, 96
checklists
    limitations of, 251
    for more than yes/no responses,
        252–254
    for self-checking, 251, 252
    value of, 250–251
children. *See* learners
choice, 57–65
    effect on literacy activity, 43–45
    as error, 60
    factors influencing, 58–59
    motivation and, 44, 55
    priorities revealed through, 59–60
    in reading, 44, 45
    teacher's role in, 58
    value of, 57–58
    in writing, 46
circle discussions, 164–165
classics, conceptions of, 95–96
classroom conversations
    circle discussions, 164–165
    constructive, 166–167
    controlling through questions, 160
    encouraging, 160–167
    teacher domination of, 159
classroom organization, adultcentric, 159

Clay, Marie, 21, 35, 39, 98, 101, 114, 119,
    140, 142, 193, 212, 213, 214
cloze, 243–244
Cole, Michael, 188
collaboration, on portfolio assessment,
    320–321
collaborative literacy, 83–84
comparisons, interpersonal, 131–133
competence
    assessment questions, 137
    children's concepts of, 130–137
    sense of control and, 136–137
competition, reflection and, 32
complexity, development of, 147–148
compound words, children's concepts
    about, 111
comprehension, 77, 78
Concepts About Print (CAP) test, 20–21,
    101–102
conceptual confusion, 108
conceptual knowledge, in writing,
    146–147
conclusions, inappropriate, 74–75
concrete discussion, in interviews,
    181–182
conferences
    as alternatives to report cards, 298,
        309–310
    parent-teacher, 298, 309–310
    parent-teacher-student conferences,
        309–310
    portfolio, 277, 279–280, 281
    "status-of-the-class," 252–253
connected knowing, 80
connections
    failure to make, 72
    inappropriate, 74–75
    making meaning through, 71–73
conscious awareness, *See also* awareness
    balancing, 33
    value of, 30–32
consonants, children's representation of
    in print, 115–116
constructed knowing, 94–95
constructive conversations, cultivating,
    166–167
constructive evaluation, 11–16
    listening and, 14–16
    observation and, 11–14
    reflection and, 16
Constructive Evaluation of Literate Activity
    (Johnston), 1
constructive knowing, 77

constructive literacy, 76–85
    assessment questions, 85
constructive self-assessment, 134–136
context
    ease of literacy activities and, 51–53
    recognition and, 73
    for self-assessment, 32–33
contrast questions, 184
control
    in evaluation settings, 20–22
    questions as, 21–22, 160
controversial knowledge, 93
conventions, children's early concepts of,
    98–101
conversations
    classroom. *See* classroom conversations
    print. *See* print conversations
coping strategies, 127
copy matching strategy, 188
corrections
    effect on learners, 19
    vs. self corrections, 29
*Couple of Kooks and Other Stories About
    Love, A* (Rylant), 79
Cowley, Joy, 198, 333
criteria
    external, 273
    internal, 273
    for moderation, 314–317
    for selecting portfolio items, 272, 273,
        278, 283, 285
    specifying in reporting systems,
        315–317
    for student self-evaluation, 35–36
critical literacy, 84–85
critical reading
    children's concepts of, 92
    separate vs. connected knowing and,
        81
    social imagination and, 79
Crooks, Mina, 124
Crooks, Terry, 27
Csikszentmihalyi, Mihalyi, 9
cultural differences
    errors and, 61, 62
    language and, 8, 14
    meaning and, 70
    in timing of responses, 22
cummings, e. e., 60

Dansereau, Donald, 246
deaf children, development of print
    awareness by, 119

decision-making process, priorities revealed through, 59
decoding, literacy and, 139–140
deep processing strategies, 133
deferential literacy, 92
democracy
    conversations in, 164
    relationships in, 82–83
    values and, 320–321
de Paola, Tomie, 246
dependency, on support, 55
descriptions, of learners, 15
descriptive questions, 183
development patterns, 138–155
Dewey, John, 304, 321
Diagnostic Reading Scales, 292
dialectical notebooks, 176
dialects, nonstandard, editing, 79
dialogue journals, 81–82, 168–176
    advantages of, 171–174
    literary, 168–170
    nonliterary, 170–171
    principle of, 176
    responding to, 174–176
dictation tests, 119–120
Dillon, James, 160
discussion. See classroom conversations
display questions, 172–173
distance, in assessment, 25
diversity
    development of, 148
    in portfolios, 267
    social imagination and, 79
double-entry notebooks, 176, 256
Dragon's Birthday, The (Mahy), 197–198, 203–204
dramatizations, translating texts into, 247
Durkin, Dolores, 240
dynamic assessment, 55

Early Reading Inservice Course (ERIC), 194–195
Easley, Jack, 29
easy texts, 213
Edfeldt, Ake, 232
editing
    for an audience, 79
    by children, 154–155
Edmiston, Pat, 237, 247
efferent reading, 239
effort, grading on, 304–305
ego, grades and, 24
ego-orientation, 133

Elkonin, Daniil, 149
emergent literacy, 140
emotional issues, learning about in interviews, 189–190
emotions, meaning and, 70
empathy, connected knowing and, 80
engagement, 322
Enright, Scott, 159
error rate, in oral reading, 212–213
    calculating, 215–216
errors
    analyzing, 60–65
    choices as, 60
    correcting, by students, 63
    counting, in running records, 213–216
    defined, 60
    detecting, by students, 63
    learning from, 60
    patterns of, 64–65
essays, 170
evaluation, See also assessment
    use of term, 2
experience
    making connections to, 71–73
    meaningfulness and, 69–71, 77–78
    social imagination and, 78–79
external criteria, for including items in portfolios, 273

Faithful Elephants (Tsuchiya), 69, 73
Fantail, Fantail (Mahy), 198
"fast-write," 320
feedback
    motivation and, 37–39
    specificity of, 39
fiction, prior experience and, 71
Fillmore, Charles, 235
Fine, Michelle, 320
finger-pointing, 231
five-finger rule, 234
Flesch Reading Ease formula, 43
flexibility, development of, 148
Flower, Linda, 238
fluency, in reading, 146
focus
    on reading and writing process, 24
    on what student has to say, 23–24
"folk process," 246
Foundling, The (Mailot), 70
Fox, Helen, 62
frame of reference, in understanding texts, 240
framing, in case studies, 290–292

Friere, Paulo, 92
Friskey, Margaret, 210, 218

gender stereotypes, critical literacy and, 84–85
genres
    awareness of, 149
    diversity in, 148
Gesell, Arnold, 139
goals
    ease of literacy activities and, 53
    for portfolios, 278–279
    reading and writing strategies and, 123–124
Goatley, Ginny, 81
Goodman, Ken, 192
grade level reading, basal readers for, 44, 55–56
grading, 297–310, See also report cards
    alternatives to, 299, 305, 306–310
    conflicts involved in, 300
    on effort, 304–305
    in middle schools, 298
    motivation and, 304, 305
    teacher decision-making involved in, 297
Graves, Don, 40, 59, 146, 179
Greedy Cat (Cowley), 333–335, 338, 339
Green, Nancy, 283
Griffin, Peg, 188
group tests, social interaction effects, 18
Guszak, Frank, 240

Haggerty, William, 335
Hansen, Jane, 40, 59
hard texts, 213
Harry Goes to Funland (Ziefert), 207
Hazzard, Susan, 20
Heath, Shirley Brice, 170
hesitations, in oral reading, 213
Hewitt, Geof, 271, 283
higher-order questions, 242–243
high frequency words, sight recognition of, 119
Holdaway, Don, 111
home journals, 306
Huey, Edmund, 233
Hull, Glynda, 64
Hungry Thing, The (Slepian and Seidler), 115
Hunia, Fran, 332

iatrogenics, 290
I Can Read (Malcolm), 209

Ihimaera, Witi, 86
imagination
    development of, 150
    social, 78–79
independence
    as characteristic of literacy
        development, 146
    importance of, 9–10
Indian Two Feet and His Horse (Friskey),
    210, 218
In the Early World (Richardson), 34
inferential questions, 241
Informal Reading Inventories (IRIs), 193,
    194
information sources, in oral reading,
    219–223
In the Middle (Atwell), 168–169
inner speech, characteristics of, 232–233
instructional level texts, 213
instructional suggestions, in case studies,
    295–296
"intelligent unrest," 16
intentions
    ascribing, 60
    inferring, understanding errors
        through, 62
interactive assessment, 55
interdependence, 10
interest inventories, 185
internal criteria, for including items in
    portfolios, 273
interpersonal comparisons, 131–133
interpretation, prior experience and, 71
intervention, in oral reading, 208–210
interviews, 178–185
    cautions about, 190–191
    concrete discussion in, 181–182
    efficiency of, 187
    information gathered through, 187–190
    questions in, 180–181, 182–184,
        329–330
    reflection in, 182
    requesting information in, 180–181
    standardized, 184–185
    tacit information gained through,
        186–187
invented spelling
    phoneme awareness and, 114
    value of, 115
    visual analysis and, 117–118
    writing development and, 117
involvement, as characteristic of literacy
    development, 146

James, William, 145
Johnson, Dale, 241–242
Johnston, Emily, 327–328
Jones, Allison, 78
journals, *See also* dialogue journals
    double-entry, 176, 256
    home, 306
    reflection through, 31–32
    teacher, for observational records,
        254–255
Juel, Connie, 73

knowing
    children's concepts of, 91–95
    connected, 80, 81
    constructed, 94–95
    constructive, 77
    procedural, 94
    received, 93
    separate, 80, 81
    silence, 92
    subjective, 93–94
knowledge
    of audience, 79
    conceptions of, 92–95
    conceptual, 146–147
    controversial, 93
    of literacy, 10, 14–15
    prior, 70–71
Kohn, Alfie, 304

Langer, Judith, 235
language
    appropriate, in case studies, 288–290
    of assessment, 14–15
    cultural differences, 8, 14
    specialized, 289
    transparency of, 7–8
language play, literacy development and,
    149–150
lax vowels, 115–116, 118, 142
learners
    control of learning process by, 136–137
    describing, 15
    effect of corrections on, 19
    logic of, 61
    as source of literacy problems,
        126
learning
    children's orientation to, 133
    process, control of, 136–137
learning disabilities, as source of literacy
    problems, 126

learning disabled students
    conceptions of knowledge by, 95
    encouraging reflection in, 32
learning texts, 213
letters, children's concepts about,
    98–101, 104, 108
library model, of reading choice, 44, 45f
listening
    active, 9, 25, 277
    empathy and, 15–16
    in interviews, 180–181
    learning from, 186–191
    received knowing as, 93
    by teacher, classroom conversation
        and, 165
lists, 250, 253, *See also* checklists
literacy
    assessment questions, 97
    children's concepts of, 86–96
    collaborative, 83–84
    constructive, 76–85
    critical, 84–85
    cultural issues, 8
    deferential, 92
    defined, 139–140
    knowledge of, 10
    learning about through interviews,
        187–190
    meaningful, 69–75
literate activity
    choice and, 43–45
    ease of
        controlling, 50–56
        factors affecting, 42–49
        manageable, 56
        overemphasis on, 56
    knowledge of, 14–15
    readability and, 42–43
literacy development, 138–155
    characteristics of, 146–155
    complexity of, 142–144, 150–155
    order of, 138–139
    predictability in, 143–144
    quantity, rate, and fluency, 145–155
    regression, 142
    theories of, 189–141
literacy strategies, 127
literal questions, 241
literary dialogue journals, 168–170
literate communities, 82
literate exchanges, 82–83
literate relationships, sustaining, 81–84
literature, conceptions of, 95–96

Little Pig (Melser), 196
logic, of children, 61
looking. *See* observation
Love You Forever (Munsch), 240
lower-order questions, 242–243
low reading group readers, lack of
    connections made by, 72
"low risk" books, 59

MacLachlan, Patricia, 247–248
McLure, Pat, 92, 165
Macrorie, Ken, 288
Mahy, Margaret, 120, 197, 199, 203
Malcolm, Margaret, 209
Mailot, Hector, 70
Man Whose Mother Was a Pirate, The
    (Mahy), 120–121
Marbe, Karl, 233
March, James, 7
Martin, Craig, 202
mastery, as motivation, 133–134
meaning
    connections and, 71–73
    cultural differences and, 70
    emotions and, 70
    experience and, 69–71
    student experience and, 77–78
    through constructive knowing, 77
meaning cues, 221–223
meaningful literacy, 69–75
meaningful relationships, 80–81
measurement, use of term, 2
Melser, June, 196
memory, development of, 148–149
mental age, reading instruction and, 139
metacognitive awareness, 234
middle schools, grading in, 298
Milliken, Mark, 267, 281, 286
miscue analysis, 192
Missing May (Rylant), 24
moderation
    benefits of, 313–314, 317–319
    criteria for, 314–317
    defined, 312
    examples, 312–313
Morphett, Mabel, 139
motivation
    children's concept of ability and, 134
    choice and, 44, 55
    ease of literacy activities and, 51–53
    feedback and, 37–39
    grading and, 304
    mastery as, 133–134

Moyes, Lesley, 203, 218
"Mud, The" (Emily Johnston), 150–155
multiple realities, constructing, 8–9
Munsch, Robert, 240
My Bike (Martin), 202

Newkirk, Tom, 92, 165
New Zealand Department of Education,
    194–195
Nicholls, John, 20
Nicholson, Tom, 188
Night (Wiesel), 76–77
Noddings, Nel, 36, 303
Nolan, Betsy, 164–165
nonfiction, prior experience and, 71
nonliterary dialogue journals, 170–171
nonsense text, 54
nonstandard dialects, editing, 79
nonverbal cues, in think-alouds, 234
notebooks. *See* dialogue journals; journals
Now One Foot, Now the Other (de Paola),
    246

objectivity, in assessment, 25
observation
    empathy and, 15–16
    of patterns, 11–14
    value of, 11, 23
observational records, 254–259
*Observation Survey of Early Literacy
    Achievement, An* (Clay), 193,
    212
Old Tuatara (Cowley), 198
Oops! (Hunia), 332–333, 336, 337
oral language development, 143–144
    imaginative storytelling, 150
    vocabulary, 150
oral reading
    appeals in, 207
    error analysis, 192, 213–216
    error rate, 212–213
    error recording, with running records,
        194–208
    information use in, 219–223
    interpreting running records, 212–231
    intervention in, 208–210
    pauses in, 210
    prediction in, 217–219
    problem-solving in, 203–205
    recording, 192–211
    recording methods, 193–194
    repetitions in, 202–203
    retelling, 245

self-corrections in, 200–202, 216–217,
    222–223
self-evaluation through, 30–31
words inserted in, 198–200
words omitted in, 196–197
words substituted in, 197–198
oral retelling, 245–247
Owl Babies (Waddell), 223–225

parents, attitudes toward report cards,
    298
parent-teacher communication
    conferences, 298, 309–310
    encouraging, 322
    report card alternatives and, 308–310
    reporting systems encouraging,
        314–315
parent-teacher-student conferences,
    309–310
patterns
    of development, 138–155
    of errors, 64–65
    of letters, children's early concepts of,
        100
    recognizing, 11–14, 73–75
    seeking, 74–75
pauses, in oral reading, 210
Pearson, David, 241–242
"pebble in the pond" effect, 142
Perry, Martha, 96
persistence, literacy development and, 146
Peyton, Joy, 171
phonetic analysis, reading and, 113–114
pictures, translating text into, 247, 248
Piggybook, The (Brown), 70
portfolio conferences
    active listening in, 277
    length of, 279–280
    recording, 281
portfolios, 263–276
    approaches to, 265–266
    assessing, 281–284, 320–321
    assessing learning progress through,
        40–41
    as assessment tools, 40–41, 283–284,
        307, 312
    benefits of, 266–267
    children's selections for, 272–274
    collaborative assessment of, 320–321
    contents of, 263–265, 270–273
    criteria for selecting items for, 36,
        272–274, 278, 283, 285
    defined, 282

portfolios (continued)
diversity in, 267
encouraging parent-teacher
communication, 314
encouraging self-evaluation with, 30
form of, 269
goals for, 278–279
home vs. school location for, 274, 286
introducing, 267–268
limiting number of items in, 267
making time available for, 274–276
managing, 268–269
modeling, 268
presenting, 275
presenting to larger audience, 280–281
purposes of, 263–264
reviewing, 275
sharing, 264–265, 266–267
standardizing, 282–283, 284–285
storing, 270
talking about, 277–287
for teachers, 264–265, 268
teacher's selections for, 273–274
value of, 286–287
positive assets, emphasis on, 36–39
Postman, Neil, 290
power
body orientation conveying, 20
in evaluation settings, 20–22
Power, Brenda, 255
praise, nonspecific, 39
predictable reading materials
drawbacks to, 55
ease of reading and, 49, 54
reading strategies, 54
predictable relationships, value of, 179
prediction
in literacy development, 143–144,
148–149
reading efficiency and, 217–219
prereading, 140
Primary Language Record (PLR), 305,
307, 312–313, 315
print
concepts about, 98–112, 143
assessment questions, 112
relationship to speech, 113–116
print awareness
checking, 101–108, 255
in deaf children, 119
relationship between speech and print,
113–116
visual analysis, 116–120

print conversations. See dialogue journals
prior knowledge, meaning and, 70–71
problem-solving, in oral reading, 203–205
procedural knowing, 94
process, vs. product, evaluating, 39–40
productive assessment, 5–6
progress, evaluating through portfolios,
40–41
proximal development, zone of, 50, 56
punctuation
children's concepts about, 110–111
development of, 143
Punished by Rewards (Kohn), 304
punishments, grading and, 303–304

questions
classification of, 241–243
contrast, 184
as control, 21–22, 160
descriptive, 183
in dialogue journals, 172–173, 174,
175–176
display, 172–173
encouraging from children, 160, 186
for evaluating reading comprehension,
240–243
higher-order, 242–243
inferential, 241
in interviews, 180–181, 182–184,
329–330
known-answer, 21–22, 160, 240–241
literal, 241
lower-order, 242–243
messages conveyed though, 182–183
structural, 183–184
student interpretation of purpose of,
21–22
text-explicit, 242
text-implicit, 242
that teach, 29
"tour," 183

rationalizations, learning about in
interviews, 190
readability
effect on literacy activity, 42–43
formulas, 42–43, 45f
reading, See also oral reading
aesthetic, 239
children's concepts of, 87–88, 96
choice in, 58–59, 234
conversations about, 160–165
critical, 79, 81, 92

diversity in, 148
ease of, 46–48, 164
efferent, 239
flexibility in, 148
focusing on process of, 24
on grade level, 44, 55–56
low-risk choices in, 58–59
as model for writing, 54
pattern recognition in, 73–74
phonetic analysis and, 113–114
prediction strategies, 54, 217–219
quantity of, 145
thinking out loud during, 233–238
reading aloud. See oral reading
reading comprehension
assessing through cloze procedure,
243–244
assessing through retelling, 244–247
assessing through translating, 247–249
evaluating, 239–249
interpretation and, 248
questions for evaluating, 240–243
reading instruction, mental age and, 139
reading level
basal readers for, 44, 55–56
choosing for children, 44–45
reading logs, 82
reading rate, 142, 145–146
reading readiness, 139–142
reading strategies, 122–129, See also
strategies
constraints on, 123–124
Read and Retell (Brown and Cambourne),
246
realities, multiple, constructing, 8–9
received knowing, 93
recognition
automatic, 74–75
development of, 148–149
of patterns, 73–75
Reed, Leslie, 175
reflection, 322, See also self-assessment
competition and, 32
constructive evaluation and, 16
development of, 149–150
dialogue journals for, 174, 176
emphasizing the positive in, 36–39
encouraging, 29, 32–33, 34–41, 182
excessive, 33
importance of, 33
in interviews, 182
self-evaluation through, 31
through journal writing, 31–32

through writing folders, 32
value of, 23
Reflective Practitioner, The (Schon), 8–9
reflective questions, 35, 174
regression, 142
relationships
    building, 178–180
    in a democracy, 82–83
    meaningful, 80–81
    sustaining, 81–84
repetition, in oral reading, 202–203
report cards, *See also* grading
    alternatives to, 301–303, 305, 306–310
    degrading students through, 303–305
    encouraging parent-teacher
        communication, 314–315
    form of, 298–300, 301
    functions of, 297, 300
    parent attitudes toward, 298
    parent involvement in, 308–310
    student involvement in, 301, 308–310
reporting systems, *See also* moderation;
      portfolios
    alternative, 301–310
    changing, 306–310
    documentary, 302
    home journals as, 306
    moderation, 314–319
    motivation issues and, 305
    portfolios as, 301
research, student concepts about, 188
respect, building, 178–179
responding, to dialogue journals, 174–176
responsibility, 7
retelling, 244–247
revision, by students, 127
rewards, grading and, 303–304
rhyme, reading ease and, 48–49
rhythm, reading ease and, 48–49
Richardson, Elwyn, 34
Rief, Linda, 76, 78, 80, 170, 248, 273,
    283, 320
role-playing, 150
Romanes, George, 145–146
Rose, Mike, 64
Rosenblatt, Louise, 239
Runner, The (Voigt), 81–82
running records, 21
    analysis sheet, 331
    beginning, 195
    cautions about, 230–231
    counting errors in, 213–216
    defined, 193

error rate, 212–213
    interpreting, 212–231
    recording
        appeals, 207
        interventions, 208–210
        pauses, 210
        problem-solving, 203–205
        repetitions, 202–203
        words inserted, 198–200
        words omitted, 196–197
        words read correctly, 195–196
        words substituted, 197–198
    recording symbols, 194f
    self-correction in, 216–217
    student reactions to, 231
    tape recorders for, 194–195
    using, 193–208, 223–229
Rylant, Cynthia, 24, 79

Sarah, Plain and Tall (MacLachlan), 248
Saturday Morning (Moyes), 203, 218
scaffolding, 55
schedules, 22–23
Schon, Donald, 9, 65
school psychologists, 178, 180
scientific method, 80–81
security, of trusting relationships, 179
"seeding" conversations, 167
Seeking Diversity (Rief), 170
self-assessment, 26–33, *See also* reflection
    constructive, 134–136
    contexts for, 32–33
    criteria, 35–36
    emphasis on the positive, 36–39
    encouraging, 9, 29–30
    evaluations by others and, 20
    importance of, 33
    reflective, 31
    by teachers, 30, 172
        portfolios for, 287
    types of, 28–29
    valuing, 29–30
self-checking, 30
self-confidence, evaluation and, 28
self-correction
    from meaning, 217
    from print, 217
    literacy development and, 146
    in oral reading, 200–202, 213, 216–217,
        222–223
    story memory and, 149
    value of, 29
self-judgment, 28–29

separate knowing, 80–81
Shockley, Betty, 306
Short, Kathy, 72
Shuy, Roger, 172, 173
sight words, dictation tests, 119–120
silence, 92
silent speech, characteristics of, 232–233
social imagination, 78–79
social interaction
    evaluation as, 17–25
    literacy development and, 150
Sokolov, Alexandr, 232
sound analysis
    assessment questions, 121
    evaluating, 119
special education, teacher referrals to, 15
specialist teachers, 179–180
specificity, of feedback, 39
speech, relationship to print, 113–116
speech delays, reading comprehension
    and, 249
spelling
    assessment of, 37–39
    invented, 114, 115, 117–118
    under various conditions, 154–155
    writing failure and, 52–53
Spiro, Rhoda, 130
Spradley, James, 183
stages, specifying in reporting systems,
    315 317
standardized interviews, 184–185
standardized portfolios, 282–283, 284–285
standardized tasks, 311
standardized tests, social interaction
    effects, 18–19
standards, student self-evaluation and,
    35–36
states, in assessment, 24–25
Staton, Jana, 171
"status-of-the-class" conferences, 252–253
stereotypes, critical literacy and, 84–85
stories
    knowledge of structure of, 149
    memory for, 149
story structures, recognition of, 73
storytelling, 150
    as retelling, 246
strategies, 122–129, *See also* reading
      strategies; writing strategies
    assessment questions, 129
    availability of, 124
    conditions of use, 126–127
    constraints on, 123–124

strategies (continued)
  coping, 127
  deep processing, 133
  knowing when to use, 124–125
  literacy, 127
  nature of problem and, 125–126
  nonproductive, 127–128
  in oral reading, 221
  thinking out loud about, 234–238
structural questions, 183–184
structure cues, 221–223
students. See learners
style, in case studies, 292–293
subjective knowing, 93–94
success, children's concepts of, 130–137
support
  drawbacks to, 55
  role of, 50
  types of, 55
sustaining relationships, 81–84
syllables, children's concepts about, 111

Taking Note (Power), 255
Tammivaara, Julie, 159
tape recorders, for running records, 194–195
task orientation, 133
teachers
  construction of multiple realities by, 8–9
  evaluative criteria of, 36
  improving assessment role of, 7
  pattern recognition by, 12
  portfolios for, 264–265, 268
  predispositions toward assessment, 14
  role in classroom conversation, 165, 167
  self-assessment by, 30, 172
  think-alouds for, 237–238
  trusting relationships with, 179
teacher-student exchanges, dialogue journals and, 172–174
teaching skills, 9–10
tense vowels, 115–116, 118, 142
Terrible Days of My Cat Cali, The (Haggerty), 335, 340
testing, See also assessment
  of reading comprehension, 239–240
  social interactions and, 6
  use of term, 2
text explicit questions, 242
text implicit questions, 242
thingification, 293

think-alouds
  benefits of, 235–237
  increasing the quality of, 233–235
  for teachers, 237–238
thinking out loud, 232–238
  characteristics of, 232–233
  in learning process, 232
time and timing
  cultural differences, 22
  in evaluation, 22–23
"tour" questions, 183
translating, 247–249
trust
  building, 178–179
  classroom conversations and, 166
  dialog journals and, 176
  importance of, 19–20
  maximizing, when asking questions, 22
  nonspecific praise and, 39
Tsuchiya, Yukio, 69

understanding
  evaluating, 239–249
  frame of reference and, 240

values, 320
Vesper, Jim, 264
videotapes, encouraging self-evaluation with, 30, 31
visual analysis
  assessment questions, 121
  of words, 116–120
visual cues, 221–223
visual memory, development of, 117
vocabulary
  development of, 150
  tests, 119
voice, in case studies, 292–293
voice-pointing, 231
Voigt, Cynthia, 81
von Neumann, J., 242–243
vowels
  children's concepts about, 108
  children's representation of in print, 115–116
  lax, 115–116, 118, 142
  tense, 115–116, 118, 142
  visual analysis of, 118–120
Vygotsky, Lev, 50, 232

Waddell, Martin, 223
Warner, Trudy, 172
Washburne, Carleton, 139

Weber, Rose-Marie, 160, 192
"weight control," for selecting items for portfolios, 271
Why Do Boys Say Girls Are Afraid of Creepy Crawlers? (Johnston), 327–328
Wiesel, Elie, 76
Wilson, Mary, 263–264
Wolf, Dennie Palmer, 96, 278
Woodcock Reading Mastery Test, 20
words
  auditory analysis of, 118
  children's concepts about, 113–120
  recognition speed, 145
  sight recognition, 119
  speech sounds and letters, 113–116
  visual analysis of, 116–118
writer's block, 64
"writer's compulsion," 146
writing
  children's concepts about, 87–91, 92, 98
  choice and, 46, 57, 59–60
  complexity in, 147–148
  conceptual knowledge in, 146–147
  critiques by classmates, 83
  in dialogue journals, 169
  dislike of, 188
  diversity in, 148
  ease of, 48–49, 51–53
  flexibility in, 148
  quantity of, 145
  reading as model for, 54
  spelling difficulties and, 52–53
  thinking out loud during, 236–238
writing folders, self-assessment and, 32
writing process
  evaluating, 39–40
  focusing on, 24
writing strategies, 122–129, See also strategies
  constraints on, 123–124
  learning about in interviews, 188–189

Yaden, David, 160
Young, Kim, 308

Ziefert, Harriet, 207
zone of proximal development, 50, 56
Zwoyer, Russell, 29